CAN A "WHITE [barcode] P9-BIK-870
AWAY WITH A "

Do you know what's meant when they talk about "coupon stripping"? What about "closing costs"? Or "decision trees"? Or "GMAT"? Or "transaction account"? Or "visible supply"? Or "internal rate of return"? Or any of the other thousands of terms and concepts that form the living language of the world of business and finance?

If you want to read, speak, and think in this language like a native, the information you're looking for is waiting here for you inside the best and easiest-to-employ reference guide on the market today.

"The terms covered range from business concepts such as leverage and development to aspects of business research such as Likert scale and Chisquare. . . . Also covers abbreviations . . . and slang terms with surprising frankness."
—*Booklist*

"The definitions are clear and the illustrations make this dictionary helpful to the person who happens on a new term." —*Choice*

JAY M. SHAFRITZ is editor of the *Dorsey Dictionary of American Government and Politics, Facts on File Dictionary of Public Administration* (one of the ALA's "outstanding reference books of 1986"), and some forty other text and reference books. DANIEL ORAN is editor of *Oran's Law Dictionary for Non-Lawyers*, and co-author of the novel *Z-Warning*.

THE NEW AMERICAN DICTIONARY OF BUSINESS AND FINANCE

Jay M. Shafritz
and
Daniel Oran

A MENTOR BOOK

MENTOR
Published by the Penguin Group
Penguin Books USA Inc., 375 Hudson Street,
New York, New York 10014, U.S.A.
Penguin Books Ltd, 27 Wrights Lane,
London W8 5TZ, England
Penguin Books Australia Ltd, Ringwood,
Victoria, Australia
Penguin Books Canada Ltd, 2801 John Street,
Markham, Ontario, Canada L3R 1B4
Penguin Books (N.Z.) Ltd, 182-190 Wairau Road,
Auckland 10, New Zealand

Penguin Books Ltd, Registered Offices:
Harmondsworth, Middlesex, England

First Mentor Printing, September, 1990
10 9 8 7 6 5 4 3 2 1

The New American Dictionary of Business and Finance
is a revised and updated edition of *The MBA's Dictionary*,
published by Reston Publishing Co., 1983.

 REGISTERED TRADEMARK—MARCA REGISTRADA

Library of Congress Catalog Card Number: 90-60117

PRINTED IN THE UNITED STATES OF AMERICA

How to Use This Book

This dictionary is a tool for anyone concerned with the language of business and finance. It contains the language of American commerce with extensive coverage of accounting, business law, finance, insurance, international trade, labor relations, management, marketing, personnel and human resources management, production and operations management, real estate and the stock market. We have also covered the slang terms and informal processes that are often more important than textbook words.

Commonplace words such as *mall, salesperson* or *supermarket* are not included because definitions of them, if needed, are so readily available in other dictionaries. After all, this is a dictionary of all the business and financial words (or meanings of those words) that are generally not found in regular dictionaries of the English language.

The entries are in strict alphabetical order with one exception: *all* abbreviations are presented at the beginning of each letter. Most words are cross-referenced under major headings. Each cross-referenced word or phrase is in **boldface.** If you cannot find the word in alphabetical order, try a more general word or try the other half if it is a compound word.

A

A 1. In a newspaper **stock** transaction table, an indication of a cash payment in addition to regular **dividends;** or an indication that the **yield** of a **money market mutual fund** may include **capital gains** (and losses) as well as current **interest.** This indicator is always lowercased (a). 2. In newspaper reports on stocks, an indicator that the stock is traded on the **American Stock Exchange.** This indicator is always uppercased (A). 3. A **bond** rating indicating that the **security** of **principal** and interest is adequate. This ranking is above triple B **(BBB)** and below double A **(AA)** and triple A **(AAA).**

AA (double A) **Standard & Poor's bond** rating indicating that the **security** is one step below the highest level (triple A, or **AAA**); that there exists a strong capacity to repay principal and interest. **Moody's** comparable rating is Aa.

AAA 1. American Accounting Association. 2. **American Arbitration Association.** 3. **Standard & Poor's** highest rating (triple A, or **AAA**) for a **bond** indicating that there exists great confidence in the **security** of the **principal** and **interest. Moody's** comparable rating is Aaa.

AAAA American Association of Advertising Agencies.

AACSB American Assembly of Collegiate Schools of Business.

ABA 1. **American Bar Association.** 2. American Bankers Association.

ABC 1. *ABC inventory control* is a system that divides **inventory** into three dollar-volume classifications, A, B, and C, with A being those items with the greatest dollar volume (those that are "most active"). The inventory manager finds an item's annual dollar volume by multiplying its cost times the number used in a year. Grouping items by dollar volume enables a company to exercise extra control where it is needed most—over that part of

7

its inventory that represents the greatest **investment.** 2.
The *ABC test* states that an employee need not be covered by unemployment insurance if the employee is an
independent worker who performs jobs free of the employer's control and away from the employer's place of
business. 3. An *ABC transfer* was a complicated exchange of mining or oil rights meant to lower taxes.
Current tax law eliminates the advantage of these transfers. 4. Audit Bureau of Circulation. It verifies newspaper
and magazine circulation claims. 5. An *ABC analysis*
groups items into three categories—important, less important, least important—as a basis for control and
treatment.

A/C Account; active account.

ACRS Accelerated cost recovery system.

ADP Automatic data processing. Usually by computer.

ADR 1. **Asset depreciation range.** 2. **American depository receipts.** 3. Automatic **dividend** reinvestment; this
allows stockholders to buy more shares of common **stock**
instead of receiving dividends.

**AFL-CIO American Federation of Labor-Congress of In-
dustrial Organizations.** The largest organization of labor
unions in the United States.

AICPA American Institute of Certified Public Accountants.

AIDA A memory device for a copy-writing formula: attention, interest, desire, action.

AIO Attitude, interest and opinion profile. It is used in
psychographics.

ALJ Administrative law judge.

ALTA American Land Title Association.

AMA 1. **American Management Associations.** 2. American Marketing Association.

ANSI American National Standards Institute.

AOG Arrival of goods.

AOQL Average Outgoing Quality Limit.

APA Administrative Procedure Act.

APB Accounting Principles Board. See **generally accepted
accounting principles.**

APICS American Production and Inventory Control Society.

APR Annual percentage rate.

APT Automatically programmed tool system.

AQL Acceptable (or acceptance) quality level. A percentage of failure rate.

ARM An **adjustable rate mortgage.**

ARQ Automatic request for repetition. An error-detection mechanism.

ASAP As soon as possible.

ASCII American Standard Code for computer representation of letters, numbers, and "typewriter" symbols. A combination of eight computer **bits** can handle all 128 standard characters.

ASE **American Stock Exchange.**

ASTM American Society for Testing and Materials.

ATM **Automated teller machine.**

AWOL Absent without official leave.

Abandonment 1. A complete and final giving up of property or rights with no intention of reclaiming them and to no particular person. For example, throwing away a book is *abandonment*, but selling or giving it away is not. And a lawsuit may be thrown out of court if it is *abandoned* by failure to take any action on it for too long a time. Abandonment of a **patent** right might occur if the inventor fails to apply for a patent or if too many other people are allowed to see the invention. 2. The practice of turning over damaged property to its insurer in order to claim its full insured value. 3. Eliminating a **fixed asset** from the books after its final retirement from service. 4. A consignee's refusal to accept a shipment because of damage. 5. *Abandonment of position* means quitting a job without formally resigning. *Abandonment of service* occurs if a public utility permanently cuts off a customer.

Abatement 1. Reduction or decrease. 2. Proportional reduction. For example, if a pot of money does not have enough to pay everyone it owes, each person may have to be satisfied with an *abatement* of his or her share. 3. Complete elimination. For example, an *abatable nuisance* is a nuisance that is easily or practically stopped or made harmless.

Abbroachment Buying up goods at wholesale to control the supply and then resell at much higher resale prices.

Ability to pay 1. A concept from **collective bargaining** referring to an employer's ability to tolerate the costs of requested **wage** and **benefit** increases. **Factfinders** and **arbitrators** frequently use the "ability to pay" concept in justifying their decisions. 2. The principle that as a person's income increases, that person should pay an increasing *proportion* of that income in taxes. **Progressive taxes,**

such as the federal government income tax, are based on this principle. 3. A standard that juries are rarely permitted to use in deciding how much money a defendant must pay a plaintiff. 4. A borrower's ability to pay back a loan. 5. A **bond** issuer's ability to generate revenue to meet its obligations to bondholders.

About Near in time, distance, quantity, or quality. *About* is an imprecise word, but not so imprecise as to legally undo a deal based on a phrase like "about a million widgets" or "about May first."

Above 1. Higher. Usually refers to a higher or **appellate** court. 2. Before. *Above cited* or *above mentioned* may mean "appears earlier on this page," "earlier in this chapter," etc. 3. *Above par* means that the price of a **security** is greater than its **face** amount. 4. *Above-the-line* is an accounting phrase meaning "out of profits"—that an expense or obligation will be charged to current income.

Abridge 1. Infringe upon. To *abridge* a right is to make the right less useful or complete. 2. Shorten or condense.

Abrogation 1. The destruction, ending, or annulling of a former law. 2. The formal cancellation of an agreement or a part of one.

Abscond Hide or sneak away to avoid arrest, a lawsuit, or creditors.

Absence 1. An employee's short-term unavailability to work, lasting at least one day or tour of duty. An *absentee landlord* is an owner or other **lessor** who does not live on the premises; usually one who cannot be reached by the tenants. 2. *Absenteeism* is unnecessary, unexcused or habitual absence from work.

Absolute 1. Complete, final, and without restrictions. 2. An *absolute advantage* is an international trade concept which holds that one nation has an *absolute advantage* over another when it can produce more of a product using the same amount of resources than the other can. See also **comparative advantage.** 3. An *absolute deed* is a transfer of land without a **mortgage** or other restrictions. 4. *Absolute liability* is responsibility for harm to another whether or not you are at fault. 5. An *absolute nuisance* is a nuisance that involves no negligent conduct. 6. *Absolute priority* refers to the fact that **creditors** must be satisfied before **stockholders.** This concept is especially relevant during **liquidations** and **reorganizations.**

Absolution Freedom or release from an obligation or a debt.

Absorption 1. The continued life of a thing (a right, a company, etc.) by its becoming a part of another thing. For example, when one business **merges** with another, the continued right of **seniority** for employees is called *absorption*. 2. *Absorption costing* is the system of allocating business costs in which all costs, whether fixed or variable, **direct** or **indirect**, are *absorbed* by the goods produced within an **accounting period.** The cost of a product consists of the costs of production allocated between the goods sold during the period and those in the ending **inventory** on some more or less arbitrary basis.

Abstinence theory of interest. See **agio.**

Abstract 1. A summary. For example, an abstract of **title** is a condensed history of the ownership of a piece of land that includes transfers of ownership and any rights (such as **liens**) that persons other than the owner might have in the land. 2. *Abstraction* is taking something (usually money) with the intent to commit fraud.

Abuse Misuse. *Abuse of discretion* is the failure to use sound, reasonable judgment as a judge or as an administrator, and *abuse of process* is using the legal process unfairly; for example, prosecuting a person for writing a bad check simply to put on pressure to pay.

Academy of Management A nonprofit organization, most of whose members are college teachers, that views itself as America's academic "voice" in U.S. management.

Accede 1. Come into a job or public office. 2. Agree, consent, or give in.

Accelerated cost recovery system An **accounting** method that uses a range of time, usually shorter than an **asset's** useful life, over which a business may take **depreciation** on the asset. The **IRS** specifies rules and percentages.

Acceleration 1. Shortening of the time before a future event will happen. An *acceleration clause* is a section of a contract that makes an entire debt come immediately due because of a failure to pay on time or because of some other failure. *Acceleration of capital* is the theory that business will not invest in production unless sales increase. And for *accelerated depreciation,* see **depreciation.** 2. *Accelerating premium pay* is a bonus **incentive** system in which pay rates rise as production **standards** are exceeded. For example, an employee who exceeds standard production by two percent may get a two percent **bonus,** while an employee who exceeds by five percent may get a ten percent bonus. 3. The *accelerator principle,* also called the *accelerator effect,* is a business cycle theory which holds that an increase in **demand** for finished products tends to create a greater increase in demand for those things that are used to make the finished product.

Acceptance 1. Agreeing to an **offer** and becoming bound to the terms of a **contract.** 2. Taking something offered by another person with the intention of keeping it. For example, the **Uniform Commercial Code** explains several ways a buyer can *accept* goods from a seller: by telling the seller that the goods received are right; by saying that the goods will be taken despite problems; by failing to reject the goods in reasonable time; or by doing something that makes it seem like the buyer now owns the goods. 3. In **negotiable instruments** law, a person's *acceptance* of a check may be by signing and depositing it, and a bank can *accept* the check by cashing it. There are technical rules of acceptance for more complicated negotiable instruments. 4. A *banker's acceptance* is a trade device in which a bank promises to pay a certain amount at a future date (a negotiable time **draft** or a guaranteed **bill of exchange.**) For example, a manufacturer in New York wishes to sell goods to a merchant in Texas on 90 days' time. The manufacturer will send the **bill of lading** to the Texas merchant's bank with a draft on the bank. The bank will accept the draft because it has assurance that the draft will be paid at **maturity.** This assurance rests either on the high credit standing of the Texas merchant or on the fact that the bank holds the bill of lading or some other document as **collateral.** The bank is liable to the drawer of the draft, but it looks, in turn, to the merchant for repayment. A draft accepted by the bank is a **banker's acceptance.** A *trade acceptance* is the same thing promised by a company instead of a bank. These are both called "*acceptance credit,*" are often used to finance international trade and are bought and sold as investments. And an *acceptance house,* also called an *acceptance bank,* specializes in lending money on the **security** of **bills of exchange** or **guaranteed** bills **drawn** on another party. 5. *Acceptance sampling* is a statistical method for deciding whether to accept or reject an entire lot on the basis of the quality of a **sample.** One hundred percent inspection is usually too expensive and very often does not yield accurate information because of inspection fatigue and other types of errors. Many tests are destructive, so acceptance sampling is often the only practical means of inspection. Acceptance sampling procedures are most efficient when used on large lots of material; this technique presumes homogeneous lots of material received from the same source. And an **acceptance trial** is the testing of newly developed equipment by agents of a purchaser to determine if prespecified performance criteria have been met.

Access 1. Opportunity to approach. For example, most city lots have *access* to the street. 2. Right to approach. For example, *access* to public records includes both their practical availability and the right to see them. 3. *Access time* is the time required for information to be inserted into or taken from the storage section of a computer. A computer with a relatively slow access time of 10 microseconds can make information transfers at the rate of 100,000 per second.

Accession 1. The right to own things that become a part of something already owned. For example, if land builds up on a riverbank, the bank's owner will also own the new land by *accession.* 2. The right to things, such as crops, produced on owned property. 3. See **accede.** 4. Any acquisition. 5. Any addition, such as an addition to an organization's workforce. The *accession rate,* also called *hiring rate*, is the number of employees added to a payroll during a given time period, usually expressed as a percentage of total **employment.** The accession rates can be computed using the following formula:

$$\text{accession rate} = \frac{\text{total accessions x 100}}{\text{total number of workers}}$$

Accident A chance event. An *accident frequency rate* is the total number of disabling injuries per million hours worked as computed by the **Bureau of Labor Statistics.** *Accident-proneness* is a concept that implies that certain kinds of personalities are more likely to have accidents than others. However, psychological research supports the claim that accident-proneness is more related to situational than personality factors. An *accident severity rate* is generally computed as the number of work days lost because of accidents per thousand hours worked. An *accidental death benefit* is a feature found in some life insurance policies that provides for payment of additional amounts to the **beneficiary** if the insured person dies as a result of an accident. When such provisions allow for an accidental death **benefit** that is twice the normal value of the **policy**, they are known as **double indemnity** provisions.

Accommodation A favor done for another person, usually involving **co-signing** to help another person get a loan or credit. An *accommodation line* is business that is accepted not on its own merits but to get other business or as part of a "package." *Accommodation paper* is a **bill** or **note** that is signed by one person as a favor to help another person get a loan. The person signing promises to pay if the person getting the loan fails to pay. An *accommodation party* is a person who signs an **accommodation paper** as a favor to another person. *Accommodation personnel* are **dummy incorporators.**

Accord 1. An agreement to pay (on one side) and to accept (on the other side) less than all a debt or obligation is worth as full payment for that obligation. For example, there is an *accord* if a person agrees to take one hundred dollars as payment in full for one hundred and fifty dollars worth of damages to an auto, and the person who did the damage agrees to pay the one hundred dollars. 2. An *accord and satisfaction* is an accord that has been completed by payment and a full **release.** 3. Any agreement.

Account 1. Any self-contained financial record-keeping system for one particular subject or type of transaction. The most common form it takes is a chronological record of changes in a **ledger.** An account total is increased or decreased by **posting debits** or **credits.** The difference between total debits and credits is the **balance** of the account. An *account in balance* is one in which the debits equal the credits. 2. A list of money paid and owed by one person or business to another. *Account activities* are transactions on accounts such as debits, credits, holds, etc. *Account analysis* is the process of reviewing an account in order to ascertain and explain profit or loss. An *account day*, also called *settlement day*, is the day designated by stock and commodity exchanges for the settlement of accounts between members. An *account payable* is a regular business debt not yet paid. An *account receivable* is a regular business debt not yet collected; for example, a store's charge accounts. An *account stated* is an exact figure for money owed, calculated by the person to whom the money is owed, and accepted as accurate by the person who owes the money. In law, the account stated operates as an admission of liability from the person against whom the balance appears and as a promise to pay. The debtor cannot question the accuracy of the computation of the account stated if it is retained beyond a reasonable time without objection. 3. A client or customer. An *account executive* is a service industry term for those employees who have direct responsibility for a client's interests. An account executive in advertising is the **agency** employee responsible for managing the campaign of a client. Sales agents for securities dealers also call themselves account executives. See **registered representative.**

Accountability The extent to which one is responsible to higher **authority**—legal or organizational—for one's actions in society at large or within one's particular organizational **position.**

Accountant A person who specializes in the accuracy of financial records. This includes setting up financial record keeping systems, filling them in, and checking up on them. These duties include **auditing, bookkeeping,** and preparing financial **statements.** Normally, persons who do just bookkeeping do not have accounting skills. The next level of skill is accountant. Some accountants are specially trained and certified as **certified public accountants** by satisfying state professional requirements.

Accountant's report 1. A written statement, also called an *accountant's certificate, accountant's opinion,* or *audit report,* prepared by an independent **accountant** or **auditor** after an **audit.** It is addressed to the owners, directors or stockholders of the audited enterprise. The auditor states briefly the nature and the scope of the examination and expresses a professional opinion as to the fairness of the appended **financial statement** in presenting the firm's financial position and operating results for the specified period. The opinion may be unqualified, or it may contain exceptions, qualifications, or other comments regarding the treatment of particular items, the limitations of the auditing procedures followed, and changes of accounting methods from those used in previous years. 2. The term *accountant's report* occasionally is used to refer to a separate report made by the public accountants who have performed an audit of the company's books. The report, often called a *management letter*, contains suggestions or recommendations for the company to improve its systems, controls, cash handling, record keeping, and the like. These matters are not of sufficient importance to require a qualification in the certificate of a public accountant.

Accounting 1. The process of analyzing business transactions and recording them in the books of account to show the results of business operations. *Accounting* includes the design, installation, and operation of the accounting system, the analysis of financial statements, budgeting methods, and the procedures for internal control. See also **cost accounting.** 2. The term *accounting* is sometimes limited to systems for setting up financial record books, especially for tax purposes. Two of the most common methods are the *accrual method* (recording debts owed to and by a company when the debt becomes a legal obligation, which may be before the money is actually paid) and the *cash method* (recording debts when paid). 3. The rendering or delivering of a formal statement by a person who is under a legal duty to account for property or money of another. Thus, accountings are made by **executors, agents,** guardians, etc. *Accounting* may also mean actually making good on money owed. For example, a court may order one partner to pay another. This is called an *accounting for profits.* 4. An *accounting change* is, generally, a change in an accounting principle (such as using a different method of determining **depreciation**), a change in an accounting estimate (inflation was greater or less than expected), a change in accounting period, or a change in the reporting entity. The correcting of errors in earlier financial **statements** is not considered an accounting change. *Accounting control* is a set of procedures that monitors the receipt and disbursement of funds and the recording of business transactions. It is an essential element in the control of cost and operations and includes

the use of **control accounts**, or their equivalent, that can
be used to verify the accuracy of groups of subsidiary
accounts. Accounting control should also provide financial data for reports required by management. See also
internal control. The *accounting cycle* is the sum of the
accounting procedures from the records made in the books
of original entry to **posting** to **ledger** accounts, making
closing entries, making adjusting journal entries, and taking a trial balance. These parts of the cycle are directed
toward the preparation of an income **statement** and a
balance sheet at the close of the **accounting period.** The
accounting cycle also refers to the time required to convert cash into merchandise inventory, to **accounts receivable**
and back to cash again. It is usually one year but may be
longer, depending upon the product involved. Where the
inventory takes more than one year to sell (for example,
wine which ages three or more years) the *accounting cycle*
will run for that period of time. An *accounting identity* is
a statement that two numerical things are equal by accepted definition; for example, **assets** equal **liabilities** plus
stockholder's **equity.** *Accounting methods* are the specific
procedures that follow from *accounting principles*. *Accounting models* are simulations of financial situations.
An *accounting period* is the length of time for which a
financial or operating report is prepared. It can range
from weekly to yearly. See also **fiscal.** *Accounting policy*
consists of the accounting methods selected by management from the available alternatives. For example, management may decide not to **capitalize research and
development** costs but to regard them as **operating expenses.** *Accounting policy* may also refer to the standard
operating procedures that a business uses to maintain its
accounts. *Accounting principles* are the basic premises
that govern most accounting theory and practice. Accounting principles are validated by general acceptance
within the accounting community; they are not immutable
in the sense of scientific laws. They arise from common
experiences, historical precedents and formulations of professional bodies and governmental agencies. They change
over the years as new techniques, business practices and
laws evolve. See also **Generally Accepted Accounting
Principles.** *Accounting rate of return* is the same as **unadjusted rate of return.** An *accounting system* is the total

structure of records and procedures that record, classify, and report information on the financial position and operations of an organization.

Accounts payable Money owed, usually to suppliers. A company groups its records of this money in one account called *accounts payable.*

Accounts receivable Money owed, usually by customers. A company groups its records of this money into one account called *accounts receivable* or *receivables.*

Accounts receivable financing 1. Using a company's **accounts receivable** as **collateral** for loans under a continuing arrangement. This usually involves higher financing costs than regular bank loans. Such financing is carried out through a formal agreement called the *underlying agreement* or *working plan*, which specifies what percentage of the value of pledged accounts receivable will be advanced by the lender (usually from 75 percent to 85 percent) and sets the over-all conditions by which each assignment will operate. Assignment of accounts receivable is made from time to time as the borrower needs funds. At such times, the borrower prepares a **schedule** of the **assigned** accounts and **executes** a **demand note** in the amount of the loan. The assignee (lender) usually stamps the assigned accounts in the company's accounts receivable **ledger**, indicating that the account has been assigned. Some states require this bookmarking to validate the assignment.   2. Selling accounts receivable outright. This is called **factoring.**

Accretion Any gradual accumulation; for example, the growth of a bank account due to continuing deposits or the interest earned, the extension of land boundaries due to the deposit of dirt by a river, the growth of trees on land, etc.

Accrual basis A method of **accounting** that shows expenses **incurred** (see also **all events test**) and income earned in a given time period, whether or not cash payments have actually changed hands during that period. Also, investments in **fixed assets** are often divided up by the time periods benefiting from these assets. This is done by **depreciation** accounting. One advantage of *accrual basis* accounting is that it helps in making comparisons between business activity of two periods. Only where all relevant expenses have been applied against the income of the period, is it possible to obtain an accurate picture of the profit or loss. One disadvantage is the possibility that some portion of a company's **accounts receivable** may never be realized as cash. See also **cash basis.**

Accruals Regular, short-term business obligations, such as employees' wages.

Accrue 1. Become due and payable but not yet paid. For example, in tax law, income *accrues* to a taxpayer when the taxpayer has an unconditional right to it and a likelihood of being able to receive it. 2. An *accrued dividend* is a share of a company's earnings that has been formally declared as payable to the stockholders, but not yet paid. *Accrued assets or income* is money earned, but not yet collected, and *accrued liabilities or expenses* are those owing, but not yet paid. In **accounting,** these are all earned or owing in the current *accounting period,* but may not actually be paid until a later one.

Accumulated (or accrued) depreciation That part of an asset's cost that is estimated to have been consumed in production. It is charged to operations.

Accumulated earnings tax A federal tax on **corporations** that pile up profits without either distributing them to stockholders in the form of **dividends** or plowing the money back into the business.

Accumulated retained earnings See **retained earnings.**

Achievement test A test designed to measure an individual's level of proficiency in a specific subject or task. A collection of achievement tests designed to measure levels of skill or knowledge in a variety of areas is an *achievement battery*.

Acid test See *quick ratio* under **quick assets.**

Acknowledgment 1. An admission or declaration that something is genuine. 2. The act of signing a formal paper and swearing to it as your act before a court official such as a **notary public.**

Acoustic coupler A device that hooks a telephone handset into a computer to allow computer communication over phone lines using a **modem.**

Acquiescence Silent agreement; knowing about an action or occurrence and remaining quietly satisfied about it or, by silence, appearing to be satisfied.

Acquisition The taking over of one company by another, or the company that has been taken over. An *acquisition charge* is a charge for paying off a loan before it comes due.

It is also called a *prepayment penalty*. An *acquisition cost* is the immediate cost of selling, **underwriting,** and issuing a new **insurance policy,** including clerical costs, agents' commissions, advertising, and medical inspection fees. *Acquisition cost* also refers to the cost paid by a retailer to a manufacturer or wholesaler for a supply of goods.

Acquittal 1. A formal legal determination that a person who has been charged with a crime is innocent. 2. A **release** from an obligation.

Acquittance A written **discharge** of an obligation. For example, a **receipt** is an *acquittance* of an obligation to pay money owed.

Across-the-board increase An increase in wages, whether expressed in dollars or percentage of salary, given to an entire workforce.

Act 1. A law passed by one or both houses of a legislature, such as Congress. 2. Something done voluntarily that triggers legal consequences. 3. An *act of bankruptcy* is any one of several actions (such as hiding property from creditors) that used to make a person liable to be proceeded against as a bankrupt by **creditors. Bankruptcy** law now provides for this sort of *involuntary bankruptcy* only when a person cannot pay debts as they come due. An *act of God* is an event caused entirely by nature alone. The *act of state doctrine* is the rule that a court in the United States should not question the legality of acts done by a foreign government in its own country.

Acting Holding a temporary rank or position. Filling in for someone else.

Action 1. A formal legal demand. *Actionable* means that an act has provided the legal grounds for a lawsuit. 2. The French term for a share of stock. 3. The trading volume and price trends of a **security.** 4. *Action planning* is the **planning** phase in which **production** preplanning is tried and tested. 5. *Action research,* in its broadest context, is the application of the scientific method to practical problems. As the basic model underlying **organization development,** action research is the process of collecting data about an ongoing organizational system to feed it back into the system, then alter a variable within the organizational system in response to this data or to test a hypothesis, and evaluate the results by collecting more data. Repeat the process as needed.

Active In use; busy. An *active account* is one which has frequent transactions. *Active assets* are assets in productive use. *Active capital* is capital in productive use. *Active listening* is a counseling technique in which the counselor listens to both the facts and the feelings of the speaker. Such listening is "active" because the counselor has the specific responsibilities of showing interest, of not passing judgment, and of helping the speaker to work out problems. An *active market* means that there is a large volume of transactions on an exchange. *Active money* is circulating currency. An *active partner* is a member of a firm who is fully engaged in its business. *Active securities* are stocks and bonds that are traded every day. An *active trust* is a trust for which the trustee must actually perform some service.

Activity charge A checking account fee.

Activity ratios Measures of how well a firm manages its resources. Also known as *operating efficiency ratios*. See **average collection period, capital turnover ratio, cash turnover ratio, fixed asset turnover, inventory turnover, ratio analysis, receivables turnover,** and **total assets turnover.**

Actual Real, substantial, and presently existing, as opposed to possible or theoretical. *Actual authority,* in the law of **agency,** is the right and power to act that a **principal** (often an employer) intentionally gives to an **agent** (often an employee) or at least allows the agent to believe has been given. This includes both **express** and **implied** authority. *Actual cash value* is the fair, usual, or reasonable cash price that something will bring on the open market; the same as **fair market value.** *Actual cost*, in a **cost accounting** system, is the true cost, with all cost factors correctly evaluated and attributed to the proper source. Actual costs rarely appear in accounting records except in one-product companies, where all the costs must be attributed to one product. Actual costs are determined after the fact, when all accounts have been settled. *Actual investment* is the spending on capital goods that occurs during a given year, as opposed to spending that was planned. *Actuals* are real **commodities** as opposed to their **futures.**

Actuarial method The way of accounting for finances in a record book. For example, the *actuarial method* described in the Uniform Consumer Credit Code is a company's method of applying payments made by a consumer first to **interest** and finance charges, then to paying off **principal** (the basic debt).

Actuarial projections Mathematical calculations involving the rate of mortality for a given group of people.

Actuary A person who specializes in the mathematics of **insurance;** for example, the possibility of a person dying by a certain age, the money that should be paid for a certain type of insurance, etc.

Ad hoc (Latin) "For this"; for this special purpose; for this one time; for example, an *ad hoc* committee is a temporary one set up to do a specific job. An *ad hoc arbitrator* is an **arbitrator** selected by the persons involved to serve on one case. Nothing prevents the arbitrator from being used again if both sides agree. *Ad hoc* or temporary, single-case **arbitration** is distinguished from "permanent" arbitration where arbitrators are named in an **agreement** to help resolve disputes that may arise during the life of the agreement.

Ad valorem (Latin) According to value. For example, an *ad valorem* tax is a tax on the value of an item, rather than a fixed tax on the type of item. An *ad valorem* tax might tax a ten-dollar hat fifty cents and a twenty-dollar hat one dollar, while a specific hat tax might tax all hats seventy-five cents regardless of price or value. An *ad valorem tariff* is a **tariff** calculated as a percentage of the value of goods clearing customs.

Adaptive control system Any device that automatically adjusts itself to its environment in order to maintain a specified level of performance.

Add-on More goods bought before old goods are paid for; often, the contract for the original goods is rewritten to include the new things. An *add-on clause* is a provision in an **installment** contract that combines payment obligations for previously bought and newly bought things so that nothing is owned "free and clear" until everything has been paid for. Several states have enacted laws to protect retail customers against the injustice of this practice. These laws provide that items originally purchased are **security** for the new debt only until the original **balance** is paid. They also provide how the payments under the new contract shall be **prorated** to the old and new purchases.

Address The identifying name or symbol that locates the place where information is stored in a computerized data system.

Adhesion "Stuck to." For example, a *contract of adhesion* is one in which all the bargaining power (and all the contract terms) are unfairly on one side. This often occurs when buyers have no choice among sellers of a particular item, and when the seller uses a pre-printed form contract.

Adjacent Near or close by. Perhaps touching, but not necessarily so. *Adjacencies* are radio or television commercials that either precede or follow each other.

Adjective law Procedural law. The rules by which courts and agencies operate as opposed to what is usually thought of as "the law" or substantive law.

Adjoining owners Persons whose land touches a particular piece of land and who may have special rights against it under local **zoning** laws and under general laws of property.

Adjudicated form A form may be called *adjudicated* if a court has called it legally binding or has interpreted it in a way that makes it useful for later users.

Adjudication The formal giving, pronouncing, or recording of a **judgment** for one side or the other in a lawsuit.

Adjudicative facts Facts about the persons who have a dispute before an **administrative agency.** These are the "who, what, where, etc." facts that are similar to the facts that would go to a jury in a court trial. They are different from the more general legislative facts.

Adjunct account An **account** that receives additions such as interest from another account.

Adjust To fix or settle. *Adjusted basis* is the worth of property for tax purposes after subtracting for **depreciation** and adding in **capital** improvements. *Adjusted cases,* according to the **National Labor Relations Board,** are cases closed as "adjusted" when an informal settlement **agreement** is executed and compliance with its terms is secured. A central element in an "adjusted" case is the agreement of the parties to settle differences without recourse to litigation. *Adjusted gross income* is a technical federal income tax phrase that means, in general, the money a person makes minus deductions such as certain travel, work, business, or moving expenses, etc. For most persons, it is the same as "gross" or total income. The phrase is used for personal taxes, not for business taxes. An *adjusted* *trial balance* is the **trial balance** taken right after adjusting **entries** are posted. An *adjuster* is a person who either determines or settles the amount of a claim or debt. For example, an *insurance adjuster* acts for an insurance company to determine and settle claims. *Adjustment assistance* is financial and technical assistance to firms, workers, and communities to help them adjust to rising import competition. *Adjustment assistance* is designed to facilitate structural shifts of resources from less productive to more productive industries. Under U.S. law qualified workers adversely affected by increased import competition can receive special **unemployment compensation,** retraining to develop new skills, and job search and relocation assistance; affected firms can receive technical assistance and loan guarantees to finance their modernization or shift to other product lines, and communities threatened by expanding imports can receive loans and other assistance to attract new industry or to enable existing plants to move into more competitive fields. For *adjustment bond*, see **bond.** *Adjustment entries* are an accounting device used at the close of a **fiscal** period to record income and expenses in the proper period and make the profit and loss **statement** show the correct income. It involves accounting for **deferred, accrued,** and prepaid income and expenses as well as for **bad debts** and **depreciation.** *Adjustment entries* are also made to correct errors discovered when the books of account are audited. They are also called *adjusting journal entries. Adjustment securities* are stocks, etc. that are issued during a **corporate reorganization.** The "adjustments" are usually changes that make the new stock worth less than the stock it replaced.

Adjustable rate mortgage A mortgage which can vary in any of its terms during the life of the mortgage as agreed on in the mortgage contract. With an adjustable rate mortgage, also called a *flexible rate loan*, the starting rate, or "initial interest rate," will be lower than the rate offered on a standard fixed rate mortgage. This is because the long-term risk is higher—the rate can increase with the market—so the lender offers an inducement to take this plan. Changes in the interest rate are usually governed by a financial **index.** If the index rises, so may your interest rate. In some plans, if the index falls, so may your rate. Examples of these indexes are the Federal

Home Loan Bank Board's national average mortgage rate and the U.S. Treasury bill rate. To build predictability into the flexible rate loan, some lenders include provisions for "caps" that limit the amount of interest that may be changed. A *periodic cap* limits the amount the rate can increase at any one time. An *aggregate cap* limits the amount the rate can increase over the entire life of the loan. Many flexible rate mortgages offer the possibility of rates that may go down as well as up. One variation of the flexible rate mortgage is to fix the interest rate for a period of time—3 to 5 years for example—with the understanding that the interest rate will then be *renegotiated*. Loans with periodically renegotiated rates are also called *rollover mortgages*. Such loans make monthly payments more predictable because the interest rate is fixed for a longer time. See also **fixed rate mortgage; renegotiable rate mortgage; rollover mortgage, variable rate mortgage** and **zero rate mortgage.**

Administered price   A price set by the seller rather than by the marketplace forces of supply and demand.

Administration   1. A collective term for all of the policymaking officials of a government.   2. The execution and implementation of public policy.   3. The time in office of a chief executive such as a president, governor or mayor.   4. The supervision of the estate of a dead person in order to pay taxes and assign assets to heirs.   5. Making and carrying out an organization's policies and plans. This is nearly synonymous with **management.** An *administrative agency* is a sub-branch of the government set up to carry out the laws. For example, the police department is a local *administrative agency* and the **IRS** is a national one. There are also non-governmental administrative agencies, such as the American Arbitration Association, but most serve a public purpose. *Administrative analysis* is the approaches and techniques that allow an organization to assess its present condition to make adjustments and improvements. *Administrative behavior* is human behavior in an organizational context. It is nearly synonymous with "organizational behavior," but not restricted to work organizations. *Administrative board* is a broad term which sometimes means *administrative agency* and sometimes means a courtlike body set up by an agency to hold **hearings.** *Administrative discretion* is a public official's right to perform acts and duties that are not precisely "covered" by a law or rules and that require the use of professional judgment and common sense within the bounds set by the law. *Administrative due process* is **due process** requirements for **administrative agencies.** These include written guidelines and other protections against the arbitrary exercise of bureaucratic power. *Administrative expense* is a group of business expenses usually classed as "general and administrative expense" and distinguished from manufacturing **expense** and **selling expense** because it is incurred in the overall direction of the business activity. *Administrative expenses* include such items as office salaries, officers' salaries and expenses, stationery and printing, office supplies, telephone and telegraph, general office expense, **depreciation** of office equipment, and rent. These vary with the nature of the business. *Administrative issues* are the non-economic concerns of **collective bargaining** such as seniority, discipline, safety, etc. *Administrative law* is either laws about the duties and proper running of an *administrative agency* that are handed to agencies by legislatures and courts, or **rules** and **regulations** set out by administrative agencies. An *administrative law judge* is an official who conducts **hearings** for an **administrative agency.** Also called "hearing officer" or "examiner." An *administrative order* is a directive carrying the force of law and issued by an *administrative agency*. *Administrative planning* is the process of deciding what an organization will do, who will do it and how it will be done. The *Administrative Procedure Act* is a law that describes how U.S. agencies must do business (hearings, procedures, etc.) and how disputes go from these federal agencies into court. Some states also have an Administrative Procedure Act. An *administrative remedy* is a means of enforcing a right by going to an *administrative agency* either for help or for a decision. Persons are often required to "exhaust administrative remedies," which means to fully submit their problems to the proper agency before taking them to court. An *administrative workweek* is a period of seven consecutive calendar days designated in advance. It usually coincides with a calendar week.

Administrator 1. An executive of an organization. 2. The manager of a government agency. 3. A person appointed by a court to supervise handing out a deceased person's **estate.**

Admiralty 1. A court that handles most maritime (seagoing) matters, such as collisions between ships and shipping claims. This is usually a federal district court. 2. Maritime law.

Admissible Proper to be used in reaching a decision; evidence that should be "let in" or introduced in court; evidence that the **jury** or an **administrative agency** may use.

Admission by investment The addition of a new partner to a partnership when the new member also contributes cash to the business.

Admissions Confessions, concessions, or voluntary acknowledgments. Statements made by a party to a lawsuit (or the party's representative) that a fact exists which helps the other side or that a point the other side is making is correct.

Admitted assets Assets of an **insurance** company recognized by a state regulatory or other examining body in determining the company's financial condition.

Adoption process A person's thinking about a new product from initial awareness through using it regularly.

Adulteration Mixing inferior, cheaper, or harmful things in with better ones (to increase volume, lower costs, etc.).

Advance 1. Pay money before it is due; lend money; supply something before it is paid for. It is generally a payment of cash or the transfer of goods for which an **accounting** must be rendered by the recipient at some later date. Common types of advances include the payment of wages, salaries, or commissions before they have been earned or before the regular payday, and advance payment to a builder to allow the start of construction. 2. An increase in price. 3. An *advance appropriation* in the Federal budget is an **appropriation** provided by the Congress one or more years in advance of the **fiscal** year in which the budget authority becomes available for obligation. *Advance appropriations* allow state and local governments, and others, sufficient time to develop plans with assurance of future funding. An *advance appropriation* is sometimes mistakenly referred to as *forward funding*, which involves an **agency** in obligating funds in the current year for outlay to programs that are to operate in subsequent fiscal years. *Advance work* is the activities of the representatives of a "personality" as they prepare for a personal appearance by the VIP for whom they work.

Advantage See **absolute advantage** and **comparative advantage.**

Adventure 1. A risky commercial venture; any commercial venture. 2. A shipment of goods by sea; any shipment of goods.

Adversary proceeding A hearing with both sides represented.

Adversary system The system of law in America. The judge acts as the decision maker between opposite sides (between two individuals, between the state and an individual, etc.) rather than acting as the person who also makes the state's case or independently seeks out evidence. This latter method is called the inquisitorial system.

Adverse Opposed; having opposing interests; against. **Adverse actions** by employers towards employees include firing, demoting, etc., and an *adverse action* in the context of **credit** can mean a refusal to grant credit in the amount or under terms requested, the termination of an account, an unfavorable change in terms that affects only some of the debtors, etc. An *adverse effect* (or impact) is a differential rate of selection (for hire, promotion, etc.) that works to the disadvantage of an applicant subgroup, particularly subgroups classified by race, sex, and other characteristics on the basis of which **discrimination** is prohibited by law. The *adverse inference rule* is an **administrative agency's** inference that, when relevant information is withheld from the agency with no good excuse, the information is *adverse* to the person or organization keeping it back. *Adverse interest* means having opposing needs and desires from those of a person with whom you are associated. An *adverse land use* is a use, such as a factory in a neighborhood of single-family homes, that harms the local properties. An *adverse opinion* is an **auditor's** statement of why a financial **statement** may not fairly present the actual financial position. An *adverse party* is a party who, when a case is **appealed,** might be hurt by a successful appeal. **Notice** of the appeal must be given to all *adverse parties* even if they were originally on the side that is now appealing. *Adverse possession* is a method of gaining legal **title** to land by occupying the land openly and continuously for a number of years set by state law and openly and aggressively claiming the right to both own and occupy the land. *Adverse selection* is the disproportionate **insurance** of **risks** who are poorer or more prone to suffer loss or make claims than the average risk. It may result from the tendency for poorer risks to seek or continue insurance to a greater extent than do better risks, or from the tendency for the insured to take advantage of favorable options in insurance contracts. *Favorable*, as compared to *adverse*, selection, when intentional, is called *skimming*.

Advertising   A **marketing** tool which has an identifiable sponsor pay for a presentation of ideas, goods, or services to inform or persuade a public. An *advertising agency* is a company that creates and places advertising for clients. An *advertising allowance* is a price reduction given by manufacturers to sellers to encourage local advertising. An *advertising campaign* is the planned use of various media to sell a product or group of products. The *Advertising Council* is a nonprofit organization that produces public service advertising. An *advertising credit* is the mention of a retailer's name in an advertisement placed by a manufacturer. An *advertising specialty* is a low-cost item imprinted with the name and address of a seller that is given to buyers; for example, key rings, calendars, pens, etc. *Comparative advertising* directly evaluates one product in relation to a competing product. *Co-operative advertising* has a manufacturer paying for a percentage of the cost of local advertising while the retailer pays the rest; particularly common in publishing. *Display advertising* is an ad in a newspaper or magazine that uses graphics or pictures. *Direct response advertising* solicits a customer to make a direct purchase by sending in a coupon or, as in TV ads, calling "now" to get something "not available in stores." *Institutional advertising* is designed more to improve a company's image than sell its products. *Image advertising* attempts to sell a product because of its association with intangible factors such as sex appeal or success. *Trade advertising* is aimed at the distributors and retailers of a product.

Advertorial   A combined "advertisement" and "editorial" in which a company presents its views on major social issues.

Advising bank   A bank, operating in an exporter's country, that handles **letters of credit** for a foreign bank by notifying the exporter that credit has been opened in his or her favor. The *advising bank* fully informs the exporter of the conditions of the letter of credit without necessarily bearing responsibility for payment.

Advisory arbitration   **Arbitration** that recommends a solution of a dispute but is not binding upon either party. This is not true arbitration, but **mediation.**

Advisory capacity   A term indicating that a shipper's **agent** or representative is not empowered to make definitive decisions or adjustments without approval of the group or individual represented. Compare to **without reserve.**

Affected class   1. Persons who suffer the present effects of past job discrimination, based on race, religion, sex or national origin. Employees may continue to be members of an *affected class* even though they may have been transferred or advanced into more desirable positions if the effects of past discrimination have not been remedied. For example, if an employee who was hired into a lower paying job because of past discrimination practices has been subsequently promoted, further relief may be required if the employee has not found his or her **"rightful place"** in the employment structure of a federal government contractor.   2. Persons who make up a "class" for a **class action.**

Affecting commerce   1. An activity that generally concerns business or commerce.   2. An activity that is likely to lead to a **labor dispute** that could obstruct the free flow of commerce.

Affidavit   A written statement sworn to before a person officially permitted by law to administer an oath. For example, an *affidavit of service* is a sworn statement that a legal paper has been "served" (mailed, handed to, etc.) upon another person in a lawsuit.

Affiliate   A person or company with an inside business connection to another company. Under **bankruptcy, securities,** and other laws, if one company owns more than a certain amount of another company's voting **stock,** or if the companies are under common control, they are *affiliates*.

Affirm   1. Make firm; repeat agreement; confirm.   2. When a higher court declares that a lower court's action was valid and right, it *affirms* the decision.   3. Reaccept and make solid a **contract** that is breakable.

Affirmative   Positive. **Affirmative action** is the requirement that an organization take specific steps to remedy the present effects of past **discrimination** in hiring, promotion, etc.; for example, by recruiting more minorities and women. *Affirmative action* also refers to any administrative action taken to right a wrong, rather than to punish anyone for causing it. *Affirmative action groups* are segments of the population that have been identified by federal, state, or local laws to be specifically protected from employment **discrimination.** Such groups include women, identified minorities, the elderly, and the handicapped. An *affirmative action plan* is an organization's written plan to remedy past **discrimination** against, or underutilization of, women and minorities. The plan itself usually consists of a statement of goals, timetables for achieving milestones, and specific program efforts. An *affirmative action program* is a formal course of action undertaken by employers to hire and promote women and minorities in order to remedy past abuses or maintain present equity. The most basic tool of an *affirmative action program* is the *affirmative action plan*. See also **reverse discrimination.** An *affirmative order* is a judge's or an **agency's** order that a person or organization not only stop doing something, but also take positive steps to undo the damage. For example, the **NLRB** might issue an *affirmative order* to a company to "make whole" a wrongfully discharged employee by reinstating the employee with full back pay and reestablishing the employee's seniority and other rights. *Affirmative recruitment* is recruiting efforts taken to assure that adequate numbers of women and minorities are represented in applicant pools for positions in which they have been historically underrepresented.

Affreightment A shipping contract.

After-acquired property Property received after a certain event, such as the date a person **mortgages** other property. Some mortgages have an *after-acquired property clause* which means that anything added to the mortgaged property is subject to the mortgage just as if it were mortgaged directly. This clause is usually inserted in corporate mortgages to give greater security to the bondholders. It may help to reduce the rate of interest on the bond issue when the financing is arranged.

After-date The **maturity** date of a **bill of exchange.**

Aftermarket 1. Secondary market, usually for **securities.** 2. The repair, upgrading, peripheral product and other needs of equipment buyers.

Against the box A **short** sale of a **security** by someone who also has a **long** position in the same security.

Agate line An advertising space measure one-fourteenth of an inch high by one column (of whatever width) wide.

Agency 1. A relationship in which one person acts for or represents another by the latter's authority. 2. Short for **administrative agency.**

Agency shop An arrangement between an employer and a **union** that requires all nonmembers of the union to pay the union as much money as if they were dues-paying members. The *agency shop* was designed as a **collective bargaining** compromise between the union's desire to eliminate "free riders" by means of compulsory membership and management's wish that union membership be voluntary.

Agent A person authorized (requested or permitted) by another person to act for him or her; a person entrusted with another's business. Some of the many types of agent include **bargaining agent;** *independent agent* (a **contractor** who is responsible for results only, who is not under the direct control of the employer, and not on the regular payroll), and *managing agent* (a company employee who runs a part of the company's business and acts with independent judgment much of the time). A person need not be called an *agent* to be one for legal purposes. Many employees are *agents.*

Agent de change A French stockbroker.

Agent provocateur An individual who is hired by an organization to create trouble for a rival organization by inducing its members to perform acts that are in the best interest of the opposition.

Aggregate Collected together. An *aggregate corporation* is a corporation with more than one stockholder; *aggregate demand* is the total market for goods or services during a given time period; *aggregate indemnity* is the maximum dollar amount payable for any disability, period of disability, or covered service under an **insurance policy;** *aggregate liability* is the total amount that an insurer will pay for liabilities assumed under a policy; the *aggregate method* is the projection of costs for a whole pension or insurance plan rather than for each individual in it; and *aggregate supply* is the total supply of goods and services available to meet *aggregate demand.*

Aggressive A **mutual fund** or individual investment **portfolio** managed for fast **capital** appreciation.

Aggressive collection Various means of collecting a **debt**, such as **attachment, execution, garnishment**, etc.

Aging schedule A list showing how long **accounts receivable** (short-term money owed to a company) have been owed and which ones are overdue. See also **collection ratio.**

Agio Extra money paid to convert from one currency to another. The *interest agio* is the difference between the interest rates of two countries. The *agio* or *abstinence theory of interest* holds that interest on savings is the result, indeed the reward of, abstinence; that is, not spending.

Agreement 1. An intention of two or more persons to enter into a contract with one another combined with an attempt to form a valid contract. An *agreement* may include the language used plus background facts and circumstances. 2. A **contract.** 3. See also **blanket, fair-share, gentlemen's, individual, interim, labor, master, model, open-end,** and **sweetheart agreements.** 4. An *agreement corporation* is a U.S. domestic state-chartered corporation principally engaged in international banking. U.S. banks may invest in such corporations provided that the corporation enters into an agreement with the **Federal Reserve** to conduct its business as the Federal Reserve may prescribe. In practice, the activities of *agreement corporations* have been restricted to those permitted **edge corporations.**

Agribusiness Farming writ large. *Agro-industry* refers to activities that are both agricultural and industrial in their character.

Air pocket A sudden weakness in the price of a particular stock.

Air rights 1. The right to build above a piece of land; for example, the right to put a building over a sunken road. 2. The right to reasonable use of all airspace above a property. For example, while airplanes may fly over a property, if they regularly fly so low as to reduce the property's value, they may have to pay for this reduction.

Airbill A **bill of lading** for shipment by air.

Aleatory contract A **contract** with effects and results that depend on an uncertain event; for example, **insurance** agreements are *aleatory*. [pronounce: a-le-a-to-ri]

Algorithm A repeatable, step-by-step procedure to solve a (usually mathematical) problem or to accomplish a task.

Algorithms for computerized applications make each step a yes-or-no decision with only two choices.

Alia (or alii) (Latin) 1. Other things. 2. Other persons.

Alienate Transfer, convey, or otherwise dispose of property to another person. The process is called *alienation* when land is transferred. An *alienation clause* is a part of an **insurance** policy that **voids** (ends) the policy if the property being insured is sold or otherwise transferred. *Alienation* was originally a concept from Marxism which held that industrial workers would experience feelings of disassociation because they lacked control of their work (and thus be ripe for revolution). The word has now lost its Marxist taint and now refers to any feelings of estrangement from one's work, family, society, etc.

All events test When taxes are paid on an **accrual basis,** income is considered to belong to the taxpayer once all events have occurred that give the taxpayer a legal right to the income and once the amount can be closely figured.

Allocation Putting something in one place rather than in another. For example, crediting all of a payment to one **account** when it is not specifically marked and the customer has two accounts at the store is called *allocation*. *Allocation of income* refers to the **IRS's determination** that income belongs to one of two companies controlled by the same persons, rather than to the other company. And *allocation* of a **position** or **class** is to assign it to a particular salary grade in the salary schedule, based on an evaluation of its relative worth. To *reallocate* is to change the existing allocation of a position or class to a different salary grade in the schedule.

Allonge A piece of paper attached to a **negotiable instrument** to provide space for **indorsements** (signatures).

Allotment A share or portion; sometimes, the dividing-up process itself. For example, an *allotment certificate* is a document that tells prospective buyers of **shares** in a company how many shares they may buy and the **schedule** of payments for the shares; and a *land allotment* is a dividing-up of a piece of land for sale as building lots. Also, *allotment* is the system by which departments control spending by lower units; a legal authorization to **incur** expenditures for a given amount for a specific purpose made on a monthly or quarterly basis.

Allowable charge The maximum fee that an insurance plan will pay a provider for a given service.

Allowable costs Items or elements of an institution's costs which are reimbursable under a payment formula. For example, both Medicare and Medicaid reimburse hospitals on the basis of certain costs, but do not allow reimbursement for all costs. *Allowable costs* may exclude, for example, uncovered services, luxury accommodations, costs which are not reasonable, etc.

Allowance 1. A financial payment to compensate an employee for the extra expense of living at a hardship post, for special clothing (such as uniforms), or for some other benefit that personnel policy allows. See also **clothing, cost-of-living, family, fatigue, hardship, housing, subsistence,** and **tax-reimbursement allowances.** 2. See **reserve.**

Allowed time The time given an employee to perform a task. It usually includes an allowance for fatigue and personal or unavoidable delays.

Alongside The side of a ship. Goods to be delivered *alongside* are to be placed on the dock or barge within reach of a transport ship's tackle so that they can be loaded aboard the ship.

Alter ego Second self. The rule that if persons use a **corporation** as a mere front for doing their own private business, a court may disallow some of the protection that the law gives to the corporation's owners. Under the *alter ego rule* the court may hold the persons individually liable for their actions taken through the corporation. See also **corporate veil** and **instrumentality.**

Alternation ranking A technique used in **job evaluation** and **performance appraisal** that ranks the highest and the lowest, then the next highest and the next lowest, etc., until all jobs have been ranked.

Alternative technology See **appropriate technology.**

Amalgamation A complete joining or blending together of two or more things into one. For example, the *amalgamation* of two **corporations** usually creates a single **board** of directors, a single company name, new company stock, etc.

American United States. The *American Arbitration Association* is an organization that supplies arbitrators who help settle labor and other disputes through **arbitration, mediation,** and other voluntary methods. The *American Assembly of Collegiate Schools of Business* is the sole accrediting agency for bachelors and masters programs in business and administration. An *American clause* is a provision in some marine **insurance** policies that makes the insurance company liable for the full amount of certain claims even if other insurance covers the same claims. *American depository receipts* are documents similar to **stock** certificates which represent shares in a foreign corporation. These shares, registered in the holder's name, are held by a foreign bank which acts as the **agent** for the domestic bank which issued the receipts. The *American Federation of Labor-Congress of Industrial Organizations (AFL-CIO)* is a voluntary federation of over 100 national and international unions operating in the United States. The AFL-CIO is itself not a union; it does no bargaining. It is perhaps best thought of as a union of unions. The *American Institute of Banking* is the educational section of the American Banker's Association. The *American Management Associations* is the largest organization for professional managers. For *American national standard,* see **industrial standardization.** *American plan* was a term used by employers in the early part of this century to encourage open or nonunion shops. By implication, the closed or **union shop** was portrayed as alien to the nation's individualistic spirit, restrictive of industrial efficiency, and generally "un-American." An *American plan* is now a hotel's policy of including meals with a room charge. The *American Production and Inventory Control Society* has a nationally recognized examination and certification program in production and inventory management. *American selling price (ASP)* is a method of valuation, required in U.S. tariff legislation for certain imports, where the **customs** value on which the appropriate **ad valorem duty** is assessed is not the actual export value of the commodity but the higher selling price in the U.S. of the competitive domestic product. The *ASP* valuation thus increases the amount of the U.S. import duty, in most cases substantially. The *ASP* valuation method is considered a **non-tariff barrier.** The *American Stock Exchange* is the second-largest stock exchange in the United States (after the **New York Stock Exchange**). It is also known as the Curb Exchange because it originally conducted business directly in the street.

Amex   American Stock Exchange.

Amicus curiae (Latin) "Friend of the court." A person who is allowed to appear in a lawsuit (usually to file arguments in the form of a brief, but sometimes to take an active part) even though the person has no right to appear otherwise. [pronounce: a-me-kus cure-e-eye]

Amortization 1. Paying off a debt in regular and equal payments. To *amortize* an ordinary loan, figure out the total interest for the whole time until the loan is paid off, add that total to the amount of the loan, and divide the total by the number of payments. *Negative amortization* occurs when monthly interest payments do not cover all of the interest cost; this unpaid interest is then added to the principal balance. 2. Breaking down the value and costs of an intangible asset (such as money owed, a **copyright**, or a **patent**) year-by-year over the estimated useful life of the asset. 3. Any dividing up of benefits or costs by time periods, primarily for tax purposes. It is generally called *amortization* for **intangibles** such as money owed, **depreciation** for physical objects used in a business, and **depletion** for natural resources such as oil.

Analog 1. An individual's counterpart or opposite number in another organization. 2. Data represented by a continuous flow of information, usually as it is received in physical form. For example, a mercury thermometer gives an *analog* reading on a glass scale, while a thermometer that reads out in numbers is *digital*.

Analogy method The estimating of costs by making direct comparisons with historical information on similar existing alternatives or their components. It is probably the most widely used method of cost analysis. Because it is basically a judgment process, it requires a considerable amount of experience and expertise if it is to be done successfully. Moreover, a judgment should always be recognized for what it is, an educated guess. Estimations of facilities acquisition costs often place heavy reliance on the *analogy method*.

Analyst A person who reviews **securities** for a brokerage firm in order to recommend that clients buy or sell them. In bigger firms *analysts* usually specialize in certain industries.

Analytical estimating A work-measurement technique that estimates the time required to perform a job on the basis of prior experience.

Anchor tenant A major retailer, such as a big department store, that draws traffic to a shopping center.

Annual Yearly. *Annual earnings* is an employee's total **compensation** during a calendar year, including basic salary or wages, all overtime and premium pay, vacation pay, bonuses, etc. The *annual percentage rate* is the true cost of borrowing money, expressed in a standardized, yearly way to make it easier to understand **credit** terms and to shop for credit. An *annual report* (or *statement*) is a report most **corporations** are legally required to provide each year to stockholders and to the government. Most companies also make it freely available to the public. The report usually contains a **balance sheet, statements** of income, spending, **retained earnings,** and other financial data, plus a breakdown of the company's **stocks** and **bonds,** an explanation of **accounting** principles used, an **auditor's** report, comments about the year's business and future prospects, etc. Parts of the report may have different names from those given here. An *annual report* may also be any yearly report of an organization. *Annualized cost* is the cost of something for a 12-month period. *Annualized costs* may be figured on the calendar year, the fiscal year, the date a contract becomes effective, etc.

Annuity 1. A fixed sum of money, usually paid to a person at fixed times for a fixed time period or for life. If for life, or for some other uncertain period of time, it is called **contingent.** 2. A *retirement annuity* is a right to receive payments starting at some future date, usually retirement, but sometimes a fixed date. There are many ways a *retirement annuity* can be paid. For example, *life* (equal monthly payments for the retiree's life); *lump sum* (one payment); *certain and continuous* (like *life*, but if the person dies within a set time period, benefits continue for the rest of that period); and *joint and survivor* (a slightly lower level of benefits, but it will continue for the life of either the retiree or the spouse).

Answer 1. The first pleading by the defendant in a lawsuit. This pleading responds to the charges and demands of the plaintiff's complaint. The defendant many deny the plaintiff's charges, may present new facts to defeat them, or may show why the plaintiff's facts are legally invalid. 2. Take on the **liability** of another person, as in to *answer* for someone's debt.

Antecedent debt   A debt that is prior in time to another transaction. In **contract** law, the prior debt may sometimes make a fresh promise to pay enforceable even if the debt itself is too old to collect. And in **bankruptcy** law, an *antecedent debt* is one owed for a long enough time before the filing of bankruptcy that it is considered a valid debt rather than an attempt to give money to one person in preference to other **creditors.**

Antedate   Predate. Date a document earlier than the date it was actually signed. This is sometimes a crime.

Anticipation   1. The act of doing a thing before its proper time or simply doing it "before" something else.   2. The right to pay off a **mortgage** before it comes due without paying a **prepayment penalty.**   3. The right under some **contracts** to deduct some money (usually equal to the current interest rate) when paying early. For example, selling terms may allow a two percent discount for payment within ten days. If the invoice is paid the first day of the discount period, an additional deduction is allowed by some vendors for the nine days' prepayment. This additional deduction is referred to as *anticipation.*   4. In **patent** law, a person is *anticipated* if someone else has already patented substantially the same thing. *Anticipations and intentions data* is information on the plans of businesses and consumers regarding their economic activities in the near future. These plans are considered valuable aids to economic forecasting, either directly or as an indication of the state of confidence concerning the economic outlook. *Anticipatory breach* is breaking a contract by refusing to go through with it once it is entered into, but before it is time actually to perform (do your side or share).

Anti-dilutive   A **potentially dilutive security** which would increase **earnings per share** or decrease loss per share if it were converted into **common stock.**

Anti-discrimination laws   1. State **insurance** laws which prohibit *insurers* from giving preferential terms or rates not warranted by the rating of the **risks** involved.   2. See **discrimination.**

Antidumping act (or duty)   See **dump.**

Anti-Racketeering Act   A federal law prohibiting extortion and other interference with interstate commerce. Also called the Hobbs Act. For example, the Act makes it a federal crime for union leaders to either blackmail employers or accept bribes for not calling strikes. See also **labor racketeer.**

Antitrust acts Federal and state laws to protect trade from **monopoly** control and from **price-fixing** and other **restraints of trade.**

Apparent Easily seen; superficially true. For example, *apparent authority* is the **authority** an **agent** (such as an employee) seems to have, judged by the words and actions of the person who gave the authority and by the agent's own words and actions.

Appeal 1. Ask a higher court to review the actions of a lower court in order to correct mistakes or injustice. 2. The process in no. 1 is called *an appeal.* An appeal may also be taken from a lower level of an **administrative agency** to a higher level or from an agency to a court.

Appearance The coming into court as a **party** (plaintiff or defendant) to a lawsuit. A person who does this *appears.*

Appellant The person who **appeals** a case to a higher court or authority.

Appellate A higher court that can hear **appeals** from a lower court.

Appellee The **party** in a case against whom an **appeal** is taken (usually, but not always, the winner in the lower court).

Applicant An individual seeking initial employment or an in-house promotional opportunity. An *applicant pool* consists of those individuals who have applied for a particular job over a given period. And an *applicant tally* is a system by which the **EEO** status of applicants is recorded at the time of application or interview. By periodically comparing applicant tally rates with rates of appointment and rejection, the progress of **affirmative action** recruitment efforts can be measured.

Applications package A set of computer **programs** to perform one type of task such as **word processing.**

Application blank Frequently the first phase of the **applicant** selection process. Properly completed it can serve three purposes: (1) it is a formal request for employment; (2) it provides information that indicates the applicant's fitness for the position; and (3) it can become the basic personnel record for those applicants who are hired. Application blanks must conform to all **EEOC** guidelines; requested information must be a valid predictor of performance. See also **weighted application blank.**

Applied costs The financial measure of resources consumed or applied within a given period of time to accomplish a specific purpose (such as performing a service, carrying out an activity, or completing a unit of work or a specific project) regardless of when ordered, received, or paid for.

Apportionment In real estate, the dividing between seller and buyer of debts the property owes (such as fuel bills) and income owed to the property (such as rent). This is usually done at the **closing.**

Appraisal (or appraisement) 1. Estimating the value of something by an impartial expert. This is not the same as an **assessment.** 2. Fixing the fair value of **stock** by a court when stockholders in a **corporation** quarrel and some must be bought out. *Appraisal remedy* (or *rights*) is the provision of law in most states giving **minority stockholders** the right to be bought out at the price the stock was before the corporation took an unusual action, such as a **merger** or sale of major **assets.** 3. The *appraisal method* of **depreciation** values **assets** by appraisals made at the beginning and end of each **accounting period,** depreciation for the period being the difference between the appraised values. When this method is used, the effect of fluctuations in **market values** should be ignored. The appraisal method is probably most practical for assets such as small tools or supplies inventories where breakage or theft are more important depreciation factors than use or the mere passage of time. 4. An *appraisal surplus* is the value of an asset beyond the amount paid for it. 5. The evaluation of employees. See **performance appraisal.**

Appraiser An impartial expert chosen to set a value on a piece of property.

Appreciation 1. The increase in value of a piece of property excluding increases due to improvements. 2. Any increase in value.

Apprentice A worker who learns, according to written or oral contractual agreement, a recognized skilled craft or trade requiring one or more years of **on-the-job training** through job experience supplemented by related instruction, prior to being considered a qualified skilled worker. The *Apprenticeship Act* is a federal law that authorizes the Secretary of Labor to set **standards** necessary to safeguard the welfare of apprentices and to cooperate with the states in the promotion of such standards. It is also called the Fitzgerald Act. The *apprentice rate* or *scale* is a schedule of rates for workers in formal apprenticeship programs that gradually permits the attainment of the minimum **journey worker** rate.

Appropriate technology A technology in which the tools, devices, and processes are developed from local resources with local talents to meet local needs within local cultural patterns. Other terms used synonymously with appropriate technology are *alternate technology, intermediate technology,* and *soft technology.*

Appropriate unit See **bargaining unit.**

Appropriation 1. A legislature's setting aside for a specific purpose a portion of the money raised by the government; for example, a *highway appropriation.* In the federal government's budget process an *appropriation* is an Act of Congress that permits federal agencies to **incur** obligations and to make payments out of the Treasury for specified purposes. An *appropriation* usually follows enactment of authorizing legislation. An *appropriation act* is the most common form of budget authority, but in some cases the authorizing legislation provides the budget authority. *Appropriations* are categorized in a variety of ways, such as by their period of availability (one-year, multiple-year, no-year), the timing of congressional action (current, permanent), and the manner of determining the amount of the appropriation (definite, indefinite). 2. A governmental taking of land or property for public use. 3. Taking something wrongfully; for example, using a person's picture and name in an advertisement without permission. 4. In private business, an *appropriation* is setting aside money for a major purchase or long-term project.

Approval A sale *on approval* means that the buyer may return the goods if they are unsatisfactory even if they are all the seller claims they are.

Aptitude The capacity to acquire knowledge, skill, or ability with experience or a given amount of formal or informal education or training. An *aptitude test* is usually a battery of separate tests designed to measure an individual's overall ability to learn. A large variety of specialized aptitude tests have been developed to predict an applicant's performance on a particular job or in a particular course of study.

Arbitrage 1. Buying **securities, commodities, goods,** or **foreign exchange** in one market and simultaneously selling the same thing in another market to take advantage of a difference in price quotations between the two markets. Because of foreign exchange restrictions, *arbitrage* in securities and commodities must usually be confined to one country. 2. Buying an item and simultaneously selling another item into which the first is convertible, in the same market. This is often done with **convertible** and **preferred stock** and bonds. When the subject of the *arbitrage* is the bonds of a company in **reorganization,** the operation is called *quasi arbitrage.*

Arbitrageur 1. A trader who practices **arbitrage;** also known as an *Arb.* 2. A trader who invests in companies that are **takeover** targets.

Arbitrary 1. Action taken according to a person's own desires; without supervision, general principles or rules to decide by. 2. Action taken capriciously, in bad faith, or without good reason.

Arbitration Formally submitting a dispute to a person (other than a judge) whose decision is usually binding. This person is called an *arbitrator.* If *arbitration* is required by law, it is called "compulsory." In labor disputes, the *arbitrator* usually holds a formal hearing and renders a decision that may or may not be binding on both sides. The *arbitrator* may be a single individual or a board of three, five, or more. When boards are used, they may include, in addition to impartial members, representatives from both of the disputants. *Arbitrators* may be selected jointly by labor and management or recommended by the Federal Mediation and Conciliation Service, by a state or local agency offering similar referrals, or by the private American Arbitration Association. See also **binding, compulsory, final offer, grievance, interest, and voluntary arbitration.** *Arbitrability* is whether or not an issue is covered by a **collective bargaining agreement** and can be heard and resolved in *arbitration.* **Arbitration acts** were laws that help (and sometimes require) the submission of certain types of problems (often **labor** disputes) to an *arbitrator.* An **arbitration clause** is a provision of a **collective bargaining agreement** requiring that disputes arising during the life of the contract over its interpretation are subject to *arbitration.* The clause may be broad enough to include "any dispute" or restricted to specific concerns. *Arbitration of exchange* is the **arbitrage** of **bills** of exchange in order to take advantage of the different values of national currencies in different international money markets.

Architectural barriers Physical aspects of a building that might hinder or prevent the employment of a physically **handicapped individual.** The lack of a ramp, for example, may prevent a person in a wheelchair from entering a building having only stairways for access.

Area A place or region. An *area* or *area-wide agreement* is one **union** making the same **labor contract** with many companies in one geographical area. This is called *area bargaining*. An *area of consideration* is the geographic area within which all candidates who meet the basic requirements for promotion to a **position** are given the opportunity to be considered. *Area sampling* is marking off a geographic test area into blocks, choosing random sample blocks, and interviewing as many persons as possible in those areas. *Area wage differences* are differing pay rates for various occupations in differing geographic areas. For *area wage survey*, see **wage survey.**

Arithmetic mean See **mean.**

Arms length Not on close terms; not an "inside deal"; not done by a lawyer, **trustee,** or other person especially responsible to a person for faithfulness. Whether a deal is *arms length* is often tested by its result: was the price paid a fair one, was it a price that would have been reached on the open market?

Arrangement with creditors A plan under the federal **Bankruptcy** Act that allows a financially weak person or company to settle debts for less than full value, to gain additional time to pay, or to otherwise keep from going under completely. See **Chapter Eleven** for **corporations** and **Chapter Thirteen** for persons and small businesses.

Array A table of numbers, especially one in order from small to big. An *array processor* is a large computer that quickly does repeat calculations.

Arrears (or **arrearages**) Money owed that is overdue and unpaid.

Articles 1. The separate parts of a document, book, set of rules, etc.; a law with several parts; or a system of rules, for example, *articles of the navy*. 2. Certain types of contracts; for example, *articles of partnership*, which set up a partnership, or *articles of association*, which set up non-stock (often non-profit) organizations. *Articles of incorporation* is the document that sets up a **corporation.** This document must be filed with the right state agency (usually the secretary of state).

Artificial barriers to employment Limitations (such as age, sex, race, national origin, parental status, credential requirements, criminal record, lack of child care, and absence of part-time or alternative working patterns/schedules) in hiring, firing, promotion, licensing, and conditions of employment which are not directly related to an individual's fitness or ability to perform the tasks required by the job.

Artificial person An entity or "thing" that the law gives some of the legal rights and duties of a person; for example, a **corporation.**

Asian dollars U.S. dollars in Asian and Pacific Basin banks.

As is In its present condition. An *as-is sale* is one in which the buyer agrees to accept the goods in the condition they are in at the time of purchase. No **warranty** applies to such a sale. The buyer bears all the risk as to the quality of the goods purchased (barring intentional fraud or misrepresentation by the seller). *As is* merchandise is frequently sold at a markdown. Terms associated with its sale include "All Sales Final," "No Returns," and the like.

Assay 1. Examine something to discover its size, weight, number, or quality. 2. The chemical testing of a metal's purity.

Assemblage Combining many things (such as small lots of land) into one.

Assembly line A production method requiring workers to perform a repetitive task on a product as it moves along on a conveyor belt or similar machine.

Assembly order costs A type of **job order cost system** used by industries engaged in the assembly of completed parts into a finished product. Assembly costs are called such because the costs of materials have already been accounted for either in the previous production of the finished parts or the purchase of completed parts, and the only remaining costs of production are those for the labor and **overhead** involved in assembling parts into finished units.

Assess 1. Set the value of something 2. Set the value of
property for the purpose of taxing it. 3. Charge part of
the cost of a public improvement (such as a sidewalk) to
each person or property directly benefiting from it. 4.
Assessable means liable to pay extra. For example, *assessable stock* is stock that may require the owner to pay
more than the original investment to keep a share in the
company; and *assessable insurance* may require the person injured to start paying higher **premiums** if a loss is too
expensive. *Assessable* also means liable to be put on the
tax rolls and taxed. 5. *Assessed valuation* is the value
placed on real estate for tax purposes by the government.
It is usually less than **market value.**

Assessment 1. Deciding on the amount to be paid by each
of several persons into a common fund. For example,
insurance companies may be *assessed* a certain amount
each to pay for a government regulatory program. 2.
The process of listing and evaluating the worth of property for taxing it. This is *not* **appraisal.** 3. A payment
beyond what is normally required of members of a
group. 4. Periodic payments by persons who have
subscribed to buy **stock** from a **corporation.** 5. Deciding
the amount of **damages** that the loser of a lawsuit must
pay. 6. An extra payment, for example, when the **IRS**
decides that you owe more taxes than you paid, or when
union members must make payments in addition to their
regular dues when a union needs funds urgently in order
to support a strike or some other union-endorsed cause.
The amount of these *assessments* is usually limited by a
union's constitution or bylaws. An *assessment center* is
not a particular place, but a process consisting of the
intense observation of a person undergoing a variety of
simulations and stress situations over a period of several
days. *Assessment centers* are a popular way of identifying
individuals with future executive potential so that they
may be given the appropriate training and development
assignments. An *assessment ratio* is the percentage of the
market value of a property at which the government
values it for tax purposes.

Assessor 1. A person who evaluates the worth of things;
usually a government official who evaluates land and buildings for tax purposes. 2. A trained observer in an **assessment center.**

Assets All money, property, and money-related rights (such as money owed) owned by a person or an organization. In a business, *capital assets* or *fixed assets* are those things that cannot be turned into cash easily (such as buildings); *current assets* or *liquid assets* are those things that can be turned into cash easily (such as cash or goods for sale); and *frozen assets* are those things that are tied up because of a lawsuit. For other types of assets, such as **quick assets**, see those words. *Asset allocation* is the moving of money among a variety of types of investments to insure the greatest overall return. *Asset coverage* is the extent to which assets serve as **collateral** for specific obligations or the ratio of all *assets* to all obligations. *Asset currency* consists of bank notes **secured** only by the general *assets* of the bank which issued them. *Asset depreciation range* is the choice of "lifetimes" the **IRS** will let you use when you claim **depreciation** on a particular *asset* (property). See **accelerated cost recovery system.** *Asset management* is a policy of reducing a company's *fixed assets* to the minimum needed for effective operations. *Asset management accounts* are money-management services offered by some banks, brokers and mutual funds. *Asset stripping* is the selling off of selected *assets* of an acquired company to pay for the debt incurred in the **acquisition.** For *asset-linked annuity*, see **variable annuity,** and for *asset turnover*, see **total assets turnover.**

Assigned account A debt owed to a company that the company uses as security for its own debt to a bank. Also called *pledged* accounts receivable.

Assigned risk A **risk** that insurance companies do not care to insure (such as a person with hypertension seeking health insurance) but which, because of state law or otherwise, must be insured. Insuring *assigned risks* is usually handled through a group of insurers (such as all companies licensed to issue health insurance in the state) and individual *assigned risks* are assigned to the companies in turn or in proportion to their share of the state's total health insurance business. Assignment of risks is common in casualty insurance and less common in health insurance. As an approach to providing insurance to such risks, it can be contrasted with pooling of such risks in which the *losses* rather than the risks are distributed among the group of insurers.

Assignment The transfer of property, rights in property, or money to another person. An *assignment for the benefit of creditors* is a voluntary transfer of property to a third party who will make a distribution to creditors. This is a relatively inexpensive way of **liquidating** a failing firm. An *assignment of income* is an attempt to have income taxed to someone else by turning over either the income or the income-producing property to that person. Tax laws make this hard to do. An *assignment of wages* is an employer paying part of an employee's salary directly to someone to whom the employee owes money. Most states limit this. When it is ordered by a court, it is called wage **garnishment.**

Associate company A company owned or controlled by a **holding company.**

Association 1. A general word meaning a group of persons joined together for a particular purpose. 2. A type of **limited partnership, trust,** or other financial entity that the **IRS** will tax as a **corporation** because it acts like a corporation.

Association agreement A model or standardized **collective bargaining agreement** put forth by an **employer association.**

Assumable mortgage A **mortgage** that can be passed on to a new owner at the previous owner's interest rate. During periods of high rates, most lending institutions are reluctant to permit **assumptions,** preferring to write a new mortgage at the market rate. Some buyers and sellers are still using *assumable mortgages,* however. This has resulted in many lenders calling in the loans under **due on sale** clauses. Because these clauses have often been upheld in court, many mortgages are no longer legally *assumable.*

Assumption The taking over of a debt. For example, the *assumption* of a **mortgage** is the taking over of a mortgage debt (for example, on a house) when buying the property. *Assumed bonds* are **bond issues** that some corporation other than the issuing corporation has agreed to take over as its obligation. The term sometimes includes any bond for which the responsiblity has been assumed by other than the original debtor corporation, but is usually restricted to bonds that have been assumed by some corporation while acquiring properties of the debtor corporation. *Assumed bonds* generally arise through a **consolidation,**

merger, reorganization or **dissolution** of minor **subsidiaries** by **parent** corporations. *Assumed bonds* differ from **guaranteed bonds** in that the obligation for *guaranteed bonds* continues to be that of the issuing corporation. An *assumption fee* is the cost charged for processing papers when a buyer takes over the payments on a prior loan to the seller.

Assumption-of-risk doctrine   In labor law, this is the rarely used concept that an employer should not be held responsible for an accident to an employee if the employer can show that the injured employee had voluntarily accepted the hazards associated with a given job.

Assurance   1. **Insurance.** *Assured* means insured or insured person.   2. A **pledge** or **guaranty.**

At risk   1. The amount of money a person could actually lose if an investment goes bad, if an **asset** is not fully insured, if an obligation comes due, etc.   2. The special risk of injury or disease of certain groups, such as coal miners' risk of black lung disease.

At the market   An **order** to buy or sell a **security** or a **commodity** at the best available price at the time the order is transmitted to the floor of the **exchange.**

At the opening   An order given to a stock broker to buy or sell securities at the beginning of trading in the security.

Attachment   1. The act of taking or seizing property to bring it under the control of the court. For example, a bank account may sometimes be *attached* to make sure that a person pays a debt that might result from a successful lawsuit. This is usually only done if the debtor is a nonresident, has gone away, is in hiding, is about to take the property away, has committed fraud, etc. For *attachment of wages,* see **garnishment.**   2. A document added onto another document.   3. A **security** interest, such as a **mortgage,** *attaches* if it is valid and can be enforced by the person who has it against the person who holds the attached property.

Attendance bonus   Extra money paid to an employee for regular attendance.

Attitude   A learned predisposition to act in a consistent way toward particular persons, objects, or conditions. *Attitude management* is the underlying premise of **public relations** that reality is not nearly as relevant as the impressions or attitudes people develop on the basis of the information they receive. Consequently, the job of public relations is to give people information so that they may develop attitudes desired by the providers. An *attitude survey* is a questionnaire, usually anonymous, that elicits the opinion of employees to determine compliance with and attitudes towards current management policies. *Attitude survey* also sometimes refers to a market survey questionnaire to determine general trends and attitudes towards ideas, persons, products, etc.

Attrition The reduction in the size of a workforce through normal processes, such as voluntary resignations, retirements, discharges for cause, transfers, and deaths.

Audit 1. An official examination and verification of an **account** or of a person's or an organization's financial situation. The two most common *audits* are the annual outside examination of a company's total financial picture by *auditors* and the inspection by the **IRS** of a person's tax records. This IRS examination can be a *field audit* (at home or place of business), a *correspondence audit*, or an *office audit* (at the IRS office). See also **auditor.** 2. An official examination of a program or an operation to see whether money has been spent properly, efficiently and with the desired results. This is the final step in the program review process, and may include a review of accounting systems, management policies, and administrative procedures. It may be done by insiders or outsiders. 3. An *audit program* is the detailed steps and procedures to be followed in conducting the *audit* and preparing the audit report. A written audit program should be prepared for each audit and it should include such information as the purpose and scope of the audit, background information needed to understand the audit objectives and the entity's mission, definition of any unique terms or abbreviations used by the entity, objectives of the audit, and the audit and reporting procedures to be followed. For *audit report,* see **accountant's report.** An *audit trail* is a cross-reference from a bookkeeping record to its source to properly explain it, document it, or check its accuracy.

Auditor An official (or an organization) who examines **accounts** and decides whether they are accurate, or who examines organizations and programs more broadly for proper functioning. An *auditor's opinion* is an expression in an auditor's report as to whether the information in the financial **statement** is presented fairly in accordance with **generally accepted accounting principles** (or with other specified accounting principles applicable to the auditee) applied on a basis consistent with that of the preceding **reporting period.**

Authority 1. Permission to act. 2. Power to act. 3. Legal right to act. The power inherent in a specific position or function that allows an incumbent to perform assigned duties and assume assigned responsibilities. See also **functional authority.**

Authorization Empowering. An *authorization card* is a form signed by a worker giving a **union** the right to represent him or her. If a union gets a majority of employees to sign cards, the company must deal with that union in **collective bargaining.** Another way a union can get these rights is through an *authorization election* by secret ballot. See also **showing of interest.** An *authorization election* is a poll conducted by the **National Labor Relations Board** (or other administrative agency) to determine if a particular group of employees will be represented by a particular union or not.

Authorized capital The total value of the shares of stock that a **corporation** is empowered to issue. This sum is generally fixed by the **articles of incorporation** and remains the same unless it is increased or reduced by amendment.

Automated clearing house (ACH) A computerized facility for clearing funds transactions among participating institutions electronically. Most ACHs are operated by the Federal Reserve. See also **electronic fund transfer systems.**

Automated teller machine An electronic terminal which handles financial transactions between a **depository institution** and its customers. Terminals can be located on or off the premises of a depository institution. See also **electronic fund transfer systems.**

Automatic Self-acting. An *automatic audit* is the **audit** performed regularly and automatically in the course of the day-to-day operations of a sound system of **internal check.** Both **external audits** and **internal audits** are designated as deliberate or selective audits; they are performed only if and as deliberately planned, and then, except in unusual instances, on a selective basis by which some but not all of the transactions and records are chosen for examination or verification. **Internal check,** on the other hand, provides for an automatic check on all transactions coming within its scope. An *automatic* (or *compulsory*) *checkoff* is an illegal procedure in which the employer deducts union dues and assessments from the pay of all employees in the **bargaining unit** without the prior consent of each individual employee. The **Labor-Management Relations Act** provides that **checkoffs** must be voluntary and initiated only upon the written authorization of each employee. An *automatic* (or *"built-in"*) *stabilizer* is a mechanism having a **countercyclical** effect that automatically moderates changes in incomes and outputs in the economy without specific decisions to change government policy. Unemployment insurance and the income tax are automatic stabilizers. An *automatic wage adjustment* is a raising or lowering of wage rates in direct response to previously determined factors such as an increase or decrease in the **Consumer Price Index** or the company's profits.

Automatic Transfer Service   A service provided by commercial banks, through which they **debit** savings accounts to cover checks written against checking accounts. In this way, depositors earn interest on their transaction balances, until actually spent.

Automatically programmed tool system (APT)   A computer language for machine-tool operations.

Automation (or **mechanization**)   The use of machines to do work that would otherwise have to be done by humans. *Automation* tends to be popularly used interchangeably with *mechanization*—the use of machines. However, a production system is not truly *automated* unless the machinery is to some degree self-regulated—that is, capable of adjusting itself in response to feedback from its earlier outputs. This attribute lessens the need for human attendants and usually means computer-controlled production or work.

Autonomous   Self-governing. *Autonomous investments* in the **private sector** are purchases such as new **capital** goods that are made without regard to current economic conditions. This is often done when new technologies allow for significant cost savings even if total sales would remain stagnant. An *autonomous investment* in the **public sector**

is one that is made independent of changes in interest rates or levels of national income. Public works and defense spending are prime examples. *Autonomous spending* is the aggregate of a nation's voluntary spending. An *autonomous tariff* is a tariff established by legislative action as opposed to one established by a treaty. An *autonomous variable* is a statistical term for those variables dependent upon factors that are other than economic in nature such as political actions, social movements, etc.

Auxiliary account An account that is closely related to another (major, or principal) account. *Auxiliary accounts* are sometimes called offset or contra accounts, if the principal account has a debit balance and the auxiliary account a credit balance, or vice versa. They are sometimes called *adjunct accounts* if the balances of the principal and auxiliary accounts are both debits or both credits.

Auxiliary agency An administrative unit whose prime responsibility is to serve other agencies of the greater organization. Personnel agencies are one example.

Avails Profits or proceeds.

Average A general mathematical term that can mean the mean, the median, or the mode. *Average collection period* is an activity ratio determined by dividing total credit sales by 365; then divide the resulting number into accounts receivable. Another method is to divide receivables turnover into 365 days. Many consider a collection period excessive if it is more than 10 to 15 days longer than those stated in selling terms. *Average deviation* is a measure of dispersion that provides information on the extent of scatter, or the degree of clustering, in a set of data. The *average cost method* is a method of assigning costs to specific units of inventory computed on any of the following basics: (1) *Simple average*. An average of the prices at which all purchases, including those in the opening inventory, were made. The average price is then multiplied by the number of units in the ending inventory. This method has the advantage of simplicity but is illogical in the sense that unit prices of both large and small purchases are given equal weight. (2) *Weighted average*. The total cost of all units purchased, divided by the number of units purchased. Implicit in the weighted average method is the assumption that sales are made proportionately from all acquisitions. (3) *Moving average*. New unit average costs are computed after each purchase. *Average earned rate* is total **earnings** for a given time period divided by the number of hours worked during the period. The *average fixed cost* is the cost of the fixed inputs of production (overhead) per unit of output. *Average incumbents* is the average workforce strength figure found by adding the workforce strengths at the beginning and end of a specified report period and dividing this sum by two. This computation is widely used in **turnover** analysis. *Average outgoing quality limit (AOQL)* is a measure of the average quality level which will result from the use of a particular **acceptance sampling** plan. The AOQL is the maximum value on an average outgoing quality chart. This chart is derived by plotting the probability of accepting a lot against different proportions of defectives per lot. The AOQL represents the worst average outgoing quality that is possible under a given plan. Individual lots, therefore, may be better or worse than the AOQL. However, if all lots were averaged over a period of time, the average quality would not exceed the AOQL. The average outgoing quality limit is used in *acceptance rectification* type plans. This type of plan calls for 100% inspection of the lot and correction of defects when the number of defects found in the sample exceeds the acceptance number. The *average propensity to consume* is the proportion of an individual's or an economy's income that is used for consumption. The *average propensity to save* is the proportion of an individual's or an economy's income that is reserved for savings. This is a useful measure of a society's capacity for economic investment and development. The *average revenue* is the total revenue divided by the quantity of a given product that is sold. The *average variable cost* is the cost of the variable inputs of production per unit of output. *Averages* are various measures of securities prices on a stock exchange. The **Dow-Jones** average of 30 industrial stocks is the best known example.

Award 1. To give or grant by formal process. For example, a jury *awards* **damages** and a company awards a **contract** to a bidder. 2. The decision of an **arbitrator** or other nonjudge in a dispute submitted to him or her.

B

B 1. In a newspaper **stock** transaction table, an indication, lowercase (b), of a payment of a stock **dividend** in addition to a regular cash dividend. 2. In newspaper reports on stocks, an indicator, uppercase (B), that the stock is traded on the **Boston Stock Exchange.** 3. A **bond** rating indicating that the **security** of **principal** and **interest** is chancy; that there is considerable uncertainty as to issuer's ability to repay. This ranking is above triple C (**CCC**) and below double B **(BB.)**

BARS Behaviorally anchored rating scales. See **behavior.**

BB (double B) **Standard & Poor's bond** rating indicating that the **security** is the highest level speculative grade; that the issuer's capacity to repay **principal** and **interest** is moderate. **Moody's** comparable rating is Bb.

BBB (triple B) **Standard & Poor's** lowest rating for an investment-grade **bond.** This is just above speculative grades of BB. **Moody's** comparable rating is Bbb.

B/E Bill of exchange.

BFOQ (or **BFQ** or **BOQ**) See **bona fide occupational qualification.**

B/L Bill of lading.

BLS Bureau of Labor Statistics.

B/M Bill of materials.

BNA Bureau of National Affairs, a publisher of **loose-leaf services.**

B-School A slang term for any school (usually graduate level) of business or management.

B/V Book value.

BV/Share Book value per **share.**

Baby bond A $25, $50, or $100 corporate or government bond.

Baby Wagner Acts State labor laws that parallel the federal **Wagner Act** of 1935.

Back To **indorse,** sign, or assume financial responsibility for something; for example, co-signing a loan **note.** Also, to supply money for a business venture. A *back bond* is a bond given by a person to the **surety** who backs the person's debt. For example, when John promises to pay Mary's debt to Sue if Mary fails to pay it, Mary may give a *back bond* to John, promising to repay any losses. *Back of the envelope calculations* are those easily arrived at without the aid of a calculator, or are rough estimates or extrapolations. A *back order* is a request for an item(s) for sale or inventory that is not immediately available. *Back pay* is the delayed payment of wages for a particular time period. *Back-selling* is a marketing effort by suppliers which seeks to encourage the purchase of goods made from their products; thus a pharmaceutical firm might extensively advertise an artificial sweetener so that consumers would seek out soft drinks containing their product. *Back-to-work movement* is striking employees returning to their jobs before their union has formally ended the strike.

Backhauling 1. Shipping from a warehouse to a customer who is closer to the producing plant. 2. Return-trip carriage of goods with what would have been an empty truck.

Backwardation A **commodities** pricing condition which sees **futures** prices progressively lower in later months. This happens when there is a greater demand for a commodity in the near term when there is a scarcity than in the longer term when greater supplies may be expected.

Backward bending supply curve The graphic depiction of the assumption that as wages increase, workers will continue to offer to work only to a point; thereafter the amount of offered labor will decline as the demand for more leisure increases relative to the demand for more income.

Bad debt A debt that has become completely uncollectable. A *bad debt* can be a tax **deduction.** There are different rules for loans due to business, investment, and personal bad debts. A typical business bad debt might be an unsecured bank loan with no monthly payments made for several months despite collection efforts. Another would be **accounts receivable** that cannot be paid. Many companies set up a *bad debt reserve* to anticipate their losses.

These reserves, or allowances, for bad debts are customary only for businesses using the **accrual basis** of accounting. When the **cash basis** is used, deductions cannot be
claimed for tax or accounting purposes since the sales
which created these debts have never been included in
gross income. A *bad debt ratio* is the ratio of bad debts to
sales for a year or some other period. The weakness of
this ratio is that the bad debts recorded for any period do
not arise from the sales and credit decisions of that period
but from those of an earlier period, thus giving little
indication of the success of the credit or collection policy
of that year.

Bad faith   Dishonesty in dealing with another person,
whether or not actual fraud is involved.

Bailment   A temporary delivery of property by the owner
to another person. Examples of *bailments* include the
loan of a book to a friend, the storage of property in a
commercial warehouse, the repair of an automobile in a
repair shop, etc. A *bailment for term* is a delivery of
property for a set length of time.

Bail-out   1. Any situation in which one person or organization saves another from financial loss.   2. A government-
sponsored rescue (by providing loans or **loan guarantees**)
of a failing private sector enterprise.   3. A conversion of
ordinary income to **capital gains,** or any other attempt by
the owner of a business to get better tax treatment of
profits.

Bait and switch   Advertising one item to get people to
come into a store and then persuading them to buy a
different item. This may be illegal if the original item was
never really available or if it was not really as advertised.
The Federal Trade Commission warns that a seller should
not publish any advertisement which contains an offer to
sell which is not a **bona fide** offer to sell that product;
which creates a false impression of grade, quality, make,
value, currency of model, size, color, usability or origin;
and which is used to switch a purchaser to another product.

Balance   1. An amount left over. For example, the difference between a debt and the payments already made on
that debt is called a *balance due.* In bookkeeping a *balance*
is the difference between the amounts in the **debit** and
credit columns. If the debit total is larger, the account has
a *debit balance.*   2. Nothing left over. For example, if the

debit and credit columns in no. 1 add up to the same amount, the account is called *in balance* or *balanced.* 3. The *balance of payments* is a country's *balance of trade* (the figure that shows the value of exports to a country compared with imports from it) plus other financial transactions such as international loans. It is a systematic record of all economic transactions between residents of a country and residents of the rest of the world (including international institutions) in a given period of time, usually a year. If such balance shows a net outflow of funds, it is said to be "unfavorable" or "in deficit"; if it shows a net inflow, it is said to be "favorable" or "in surplus." A persistent substantial deficit usually results in a **depreciation** of the currency in question on the world exchange markets. A *balance sheet* is a complete summary of the financial worth of a company, broken down by **assets** and **liabilities.** It is called a balance sheet because total assets balance with, or are equal to, total liabilities plus net worth. A corporation's annual balance sheet will show what it owns and owes as of a given day and will include **stockholder's equity** as a separate item. *Balance sheet ratios* refer to relationships between various balance sheet items. A *balanced budget* is a budget in which receipts are equal to or greater than outlays. A *balanced inventory* is the ideal situation in which **inventory** items on hand or in transit are just sufficient to meet anticipated production or sales needs for a specific period set by management.

Balloon payment (or **balloon loans**) A loan in which the last payment is much larger than any of the other regular payments. This gives the customer a feeling that low payments will pay off a debt, because the *balloon payment* at the end is not as noticeable. The federal Truth-in-Lending law requires the clear disclosure of a balloon payment, and many state laws prohibit them entirely. Balloon **mortgages** have a series of equal monthly payments and a large final payment. Although there usually is a fixed interest rate, the equal payments may be for **interest** only. The unpaid balance, frequently the **principal** or the original amount borrowed, comes due in a short period, usually 3 to 5 years. If you can't make that final payment, you will have to **refinance** (if refinancing is available) or sell the property. Some lenders guarantee refinancing when the *balloon payment* is due, although they do not guarantee a certain interest rate.

Ballpark figure A rough estimate, often too optimistic.

Bank A business establishment that is authorized by state and federal laws to **discount** and deal in **negotiable instruments,** to lend money, to receive deposits, and to buy and sell **foreign exchange.** There are three principal types of banks that perform important services for businesses: **commercial banks, savings banks,** and **trust companies.** For *bank acceptance,* see **acceptance.** For *bank book,* see **passbook.** A *bank note* or *bank bill* is a document that promises to pay a certain sum of money to the **bearer** on **demand** and is intended to serve as money. A *bank charge* is a **debit** memorandum or notice of a charge made by a bank against an account. The notice shows the amount, reason, and authority for the charge. Bank charges are made for such reasons as checks returned by other banks, collection expenses, issuance of certified checks, etc. Service charges based on activity in an account (the number of checks issued and deposits made) are a frequent type of bank charge. *Bank credit* is a written promise by a bank (based on a **credit** rating or on **security**) that a person may borrow up to a certain amount from the bank. A *bank discount* is a deduction made in advance from the amount of a loan by the bank, as a charge for the use of the money. Bank discount is usually computed as simple **interest** on the amount due at **maturity.** The amount received from the bank—amount due at **maturity** less the discount collected in advance—is called the "proceeds." A *bank draft* is a check or similar document made out by a bank officer to take out funds from the bank or from another bank where the bank has funds. The *Bank Holding Company Act* is a federal law that places restrictions on companies that have partial control of more than one bank. A *bank holiday* is any of the traditional legal holidays or other special occasions when banks as well as most, but not all, other businesses remain closed. *Bank paper* is a commercial document (such as a bank note or bill of **exchange**) good enough to be **discounted** (bought by a bank or used as **collateral** for a bank loan). The *Bank Secrecy Act* is a federal law that requires banks to report all large cash transfers, and requires persons to report all carrying or sending of large amounts of money in or out of the country and to report on any foreign bank accounts. *Bankwire* is an electronic communication network similar to the **Fedwire** but owned by an association of banks and used to transfer messages between subscribing banks. A *banker's lien* is a bank's right to take for its own the money or property left in its care by a customer if the customer owes an overdue debt to the bank and if the money, to the bank's knowledge, belongs fully to the customer.

Bankruptcy The procedure, under the Federal Bankruptcy Act, by which a person is relieved of all debts once the person has placed all property and money under the court's supervision or by which an organization in financial trouble is either restructured by the court or ended and turned into cash to pay **creditors** and owners. *Bankruptcy* is a legal word and, while triggered by **insolvency** does not mean the same thing. A bankruptcy can be *voluntary* (chosen by the person in financial trouble) or *involuntary* (caused by the person's creditors). Bankruptcies are handled by the federal district courts. A typical bankruptcy involves a **trustee** appointed by the court who takes charge of the *bankrupt's* property, gets a list from the bankrupt of all debts owed, and distributes the property proportionally among those creditors who file and prove their claims. When this is done, the court allows the bankrupt to keep some personal property and grants a **discharge** which frees the bankrupt from all listed debts. This is done under **Chapter Seven** of the Bankruptcy Act. See also **Chapter Eleven** for business reorganizations short of full bankruptcy and **Chapter Thirteen** for personal and small business "partial" bankruptcies with special plans.

Bar code A series of lines of varying thicknesses that can be scanned by an optical device and fed into a computer. The *Universal Product Code* on most consumer goods is a bar code that contains product and manufacturer information.

Bargaining This usually refers to *labor* negotiations. For the various *bargaining* words, see the following: **blue sky, coalition, collective, crisis, good-faith, individual, industry wide, joint, pattern, productivity,** and **sunshine bargaining.** A *bargaining agent* is a union organization (not an individual) that is the exclusive representative of all the workers, union as well as non-union, in a **bargaining unit.** Employers may voluntarily agree that a particular union will serve as the *bargaining agent* for their employees, or the decision on representation can be settled by secret ballot election conducted by the federal **National Labor Relations Board** or a counterpart state agency. For *bargaining agreement,* see **labor agreement.** *Bargaining rights* are the rights that all workers have to bargain collectively with their employers. *Bargaining theory* is the sum of several approaches to the study of how people negotiate and how to negotiate successfully. These approaches include mathematical modeling, **game theory,** various schools of psychology, and the study of bargaining in many different settings. The *bargaining theory of wages* is the theory that wages are based on the supply and demand for labor, that wages can never be higher than a company's break-even point or lower than bare subsistence for the workers, and that the actual "price" of labor is determined by the relative strengths—the bargaining power—of employers and workers. While the *bargaining theory* does not explain wage determination over the long run, it is generally accepted as the most pragmatic explanation of short-run wage determination. A *bargaining unit* is made up of those employees in a company who have a "mutuality of interest and are best treated as one group for purposes of being represented by a union." This is usually the union that an employer has recognized or an **administrative agency** has certified for **collective bargaining.** All of the employees, both union and non-union, in a *bargaining unit* are subsequently covered in the labor contract that the union negotiates on their behalf. *Bargaining units* may be as small as the handful of workers in a local shop or as large as the workforce of an entire industry.

Barometer A business index (such as the unemployment rate) that shows general economic trends; or a stock that tends to go up (or down) in price when the general stock market goes up (or down). *Barometric forecasting* is the use of **leading indicators** to predict economic trends.

Barriers to entry Impediments to further competition in an industry whether they be legal (critical patents owned by others); economic (start-up costs too high); political (unstable government); or social (the market has established brand preferences).

Barter An exchange of things for other things, as opposed to a sale of goods or services for money.

Base Basic or underlying; that upon which something is added or calculated. The *base level* is the price below which a stock or other security will not generally fall because its low price will create demand. A *base period* is a minimum time something must happen before something else can legally happen (for example, the time that an employee must work before becoming eligible for state **unemployment insurance** benefits) or it is a time period used for financial comparison and calculations based on a fixed standard. *Base points* are the minimum point values given to the factors in a **job evaluation** system. A *base price* is the cost of something such as an automobile before "extras" are added such as air conditioning. A *base salary* (or *base rate*) is a worker's standard earnings before the addition of overtime or **premium** pay. *Base time* is the time required for an employee to perform an operation while working normally with no allowance for personal or unavoidable delays or **fatigue.**

BASIC An acronym for Beginners' All-purpose Symbolic Instruction Code, an introductory computer language.

Basic Underlying. A *basic patent* is for an entirely new and unpredicted process or product; a **patent** that may open up a whole new field of discovery; a *pioneer patent*. A *basic workday* is the number of hours in a normal workday, as established by collective bargaining agreements or law. **Premium** payments must usually be paid for time worked in excess of the *basic workday*. The eight-hour day is widely accepted as the standard basic workday. A *basic workweek* is the number of hours in a normal workweek, as established by collective bargaining agreements or law. Premium payments must usually be paid for time worked in excess of the *basic workweek*. The 40-hour week is widely accepted as the standard *basic workweek*.

Basing-point system A method a vendor uses for computing the delivered price of products by incorporating freight shipping charges from a basing point—*not* the shipping point, but a point selected by the shipper which determines freight charges to include in the delivered price. The use of the *basing-point system* makes the freight charges to a customer either higher or lower than the actual freight rate for the shipments. When the freight charge is higher than the actual, the seller is charging "phantom freight." When the charge is lower, the seller is "absorbing freight." This method of arriving at delivered prices can be used by a group of competing sellers to produce identical delivered prices at any delivery point. When this happens the Federal Trade Commission Act is violated.

Basis 1. The assumed cost of property used in calculating gain or loss for tax purposes when property is sold or exchanged. This is usually, but not always, purchase price. Sometimes it is original cost plus **improvements** minus **depreciation,** sometimes the cost to the person who gave the current owner the property, and sometimes another cost. 2. The difference between the **spot price** and the price of the **futures** contract in a **hedging** transaction on a **commodity exchange.** A seller is said to be *short of the basis* if selling spot goods hedged by the purchases of futures. Someone who is *long of the basis* has bought spot goods and hedged them by the sale of futures. 3. A *basis point* is one percent of one percent.

Basket buy A purchase of several different things for one price.

Basket of currencies A way of determining the value of a unit of an artificial international currency. In order to reduce as much as possible the fluctuations in the value of an international currency such as the **Special Drawing Rights** of the International Monetary Fund or the **European Currency Unit,** the unit is pegged to the value of a combi nation, or *basket*, of several currencies rather than just one. Baskets are usually weighted; i.e., a strong currency will represent a larger percentage of the value of the unit than a weak currency.

Batch costing A **cost accounting** method used by industries that process raw materials in batches or runs. Whenever a quantity of raw materials is run through a plant, the cost of the materials and often all operating expenses of the plant or process during the treatment period are considered as attaching to the materials being processed.

Batch processing Gathering related documents for simultaneous handling by a computer in one **run** for changes, computations, etc. See also **real time processing.**

Bath A big loss. "Taking a bath" is losing big in a stock or business deal, and a "big bath" is a company's abandoning of an unprofitable line of business and taking a **write-off** for taxes.

Baud Signals sent and received per second. It is a measure of, and way of standardizing, the flow speed of computer data over telecommunications lines and is usually expressed in **bits** per second.

Beachhead A small portion of a new market for goods and services.

Bear market A general drop in stock or other security prices; a *bear* is someone who thinks the market will fall. A *bear position* means that someone has arranged investments to take advantage of what he or she believes to be a forthcoming bear market.

Bear raiding An illegal attempt by a group of investors to drive down the price of a stock by a rapid series of sales. A *bear clique* seeks the same result by selling **short**. A **bear hug** is an offer to buy the stock of a corporation at such a premium over the market price and at such favorable terms that there is no choice but to accept.

Bearer 1. A person in possession of a **negotiable instrument** (for example, a check) that is made out "payable to bearer," that is indorsed in **blank** (signed, but no name filled in on the "payable to" line), or that is made out to "cash" or otherwise indicates that no one specific person is meant to cash it. 2. A person in possession of a **bond** that is not registered in the name of the owner but is payable to anyone who holds it. Such bonds are completely **negotiable** by delivery.

Bearer instrument (or **paper**) A check or other financial document as described in **bearer.**

Bedaux Plan (or **point system**) A wage incentive plan in which the bonus earned for incentive effort is divided between the employee and management.

Beggar-thy-neighbor policy A course of action through which a country tries to reduce unemployment and increase domestic output by raising **tariffs** and instituting non-tariff measures that impede imports.

Beginner's rate A wage rate for an inexperienced employee. Once a previously established training period is successfully completed, an employee is entitled to the regular rate of pay.

Behavior   The actions of people, machines or systems. *Behavior modeling* is training, usually for first- or second-line supervisors, that uses videotapes and role-playing sessions to give supervisors an opportunity to improve their supervisory abilities by imitating "models" who have already mastered such skills. *Behavior modification* (or *B Mod*) is the use of positive or negative **reinforcements** to change the behavior of individuals or groups. *Behavior models* are diagrams used by social scientists to better explain their theories of human behavior. See, for example, **managerial grid**. *Behavioral sciences* is a general term for all of the academic disciplines that study human and animal behavior by means of experimental research. *Behavioral technology* is an emerging discipline that seeks to meld together the technical and human aspects of the workplace. It places equal emphasis on the social and the technological sciences to foster the individual's fullest use as both a human and technical resource. *Behaviorally anchored rating scales* are a performance-evaluation technique that is premised upon the scaling of **critical incidents** of work performance.

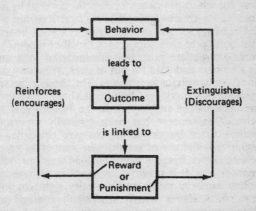

Benchmark   Any **standard** that is identified with sufficient detail so that other similar things can be compared as being above, below, or comparable to the "benchmark" standard. For example, a *benchmark position* is a job used as a frame of reference in the evaluation of other positions. *Benchmark* also refers to a computer **program** used to test the speed and accuracy of computers.

Beneficial interest The right to profits resulting from a contract, estate, or property rather than the legal ownership of these things.

Beneficial owner The true owner of a **security** which may, for convenience, be recorded under the name of a **nominee.**

Beneficiary Anyone who benefits from something or who is treated as the real owner of something for tax purposes; for example, a person who is eligible to receive, or is receiving, benefits from an insurance policy.

Benefit 1. Any advantage, profit, or privilege. 2. Money paid by an insurance company, a retirement plan, an employer (other than wages), etc. 3. Any non-salary advantage of employment. 4. For *benefit-cost analysis*, see **cost-benefit analysis.** A *benefit district* is a method for financing the construction of public works in which those who directly benefit are charged for the construction costs. For example, sidewalks are often financed through increases in property taxes of residents through whose property the sidewalk passes. A *benefit period* is the period of time for which payments for *benefits* covered by an insurance policy are available. While a *benefit period* is usually defined by a set unit of time, such as a year, benefits may also be tied to such things as a "spell of illness." *Benefit plans* are welfare programs administered by a union for its members and paid for out of dues, voluntary contributions, or special assessments. The *benefit principle of taxation* is the concept that taxes should be levied upon the taxpayers in proportion to the *benefits* that they receive. This concept has been generally superseded for income taxes by the **ability to pay** principle. *Benefit seniority* is the use of **seniority** in computing an employee's economic fringe benefits such as pensions, vacations, bonuses, etc. It is possible for a person to have different *benefit seniority* rights and seniority rights to job security. 5. A *direct benefit* is a result attained which is closely related to a project or program in a cause and effect relationship; for example, an increase in literacy as a result of a reading program. An *indirect benefit* is a result which is attained circuitously; for example, a decrease in crime due to increased literacy arising from a reading program. See also **externalities.** A *principal benefit* is a result attained toward accomplishing the major goals or objectives of a program. For example, increases in employment rates and income per capita could be the *principal benefits* derived from an increase in literacy resulting from a reading program. A *social benefit* is a result attained for society as a whole. A *subsidiary benefit* is a result which is a lower-priority objective or goal of a program. For example, a decrease in welfare rolls would be a *subsidiary benefit* as newly literate populations become employable as a result of a reading program.

Best use The value a piece of property would have if it were used in the most lucrative way. See **highest and best use.**

Beta A statistical measure, the *beta coefficient*, of how closely the value of a stock (and the money it pays its owners) parallels that of the stock market generally. *Beta* figures are often used to describe the variability of an entire **portfolio** of stocks.

Better Business Bureau A local business-supported organization that handles complaints about business practices, provides consumer information, and generally promotes ethical business dealings. National standards and support for these local bureaus are provided by the Council of Better Business Bureaus.

Betterment 1. An improvement rather than a repair. 2. A *betterment act* (or *betterment theory*) is a law (or a legal rule) that allows a tenant to recover the cost of necessary permanent improvements to property from the landlord.

Biannual Twice a year. See also **biennial.**

Bias The tendency of a selection device to err in a particular direction. A *biased sample* is a sample that does not truly represent the total population from which it was selected. *Bias* may originate from poor design of the sample, from deficiencies in carrying out the sampling process, or from an inherent characteristic of the estimating technique used. Also a survey questionnaire could be *biased* if it allows only the responses desired by the questioner. See also **sample.**

Bid 1. An offer to pay an asking price at an auction. *Bidding up* or *by-bidding* is artificially raising the price at an auction by an insider who has no real intention of actually buying. 2. An offer to perform work or supply goods at a given price. An *open bid* reserves the right to reduce the price to meet the competition. 3. *Bid and asked* is the range of prices quoted in an **over-the-counter** exchange of **stock.** *Bid* is the selling price and *asked* is the purchase price. The difference is dealer profit. Another way of looking at it is that *asked* is the average price asked by those persons recently willing to sell, and *bid* is the average price bid by those persons recently willing to buy. *Bid shopping* (or *peddling*) is disclosing low *bids* on **contract** work in order to get lower ones from other persons. 4. An application for a new (usually vacant) job with the same employer.

Biennial Once every two years. See also **biannual.** A *biennium* is a two-year period such as a spending period for a state with a legislature that meets only once every two years.

Big Large. *Big board* is a popular term for the listing of stock prices at the **New York Stock Exchange.** *Big Eight* is a slang term for the eight largest public accounting firms. *Big Three* is the three largest American auto makers: General Motors, Ford, and Chrysler. *Big ticket* means high priced (and usually large sized).

Bilateral contract A deal that involves promises, **rights,** and **duties** on both sides. For example, a **contract** to sell a car is *bilateral* because one person promises to turn over the car and the other person promises to pay for it.

Bilateral monopoly A market condition in which there is only one buyer and one seller.

Bill 1. A type of **negotiable instrument** promising the payment of money; for example, a *bill of exchange* (a written **order** from A to B, telling B to pay C a certain sum of money). 2. A statement of money owed for goods or services. 3. A more general list such as a **bill of lading** or a **bill of materials.**

Bill of lading A document given by a railroad, shipping company, or other **carrier** that lists the goods accepted for transport and sometimes lists the terms of the shipping agreement. It serves not only as a contract to transport but also as a receipt and a document of **title.** The two basic types of bills of lading are the *straight bill* and the *order bill.* The straight bill of lading gives title to the **consignee** only. It is not **negotiable** and is thus not good **collateral** for a loan. The order bill of lading, however, is negotiable, and upon proper **indorsement** is good collateral for a loan. An *inland bill of lading* is used in transporting goods overland to an exporter's international carrier. An *ocean bill of lading* indicates that the exporter consigns a shipment to an international carrier for transportation to a specified foreign market. A *through bill of lading* covers both the domestic and international carriage of an export shipment. An air waybill, for instance, is essentially a *through bill of lading* used for air shipment.

Bill of materials A list of parts needed to manufacture a product; the final phase of planning a product by **product engineering.** The bill of materials usually includes a description of the material, the quantity needed, the order number (production or sales order number), the place to be delivered, the time to be delivered, the unit cost, and the financial account to be charged.

Billing cycle The regular time interval (often one month) between dates when bills are sent out to customers.

Billing error A mistake in a periodic statement due to a charge made by someone not authorized by the credit cardholder, an error in arithmetic, a failure to reflect a credit, a charge for which the cardholder requests clarification or other instances as defined by the **Fair Credit Billing Act.**

Billings 1. The total amount that an advertising agency charges its clients for services, or a subset of fees paid for advertising; for example, billings for network radio spots. *Value billing* has an agency charging a client what the advertising is worth to the client rather than a rate determined by standard criteria. 2. The accounting function of submitting invoices.

Binary number A number using only the digits 0 and 1. The *binary number system* is used by computers because each logical or electrical choice can be "yes-no," "on-off," etc. Normal *decimal* numbers (based on ten fingers) can be *binary coded* for computer use, as can alphabetic letters.

Binder 1. A temporary, preliminary insurance contract. 2. The agreement made when a deposit is paid on a home purchase.

Binding A provision in a trade agreement that no **tariff** rate higher than the rate specified in the agreement will be imposed during the life of the agreement without payment or compensation.

Binding arbitration Almost a redundancy! **Arbitration,** unless it is *advisory*, is by its nature binding upon the parties.

Bi-partite board A labor-management committee established as part of a **grievance** process in order to resolve a dispute short of **arbitration.**

Birdyback Transporting container trucks by air. See also **fishyback.**

Birth leave Paid time off upon the birth of a child. This is generally available only to men. Women would take **maternity leave.**

Bit Short for "binary digit," a single 0 or 1 character (symbol) in the **binary number** system. This is the smallest unit of computer memory storage. See also **byte.** *Bit density* is the number of bits stored in a given physical storage size (bits per inch) and *bit rate* is the speed bits are transmitted (bits per second).

Bituminous Coal Act A federal law that regulates the sale of bituminous coal in interstate commerce and provides **collective bargaining** rights for coal miners.

Black Dark or bad. A *black box* is a device or process with unknown internal workings or hidden steps but known inputs and results. *Black capitalism* is a term used to describe businesses owned by Blacks. *Black Friday* is a term given to a very bad day in the stock market. September 24, 1869, was the original black Friday. Because other sharp stock market drops have occurred on a Friday (most notably in 1873 and 1929), the phrase has grown to mean any bad day for investors. For *black leg,* see *scab.* A *blacklist* is a list of persons to be avoided, such as a list circulated by merchants of persons who cannot be counted on to pay their bills. Also, the early union movement found that employers were using "don't hire" lists of men who joined unions. But the **National Labor Relations Act** made such *blacklisting* illegal. In the 1950s, many in the entertainment industry were *blacklisted* and thus denied employment for alleged "un-American" activities. *Black-lung disease*, or pneumoconiosis, is the chronic and disabling occupational disease (mostly of miners) resulting from the inhalation of dusts over a long period of time. *Black market* is a term given to buying or selling in violation of government regulations. *Black money* is income which, for tax purposes, is unreported.

Blank 1. A space left in a written or printed document. 2. A printed document (a "form") with spaces to be filled in; a model document. 3. *Blank indorsement* is signing a **negotiable instrument,** such as a check, without specifying to whom it is being signed over (leaving a blank in that space) and thus not limiting who can cash it.

Blanket Covering most (or many) things. A *blanket agreement* is a **collective bargaining** agreement that is based on industrywide negotiations or negotiations covering a large geographic area within an industry. A *blanket mortgage* is a single mortgage on two or more parcels of real property. It may include an **after-acquired property clause.** A *blanket order* is a contract for the delivery of a large quantity of goods over a long period, usually a year. This allows the buyer to cut the cost of order processing and to get large discounts and gives the seller a firm order for a specified amount for an entire year. A *blanket policy* is a broad type of insurance coverage, most commonly used in fire and burglary insurance. A blanket fire insurance policy may be written to cover a building and its contents, without any definite proportion of the insurance being carried on the building or its contents; two or more buildings at different locations; contents at several locations. The term *blanket policy* is also used in group insurance and in garage liability insurance.

Blind entry An incomplete **entry** in an **account** book. A *blind entry* might state only the amounts **debited** and **credited,** but not an explanation for the entry. A *blind entry* to a **ledger** is not supported by a **voucher** or other record.

Blind trust The placement of major assets in a trust designed to prevent the owner from influencing or even knowing about its management. This is done when the owner wants to avoid the appearance of a **conflict of interest.**

Blip A brief and meaningless change in a **leading indicator.**

Block A large quantity of identical **securities** such as stock. *Block positioning* is a **broker's** buying a part of a large block of stock from a client because it cannot be sold immediately and then selling it off piece by piece. The *blockage rule* holds that the value of large blocks of stock for tax purposes may be lower than the sum of the values of each share because it is often hard to sell large blocks all at once without driving down the value of the stock.

Block method A system for controlling a large number of
subsidiary **accounts** by establishing sub-control accounts.
Under the *block method*, **accounts receivable** would be
divided into several groups with each group being controlled by its own sub-control account. This simplifies
error discovery. An error showing up in a sub-control
account could be found by tracing only the block controlled by that account without having to check the other
blocks. This system is also useful in firms which use a
cycle billing system, enabling customer statements to be
mailed block by block as the alphabetical groups of accounts are prepared each month.

Blocked 1. Money is *blocked* when there are government
restrictions on taking it out of the country or exchanging
it for foreign currency. 2. *Blocked* also refers to bank
accounts, checks, and other financial documents that are
temporarily kept from payment for any reason.

Blue Colored blue. A *blue chip* is a large company with a
history of stability and profits. For *blue-circle rate*, see
green-circle rate. *Blue-collar workers* are those workers,
both skilled and unskilled, engaged primarily in physical
labor. *Blue Cross* is a nonprofit, tax-exempt health service prepayment organization providing coverage for health
care and related services. *Blue Shield* is a nonprofit,
tax-exempt health insurance plan which provides coverage of physician's services. It is often integrated with **Blue
Cross**. *Blue sky bargaining* is unreasonable and unrealis-
tic negotiating demands by either side, made usually at
the beginning of the negotiating process. The only "useful" purposes of such bargaining are to satisfy an outside
audience that their concerns are being attended to; delay
the "real" negotiations because such a delay is thought to
hold a tactical advantage; and provide a basis for compromise as the negotiations progress. A *blue sky law* is a law
regulating and supervising sales of stock and other activities of investment companies to protect the public from
fly-by-night or **fraudulent** stock deals. Most state laws
require the licensing or registration of dealers and brokers
including proof of financial responsibility, and state registration of offerings to sell securities. States usually have
the power to stop stock sales as well as prosecute for
fraud.

BMod See **behavior modification**.

Board 1. A publically appointed or elected group of persons chosen to oversee a public function. For example, a *board of aldermen* is the governing body of some local governments; a *board of supervisors* runs some county governments; a *board of elections* runs many elections; the *Board of Patent Appeals* reviews decisions in patent application cases; and a state professional licensing *board* examines the qualifications of various specialists. 2. A private governing body or looser-knit organization. For example, a **board of directors** is the group that runs a corporation, and a *board of trade* is an association of merchants with common interests. Also, a *board of governors* might run a stock exchange or a *public* organization such as the Federal Reserve System.

Board basket A desk file kept by a **corporation secretary** with collected notes and material to be used at the next meeting of the corporation's **board of directors.** Shortly before the meeting, the secretary makes up the agenda for the meeting from the material in the basket, numbering the documents in the file to correspond with the numbers of the subjects listed on the agenda.

Board lot **Round lot.**

Board of directors A group of individuals elected by stockholders, who, *as a body*, manage a corporation. Any person who is legally competent to contract can be a director, unless a **statute, charter** or **bylaws** provides otherwise. Ownership of stock is generally, but not always, a requirement. "Inside" directors have ownership interests or management employment with the company and "outside" directors do not. Many boards of larger companies have both to insure some persons with an intimate knowledge of company operations and other persons with a broader, more independent perspective. The charter of a corporation usually names the first board of directors; statutes usually give stockholders the right to elect directors annually thereafter; and terms of office are usually fixed by bylaws. The directors have power to conduct the ordinary business activities of the corporation. They are free to exercise their independent judgment upon all matters before them, without interference by the stockholders except in matters requiring stockholders' consent. In many states the laws provide that matters affecting all the property of the company be referred to the stockholders;

for example, a sale of the assets, lease of all the assets, consolidation or merger, or amendment of the charter to increase or decrease **capital stock.** Directors must act in **good faith** and with reasonable care, and must handle the affairs of the corporation with the prudence that an ordinary person would use. They are *not* personally liable for losses resulting from accident or mistakes of judgment. Their relation to the corporation is **fiduciary** and they are accountable to it for any secret profits. Generally, directors can bind the corporation by their acts only when they are assembled in a meeting. Bylaws usually provide for the place of the meeting and the method of calling it. A majority of the members of the board is necessary to constitute a **quorum.** A director cannot usually vote by **proxy** or vote on any matter in which personally interested. Directors of most large corporations perform a variety of functions. They safeguard the assets of the company from improper use; establish the company's major objectives; adopt long-term budgets, plans and policies; select all higher officers and executives; make all major decisions; and monitor both financial and operating results. The chairperson, in addition, coordinates overall board planning and, if also the chief executive officer of the company, runs the business.

Boardroom 1. The place where a **board of directors** or other governing board meets. 2. An assigned room in a **brokerage** office in which the high, low and current prices of leading or active stocks are posted upon a large board or displayed electronically during trading hours, for the benefit of customers and public.

Bogey An easily exceeded informal standard that employees may establish in order to restrict production.

Bogus False and intended to deceive. For example, a *bogus check* is a check given by a person who has no active account at the bank named on the check.

Boiler plate A form for a document, such as those sold by a stationery store. The term implies standardization or lack of tailoring to the individual problem.

Boiler-room sales High-pressure sales of stock, usually by telephone, and often of doubtful value.

Bona fide (Latin) Honest; in good faith; real. For example, a *bona fide purchaser* in commercial law is a person who buys something honestly, pays good value, and knows of no other person's claim to the item bought; and in labor law, a *bona fide union* is one that was freely chosen by employees and that is not unreasonably or illegally influenced by their employer. A *bona fide occupational qualification* (BFOQ or BOQ) is a *necessary* occupational qualification. **Title VII** of the **Civil Rights Act** of 1964 allows employers to **discriminate** against job applicants on the basis of religion, sex, or national origin if they lack a BFOQ. However, what constitutes a BFOQ has been interpreted very narrowly by the **EEOC** and the federal courts.

Bond 1. A document that shows a debt owed by a company or a government. The company or government agency promises to pay the owner of the bond a specific amount of interest for a set period of time and to repay the debt on a certain date. A bond, unlike a **stock,** gives the holder no ownership rights in the company. Examples of this type of bond include *adjustment bond* (**issued** when a corporation is reorganized); *convertible bond* (can be turned into stock); *coupon bond* (with coupons that are clipped and presented for interest); *debenture bond* (backed by the general credit of a company or government, rather than by specific property); *guaranteed bond* (backed by a company other than the one that put it out); *high yield bond* (a euphemism for **junk bond**); *industrial development bond* (put out by a local government to build business facilities that are then leased to pay off the bond); *junk bond* (issued by a company whose credit rating is less than **investment grade**); *municipal bond* (put out by state and local governments to finance government projects; the interest paid on these is usually exempt from taxes); *payment-in-kind bond* (pays interest due with more bonds instead of cash); *registered bond* (the bond owner's name is kept by the company); *serial bond* (several bonds issued at the same time with different payback times); *series bond* (of the same exact type, but put out at intervals); *strip bonds* (have been repackaged by a dealer so that receipts to interest and principal payments can be sold separately); *term bond* (all come due at the same time); and *U.S. savings bond*. 2. A document that promises to pay money if a particular future event happens, or a sum of money that is put up and will be lost if that event happens. Examples of this type of bond include *attach-*

BOND RATINGS

Standard & Poor's	Moody's
AAA	Aaa
AA	Aa
A	A
BBB	Bbb
BB	Bb
B	B
CCC	Caa
CC	Ca
C	C
D	

ment bond (to get back property that has been attached [see **attachment**] and guarantee that the person who attached it will be paid if you lose the lawsuit concerning the property); *completion bond* (to make sure that a builder finishes a job properly and within a time limit); and *fidelity bond* (to protect a business against an employee's stealing). 3. For other types of bonds such as **assumed bond** and **back bond,** see those words. 4. Other words frequently used when discussing *bonds* are *bond bank* (an arrangement whereby small units of government within a state pool their long-term debt in order to create a larger bond issue at more advantageous rates); *bond conversion* (exchanging bonds for stock); *bond discount* (the reduced amount a bond sells for when cheaper than its **face** price); *bond fund* (a **mutual fund** that invests in bonds rather than **stocks**); *bond issue* (all the bonds put out at one time); *bond premium* (the extra amount a bond sells for if it costs more than its face price); and *bond rating* (the appraisal of soundness and value given to bonds by one of several rating companies such as **Standard and Poor's** and **Moody's.** Rating systems differ, but the highest rating given is often **AAA** and the lowest rating of an "investment-quality" bond is often **Baa**). A **fallen angel** is an **investment-grade** bond whose rating has fallen to **speculative grade.** A **split bond** is a **zero-coupon** bond that converts to a cash-paying bond before maturity.

5. *Bond anticipation notes* (BANs) are a form of short-term borrowing used to accelerate progress on approved **capital** projects. Once the revenues for a project have been realized from the sale of long-term bonds, the BANs are repaid. BANs may also be used to wait until the bond market becomes more favorable for the sale of long-term securities.

Bonded warehouse A special storage place for goods that are held until a federal tax is paid for the right to sell the goods. This system is used for alcoholic beverages and imported goods stored for possible reexportation (without **duty**).

Bonding A contract involving three parties: the **insurance** company, the **beneficiary** (who sometimes pays the **premium**), and the **principal** against whose acts the beneficiary is **indemnified.** The insurance company promises to pay the beneficiary for **damages** due to the failure of performance or dishonesty of the principal. The amount of reimbursement is usually limited, as are the types of losses covered by the insurance contract.

Bonus Any compensation that is in addition to regular wages and salary. Because *bonus* has a mildly paternalistic connotation, it has been replaced in some organizations by "supplemental compensation." See also **non-production, production,** and **step bonus.**

Book inventory An **inventory** in which the number of units or their dollar value (or both) are obtained from the books and records rather than by actual count. When a physical inventory is taken, the *book inventory* figures are adjusted to those determined by actual count.

Book value 1. Net worth; clearly proven **assets** minus **liabilities.** 2. The worth of something as recorded on a company's **financial statement,** as distinguished from its market or intrinsic value. The book value of **fixed assets** is usually cost plus any additions or improvements less **accumulated depreciation.** The *book value* of **common stock** is determined by dividing the net worth of the corporation (the excess of assets over liabilities) by the number of shares outstanding. **Treasury stock** is eliminated in the calculation of the net worth. If the corporation has **preferred stock** outstanding, its **liquidation** value is deducted from net worth before the book value of the common stock is determined.

Booking An agreement with a steamship company for the carriage of freight.

Bookkeeping Writing down the financial transactions of a business in a systematic way. See **accounting.**

Books of original entry Any **journal** in which **transactions** are initially recorded for subsequent posting in the **ledgers** (books of final entry.)

Boom A strong upturn in the economy. *Boom and bust* is the classic but now fading description of **business cycles.**

Boot 1. Something extra thrown into a bargain. 2. Put a **program** into a computer.

Bootleg wages Wages above **union scale** that an employer might pay in a tight labor market in order to retain and attract employees, as well as wages below union scale that an employee might accept in lieu of unemployment.

Bootstrap sale Using the **assets** of a newly bought company to pay part of the cost of buying the company.

Border tax adjustment The remission of taxes on exported goods, including sales taxes and **value added** taxes, designed to ensure that national tax systems do not impede exports. The **GATT** permits such frontier adjustments on exports for indirect taxes, on the grounds that these are passed on to consumers, but not for direct taxes (e.g., income taxes assessed on producing firms). The United States makes little use of *border tax adjustments*, since it relies more heavily on income (or direct) taxes than most other governments.

Bottom line 1. The final profit or loss figure for a transaction or for a time period. 2. The ultimate combined result of several individual actions or a series of actions. 3. A final conclusion without supporting facts or logic. 4. Responsibility for something.

Bottom out A stock market phrase for the time when prices reach their lowest point during a given economic cycle. **Securities** analysts are always looking for the "bottom" because that's the best time to buy—assuming, of course, that it is not a "false bottom."

Bottomry A loan to repair or equip a ship.

Bottom-up management A catchphrase describing a philosophy of **participative management.**

Bought and sold notes A **broker's** notifications to a buyer and a seller that a transaction has taken place.

Boulwareism An approach to **collective bargaining** in which management makes a final "take-it-or-leave-it" offer that it believes is both fair and is the best it can do. The concept is named for Lemuel R. Boulware, a vice-president of the General Electric Company, who pioneered the tactic in the 1950s. If the final offer is rejected by the union, management grants the benefits of the offer to all non-union workers and assures the union that there will be no retroactive benefits when the union finally accepts the "final" offer. Because this tactic called for management to communicate directly to the workers, circumventing the union, it was challenged as an unfair practice. Boulwareism, as used by General Electric, was found in violation of the **National Labor Relations Act.**

Bound rates Most **favored nation** tariff rates resulting from **GATT** negotiations and thereafter incorporated as integral provisions of a country's schedule of concessions. The *bound rate* may represent either a reduced rate or a commitment not to raise the existing rate (a ceiling **binding**). If a GATT contracting party raises a tariff to a higher level than its *bound rate*, the beneficiaries of the binding have a right under the GATT to retaliate against an equivalent value of the offending country's exports, or to receive compensation, usually in the form of reduced tariffs on other products they export to the offending country.

Boycott The refusal to do business with and the attempt to stop others from doing business with a company. In labor law, a *primary boycott* involves a union and an employer while a *secondary boycott* involves companies that do business with (usually by buying from) the union's employer. A *group boycott* is an agreement among two or more companies not to do business with a specific firm. They are almost always illegal, regardless of the reason for the boycott. (A single firm may normally, on its own, refuse to deal with another firm.)

Bracket See **tax rate.** *Bracket creep* is the tendency for **progressive** taxes to increase with **inflation** because taxpayers automatically move into higher tax brackets without a corresponding increase in real income.

Brainstorming A word frequently used to describe any group effort to generate ideas. It has a more formal definition— a creative conference for the sole purpose of producing suggestions or ideas that can serve as leads to problem solving.

Branch accounting A method of **accounting** used by many large companies maintaining sales organizations in territories distant from the main office or factory. Under this method, the branch keeps a complete set of books and functions in some respects as an independent business. In place of the proprietorship accounts of an independent business, the branch would have an **account**, usually titled *Home Office Account*, which is **credited** with everything received from the home office and **debited** with everything sent to the home office. The **contra account** in the home office, titled *Branch Current Account*, is debited with everything sent to the branch and credited with everything received from the branch.

Brand A name, symbol or design that distinguishes the products or services of one seller from another. *Brand extension* is the bringing out of products related to a successful brand; for example, the makers of Levi jeans also produce Levi socks and Levi boots. The *brand leader* is the leading product in its field. A *brand manager* is responsible for a subset of a line of products; for example, a new breakfast cereal from General Mills. A *brand name* consists of words or letters which identify a product; for example, Sara Lee for cake and M&M's for candy. *Brand preference* or *brand loyalty* is the degree to which customers will choose one brand over another. *Brand recognition* is the degree to which potential customers have heard of the brand name. Sometimes manufacturers will create *fighting brands* designed to meet lower priced competition without detracting from the appeal of the original higher priced product. A *manufacturer's brand* or *national brand* is a brand created for national distribution. This is in contrast to a *private brand*, which is used by a wholesaler or retailer of the same product. *Multiple branding* occurs when a company sells the same product under differing brand names.

Brass A slang term of military origin which now refers to the key executives in an organization.

Breach To break. *Breach of contract* is a failure, without legal excuse, to perform any promise or to carry out any of the terms of a **contract**. *Breach* also includes refusing to perform your part of the bargain or making it hard for the other person to perform his or her part of the bargain. *Breach of trust* is a failure of a **trustee** to do something that is required. This includes doing things illegally, negligently, or even forgetfully. *Breach of warranty* occurs when a **warranty** made by a seller of goods proves to be false; the warranty is said to be *breached*. A buyer can then choose to do one of four things: accept the goods and claim a reduction in the purchase price; keep the goods and sue for **damages;** refuse to accept them and bring an action for damages; or **rescind** the contract and recover any part of the purchase price already paid.

Break-even analysis   Any method of analyzing the interrelationships of cost (both **fixed** and **variable**), volume, and profit. It enables management to determine how profits are affected by changes in such areas as production, sales, and distribution. The *break-even point* is the sales volume level at which revenues equal total costs.

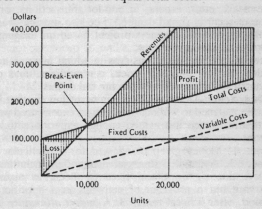

Break-Even Analysis

Bridge job   A position specifically designed to help persons move from one classification or job category to another; an integral part of many **career ladders** and upward mobility programs.

Bridge loan   Temporary, short-term financing; for example, to buy a new house before the old one can be sold.

Broad form (or **policy**)   A type of homeowner's insurance that covers more **risks** than the basic form.

Broad market   An active market, in which trading is spirited, in contrast to a dull or listless market where movement is slow or "narrow."

Brocage Brokerage. The duties of a **broker.**

Broken time A daily work schedule that is divided by a length of time considerably in excess of the time required for a normal meal break; for example, work from 6 to 10 A.M. and then from 2 to 6 P.M.

Broker An **agent** who is employed by different persons to buy, sell, make bargains, or enter into **contracts.** For example, an *insurance broker* sells insurance for more than one company; a *real estate broker* acts for the seller or buyer of land and buildings; and a *securities broker* buys and sells stocks, bonds, etc., for others. Brokers often specialize. For example, securities brokers may specialize in the securities of one business group (steels, chemicals, etc.); others, in **odd-lot** transactions, or one type of security (bond dealers). See also **outside broker.**

Bubble A gigantic business project based on exaggerated hopes and unsound claims.

Bucket shop An illegal business in which persons accept orders to buy and sell stock, commodities, and other securities without actually placing the orders.

Buddy system An on-the-job training technique that has a trainee assigned to work closely with an experienced worker until the trainee has gained enough experience to work alone.

Budget 1. Money given or allowed for a particular purpose. 2. A detailed financial plan, often including detailed income, work and resource-allocation plans for carrying out a program of activities in a specific time period, often a **fiscal year.** 3. A *budget allowance* is the amount that is apportioned to each function included in the budget. A company's *budget committee* is a group which usually includes the chief executive and the head of each primary functional division such as sales, manufacturing, accounting, etc. The *budget committee's* function is the review and approval of overall company budgets before installation and, at later dates, review of operating results against budget estimates. In many instances the **controller** is the chairperson of the *budget committee.* The *budget cycle* is the timed steps of the budget process including preparation, approval, execution and audit. A *budget deficit* is the amount by which budget outlays exceed receipts for any given period. *Budget directives* are the formal statements of management on budget ob-

jectives and policy, issued for guidance in budget preparation. A *budget period* is the length of time for which a
budget is effective. There is no uniformity in budget periods; their length is usually influenced by the type of
budget to which they apply. **Capital budgets** may cover
periods of one to ten years. The usual period for **operating budgets** is one year, usually called a "budget year" or
"fiscal year." A *budget program* (or *system*) is a management mechanism for forecasting realizable results over a
definite period or periods, for planning and coordinating
the various operations and functions of the business to
achieve realizable results, and for so controlling and limiting any variations from the approved plan of action that
the desired results are realized. *Budget receipts* are monies received by a government from its public. *Budget
reports* furnish information for purposes of **budgetary
control.** They are made by each organizational unit that
has a *budget allowance.* These reports may be prepared
for a section, a department, or for an entire operating
division. Although their complexity varies, all *budget reports*
have a common purpose—to indicate budgeted and actual
costs and to explain any *budget variances.* A *budget
surplus* is the amount by which a government's budget
receipts exceed its budget outlays for any given period.
A *budget variance* is the difference between a *budget
allowance* and actual costs or outlays.   4. For **cost-based
budgeting, incremental budgeting, line-item budgeting,
operating budget, program budgeting,** and **zero-base
budgeting,** see those words. Also see **accounting** and
finance.

Budgetary control   The regulation and guidance of business
activities achieved by the use of a **budget.** Of course, the
mere fact that a budget exists is no guarantee that it will
be followed. Something is needed that will enable management to compare actual performance with the budgeted **standards.** This is accomplished through the use of
various types of *budget reports.* The required information
may be presented in many ways but, in general, budget
reports contain the following information: the *budget allowance*, actual cost, amount or percentage of variance
and explanations of any variances. Standards are usually
set for variance reporting. For example, variances from
budget of five percent or under may not require explana-

tion. This procedure might be followed because the *budget allowances* themselves are only estimates, and the benefits that might be derived from the explanation would probably not be justified by the cost of the investigation.

Budgeting The planning phase in the establishment of a **budget.**

Buffer 1. Organizational procedures or structures that absorb disruptive inputs and thus protect the continuity or equilibrium of some core group. For example, people in positions near the boundaries of organizations often absorb a wide variety of messages and demands. These inputs are filtered, processed, and passed to the "technical core" of the organization in a sequential and routine form. Because the inputs have been buffered the central work processes are not disrupted. 2. *Buffer stocks* are **commodities** purchased by a country and sold only when necessary to stabilize market fluctuations in the prices of the *buffered* commodities. For example, goods from a stockpile may be sold when prices reach predetermined ceiling prices and purchased to add to the stocks when prices reach floor prices. The *Buffer Stock Financing Facility* is a permanent special-purpose unit of the **International Monetary Fund** established to help IMF members with **balance of payments** difficulties finance their contributions to *buffer stocks* that are maintained under international arrangements to stabilize world markets of primary commodities (e.g., cocoa, sugar, tin, etc.).

Bugs Errors which occur in the **programs** of computers. *Debugging* techniques are used to eliminate these errors.

Building code Rules and standards for the construction or use of buildings. Some codes are part of local law and others are statewide or national, such as the requirements of **FHA**-financed housing.

Building line A certain distance inside the border of a lot, outside of which no building may extend.

Building society A British savings and loan association.

Built-in stabilizers Features of the economy (such as unemployment benefits, welfare payments, etc.) that automatically act to modify the severity of economic downturns.

Bulk transfer According to the **Uniform Commercial Code,** a *bulk transfer* is "not in the ordinary course of business" and of "a major part of materials, supplies, or other inventories." Rules against *bulk sales*, *bulk mortgages*, or *bulk* *transfers* are to protect a merchant's **creditors** from being cheated.

Bull market A general rise in stock or other **security** prices. A *bull* is someone who thinks the **market** will rise.

Bull trap A stock market rally that will fail.

Bump (or **bumping**) A layoff procedure that gives an employee with greater **seniority** the right to displace or *bump* another employee. Sometimes *bumping* rights are restricted to one plant, office, or department. Because of legally guaranteed bumping rights, the laying off of a single worker can lead to the sequential transfers of a dozen others.

Burden of proof The requirement that to win a point or have an issue decided in your favor you must show that the weight of evidence is on your side, rather than "in the balance."

Bureau of the Census The nation's general purpose statistical agency, located in the Department of Commerce. Its various reports on population characteristics, manufacturing, retail and wholesale trade, construction, imports, exports, shipping, etc., are invaluable sources of economic analysis and marketing research.

Bureau of Economic Analysis The agency of the Department of Commerce responsible for preparation, development, and interpretation of the **gross national product,** the U.S. **balance of payments** and other national economic accounts. The data and analyses prepared by the BEA are disseminated mainly through its monthly publication, the *Survey of Current Business*.

Bureau of Labor Statistics (BLS) An agency responsible for the economic and statistical research activities of the Department of Labor; the government's principal fact-finding agency in the field of labor economics.

Bureaucracy An organization characterized by a **chain of command** with fewer people at the top than at the bottom; well-defined positions and responsibilities; fairly inflexible rules and procedures; "red tape" (many forms to be filled out and difficult procedures to go through); and delegation of authority downward from level to level.

Burnout A worker's feeling of mental and physical fatigue that causes indifference and emotional disengagement from his or her job.

Bursar A **treasurer** or person who dispenses money.

Business An activity where individuals, at the risk of loss, seek profit; one's occupation, profession or trade; a commercial organization such as a store or factory; patronage by customers; or the academic study of profit seeking. A *business agent* is a nonemployee who represents a company commercially (sometimes, any sales **agent**) or a full-time officer of a local union, elected or appointed, who handles **grievances,** helps enforce agreements, and otherwise deals with the union's financial, administrative, or labor-management problems. *Business capital spending* is private spending for new **plant** and equipment; considered a **lagging indicator.** A *business combination* is one company acquiring all or part of another with the intention of eliminating any overlapping functions, combining resources, and creating one **accounting entity.** For the mutually exclusive means of accounting for such combinations, see **pooling of interest method** and **purchase method.** *Business cycles* are the recurrent phases of expansion and contraction in overall business activity, measured by such things as the **gross national product.** Although no two *business cycles* are alike, they all are thought to follow a pattern of *prosperity, recession (depression), recovery. Business expenses,* in tax law, include any expense necessary for producing income, not only those expenses that are a part of a trade or business. The IRS has complex rules for deciding whether or not these expenses may be deducted from taxable income. Two areas of particular confusion are entertainment expenses and whether or not a collection (stamps, coins, etc.) is an investment or a hobby. *Business interruption insurance* protects against loss of earnings resulting from interruption of business caused by damage to or destruction of property. It meets payrolls, taxes, and other fixed expenses not provided for in the policies covering the actual physical damage to business property. The *business judgment rule* is the principle that if persons running a corporation make honest, careful decisions within their corporate powers, no court will interfere with these decisions even if the results are bad. *Business life insurance* is life insurance on a key employee, partner, or proprietor, used for business purposes. This insurance is purchased by the firm, owned by it, and payable to it as **beneficiary.** *Business logistics* includes those inventory, production and traffic management activities which seek the timely placement of goods at the proper place and in the appropriate quantities. *Business necessity* is the major legal defense for using an employment practice that effectively excludes women or minorities. *Business papers* are original sales documents such as **invoices**. For *business policy*, see **corporate strategy**. A *business risk* is the risk inherent in a firm's operations. *Business risk* plus *financial risk* equals total *corporate risk*. *Business risk* also refers to any investment strategy which tolerates moderate risk for modest gains. This is in marked contrast to a *speculative risk*, which could be a total loss or eventually offer great profit. *Business transfer payments* are funds paid by the business sector to persons for which no goods or services are received in return. These include corporate gifts to nonprofit institutions, consumer bad debts, etc. A *business trust* is a company set up in the form of a **trust** that is similar to a **corporation** in most ways. One difference is that the **trustees** are permanent, but a corporation's **directors** are usually elected for a year or a few years. *Business unions* are the conservative U.S. trade unions. They have been called "bread-and-butter" or "business" unions because they have tended to concentrate on gaining better wages and working conditions for their members rather than devoting significant effort to political action as many European unions have done.

Buy American acts   Various state and national laws that require government agencies to give a preference to American-made goods when making purchases. Similar "buy national" practices are being used also by all the major trading partners of the United States. They are counted among the **nontariff barriers** to trade.

Buy and sell agreement   An agreement among partners or owners of a company that if one dies or withdraws from the business, his or her share will be bought by the others or disposed of according to a prearranged plan.

Buy-down   A mortgage interest rate subsidy during the first few years of the loan provided by a developer or some other third party. With a *consumer buy-down*, the buyer makes a sizable down payment, and the interest rate granted is below market. In other words, in exchange for a large payment at the beginning of the loan, one may qualify for a lower rate on the amount borrowed. Frequently, this type of mortgage has a shorter term than those written at current market rates.

Buy-in 1. A slang term for joining a business venture. 2. A stock exchange policy which charges the seller of a security who does not deliver it when required any loss that a broker might experience if the same security must be bought elsewhere.

Buying patterns Statistical evaluations of trends in consumer purchasing used for **marketing** decisions.

Buy outright Purchase something for cash, without a mortgage or other credit arrangements.

Buyer 60 contract A purchase of stock at higher than the going price with the right to pay for the stock sixty days later.

By-bidding See **bid**.

Bylaws **Rules** or **regulations** adopted by an organization such as a corporation, club, or town. *Corporate bylaws* are rules made by a corporation to regulate its affairs and to define and determine the rights and duties of its stockholders in their relation to the corporation and among themselves, and the rights, powers, and duties of the directors and officers. *Bylaws* are limited by the **articles of incorporation** and by law. The power to adopt and amend *bylaws* is generally exercised by the **stockholders,** but sometimes by the **directors** or officers.

By-product A product of secondary importance, obtained from the processing of a primary product. Revenues from the sale of *by-products* are often regarded as reductions in the cost of producing the primary product.

Byte A combination of **bits** that forms a regular unit of usable computer data.

C

C 1. In a newspaper **stock** transaction table, an indication, lowercase (c), of a **liquidating dividend;** or an indication that the **yield** of a **money market mutual fund** is chiefly or entirely exempt from federal income taxes. 2. A **bond** rating indicating very poor prospects that **principal** and **interest** will ever be repaid.

CC **Standard & Poor's** bond rating (double C) for a highly speculative bond; possibly in or close to **default. Moody's** comparable rating is Ca.

CCC **Standard & Poor's** rating (triple C) for a bond that is vulnerable to **default. Moody's** comparable rating is Caa.

CA Callable in the context of **bonds.**

CAD/CAM Computer-assisted design/Computer-assisted manufacture.

CAF Cost and freight.

CBOE Chicago Board of **Options** Exchange.

CCC **Commodity Credit Corporation.**

CCH Commerce Clearing House. A publisher of **loose-leaf services.**

CD **Certificate** of deposit.

CEA Council of Economic Advisers.

CED Committee for Economic Development.

CEO **Chief executive officer.**

CF&I (or **CIF**) The price includes cost, freight, and insurance (all paid by seller).

CFR **Code of Federal Regulations.**

CFTC **Commodity Futures Trading Commission.**

CHIPS **Clearing House Interbank Payment System.**

Chq. Cheque; check.

CIA 1. Central Intelligence Agency. The U.S. international spying organization. 2. Cash in advance.

Ck. Check.

Cl. Clause.

CMO A collateralized mortgage obligation; a bond backed by a package of mortgages.

COB See **close.**

COD Cash on delivery. The price of goods or the delivery charges are paid to the person who delivers them.

COGSA Carriage of Goods by Sea Act.

COLA 1. **Cost of living adjustment.** 2. **Cost of living allowance.**

CPA 1. Certified public accountant. See **accountant.** 2. *CPA* (or *CPM* or *CPS*) is Critical Path Analysis (or Method or Scheduling), a diagram using arrows to show the flow of a project and to plan it. *CPA* usually assumes that the timing for actions is known. It is useful to analyze cost versus completion time. See also **PERT.**

CPI Consumer Price Index.

CPM Critical path method. See **CPA.**

CP/M An older computer **operating system** that allows access to many standard **programs.**

CPSC Consumer Products Safety Commission.

CPU A computer's central processing unit that contains facilities for control, memory and calculations.

CRT Cathode ray tube. A television type information display, usually part of a VDT (video display terminal).

Cafeteria plan Any **(benefit)** program that allows employees to choose their **fringe benefits** within the limits of the total benefit dollars for which they are eligible. This allows each employee to have, in effect, an individualized benefit program. Also called *smorgasbord plan.*

Call A formal demand for payment according to the terms of a contract. For example, a **contract** or **option** that allows its owner to buy a certain number of **shares** of **stock** at a certain price or by a certain day is a *call.* Also, the demand by a company that persons who promised to buy stock now actually come up with the money is a *call.* A *call-back* is a manufacturer's recall of a malfunctioning product. *Call-back pay* is compensation, often at **premium** rates, paid to workers called back on the job after completing their normal shift. Contract provisions sometimes provide for a minimum number of hours of *call-back pay* regardless of the number of hours actually worked. *Call-in pay* is wages or hours of pay guaranteed to workers (usually by contract provision) who, upon reporting to work, find no work to do. A *call-off* is an inventory management process whereby supplies are contracted for but not delivered until *called off* by the purchaser. A *call premium* is the amount over the **par** or **face** value of a **bond** or other **security** that a company must pay when the company calls it in for repurchase. *Callable* means subject to being gathered in and paid for. *Callable bonds* may be paid off before **maturity** (coming due) by the company that put them out. This is often done when interest rates go down. Some *preferred stock* is also *callable*. And *callable* **capital** is money promised to an enterprise but not yet paid in. A *called meeting* is a special-purpose meeting, as distinguished from a periodically scheduled regular meeting.

Cancel 1. Wipe out, cross out, or destroy the effect of a document by defacing it (by drawing lines across it, stamping it *canceled*, etc.). 2. Destroy, **annul,** set aside, or end. The process is called *cancellation*. 3. Under the **Uniform Commercial Code,** *cancellation* means ending a **contract** because the other side has **breached** (broken) the agreement.

Canvass Solicit sales orders, votes, opinions, etc., by going door-to-door or phoning.

Cap A ceiling on the amount of **interest** that can be charged on an **adjustable rate mortgage. See payment cap.**

Capability profile A formal appraisal of an organization's **assets** and **liabilities** in dealing with the opportunities and dangers presented by its external environment. This is usually prepared as part of a **situation audit** for **strategic planning** purposes.

Capacity Either the ability to do something or the legal right to do something. *Capacity costs* are fixed costs (see **fixed charges**) that give a business the ability to produce or sell goods and services. *Capacity building* is strengthening the capability of leaders and administrators to plan, implement, manage or evaluate policies, strategies or programs. A *capacity utilization rate* is the percentage of plant and equipment actually being used for productive purposes during a given time period. Statistical data on capacity utilization is available each month from the Department of Commerce and is an important **leading indicator** for the national economy.

Capital 1. The designation applied in economic theory to one of the three traditional *factors of production,* the others being land and labor. *Capital* can refer either to physical capital, such as plant and equipment, or to financial resources in general. 2. Relating to wealth, especially to wealth or assets held for a long time. For example, *capital assets* (almost all property owned other than things held for sale; *personal capital assets* include personally owned stocks, land, trademarks, jewelry, etc., and *business capital assets* are described under **assets**); *capital budget* (a list of planned spending on large, long-term projects to be specially financed. *Capital budgets* typically cover five- to ten-year periods and are updated yearly); *capital charges* (money needed to pay off an investment's **interest** plus **amortization**); *capital cost* (an improvement to property that can be depreciated by taking tax **deductions** little by little during the life of the **improvement**); for *capital depreciation,* see **depreciation;** *capital expenditure* (any spending producing a benefit to be charged to later **accounting** periods); *capital gains tax* (a tax on the profit made on the increase in value of a *capital asset* when it is sold; to qualify for a low *capital gains* rate, property must be held for a certain length of time); *capital goods* (things used to produce other things, rather than for final sale); *capital improvement* (any modification, addition, restoration or other improvement which increases the usefulness, productivity, or serviceable life of an existing building, structure, or major item of equipment, which is classified for accounting purposes as "fixed asset," and the cost of which increases the recorded value of the existing building, structure, or major item of equipment and is subject to **depreciation**); *capital intensive* (any production process requiring a large proportion of capital relative to labor); *capital market* (the way long-term **securities** such as **bonds** are bought and sold); *capital movements* (the flight of capital from one country to another); *capital output ratio* (the ratio of net total investment to changes in output); *capital rationing* (a company's choice among long-term projects because of a shortage of funds or the inability to borrow at good interest rates); *capital return* (payments received that are not taxed as income because they are merely the return of money paid out); *capital stock* (all stock put out by a corporation in exchange for money invested in the company; a *capital stock tax* is a tax on the **face** or

par value of the stock); *capital surplus* (money paid into a corporation by shareholders over the par value of the stock); and *capital structure* (the amount of a company's assets compared to its long-term debt and to its short-term debt).

Capital account 1. An **account** which indicates the **equity** that the owners of a firm have as of the close of each accounting period. 2. In international finance, that part of the **balance of payments** that comprises short- and long-term international financial flows, such as those associated with investment in government and private **securities**, direct investments abroad and foreign bank deposits. See also **current account.**

Capital turnover ratios Ratios designed to indicate efficiency in the use of **capital** by measuring the amount of sales activity in relation to the amount of investment employed to support such activity. Generally, the higher the ratio, the greater is the efficiency in the use of capital. *Turnover of working capital* is measured by dividing sales, less deductions for returns, discounts, and allowances, by net **working capital** (excess of **current assets** over **liabilities**). The resulting ratio will indicate the number of dollars of sales produced by each dollar of net working capital within a given period. Sometimes the **gross** sales figure is used to obtain the ratio. In either case, the ratio will vary from industry to industry, and what may be too low for one firm may be too high for another. *Turnover of net worth* is measured by dividing sales by **net worth.** This ratio indicates the efficiency in the use of **equity capital** for a given period. The ratio presumably increases as efficiency increases; however, a ratio that is excessively high in comparison with past ratios for the same firm or current ratios of other firms engaged in the same business may indicate an insufficiency of equity capital rather than extreme efficiency. *Turnover of capital* is measured by dividing sales by total capital. The resulting ratio will indicate how many dollars of investment are required to support each dollar of gross revenue.

Capitalism Private ownership of most means of production and trade combined with a generally unrestricted marketplace of goods and services.

Capitalization 1. The aggregate value of ownership **capital,** as represented by the **par** value of corporate stock outstanding, and borrowed capital, as represented by bonds or other similar evidence of long-term debt outstanding. 2. Sometimes the concept of "surplus" is incorporated into the definition of *capitalization.* Thus capitalization would be the total of **equity** capital (stock), funded **debt** (bonds, etc.), and surplus (see **retained earnings**). It is often necessary, for example, to compare funded debt with total capitalization. If surplus should represent the bulk of stockholder interest in the corporation, then it would be misleading to exclude surplus from total capitalization. 3. In **accounting,** *capitalization* is also used to describe different accounting procedures involving **stock dividends,** the payment of **arrearages** on **cumulative preferred stock,** etc. 4. For *capitalization of income*, see **capitalize.** For *capitalization rate*, see **discounting.** A *capitalization ratio* is the proportion of **bonds** and of each type of **stock** put out by a company compared to its total financing. A *bond ratio*, for example, might show that twenty percent of the company's finances comes from (and is tied up in) bonds.

Capitalize 1. Treat the cost of something (a purchase, an improvement, etc.) as a **capital** asset. 2. Issue **stocks** or **bonds** to cover an investment. 3. Figure out the **net worth** or **principal** on which an investment is based. For example, figure out what the sale price should be for a **mortgage** that brings in a hundred dollars a month for ten years. (This figure will be *much* less than one hundred dollars times twelve months times ten years.) 4. See also **capitalization.**

Capitation tax A tax on a person at a fixed rate, regardless of income, assets, etc.; a "head tax."

Captive shop Any production unit whose output is used almost entirely by the company owning it.

Career A person's total work history. *Career counseling* is guidance in achieving occupational training, education, and career goals. A *career curve* is a **maturity curve.** *Career development* is systematic development to increase an employee's potential for advancement and career change. It may include classroom training, work experience, etc. This may include *career negotiation* between employee and employer. A *career ladder* is a series of

classifications in which an employee may advance through training or on-the-job experience into successively higher levels of responsibility and salary. *Career management* is that aspect of personnel management concerned with the occupational growth of individuals within an organization. *Career* (or *job*) *mobility* is the degree to which an individual is able to move or advance from one position to another. A *career path* is the direction of an individual's career as indicated by career milestones. An employee following a career path may proceed up a single *career ladder* and then beyond it into a supervisory or executive position, or an employee may move from one career ladder to another. A *career pattern* is the sequence of occupations of an individual or group of individuals. *Career planning* is the personal process of planning one's life work. A *career promotion* is a promotion made on the basis of merit, but without competition from other employees.

Carnet A customs document permitting the holder to carry or send merchandise temporarily into certain foreign countries (for display, demonstration, or similar purposes) without paying **duties** or posting **bonds.**

Carrier 1. A person or organization that transports persons or property. A *common carrier* does this for the general public. A *contract carrier* offers transportation to a limited group of users. An *industrial* or *private carrier* is a privately owned rail, water, or pipeline facility. *Participating carriers* handle one shipment together at a joint rate. A *carrier's lien* is the right of a shipping company or other mover of property to hold the things shipped until the shipping costs have been paid. 2. An insurance company.

Carry back (and **carry over**) A tax rule that allows a person or company to use losses to reduce taxes in the years prior to (or the years following) the loss.

Carrying charges 1. The costs of owning property, such as land taxes, mortgage payments, etc. 2. **Interest.** 3. A service charge to **installment** buyers to meet the extra expense of carrying the deferred account. This charge is in addition to the purchase price and interest charge. *Carrying charges* may include bookkeeping and collection costs, insurance costs, etc. 4. The charge made by a **broker** for carrying customers' transactions on **margin.** 5.

The costs of financing an order and maintaining **inventory** after the order is received. Inventory carrying costs include charges for interest, taxes, insurance, **obsolescence, depreciation,** and storage.

Cartel A **close** (often formal) association of companies carrying on the same or similar businesses. The companies limit competition among themselves and drive out competition by others.

Cash 1. Money plus all negotiable checks. 2. Money only. 3. Immediate, as opposed to prepaid or deferred payment. 4. A *cash account* is a type of **account** with a **securities broker** or dealer in which the customer must pay the full amount due for purchases within a short period of time, usually five business days. *Cash against documents* refers to payment for goods in which a **commission house** or other intermediary transfers **title** documents to the buyer upon payment in cash. *Cash-and-carry* refers to a retail or wholesale outlet which offers a discount for a "no frills" cash only service. A *cash audit* is an examination of cash transactions, the recording of cash receipts and disbursements, and cash in banks and on hand. *Cash basis* is a system of **accounting** that shows a profit or loss when the money actually comes in or goes out. See also **accrual basis.** A *cash book* is a journal in which cash receipts, disbursements, or both are recorded. A *cash budget* is a summary of the estimated cash income and disbursements over the budget period. The cash budget usually is prepared by month for the budget year in advance. A *cash card* guarantees a discount to a customer if retail purchases are paid by cash instead of by credit card. A *cash cow* is a business or product line that continuously generates profits. A *cash cycle* is the time between a company's payment for raw materials (or wholesale goods) and its collection of payment for the finished product (or for the goods' resale). A *cash discount* is a price reduction for payment in cash, for immediate payment, or for payment before a certain specified time. A discount of "2/10, net 30" means that the seller will reduce the customer's bill by 2 percent for submitting payment within 10 days. Otherwise, the customer pays the full amount in 30 days. And a discount of "3/10 net **EOM**" means that the customer can deduct 3 percent for payment by the 10th of the month following the date of the invoice. A *cash* *dividend* is an ordinary **dividend** as opposed to a **stock dividend** but it is paid by check, not in cash. *Cash flow* is what is taken in minus what is paid out in a given time period. When **accounting** is performed on the **accrual basis,** cash flow for the period is not the same as net income for that period. Cash flow is sometimes defined as a company's **net** profits plus **depreciation.** *Free cash flow* is the maximum amount of cash a company would have available after making only the most minimum capital expenditures to stay in business. *Cash in advance* refers to payment for goods in which the price is paid in full before shipment is made. This method is usually used only for small purchases or when the goods are built to order. A *cash market* is a **spot market** as opposed to a **futures** market. To *cash out* is to sell. A *cash price* is the price at which a merchant sells (or would sell) goods or services to consumers when no credit is given. If the merchant charges a higher price than his or her normal *cash price*, federal law may call the difference interest for credit. A *cash projection worksheet* shows cash at the beginning of a period, the estimated cash inflows and outflows during the period projected, and cash at the end of the period. It

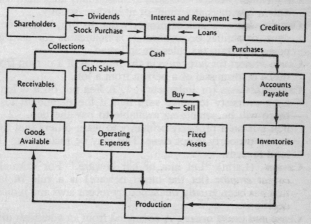

Flow of Funds Through a Firm

shows excess cash that should be invested or shortages of cash that should be covered. A *cash report* shows a company's top officers the daily or weekly cash position. While always important, it is critical to companies in a tight cash position. A *cash sale* in a **securities** transaction is a sale that takes place on the floor of the **exchange** and requires that the securities be delivered on the same day. The *cash surrender value* is the amount a life insurance policyholder receives upon cancellation of the policy. The cash surrender value also indicates the maximum amount that can ordinarily be borrowed on a life insurance policy at a given time. A *cash turnover ratio* is an **activity ratio: net** sales divided by the sum of cash plus **marketable securities.** *Cash value* is the same as **market value,** the price something would bring if it sold for cash on the open market. *Cash with order* refers to payment for goods in which the buyer pays when ordering and in which the transaction is binding on both parties.

Cashier's check   A **certified check** made out in the bank's own name and signed by a bank official. Banks issue them to pay their obligations and to transfer funds. They are also sold to customers. A cashier's check does not reveal the name of the **drawer** and is sometimes bought because of this.

Casual labor   Employees who are essentially unskilled, used only a few days at a time, or needed seasonally.

Casualty loss   A loss of property due to fire, storm, accident, or similar occurrence. It is **deductible** for tax purposes if certain tax rules are followed.

Cause   Short for *just cause* in the removal of a person from office or dismissal of a person from a job.

Cautionary lien (or **judgment**)   1. A **lien** put on a defendant's property to make sure that if the defendant loses there will be something available to pay the lien.   2. A lien put on a property primarily to warn others that **title** to the property is not **clear.** This may be recorded in the land records.

Caveat   (Latin) "Let him or her beware." For example, *caveat emptor* (let the buyer beware) is a rule of law that has been greatly weakened by recent laws and judicial decisions.

Cease and desist order   A command from an **administrative agency** that is similar to a court's injunction. It is frequently issued in **unfair labor practice** cases and requires the charged party to stop conduct held to be illegal and take specific action to remedy the unfair labor practice.

Ceiling An upper limit, for example, of ability measured by a test. A test has a low ceiling for a given population if many examinees obtained perfect scores; it has a high ceiling if there are few or no perfect scores. A *ceiling price* is a price above which something has not, cannot, is not likely to, or is not permitted to, rise; for example, the highest price a **security** is likely to reach in the near term or the maximum price that can be charged for a good or service under government regulation. The *glass ceiling* refers to the phenomenon that seems to keep women from rising to the top ranks in business and the professions. See also **job ceiling.**

Census Bureau See **Bureau of the Census.**

Central In the center. A *central bank* in most countries is the central monetary authority. Functions may include issuing a country's currency, carrying out a nation's monetary policy, and managing the level of the country's foreign exchange reserves and the external value of its currency. In the United States, the **Federal Reserve System** functions as the central bank. It also holds the **reserves** of other banks and re-lends them. The *Central Bank for Cooperatives* is a federal lending agency for associations of farmers, ranchers and the like. For *central hiring hall,* see **hiring hall.** A *central labor union* is an association of local labor unions in a specific geographic region. The *central limit theorem* is the idea that large random **samples** will have statistical properties similar to the population from which they are drawn and, in many cases, will follow normal distribution. For *central processing unit,* see **CPU.** A *central tendency* is a series of statistical measures that provide a representative value for a distribution, or, more simply, refer to how scores tend to cluster in a distribution. The most common measures of central tendency are the **mean,** the **median,** and the **mode.** *Centralization* is any process by which the **power** and **authority** in an organization or polity is concentrated.

Certificate A written assurance that something has been done or some formal requirement has been met. A *certificate of acknowledgment* is a confirmation made out by a public official such as a notary; a *certificate of conve-nience and necessity* is an operating license for a public utility such as a bus or gas company; a *certificate of deposit* is either a written receipt for a bank deposit or a bank deposit for a certain number of months or years that is permitted to pay a higher rate of interest than an ordinary **demand** savings account; for *certificate of incor-poration,* see **article of incorporation;** a *certificate of inspection* is a document certifying that merchandise (such as perishable goods) was in good condition immediately prior to its shipment; a *certificate of manufacture* is a statement (often notarized) in which a producer of goods certifies that manufacture has been complete and that the goods are now at the disposal of the buyer; a *certificate of occupancy* permits a building or apartment to be used because it meets building, **zoning,** or health requirements. A *certificate of origin* is the formal declaration required of all importers as to the origin of their goods. This is needed to establish **tariff** rates. Often this information is also attached to the goods themselves.

Certificate of stock   A document made and issued by a corporation or **joint stock company,** formally declaring that the person named on it owns the stated number of **shares of stock;** written evidence of ownership of an interest in a company, and of the rights and liabilities that such owner-ship signifies. Stock certificates are often **negotiable.** The form and contents of stock certificates must comply with requirements in the **charter, by-laws,** and **statutes.** The items most frequently included in the *certificate of stock* are the number of the certificate; the name of the regis-tered holder; the number of shares that the certificate represents, and the **class;** the designations, preferences, and special rights of the particular class of stock and the limitations, restrictions, and qualifications; the name of the corporation issuing the stock; the state of incorpora-tion; the total number of authorized shares and the **par** value or, if shares have no par value, a statement to that effect; the date of issuance of the certificate; the signa-tures of the officers authorized for that purpose; and the **corporate seal.**

Certification   Endorsement or approval. A *certification mark* is a mark or label placed on goods by an organization (other than the manufacturer or seller of the goods) to show that the goods meet the organization's quality standards, come from a particular region, or were made by certain unions, etc. The mark is the property of the organization and its use is protected by law. A *certification proceeding* is a process by which the **National Labor Relations Board** or other **administrative agencies** determine whether a particular union is the majority choice, and thus the exclusive **bargaining agent** for a group of employees in a given **bargaining unit.** *Decertification* is the opposite process. See also **occupational certification.**

Certified Approved. A *certified check* is a check that a bank has marked as "guaranteed cashable" for its customer, both as to signature and amount. In most situations, it is as good as cash. A *certified employee organization* is a union that an **administrative agency** has certified as the official representative of the employees in a **bargaining unit** for the purpose of collective negotiations. Such certification is usually the direct result of a **representation election.** A *certified financial statement* has been examined and reported upon with an opinion expressed by an independent public or **certified public accountant.** *Certified funds* are bank deposits held in suspension and awaiting claims by a certified check. *Certified mail* is ordinary mail that provides a receipt to the sender attesting to delivery. A *certified public accountant (CPA)* is an **accountant** *certified* by a state government as having met specific educational and experience requirements.

Certiorari (Latin) "To make sure." A request for *certiorari* (or "cert." for short) is like an **appeal,** but one which the higher court is not required to take for decision. It is literally a writ from the higher court asking the lower court for the **record** of the case. Most cases that reach the U.S. Supreme Court do so because the Supreme Court itself has "granted certiorari." [pronounce: *sir*-sho-*rare*-ee]

Cessionary bankrupt A person who gives up everything he or she owns to be divided among **creditors.**

Chain Connected links. *Chain banking* is the control of three or more banks by those who commonly own enough stock in each of them to install common policies. A *chain discount* is a discount on an already discounted price, so that the total discount is not as much as the sum of the discount percentages. *Chain of command* is a descriptive phrase for the **authority** systems commonly found in the

hierarchies of work or military organizations. A *chain of title* is a list of the consecutive passing of the legal right to a piece of land. *Chain picketing* is either a tightly grouped, moving picket line to prevent anyone from crossing or picketing several retail outlets of one company. For *chain referral*, see **pyramid sales scheme.**

Chairman (or **chairperson, chairwoman** or **chair**) **of the board** The highest-ranking person in a corporation, usually elected by the other board members.

Chamber of commerce A local association of businesses that promotes the area's trade. Also called *board of trade*.

Change agent An **organization development** consultant or facilitator.

Change in business inventories The value of the increase (or decrease) in the physical stock of goods held by the business sector valued in current period prices. These inventories are in three stages of production: raw materials, semifinished goods, and finished goods ready for sale or shipment. An inventory increase is regarded as investment because it represents production not matched by current consumption; an inventory decrease is regarded as "negative investment" because it reflects consumption in excess of current production.

Change in financial position See **statement.**

Channel (of trade or **distribution)** The path a product takes from manufacturer to consumer, primarily the company-to-company path that ownership of the product takes.

Chapter Eleven A **reorganization** of an **insolvent** (broke) **corporation** under the federal **bankruptcy** laws, supervised by a federal bankruptcy court, in which ownership is transferred to a new corporation made up of old owners and **creditors.** In some cases the business can continue to operate during the process.

Chapter Seven See **bankruptcy.**

Chapter Thirteen A procedure under the federal **bankruptcy** laws for an individual or small business in financial trouble to pay off only a proportion of its debts (called a *composition*), get extra time to pay them (called an *extension*), or both. This process used to be called a *wage earner's plan*, but is now called a *rehabilitation* because the person's **credit** and finances are made good again. Payments may be made from a regular source of income or from a combination of income and the sale of property. Once the court approves the plan, all unsecured **creditors** must accept it, and even **secured** creditors may have to take less **interest** on their debts.

Charge 1. A **claim,** obligation, burden, debt, **debit,** or **liability.** 2. Paying for something "on time." See **charge account.** 3. A formal accusation.

Charge-off Lowering the value of something in a company's records. For example, when a debt becomes too difficult to collect, it may be charged off (also called *write-off*).

Charge account A form of consumer credit which permits consumers to make current purchases without immediate payment. Some firms state that bills are payable within ten days following receipt of the statement; others, by the tenth of the following month; others, before the next billing; etc. Some stores use a charge card for customer identification, some do not, and some rely on general credit cards for charge transactions.

Charismatic leadership Leadership that is based on the compelling personality of the leader rather than upon formal position.

Charitable Philanthropic. A gift or organization is *charitable* for tax purposes if it meets several tests. A gift must be made to a government-qualified nonprofit organization to benefit humankind in general, the community in general, or some specific type of people (so long as the individuals are not specified). Also, the organization's and the gift's purpose must be for the relief of poverty; protection of health or safety; prevention of cruelty; government; or advancement of education, religion, literature, science, etc. A qualified organization must use its money and staff to advance these purposes, rather than to benefit specific individuals. With few exceptions, it may not lobby or otherwise try to influence legislation. If the gift and the organization meet these standards, the giver may deduct the gift from income and the organization is exempt from paying taxes. A *charitable remainder trust* is a trust that gets money (or property) for charitable purposes after others get use of the money first. A *charitable trust* is any trust set up for a public purpose such as a school, church, charity, etc.

Chart of accounts The list (by name, number, classification, etc.) of all of the accounts that an organization maintains.

Charter   1. An organization's basic starting document, such as a corporation's **articles of incorporation,** combined with the law that gives the right to **incorporate** or otherwise exist. A *city charter* spells out the purposes and powers of a *municipal corporation.*   2. Renting a ship or other large means of transportation. A *charter party* is a written contract between the owner of a vessel and a *charterer* who rents use of the vessel or a part of its freight space. The contract generally includes the freight rates and the ports involved in the transportation.

Chartered accountant   An English certified public **accountant.**

Chartist   A **securities** analyst who attempts to forecast future prices by studying charts of past price movements.

Chattel   Personal property or animals. Any property other than land. A *chattel mortgage* is a **mortgage** on personal property, and *chattel paper* is a document that shows both a **debt** and the fact that the debt is **secured** by specific goods.

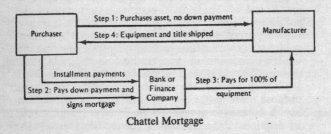

Chattel Mortgage

Check   A document in which a person tells his or her bank to pay a certain amount of money to another person. It is a type of **negotiable instrument.** *Check payment ordering* is sending a signed blank check (limited in amount) with a small order for goods when the precise price is not known. *Check trading* is a bank loan; the borrower receives a check in exchange for agreeing to pay back its amount plus interest, usually in installments.

Check clearing   The movement of checks from the banks and other depository institutions where they are deposited back to those on which they are written, and funds movement in the opposite direction. This process results in **credits** to the accounts of the depository institutions of deposits and corresponding **debits** to the accounts of the paying depository institutions. The **Federal Reserve** operates a nationwide check clearing system, including numerous *regional check processing centers* to facilitate the process. Many checks are also *cleared* by private sector arrangements either directly between institutions, through **correspondents** or through **clearing house** associations. Check-like **negotiable orders of withdrawal** and **share draft** payment orders may be cleared through the Federal Reserve. See also **electronic fund transfer systems.**

Checkoff A **union security** provision, commonly provided for in the **collective bargaining** agreement, that allows the employer to deduct union dues, **assessments,** and initiation fees from the pay of all union members. The deducted amounts are delivered to the union on a prearranged schedule. The **Labor-Management Relations Act** requires that union members give written permission for these fees to be deducted.

Cherry picking Highly selective buying or selling.

Chicago Board of Trade A **commodity** exchange; the world's largest grain exchange.

Chief executive officer (CEO) The individual who is personally accountable to the **board of directors** or an electorate for the activities of an organization or jurisdiction.

Child labor The employment of children below the legal age limit. The **Fair Labor Standards Act** contains strong child-labor prohibitions.

Chilling 1. Employment practices, government regulations, court decisions, or legislation (or the threat of these) that prevent the free exercise of individual employment rights, thereby creating a *chilling effect.* This tends to keep minorities and women from seeking employment and advancement in an organization even in the absence of formal bars. Other *chilling effects* may be positive or negative, depending upon the "chillee's" perspective. For example, even discussion of proposed regulations can *chill* employers or unions into compliance. 2. Holding down the sales price of an item to get it cheaply (usually at an auction and usually by telling lies about the property's value).

Choate Complete; valid against all later claims. For example, a *choate* **lien** is one that needs nothing more to be done to make it enforceable.

Christmas bonus   See **nonproduction bonus.**

Chronic unemployment   Unemployment lasting longer than six months.

Churning   The act of a **broker** who makes more trades (for example, of stock) than are beneficial to a customer's **account** in order to increase the broker's own **commissions.**

Circular combination   The uniting of companies that make allied or supplementary, non-competing products that use the same distribution outlets. When a company starts to make products allied or supplementary to its original line of products, or, having its own outlets, becomes a distributor of such items for other manufacturers, the additional activity is known as *circular expansion*. See **integration.**

Circular note   See **letter of credit.**

Citation   1. A notice to appear in court or risk losing a right.   2. A notice of a violation of law.   3. A reference to a printed authority and where it is found.

Citizen   1. A person born in or naturalized in the U.S.   2. A person is a *citizen* of the state where he or she has permanent residence, and a corporation is a *citizen* of the state where it was legally created.

Civil   1. Not criminal. For example, a *civil action* or *civil suit* is a lawsuit that is brought to enforce a right or gain payment for a wrong, rather than a court action involving the government trying to punish a crime; in general, a lawsuit brought by one person against another.   2. Having to do with the government.

Civil rights   The rights of all citizens that are guaranteed by the Constitution; for example, freedom of speech. The *Civil Rights Acts* are federal laws passed after the Civil War and during the last four decades that prohibit discrimination based on race, color, age, sex, religion, or national origin.

Claim   1. A request to an insurer for payment of **benefits** under an **insurance** policy.   2. A demand for something.

Claim for relief   The core of a modern **complaint** (first pleading in a lawsuit). It may be a short, clear statement of the claim being made that shows that if the facts **alleged** can be proved, the plaintiff should get help from the court in enforcing the claim against the defendant.

Claim of right doctrine   A rule in tax law that if a person receives money under a *claim of right* (the assertion or honest impression that it belongs to or was owed to the person), he or she must pay taxes on the money that year even if there is a good chance that it must be returned later.

Class 1. A unique **position** or a group of positions sufficiently similar in duties and responsibilities that the same title may be used to designate each position in the group, the same salary may be equitably applied, the same qualifications required, and the same examination used to select qualified employees. See **group of classes, series of classes, specification,** and **title.** 2. Any well-defined group. See **class action.**

Class action A lawsuit brought for oneself and all other persons in the same situation. To bring a *class action* you must convince the court that there are too many persons in the **class** (group) to make them all individually a part of the lawsuit and that your interests and legal claims are the same as theirs, so that you can adequately represent their needs.

Class directors Corporate **directors** whose terms of office are staggered. This assures continuity of leadership and makes takeover attempts more difficult.

Class specification See **specification.**

Classification standards Descriptions of classes of positions that distinguish one **class** from another in a series. They are, in effect, the yardstick or **benchmark** against which positions are measured to determine the proper level within a series of titles to which a position should be assigned.

Classified stock **Securities** divided into categories that have differing rights. For example, Class A may have voting rights while Class B does not.

Classify Group positions according to their duties and responsibilities and assign a class **title.** To reclassify is to reassign a position to a different class, based on a reexamination of the duties and responsibilities.

Clayton Act A federal law, passed in 1914, that extended the **Sherman Act's** prohibition against **monopolies** and price discrimination. Certain leases and terms of sale that force a buyer not to deal with a competitor may be illegal under the *Clayton Act.* In addition, some mergers and acquisitions involving actual or potential competitors, or buyers and sellers, may violate the *Clayton Act.* Such activities are not always unlawful, but the courts test whether their effects "may be to substantially lessen competition or tend to create a monopoly in any line of commerce." A key provision of the *Clayton Act* authorizes individual victims of antitrust violations to sue for themselves to recover triple the amount of their damages, or to obtain a court order prohibiting the anticompetitive practice in the future.

Clean Pure or neat. A *clean bill* is either a **bill** that has been substantially rewritten by a legislature committee, or any bill (such as a **bill of lading**) that is clear and in final form with no marginal notation or other qualifying words. *Clean hands* means acting fairly and honestly. A *clean-up clause* is a part of an ongoing loan agreement that requires all loans to be paid off by a certain time, after which no new loans will be given for a short time, the *clean-up period. Clean-up time* is time during the normal work day when employees are allowed to cease production in order to clean themselves, their clothing, or their workplace. *Clean-up-time* allowances are frequently written into union contracts.

Clear 1. Final payment on a check by the bank on which it was drawn *clears* the check. The process of sending it to that bank and making payment is called *clearing*. See **check clearing.** 2. Free from doubt or restrictions; for example, *clear title* is complete legal ownership. 3. Free of taxes; free of **liens** or other **encumbrances;** free of any claims at all. 4. Transact, finalize, and adjust the peripheral details of a deal. See **clearinghouse.**

Clearance card 1. A document given to a ship by **customs** authorities allowing it to leave port. 2. A document given to a worker leaving a job that states the worker was a good worker (or at least in good standing) when employment ended.

Clearinghouse 1. A place where, or a method by which, banks in an area exchange checks received for deposit. Banks that use the facilities of the *clearinghouse* usually form a voluntary association. If the amount of checks received by a bank exceeds the amount sent by it to the clearinghouse, that bank has an *unfavorable* balance and is a net debtor; it must pay the difference to the clearinghouse. Conversely, if the amount of checks sent to the clearinghouse by a bank exceeds the amount received by it, that bank has a *favorable* balance and receives the difference from the clearinghouse. Thus the settlement is made with a minimum of payments. A *clearinghouse agent* is a clearinghouse member who **clears** items for a non-member. *Clearinghouse funds* are funds transferred by check. The *Clearinghouse Interbank Payment System (CHIPS)* is a computerized facility for international fund transfers between U.S. and foreign banks. A *clearing union* has central banks of member countries clear international payments. The **International Monetary Fund** functions as a clearing union in some respects. 2. A separate, independent organization established for the sole benefit and use of members of a **commodity exchange** to **clear** trades between brokers, handle the adjustment of any money differences growing out of cleared trades, provide an impartial and prompt adjustment of **margins** between brokers, and direct the making of deliveries on **futures** contracts.

Clifford trust A **trust** that is set up to give the income to someone else, eventually return the **principal** (original money put in) to yourself, and get tax benefits while the trust exists.

Clock card A form designed to be used with a time clock.

Close Restricted. A *close* (or *closed*) *corporation* is a corporation whose stock is held by a limited group; its shares are ordinarily not sold in the **securities** markets. Usually a closed corporation is small, but there are some closely held large companies. The stockholders are usually the directors, officers, and managers of the business. The *close of a market* is a specified period at the end of a commodity trading session during which all trades are said to have been made *at or on the close*. *Close of business (COB)* followed by a date means the end of the normal business day; for example, 5:00 P.M. A *closed mortgage* is a **mortgage** that cannot be paid off in advance (before **maturity**) without the mortgage-holder's agreement. See also **open-end mortgage**. A *closed-end mortgage* is a **mortgage** that allows no additional borrowing under the same agreement. See **open-end mortgage**. A *closed economy* has no foreign trade. A *closed shop* is a union security provision that requires an employer to hire and retain only union members. The **Labor-Management Relations Act** made *closed shops* illegal. A *closed anti-union shop* is a work organization that will not hire current or prospective union members. Such a tactic is illegal if the organization is engaged in interstate commerce. A *closed union* is a union that formally bars new members or makes becoming a member practically impossible in order to protect the job opportunities of its present members. For *closed-end credit*, see **consumer credit**. A *closed-end investment company*, unlike a **mutual fund,** does not continuously offer to buy back its shares at the option of its shareholders. Such a company also does not continuously offer to sell its shares. After an initial sale by the company, the shares are traded like the shares of any other public corporation. Their price may fluctuate in response to changes in the value of a company's portfolio and the supply of and demand for its shares. When shares of such companies are traded with the services of a **broker,** it is customary for a **commission** to be charged. For *closely held corporation,* see **close corporation.**

Closing 1. The final meeting for the sale of land at which all payments are made, the property is formally transferred, and the **mortgage** is fully set up by filling out all necessary papers for the mortgage lender. *Closing costs* are all charges for finishing the deal, such as transfer taxes, mortgage fees, credit reports, etc. These costs are all set down on a *closing statement* also known as a **settlement sheet.** 2. The completion of a sales presentation that results in an order to buy. 3. *Closing entries* are the final adjusting entries of a **fiscal** period which result in net profit and loss postings to **equity** accounts. 4. For *closing range,* see **opening range.**

Clothing allowance Funds provided by employers to employees so that they can buy special clothing, such as uniforms or safety garments.

Cloud on title A **claim** or **encumbrance** against property which, if valid, would lower its value or add difficulties to its legal ownership.

Coaching Face-to-face discussions with a subordinate in order to effect a change in his or her behavior. *Coaching analysis* consists of analyzing the reasons why unsatisfactory performance is occurring.

Coalition bargaining (or **coordinated bargaining**) An employer negotiates with a group of unions whose goal is to gain one agreement covering all or identical agreements for each. *Coordinated bargaining* differs only in that bargaining sessions take place simultaneously at differing locations.

COBOL   An acronym for *Common Business Oriented Language*, a procedure-oriented computer programming language that resembles standard business English.

Cobuyer   A vague term that includes both persons with and without an ownership right in the thing purchased.

Code   A collection of laws or principles, especially a complete, interrelated and exclusive set of laws. A *code of ethics* is a statement of professional standards of conduct to which the practitioners of many professions say they subscribe. The *Code of Federal Regulations* is the compilation of all the **rules** and **regulations** put out by federal **agencies.** It is updated each year and divided into subject areas.

Codetermination   Union participation in all aspects of management even to the extent of having union representatives share equal membership on an organization's **board of directors.** In Germany, where *codetermination* is often legally required, the process is called *Mitbestimmungsrecht*, literally meaning "the right of codetermination."

Coding   Changing raw data into standardized form for (usually computerized) analysis.

Coemption   Buying up all of a particular thing.

Cognovit note   A written statement that a debtor owes money and *confesses judgment*, or allows the creditor to get a **judgment** in court for the money whenever the creditor wants to or whenever a particular event takes place (such as a failure to make a payment).

Coincident indicator   An economic **time series** which measures such factors as **gross national product,** unemployment, industrial production, personal income, etc., that provides a determination of when the **business cycle** reaches its various levels. See also **leading indicator.**

Coinsurance   1. A division of **risk** between an insurance company and its customer on all losses less than 100 percent if the amount of insurance is less than the value of the property. For example, if a watch worth 100 dollars is insured for 50 dollars and suffers 50 dollars worth of damage, the company will pay only 25 dollars.   2. Any sharing of an insurance risk between insurance company and customer. For example, a health insurance policy may provide that the insurer will reimburse a specified percentage (usually 80 percent) of all, or certain specified covered medical expenses in excess of any **deductible** amounts payable by the insured.

Cold-storage training The preparation of employees for jobs in advance of the need for them in these particular jobs.

Collapsible corporation A company set up to earn money by building up its **assets,** then going out of business and distributing its profits back to the owners. The **IRS** has rules that limit this sort of deal by preventing the owners from converting what would otherwise be **ordinary** income (taxed at a high rate) into **capital** gains (taxed at a low rate).

Collateral 1. Money or property put up as backing for a loan. For example, *collateral trust bonds* are **bonds secured** entirely by a **pledge** of other **securities** such as stocks and bonds of **subsidiary** corporations or those held for investment. Sometimes leaseholds, rents, franchises, and patents are offered as additional *collateral.* The primary purpose of the pledge of the securities and other collateral is to enable the trustee to reimburse the bondholders should the corporation fail to pay the bond obligation when it comes due. For **collaterized mortgage obligation** see **CMO.** 2. "On the side." For example, a *collateral warranty* is a **warranty** of **title** to land made by someone other than the person selling it. Such a promise can be enforced only by the present buyer, not by others who later buy the land.

Collection agency A firm that specializes in collecting overdue **accounts receivable.**

Collection papers All documents (commercial **invoices, bills of lading,** etc.) submitted to a buyer for the purpose of receiving payment for a shipment.

Collection ratio A comparison of **accounts receivable** and sales that shows a business's debt-collecting efficiency. See also **aging schedule** and **ratio analysis.** For *collection period ratio* see **average collection period.**

Collection system The procedures established by a credit manager for the prompt collection of **accounts receivable.** Usually included is a method of classifying receivables according to the length of time they have been **outstanding.**

Collections forecast An estimate of collections for a given period based on past sales and collection experience.

Collective Group. *Collective bargaining* is a comprehensive term that encompasses the negotiating process that leads to a contract between labor and management on wages, hours, and other conditions of employment as well as the subsequent administration and interpretation of the signed contract. *Collective bargaining* is, in effect, the continuous relationship that exists between union representatives and employers. The four basic stages of collective bargaining are the establishment of organizations for bargaining, the formulation of demands, the negotiation of demands, and the administration of the **labor agreement.** For *collective bargaining agreement,* see **labor agreement,** and for *collective bargaining unit,* see **bargaining unit.** A *collective mark* is a distinctive design used to indicate membership in an organization, such as a union. A *collective work,* under **copyright** law, is a collection of individual works by different persons, such as an issue of a magazine or an encyclopedia.

Collusion Secret action taken by two or more persons together to cheat another or to commit fraud. For example, it is *collusion* if two persons agree that one should sue the other because the second person is covered by insurance.

Color Appearance or semblance; looking real or true on the surface, but actually false. For example, acting *under color of law* is taking an action that looks official or backed by law, but which is not. In most cases ("color of authority," "color of office," etc.) *color* implies deliberate falseness, but in other cases ("color of right," "color of title," etc.) *color* implies no attempt to deceive.

Comaker A second (or third or more) person who signs a **negotiable instrument,** such as a **check,** and by doing so promises to pay on it in full.

Combination 1. A group of persons working together, often for an unlawful purpose. 2. A putting together of inventions, each of which might be already **patented** but which by working together produce a new, useful result. This *combination* might get a patent.

Combined statements Financial statements of commonly controlled companies or a group of unconsolidated **subsidiaries.** They are distinguished from **consolidated statements** in that there is no assumption of a controlling interest over the affiliated group.

Comer A slang term for a younger manager who seems to have the potential of assuming top management responsibilities.

Comfort letter A letter from an **accounting** firm saying that, upon informal review, a company's financial records seem to be in order, although full, official approval requires an **audit.**

Commerce 1. Department of Commerce. The cabinet department that promotes U.S. trade, economic development, and technology. It includes the **patent** office and many scientific and business development branches. 2. Trade.

Commerce clause The part of the U.S. Constitution that allows Congress to control trade with foreign countries and from state to state. This is called the *commerce power* (Article One, Section Eight of the Constitution). If anything "affects interstate commerce" (such as labor unions, product safety, etc.), it is fair game for the federal government to **regulate** what goes on or even to take over all regulation. See **pre-emption.**

Commercial Having to do with business. A *commercial attache* is the commerce expert on the diplomatic staff of his or her country's embassy or large consulate. A *commercial bank* is a bank whose primary function is the acceptance of **demand deposits** and the extension of short-term credit. However, a *commercial bank* may have a variety of other functions, such as the acceptance of **time deposits** and the adminstration of **trusts.** For *commercial code*, see **Uniform Commercial Code.** *Commercial insurance* is either insurance against a business loss due to another company's failure to perform a contract or insurance against general business losses beyond the company's control. A *commercial invoice* is an itemized list of goods shipped, usually included among an exporter's **collection papers.** *Commercial paper* includes all **negotiable instruments** related to business; for example, **bills** of exchange. Sometimes, the word is restricted to a company's short-term **notes,** also called *commercial finance paper.* These are corporate **promissory notes** that raise short-term (usually 30–90 day) cash, sold through intermediaries such as brokers, finance companies and banks. A *commercial paper house* either acts as a **broker** for commercial paper or buys and resells it. A *commercial unit* is an item or group of goods which, if separated, would lose value; for example, a two-part machine or a suite of furniture.

Commission 1. A written grant of authority to do a particular thing, given by the government to one of its branches or to an individual or organization. 2. An organization like one mentioned in no. 1. 3. Payment to a salesperson based on the amount of sales or on a percentage of the profit. 4. The fee charged by **brokers** as compensation for their services in purchasing or selling **securities** or **commodities** for the benefit, and at the direction, of their customers. For many years, brokers throughout the country adhered to a "fixed" schedule of commission rate charges. An individual investor had no choice but to pay the prevailing commission rate, since any broker dealt with would impose the same charge for a particular transaction. However, that situation changed after the **SEC,** in May 1975, abolished the practice of "fixing" commission rates at a uniform level (an action later written into law by Congress). Today, commission rates are negotiable and the commission charged for a particular transaction may vary substantially from firm to firm. Most firms maintain established commission rate schedules, but sometimes they will agree to "discount" their regular rates on large orders, or for active customers. In addition, there is a group of firms known as *discount brokers* who usually provide fewer services and charge lower rates. These brokers, generally speaking, offer discount rates to every customer on every transaction. 5. A *commission house* is a **commodity broker.** A *commission merchant* is a **factor.**

Commissioner 1. The name for the heads of many government **boards** or **agencies.** 2. A person appointed by a court to handle special matters, such as to conduct a court-ordered sale or to take testimony in complicated, specialized cases. 3. For *commissioners of conciliation,* see **conciliation.**

Committeeman (or **Committeewoman**) A worker chosen by co-workers to represent the union membership in the handling of **grievances,** the recruitment of new union members, etc. See **steward.**

Commodity 1. Anything produced, bought, or sold. For example, a manufacturing company's *commodity income statement* breaks down total costs and income by each product produced. 2. Any raw product or partially processed material. For example, a *commodity agreement* is an international understanding, formally accepted by the principal exporters and importers, regarding international trading of a raw material and usually intended to affect its price. The *Commodity Credit Corporation* is the federal agency that stabilizes the price and supply of crops by making loans and **price support** payments, controlling acreage under production, etc. A *commodity exchange* is an organization of dealers who sell goods for shippers, wholesalers, commission merchants, producers, and speculators. They buy for exporters, millers, manufacturers, speculators, and any others who purchase goods in large quantities. Other services include the arbitration of trade disputes, the gathering and distribution of market information, and the specification of grade requirements for the commodities dealt in. The exchange may also minimize the danger of market fluctuation by trading rules that place a limit on the extent of a price advance or decline in any one day's trading. The exchange itself has no dealings in the commodities handled by its members. An exchange may deal in contracts for the immediate **(spot)** sale of a commodity or deal in **futures.** The *Commodity Futures Trading Commission* is the federal agency that **regulates** contracts to buy and sell future supplies of raw products such as corn, silver, etc. 3. A farm product such as corn. 4. *Commodity money* is a medium of exchange that has a use in addition to its use as a means of payment; examples include gold, silver, horses, oxen, etc. For a contrast, see **credit money.**

Common Ordinary, usual or shared. For *common carrier,* see **carrier.** A *common external tariff* is a **tariff** rate uniformly applied within a regional grouping of countries, such as the European Economic Community, to imports from countries outside the region. For example, the EEC permits free internal trade, but applies *common external tariffs* against many products imported from nonmember countries. A *common labor rate* is a wage rate for the least skilled physical or manual labor in an organization; usually an organization's lowest rate of pay. *Common law* is either judge-made law (as opposed to legislature-made law) or law that has its origins in England and grows from ever-changing custom and tradition. For example, the *common law of the shop* (or industrial relations common law) is the total body of law established by judicial **precedent** that applies to the workplace. And a *common law trust* is a **business trust.** The *Common Market* is formally called the *European Economic Community*, but usually called either the Common Market or the EEC. Other regions also have *common markets* (examples include the Andean Pact and the East African Common Market) but the EEC is *the* common market. A *common scheme* (or plan or design) is dividing a piece of land into lots with identical restrictions on land use. *Common situs picketing* is **picketing** an entire construction site by a union having a dispute with one of the **contractors** doing work. This is generally illegal. A *common-size balance sheet* is a device sometimes used in analyzing **balance sheets.** The ratios of each **asset** to total assets and the ratios of each **liability** and net worth item to total liabilities and capital are computed. A statement of this type is known as a *common-size statement*, because the totals of all statements so constructed are equal to 100 percent and are, therefore, of a common size. It is often set up in comparative form so as to compare the company's balance sheet at different times or to compare two different enterprises of varying magnitude. A *common-size income statement* is a statement in which a percentage comparison is made of each item listed on the income statement with the total representing net sales. It is an accounting for the use of the income from sales and may be shown graphically in a pie chart as the disposition of the sales dollar. The common-size income statement is often set up in comparative form so as to spot trends or unusual distortions from year to year. *Common stock* is **shares** in a **corporation** that depend for their value on the value of the company. These shares usually have voting rights (which other types of company stock lack). However, they earn a **dividend** (profit) only after all other types of the company's obligations and stocks have been paid. Common stock represents the basic ownership of the corporation. With only nominal exception, all corporations have common stock. Some corporations have common stock only; others have common and **preferred** or a variety of hybrids. A *common stock equivalent* is a **security** which can, under prescribed conditions, be exchanged for *common stock.* A **warrant** is one example. A *common trust fund* is a **fund** used for the accumulation of collective investment assets by a bank or trust company acting in its capacity as trustee for a variety of trusts.

Communication The process of exchanging information, ideas, and feelings between two or more individuals or groups. *Horizontal communication* refers to such an exchange among peers or people at the same organizational level. *Vertical communication* refers to such an exchange between individuals at differing levels of the organization. *Communication intelligence* is intercepting others' messages by wiretapping, radio surveillance, and other means. *Communications theory* seeks to explain how information (meaning all social interactions) is sent, received, stored and used by an organization or a nation.

Community of interest 1. A formal or informal grouping of otherwise unaffiliated persons, organizations, or corporations to pursue policies to their mutual advantage. Fidelity to the common purpose may be based upon family relationship, personal friendship, business economy, or any common need. A community of interest, for example, may be effected by an exclusive contract between two corporations for the purchase by one of raw materials marketed by the other. *Community of interest* arrangements played an important role in the development of railroad, industrial and utility **combinations,** and many of the present **subsidiaries** of motor and steel corporations were originally related to the **parent** company solely through purchase and sales contracts. See also **interlocking directorate.** 2. A criterion used to determine whether a group of employees is an appropriate **bargaining unit** in labor law.

Community Reinvestment Act (CRA) Statement A description available for public inspection at each bank office indicating, on a map, the communities served by that office and the types of credit the bank is prepared to extend within the communities served.

Community wage survey Any survey to ascertain the structure and level of wages among employers in a local area.

Company Any organization set up to do **business.** A *company doctor* is a consultant or manager who seeks to reinvigorate a sick firm. *Company loans* are loans made to employees by a company. Such loans are usually in response to an emergency, usually of short duration, and usually without interest. A *company spy* (or **labor spy**) is someone hired by an employer to report on what is happening within a union. A *company store* is a store operated by an organization for the exclusive use of employees and their families. The largest company store in the world is the U.S. military's PX (Post Exchange) system. *Company town* is the slang term for any community whose economy is dominated by one employer. True company towns, where the company literally owns all of the land, buildings, and stores, are practically nonexistent in the modern U.S. A *company union* is a union organized, financed, or otherwise dominated by an employer. The **National Labor Relations Act** outlawed employer interference with unions, thus relegating company unions to history.

Comparable worth Providing equitable compensation for performing work of a comparable value as determined by the relative worth of a given job to an organization. The basic issue of comparable worth is whether **Title VII** of the **Civil Rights Act** makes it unlawful for an employer to pay one sex at a lesser rate than the other when job performance is of comparable worth or value. For example, should graduate nurses be paid less than gardeners; or should beginning librarians with a master's degree be paid less than beginning managers with a master's degree? Historically, nurses and librarians have been paid less than occupations of *comparable worth* because they were considered "female" jobs. Comparable worth as a legal concept and as a social issue directly challenges traditional and **market** assumptions about the worth of a job.

Comparative advantage A country or a region has a *comparative advantage* in the production of those goods it can produce relatively more efficiently than other goods. Modern trade theory says that regardless of the general level of the country's productivity or labor costs relative to those of other countries, it should produce for export those goods in which it has the greatest *comparative advantage* and import those goods in which it has the greatest *comparative disadvantage*. The country that has few economic strengths will find it advantageous to devote its productive energies to those lines in which its disadvantage is least marked, provided the opportunity to trade with other areas is open to it.

Comparative statements   1. Financial **statements** of the same company that cover two or more consecutive years so that increases (or decreases) in the various component items are easy to analyse. These include comparative **balance sheets** with parallel columns of figures. **Annual reports** usually have these.   2. Financial statements of different companies. *Comparative analysis* usually refers to the computation and comparison of ratios from the financial statement to corresponding "standard" ratios of companies in the same line of business. See **ratio analysis.**

Compensable factors   Various **elements** of a job that, when put together, both define the job and determine its value to the organization.

Compensable injury   A work-related injury that qualifies an injured worker for **workers' compensation** benefits.

Compensating (or **compensatory**) **balance**   1. A minimum amount of money that a person or company must keep in a non-interest checking account to **compensate** a bank for loans or other services.   2. Any required bank balance.

Compensation   1. Payment for loss, injury, or damages.   2. Payment of any sort for work or services performed.   3. The principle that any country that raises a **tariff** above its **bound rate** or withdraws a **binding** on a tariff or otherwise impairs a trade **concession** must lower other tariffs or make other trade concessions to *compensate* countries whose exports are affected.

Compensation management   The selection, development, and direction of the programs that implement an organization's financial reward system.

Compensatory damages   Payment for the actual loss suffered by a plaintiff, as opposed to **punitive damages.**

Compensatory time   Time off instead of **overtime** pay.

Competitive   A *competitive area* is an area in which, during **layoffs** or **reductions-in-force,** employees of large organizations are sometimes restricted, when competing for retention; in effect, the commuting area to which they are assigned. *Competitive bidding for security issues* is the process by which groups of **investment bankers bid** for the purchase of an **issue** of **securities,** as contrasted with private negotiation. In competitive bidding, the issuer sets up the terms of the offering, with or without outside financial

advice. In a negotiated offering the investment banker negotiates and agrees with the issuer concerning the type of
security best suited to the issuer's **capital structure** and to
the existing temper of the securities markets. *Competitive
bidding* is required in most states for **municipal bonds** and
other types of public and semi-private securities. A *competitive level* is all positions of the same grade within a
competitive area which are sufficiently alike in duties,
responsibilities, pay systems, terms of appointment, requirements for experience, training, skills, and aptitudes that
the incumbent of any of them could readily be shifted to
any of the other positions. A *competitive promotion* is the
selection for promotion made from the employees rated
best qualified in competition with others, all of whom
have the *minimum* qualifications required by the **position.**
Competitive seniority is the use of **seniority** in determining an employee's right, relative to other employees, to
job-related "rights" that cannot be supplied equally to
any two employees. *Competitive wages* are rates of pay
that an employer, in competition with other employers,
must offer if he or she is to recruit and retain employees.

Competitiveness The ability of the United States to compete economically with the other developed nations in the
Western world—especially Japan. In the late 1980s, the
term became an abbreviated way of referring to the concern for a comprehensive national **industrial policy,** to the
persistent problem of the lagging productivity of American workers and to an increasingly unfavorable U.S. **balance of trade.**

Complaint 1. The first main paper filed in a **civil** lawsuit. It
includes, among other things, a statement of the wrong or
harm done to the plaintiff by the defendant, a request for
specific help from the court, and an explanation why the
court has the power to do what the plaintiff wants.
2. Any official "complaint" in the ordinary sense. 3. A
complaint examiner is an official designated to conduct
discrimination complaint hearings.

Complex capital structure A corporation's **capital structure**
is *complex* when it has issued both **common stock** and
common stock equivalents or other **potentially dilutive
securities.** See **simple capital structure.**

Compliance Acting in a way that does not violate a law.
For example, when a state gets federal money for a state

project, the project must be in *compliance* with the federal law that provides the money and, sometimes, with the **regulations** of the federal agency that provides it.

Compliance agency 1. Any government agency that administers laws or regulations relating to **equal employment opportunity.** 2. A federal agency delegated enforcement responsibilities by the **Office of Federal Contract Compliance Programs** to ensure that federal contractors adhere to **EEO** regulations and policies.

Component operating company See **subsidiary.**

Composition A formal agreement involving a **debtor** and several **creditors** in which each creditor will take less than the whole amount owed as full payment. For a *composition in bankruptcy*, see **Chapter Thirteen.**

Compound 1. Combine parts or ingredients into a whole. For *compound duty* or *tariff*, see **duties.** 2. Compromise. Rid oneself of a debt by convincing the creditors to accept a smaller amount. 3. *Compound interest* is **interest** on interest. Add interest to the **principal** (the main debt) at regular intervals and then compute the interest on the last principal plus interest.

Comprador 1. An Asian term for a native agent used by foreign (originally colonial) businesses as an intermediary. 2. Business interests in the **Third World** who have close ties to **First World** counterparts. Marxists use this term in a critical way to suggest the continued exploitation of Third World workers by *compradors* who represent the old colonial powers.

Compressed time The same number of hours worked in a week spread over fewer days than normal.

Comp. time See **compensatory time.**

Comptroller See **controller.**

Comptroller of the Currency The head of the U.S. Treasury office that regulates National banks. See **Federal Reserve Board.**

Compulsory Forced. *Compulsory arbitration* is a negotiating process in which the parties are required by law or contract to **arbitrate** their dispute. For *compulsory checkoff*, see **automatic checkoff.** *Compulsory process* is official action to force a person to appear in court or to appear before a legislature as a witness. This is usually by **subpoena,** but sometimes by arrest.

Concentration banking See **lockbox system.**

Concept testing Evaluating probable public acceptance of a product idea before developing the product itself.

Conception In **patent** law, *conception* is an inventor's completed idea for an invention. The *date of conception* is the day this idea, and not merely its general principles, is put down on paper. See **reduction to practice.**

Concessions In **GATT** trade negotiations, those reductions a country offers to make in its own **tariff** and non-tariff import barriers to induce other countries to make reductions in barriers to its exports.

Conciliation The process of bringing together two sides to agree to a voluntary compromise. See **mediation.**

Conciliator A person who keeps disputing parties in negotiations until they reach a voluntary settlement. The **Federal Mediation and Conciliation Service** has **Commissioners of Conciliation** located in its various regional offices available to assist parties in the settlement of labor-management disputes.

Condemnation 1. A governmental taking of private property with payment, but not necessarily with consent. 2. A court's decision that the government may seize a ship owned privately or by a foreign government. 3. An official ruling that a building is unfit for use.

Condition A future, uncertain event that creates or destroys rights and obligations. For example, a contract may have a *condition* in it stating that if one person should die, the contract is ended. Conditions may be **express** or **implied.**

Conditional Depending on a **condition;** unsure; depending on a future event. For example, a *conditional sale* is a sale in which the buyer must wait for full ownership of the

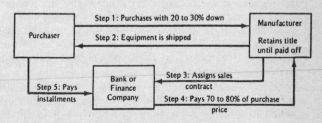

Conditional Sales Contract

thing bought until it is fully paid for. *Conditionality* is a collective term for objectives and policies which the **International Monetary Fund** expects a member to follow as *conditions* for the member's using any of the Fund's lending facilities.

Condominium Several persons owning individual pieces of a building (usually an apartment house) and managing it together.

Conduit A company, **trust,** estate, etc., is considered a *conduit* for tax purposes if certain tax benefits or consequences (such as long-term capital losses) merely *pass through* on their way to the actual owners of the company, trust, etc.

Conference Board An independent, nonprofit business research organization.

Confession of judgment A process in which a person who borrows money or buys on **credit** signs in advance to allow the lawyer for the lender to get a court judgment without even telling the borrower. See **judgment** and **cognovit note.**

Confidential relation Any relationship where one person has a right to expect a higher than usual level of care and faithfulness from another person; for example, client and attorney, child and parent, employee and employer. Another name for these relationships, if a strong duty exists, is a **fiduciary** relationship.

Confirmation 1. Formal approval, especially formal written approval. 2. A notice that something has been received, sent, ordered, etc. 3. Agreeing that something is correct; for example, a document in which a company's supplier or customer verifies financial figures or item counts for a review of the company's **books** by an **auditor.** 4. The transfer of legal **title** to land to a person who has possession of the land. 5. A **contract** that reaffirms a prior agreement that might have been otherwise difficult to prove or enforce. 6. The approval of a presidential appointment by Congress.

Confiscation The government's taking of private property without payment. Government action may be called *confiscation* if it has nearly the effect of confiscation; for example, when an electric company is not permitted to charge enough to ever make a profit. See also **condemnation.**

Conflict Clash. *Conflict of interest* is being in a position where your own needs and desires could possibly lead you to violate your duty to a person who has a right to depend on you. A conflict need not even be intentional. For example, a judge who holds XYZ stock may be unconsciously influenced in a case concerning the XYZ Company. *Conflict of laws* is the situation that exists when the laws of more than one state or country may apply to a case and a judge must choose among them. *Conflict of laws* is also the name for the legal subject of the rules to use in making this choice.

Conformed copy An exact copy of a document with written explanations of things that could not be copied. For example, the handwritten signature and date might be replaced on the copy by the notation "signed by Jonah Brown on July 27, 1990."

Confrontation meeting An **organization development** technique that has an organizational group (usually the management corps) meet for a one-day or more effort to assay their organizational health and agree on positive steps for its improvement.

Confusion 1. Mixing or blending together. For example, *confusion of goods* is a mixing together of the property of two or more persons with the effect that it is not possible to tell which goods belong to which person. 2. **Merger.** When a **creditor** and a **debtor,** a landlord and a tenant, etc., become the same person, usually because of an inheritance, and separate legal rights and duties become one, often ending the duty.

Conglomerate A company that owns, or is made up of, companies in many different industries.

Consent decree (or **order**) A settlement of a lawsuit or prosecution in which a person or company agrees to take certain actions without admitting fault or guilt for the situation causing the lawsuit.

Consent dividend A **dividend** which is immediately returned to the **corporation** by the **stockholders** as a contribution to **capital.** *Consent dividends* are a method by which personal **holding companies** may obtain the deduction for dividends paid without impairing their **cash** position. The law provides, however, that if the consent of the shareholders is obtained, the corporation does not have to go through the formality of declaring and paying a dividend which is immediately returned to it. For the corporation, the consent dividends are considered as **paid-in surplus** or as a contribution to capital, with a corresponding reduction in its **retained earnings** or profits. For the shareholders, the amount of the consent dividends is taxable in the same manner as a cash dividend. Because the consent dividend is reinvested by the shareholder, the **basis** of the stock is correspondingly increased.

Consequential damages   Indirect losses or injuries; results of a wrongful act that do not show up immediately or upon superficial examination; for example, the loss of business a taxi-driver suffers from an accident that damages the taxi.

Consideration   The reason or main cause for a person to make a **contract;** something of value received or promised to induce (convince) a person to make a deal. Without *consideration* a contract is not valid. For example, if Ann and Sue make a deal for Ann to buy a car from Sue, Ann's promise to pay a thousand dollars is *consideration* for Sue's promise to hand over the car and vice versa.

Consignment   Handing over things for transportation or for sale, but keeping ownership. In the case of shipping merchandise for sale, the owner is the *consignor* and the receiving seller is the *consignee*, usually a **factor. Title** and control of the selling price usually remain with the *consignor*, as does absent *consignee's* insurance, **risk** of loss.

Consol   1. A **bond** that keeps on paying **interest** forever and never gets paid off.   2. An abbreviation for *consolidated*.

Console   The user control portion of a computer, usually containing a keyboard.

Consolidation   1. The combining of two or more **corporations** into a new corporation under applicable state laws. When *consolidation* takes place, the consolidating corporations cease to exist. Those stockholders who voted against the consolidation plan and refuse to abide by it may usually obtain cash for the appraised value of their shares of stock in the consolidating corporation. The new corporation is also liable for all debts of the consolidating corporations. See **merger.**   2. The firming up of **securities** prices after a substantial move either up or down.   3. For *consolidated decision packages,* see **decision packages.** *Consolidated statements* are financial statements of legally separate companies combined as if they were one company. See **statement** of income. A *consolidation loan* is the combining of several debts into one, usually to reduce the dollar amount of payments made each month, by extending them over a longer period of time, but sometimes to reduce the total **interest.**

Constant dollar Current costs or prices as measured in preinflated dollars of a set prior year. A *constant dollar* is a dollar value adjusted for changes in prices. Constant dollars are derived by dividing **current dollar** amounts by an appropriate price **index,** a process generally known as *deflating.* The result is a constant dollar series as it would presumably exist if prices and transactions were the same in all subsequent years as in the *base* year. Any changes in such a series would reflect only changes in the real volume of goods and services. *Constant dollar accounting* is the same as general price-level accounting.

Constant payment mortgage The usual type of homeowner's **mortgage,** in which equal monthly payments are made, with the proportion of each payment going to **principal** increasing and **interest** decreasing until the mortgage is paid off. (Contrast this with a **direct reduction mortgage.**)

Construction A decision (usually by a judge) about the meaning and legal effect of ambiguous or doubtful words that considers not only the words themselves but also surrounding circumstances, relevant laws and writings, etc. (Looking at just the words is called interpretation.)

Construction draw A type of **mortgage** or other agreement in which a builder gets money as it is needed for building.

Constructive True legally even if not factually; "just as if"; established by legal interpretation; inferred; implied. For *constructive contract,* see **quasi-contract.** A *constructive discharge* may occur if an employer makes conditions of continued employment so intolerable that an employee "voluntarily" leaves. The employer may still have violated **Title VII** of the Civil Rights Act of 1964, which generally prohibits employers from discharging employees because of their race, color, sex, or national origin. A *constructive eviction* might occur when a landlord fails to provide heat in winter. This means that the tenant might be able to treat the legal relationship between landlord and tenant *as if* the landlord had tried to throw the tenant out without good reason. This might give the tenant the right to stop paying the rent. *Constructive knowledge* (or *notice*) is knowledge that a person in a particular situation should have; that the person would have if he or she used reasonable care to keep informed; that is open for all to see; for example, knowledge of a properly recorded mortgage on a house you plan to buy. *Constructive possession* is, for example, ownership of a **warehouse receipt** for goods represented by the receipt. The holder of the receipt lacks actual personal occupancy or possession of the property. *Constructive receipt of income* occurs when a person gains actual control of income and will be taxed on it whether he or she actually takes the cash. For example, taxes must be paid in the year that savings account interest is earned, not in the later year it might actually be collected.

Consular invoice A special form required by many countries, including most of Latin America, for **customs** and statistical purposes. It must show all details of the goods including origin, the name and flag of the carrying vessel, date of shipment, ports or points of shipment and destination, and a sworn declaration to the truth of the information that it contains.

Consultant An individual or organization temporarily employed by other individuals or organizations because of some presumed expertise. *Internal consultants* are often employed by large organizations to provide consulting services to its various units.

Consumer A person who buys (or rents, travels on, etc.) something for personal, rather than business, use. *Consumer credit* is money, property, or services offered "on time" to a person for personal, family, or household purposes. It is *consumer credit* if there is a finance charge or if there are more than four **installment** payments. There are two types of *consumer credit*: *open-end credit* and *closed-end credit*. Examples of *open-end credit* include bank and gas company credit cards, stores' revolving charge accounts and cash-advance checking accounts. In open-end credit, the creditor reasonably expects the customer to make repeated transactions; the creditor may impose a finance charge from time to time on the unpaid balance; and as the customer pays the outstanding balance, that amount of credit is, generally, once again made available to the customer. *Closed-end credit* includes all consumer credit that does not fit the definition of *open-end credit*. It consists of both sales credit and loans. In a typical *closed-end credit* transaction, credit is advanced for a specific time period, and the amount financed, finance charge, and schedule of payments are agreed upon by the lender and the customer. The *Consumer Credit Protection Act* is a federal law, adopted with changes by many states, requiring the clear disclosure of *consumer credit* information by companies making loans or selling on credit. The act requires that **finance charges** be given as a standard **annual percentage rate** (APR), gives consumers the right to back out of certain deals, **regulates** credit cards, restricts wage **garnishments**, etc. It is also called the *Truth-in-Lending Act*. A *consumer lease* is a lease of personal property to a private individual. According to the Federal Trade Commission, a consumer lease must be for personal, family or household purposes and must be for a term of more than four months. (Renting a car for a weekend is, therefore, not a "consumer lease.") The term includes leases when the customer has the option to buy at the end of the lease, but it does not include leases where the customer will have to pay more than $25,000. The *Consumer Price Index (CPI)* is a monthly economic **index** prepared by the **Bureau of Labor Statistics** which measures the change in average prices of the goods and services purchased by urban wage earners and their families. It is widely used as an indicator of changes in the cost of living, as a measure of inflation (and deflation, if any) in the economy, and as a means for studying trends in prices of various goods and services. The *Consumer Product Safety Commission (CPSC)* is a federal agency created to protect the public against unreasonable risks of injury from consumer products. *Consumer sovereignty* is the concept that as consumers decide which goods and services to purchase, they directly affect the nature of the goods and services that will be offered to them in the future. *Consumer surplus* is the difference between the value a consumer places on a purchased product and the actual price paid for it. *Consumer taxes* are taxes levied by all levels of government against the tax base of consumer spending. The two most prevalent types of consumer taxes are taxes on retail sales and taxes on selected commodities. *Consumerism* is a political movement which seeks to extend greater protections to the consumers of goods and services by requiring more government regulation of the quality and safety of products. *Consumer's risk* is the risk that a lot of goods will be accepted by a sampling plan even though it is bad.

Consumption 1. The use of raw materials and labor in the production process. 2. The use of goods and services to satisfy needs. 3. Consumer spending for goods and services. The *consumption function* is the relationship between consumption and available income in which it is assumed that the level of income will determine the level of consumption.

Containerization The use of large, usually standard truck-sized containers, to ship goods easily by a combination of truck and rail, truck and ship, etc.

Contingent Possible, but not assured; depending on some future events or actions *(contingencies)* that may or may not happen. *Contingency analysis* is a technique for exploring the possible effects of errors in major assumptions. It is designed to cope with significant quantitative uncertainties. The procedure is to vary the assumptions about important aspects of the problem and examine the changes in results of the analysis due to these changes in the assumptions. *Contingency management* (or **situational management**) is any management style that recognizes that the application of theory to practice must necessarily take into consideration, and be contingent upon, the given situation. A *contingency reserve* is a fund of money set aside by a business to cover possible unknown future expenses such as a **liability** from a lost lawsuit. A *contingent fee* is a payment to a lawyer of a percentage of the possible "winnings" from a lawsuit rather than a flat amount of money. A *contingent liability* is a possible future claim against a business. Disclosure of *contingent liabilities* is essential to determine the prospective financial condition and current position of a company. Failure to disclose them in a **balance sheet** or profit-and-loss **statement** prohibits due consideration in a credit or investment analysis. A *contingent source* is any source on which business activity depends for **inventory,** machine tools, labor, and the like. This means that any link—from the beginning to the end of the entire business effort—on which the delivery of the completed project depends, is a contingent source. Financial resources, therefore, are one of the basic contingent sources. Sources which depend on a contingent source are called *using sources*. A using source in a particular manufacturing process becomes a contingent source for the next operation. *Contingent sources* are also referred to as "feed-in" sources. *Contingent voting stock* is **preferred stock** that has no voting rights unless there is a failure to pay dividends for a certain period of time, a failure to maintain net assets up to a prescribed standard, or a failure of the corporation to redeem preferred stock or to make **sinking fund** payments. See **voting stock.**

Contra (Latin) Against; on the other hand; opposing. In **accounting,** *contra accounts* are set up to show subtractions from other **accounts,** and *contra balances* are account **balances** that are the opposite (positive or negative) of what usually appears.

Contraband Things that are illegal to import or export or that are illegal to possess.

Contract An agreement that affects the legal relationships between two or more persons. To be a *contract*, an agreement must involve at least one promise, **consideration** (something of value promised or given), persons legally capable of making binding agreements, and a reasonable amount of agreement between the persons as to what the contract means. A contract is called **bilateral** if both sides **expressly** make promises (such as the promise to deliver a book on one side and a promise to pay for it on the other) or **unilateral** if the promises are on one side only (usually because the other side has already done its part). According to the **Uniform Commercial Code,** a contract is the "total legal obligation which results from the parties' agreement," and according to the *Restatement of the Law of Contracts*, it is "a promise or set of promises for the breach of which the law in some way recognizes a duty." For different types of contracts, such as **output, quasi,** etc., see those entries. A *contract bar* is an existing **collective bargaining** agreement that bars a **representation election** sought by a competing union. The *contract clause* is the provision in Article I of the U.S. Constitution that no state may pass a law abolishing contracts or denying them legal effect. For *contract for deed,* see **land sales contract.** A *contract grade* is the grade specified for a certain **commodity** by the rules of a **commodity exchange** to be used for delivery on a **futures** contract. The grade is set by the exchange rather than by individual contract negotiation. Certain other grades of the same commodity may be deliverable on a futures contract at differential prices. *Contract labor* is workers imported from a foreign country for employment with a specific employer. For *contract sale*, see **conditional sale.** *Contracting-out* is having work performed outside an organization's own work force. A *contractor* is a person who takes on work (often building or related work) and has control over his or her own work, method, details, etc. A *prime contractor* or *general contractor* is in charge of the whole project and makes *subcontracts* with others for parts of the job.

Contrarian An investor who goes against current trends.

Contribution (and **contributory**) 1. The sharing of payment for a **debt** (or **judgment**) among persons who are all **liable** for the debt. 2. The right of a person who has paid an entire debt (or judgment) to get back a fair share of the payment from another person who is also responsible for the debt. For example, most **insurance** policies require that if another insurance company also **covers** a loss, each must share payment for the loss in proportion to the maximum amount each covers. 3. A *contribution margin* is the excess of **net** *sales* over a firm's **variable costs.** The *contribution margin ratio* is the *contribution margin* divided by *net sales.* 4. A *contributory* is a person who must pay up in full the price of stock owned in a company because the company is going out of business and owes money. A *contributory group insurance plan* or *contributory pension plan* is any **pension** or insurance program that has employees contributing a portion of the cost, with the employer (or, sometimes, the union) paying the rest. 5. For *charitable contribution*, see **charitable.**

Control 1. That aspect of **management** concerned with the comparison of actual versus planned performance as well as the development and implementation of procedures to correct substandard performance. Control, which is inherent to all levels of management, is a **feedback** process which ideally should report only unexpected situations. This is the essence of **management by exception.** Some management control systems regularly report critical indicators of performance so that management will have ad-

vance notice of potential problems. 2. An **accounting**
method such as **internal check** which is designed to protect assets and ensure the accuracy of accounts. 3. An
accounting process such as **responsibility accounting** or
cost centers for reporting financial data on a systematic
basis. 4. A person, group, object, etc. used as a basis of
comparison with another person, etc. being tested.

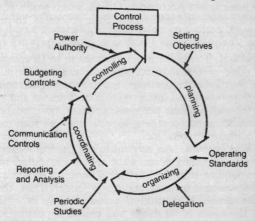

Control chart A graphic device which shows, on the basis
of **sample** information, whether or not a process is under
statistical control. The concept of statistical control is a
measure of process variability. If the quality of output is
stable, the process is presumed to be operating normally.

Controllable costs Those costs subject to direct control by
some member of management. The term may also be
used to designate those costs that an individual has the
authority to incur. The issue of *cost controllability* arises
when costs are used as an index of managerial efficiency.
A department head may be judged by an ability to hold
costs to budgeted levels. For such a manager, the costs
incurred within the department may be controllable but any
service department costs distributed to the department are
not under control. An **accounting** system that emphasizes
cost controllability must take into account the distinction
between controllable and uncontrollable costs for each
center of responsibility. See **responsibility accounting.**

Controlled account Any **brokerage** account for which trading is directed by a person other than the holder of the account; for example, where **power of attorney** is given to another individual.

Controller (or comptroller; pronounced "controller") The financial officer of a company or a government agency. For example, the *Comptroller General* of the U.S. heads the Government Accounting Office, which **audits** government agencies and investigates their problems. In private industry, a *controller* is an officer of a large or medium-sized corporation who has the technical skills of an **accountant.** The office is not essential to small companies and none of the state corporation laws require it. The basic functions of a controller are to supervise **accounting,** the preparation and interpretation of financial and statistical data for business purposes, **auditing,** tax preparation, and, in some corporations, support services such as typing, communications, etc.

Controlling account An account in the general **ledger** that shows in summary form what appears in detail in the corresponding subsidiary ledger. There is a separate controlling account for each subsidiary ledger. Thus, the **accounts receivable** controlling account shows in summary form the totals of all **debits** and **credits** appearing in the customers' accounts in the accounts receivable ledger.

Controls Devices by which regulatory bodies seek to keep the economy healthy. Through the **Federal Reserve System,** for example, such controls as **margins** used in stock transactions may expand or contract credit. The Secretary of Agriculture administers *controls* over sugar with import **quotas.** There are also controls over farm acreage, loans against crops, etc., and in times of crisis, direct controls to allocate materials and set prices.

Convenience Ease. *Convenience foods* are heavily processed to require little preparation time. *Convenience goods* are personal consumption products that are routinely bought without great regard to price (cigarettes, magazines, ice cream, etc.). A *convenience store* sells a limited variety of groceries and staples, is often located away from large shopping centers in areas of dense housing, and stays open long hours.

Conventional 1. Usual or ordinary 2. Caused by an agreement between persons rather than by the effect of a law.

For example, a *conventional mortgage* is one that involves just a person lending and a person borrowing money on a house as opposed to a mortgage involving a government subsidy or guarantee; a *conventional lien* is one created by an agreement, rather than by a law or a lawsuit; and a *conventional tariff* is established through the "conventions" (agreements) that result from tariff negotiations under **GATT** auspices.

Conversion 1. Any act that deprives an owner of property without that owner's permission and without just cause. For example, it is *conversion* to refuse to return a borrowed book. 2. The exchange of one type of property or rights for another; for example, turning in one type of **stock** to a company and getting another in return. (The *conversion ratio* or *rate* would be the number of shares one receives for each share turned in and the *conversion price* would be the value of each new share.) Also, exchanging one type of insurance coverage for another (changing a group health policy for an individual one or changing a *term* life insurance policy for *whole life*). A *conversion clause* is a provision in some **adjustable-rate mortgages** that allows a change to a fixed-rate mortgage at some predetermined time. See **convertible.**

Convertible Freely and completely exchangeable. *Convertible bonds* are **bonds** that give their holders the right to exchange or convert their bonds into **common stock** under stipulated conditions and whenever they find conversion to their advantage. Occasionally the bonds are convertible into some **security** other than common stock. The advantage of convertible bonds to the issuing company is that the bond buyer is induced to accept a lower rate of interest and the marketability of the bond is enhanced by the conversion privilege. If the privilege is exercised, the corporation enjoys a reduction of its **fixed charges** and an increase in credit standing because of the conversion of a debt into common stock equity. The bondholder that cannot assume the risks of stock ownership may realize a profit by selling the bonds when, and if, their prices rise because of an increase in the value of the stock into which it can be converted. *Convertible currency* is currency that is freely exchangeable into the currency of any other nation. A country's currency is convertible if the government of that country allows the completely free use of that currency for the purchase of currencies of other nations. Currency becomes *unconvertible* when a government orders that neither its citizens nor foreigners possessing domestic currency shall buy foreign exchange except for approved purposes or in limited amounts. *Convertible currency* may also mean currency that may be redeemed in gold or other precious metal. *Convertible preferred stock* is a class of **preferred stock** that gives its holders the privilege of converting their stock into some other form of **security.** Usually, conversion is at the option of the stockholder and permits the exchange of **senior** securities for **junior** securities of the same company within a specified time. Convertible preferred stock is ordinarily convertible into a fixed number of **common** shares. The advantages are similar to those of convertible bonds. See **conversion.**

Conveyance   A transfer of **title,** in particular, to land.

Cooked books   Financial records and reports that do not reflect the true situation. This may be legal. For example, companies may present different views of their tax liabilities to **stockholders** and to the **IRS** which obscure the differences with technicalities.

Cooling-off period   1. A period of time in which no action of a particular sort may be taken by either side in a dispute; for example, a period of a month after a union or a company files a **grievance** against the other. During this period the union may not strike and the company may not **lock out** the employees. The national emergency provisions of the Labor-Management Relations (Taft-Hartley) Act of 1947 call for an 80-day *cooling-off period* in the event of a "national emergency."   2. A period of time in which a buyer may cancel a purchase. Many states require a three-day cancellation period for door-to-door sales. The *cooling-off rule* is the **FTC's** requirement that if you make a sale, lease, or rental away from your place of business (generally by going door-to-door), costing $25.00 or more, you must allow the consumer to cancel the sale within three days.

Cooperative   1. An organization set up to help the persons who form it and who use it. The word covers many different types of organizations set up for many different purposes. Cooperatives include *apartment co-ops* (an apartment building owned by residents who **lease** the individual apartments; see also **condominium**); *consumer co-ops* (stores, utilities, health facilities, etc.); *marketing co-ops* (for example, one set up by milk producers in a certain area); *financial co-ops* (like **credit unions**); etc. Organizations like **labor unions** and **trade** associations may also be called *cooperatives*.   2. *Cooperative education* is an educational process in which students alternate formal studies with actual work experience. It is distinguished from other part-time employment in that successful completion of the off-campus experience becomes a prerequisite for graduation.   3. A *cooperative financing facility* is a program through which the U.S. **Export-Import Bank** finances exports of U.S. goods and services jointly with selected non-U.S. financial institutions. This is usually based on a 50-50 sharing of financing and of risks.

Coordinated bargaining   See **coalition bargaining.**

Coordination of benefits   Provisions and procedures used by insurers to avoid duplicate payment for losses insured under more than one **insurance policy.** For example, some people have a duplication of **benefits,** for their medical costs arising from an automobile accident, in their automobile and health insurance policies. A coordination of benefits or anti-duplication clause in one or the other policy will prevent double payment for the expenses by making one of the insurers the *primary payer*, and assuring that no more than 100 percent of the costs are covered.

Copayment   A type of *cost sharing* in which insured persons pay a specified flat amount per unit of service or unit of time (e.g., $2 per visit, $10 per inpatient hospital day), their insurer paying the rest of the cost. The *copayment* is incurred at the time the service is used. The amount paid does not vary with the cost of the service (unlike **coinsurance,** which is payment of some percentage of the cost).

Copy   The written text of an advertisement, book, label, etc. (sometimes, the spoken part or the whole advertisement). A *copy editor* makes copy ready for typesetting. *Copytesting* is research designed to measure the effectiveness of advertising copy. The *copy thrust* or *copy strategy* is the basic message that is to be communicated by the copy. A *copywriter* writes copy for advertisements. A *copy chief* supervises copywriters. When a copy chief is responsible for both copy and pictures, he or she then becomes a *creative director*.

Copyright The author's (or other originator's) right to control the copying and distributing of books, articles, movies, etc. This right is created, regulated, and limited by federal statute. The symbol for copyright is ©. The legal life of a copyright is the author's life plus fifty years or a flat seventy-five years for one held by a company. A copyright involves the form of expression rather than the subject matter of the writing. A description of a machine could be copyrighted as a writing, but this would only prevent others from copying the description—it would not prevent others from writing a description of their own or from making and using the machine. Copyrights are registered in the Copyright Office in the Library of Congress.

Corner 1. Owning enough of some **stock** or **commodity** to have control over the selling price in the general marketplace. 2. Owning contracts for more future delivery of a commodity than is produced of that commodity. When the persons who have promised to deliver cannot do it, the price shoots sky high and the person with the *corner* greatly profits.

Corporate Belonging to a **corporation.** The *corporate coat of arms* is a company's **logo** or other symbol of identity. The *corporate culture* is the society within a company as reflected by its shared values, beliefs, assumptions, **norms,** and patterns of behavior; the unseen force behind organizational activities. The *corporate identity* is the total image of the corporation as perceived by customers, employees and the public. The *corporate ladder* is the **hierarchical** sequence of **management** positions in a corporation from management trainee to **chairman of the board.** *Corporate powers* of every corporation include three classes: *express*, *incidental*, and *implied*. The *express powers* are those specifically given to it by the corporation laws of the state in which it is organized and by the provisions of its charter. The *incidental powers* are those that are inherent in the very nature of corporate existence. They include the power of corporate succession, or the right to continuing existence irrespective of changes in corporate membership; the power to sue, and be sued; the power to purchase, hold, and convey real and personal property for corporate reasons; the power to have a seal; and the power to make bylaws for its government. The *implied powers* are those that are reasonably necessary to enable the corporation to accomplish its purposes. For example, a corporation has the implied power to borrow money, make ordinary contracts, execute promissory notes, etc. *Corporate powers*, however, cannot be extended to enterprises or operations different from those within the original charter. *Corporate profits after taxes* are the earnings of corporations organized for profit after liability for state and federal taxes has been deducted. *Corporate profits before taxes* are the **net** earnings of corporations organized for profit measured before payment of state and federal profit taxes. They are, however, after payment of *indirect* business taxes, and are reported without deduction for **depletion** charges and exclusive of **capital gains** and losses and intercorporate dividends. *Corporate profits tax liability* is the state and federal taxes levied on corporate earnings, usually recorded on an **accrual** basis. That is, they are assigned to the period when the profits were earned, rather than the period when the taxes are actually paid. For *corporate reorganization,* see **Chapter Eleven.** A *corporate seal* is a mark adopted by a corporation for use on written documents. Most states require corporations to make and use a corporate seal and usually permit the corporation to alter or renew it at will. A *corporate state* is a government presumably insensitive to human values. *Corporate strategy* is decision-making in support of corporate goals and operating policies, often used interchangeably with *corporate policy formulation* to describe the process by which top management: appraises the present situation, chooses a course of action, implements its new policies, and evaluates the results in order to start the policy cycle over again. This process is heavily dependent upon **strategic management** and **planning.** This subject, usually taught as *business policy*, tends to take a top management perspective, to be limited to problems of critical importance to the survival of the firm, and to integrate the various areas of management. The *corporate veil* is the legal assumption that actions taken by a corporation are not the actions of its owners, and that these owners cannot usually be held responsible for corporate actions.

Corporation An organization that is formed under state or federal law and exists, for legal purposes, as a separate being or an **artificial person.** It may be public (set up by the government) or private (set up by individuals), and it may be set up to carry on a business or to perform almost any function. It may be owned by the government, by a few persons, or by the general public through purchases of stock. Abbreviated "corp." A private business corporation must be organized strictly in compliance with the laws of the state in which it is incorporated. The laws vary, but all of them provide that a certain number of persons, generally three or more, may form a corporation by filing in the office of a designated state official a statement giving certain specified information, paying initial taxes and filing fees, and holding certain organization meetings at which specified details or organization must be completed. The required statement is known as the "articles of incorporation," the "certificate of incorporation," or the corporate "charter." A corporation is referred to as a "domestic" corporation in the state in which it is incorporated; as a "foreign" corporation in any other state; as an "alien" corporation if incorporated in a country outside the United States and its territories. A corporation has certain fundamental characteristics that have made it the most popular form of business organization. These are: transferability of shares; continuous succession; and limited liability. The ownership of the corporation is represented by its **capital stock,** which is divided into identical units or groups of identical units called shares. These shares are represented by written instruments called **certificates** of stock. The owners of the shares are called the **stockholders.** Every stockholder has the right to transfer shares. Since the shares of stock of a corporation can be transferred by sale or otherwise from one owner to another without affecting the corporate existence, the corporation enjoys continuous succession. The existence of the corporation is not disturbed by death, insanity, or bankruptcy of individual stockholders or by change of ownership. The **liability** of the stockholders is limited as follows: the owner of **fully paid stock** ordinarily has no liability to creditors; the owner of stock that has not been fully paid is liable, in case of **insolvency** of the corporation, to pay, as far as is necessary to satisfy creditors, the amount required to make the stock fully paid. A share of stock is considered fully paid when the corporation has received the full **par** value, or if the stock is without par value, when it has received the price fixed for it on original issuance. In a corporation—particularly a large corporation with many stockholders—those who have contributed to the capital of the business do not ordinarily conduct its affairs. Management is concentrated in the hands of a **board of directors,** elected by the stockholders, who may own only a small portion of the stock. Stockholders cannot bind the corporation by their acts merely because they are stockholders. *Disadvantages* of a corporation include additional taxes, greater government supervision, and limitation of the types of permissible activities. See **partnership** and **sole proprietorship** for the other major ways of owning a business.

Corporation kit   When a **corporation** is organized, the attorney who sees to the details of incorporation obtains for it what is called a *corporation kit.* This consists of the essential documentary material required by every corporation, and usually includes a stock **certificate** book, or stock book, a **transfer** book, and **stock ledger,** a minute book, and a **corporation seal.** These kits can be purchased from legal stationers, and are standardized and inexpensive. They are usually adequate for *small* business corporations.

Correspondent   1. A person who collects **mortgage** loan payments for the lender.   2. One bank or other financial institution that performs regular services for another.

Corrupt practices act   1. A state law that **regulates** political campaign methods and spending.   2. A federal law that regulates international corporate financial activities, prohibits bribery, etc.

Cosigner   A general term for a person who signs a document along with another person. Depending on the situation and on the state, a cosigner may have *primary* responsibility (for example, to pay a debt if the person who made the cosigned loan comes first to the cosigner for the money) or only a *secondary* responsibility (to pay a debt only after the person who took out the loan doesn't pay).

Cost   The value of things used up or expended in producing or acquiring a good or a service. Also whatever must be given up to adopt a course of action. For a contrast, see **expense.** *Cost accounting* is a method in which manufacturing costs are accumulated and distributed to production on an equitable basis. Cost accounting techniques may also be applied to the non-manufacturing functions of a business to control costs and promote efficiency. In addition to information on current costs, the cost accounting system can also be used to provide data on historical costs and estimated future costs. The following functions are basic to any type of cost accounting system: classifying costs, recording costs, allocating costs to product or activity, and summarizing and reporting costs to management. For a description of individual cost systems, see **standard cost system, job order cost system, batch costing.** *Cost analysis* is determining the actual or estimated costs of relevant spending options. This is an integral part of economic analysis and program analysis. Its purpose is to translate the real resource requirements (equipment, personnel, etc.) associated with alternatives into estimated dollar costs. The translation produces direct one-dimensional cost comparisons among alternatives. *Cost and freight* means that the price quoted includes cost and freight, but not insurance or any other charge. *Cost-based budgeting* is budgeting in terms of costs to be incurred; that is, the resources to be consumed in carrying out a program, regardless of when the funds to acquire the resources were obligated or paid, and without regard to the source of funds. For example, inventory items become costs when they are withdrawn from **inventory,** and the cost of buildings is distributed over time, through periodic **depreciation** charges, rather than in a lump sum when the buildings are acquired. *Cost-benefit analysis* is any process by which organizations seek to determine the effectiveness of their spending, in relation to both tangible and intangible costs, in meeting **policy** objectives. A *cost center* is an accounting device by which all related costs attributable to some "center" within an institution, such as an activity, department, or program, are segregated for **accounting** or reimbursement purposes. *Cost centers* may also refer to separate operating divisions or subsidiaries. *Cost effective* has two meanings. First, that benefits exceed (or will exceed) costs; profits exceed (or will exceed) losses. Or, second, the alternative course of action with the highest benefits-divided-by-costs ratio is called *cost effective*. *Cost-effectiveness analysis* is an analytical technique used to choose the most efficient method for achieving a program or **policy** goal. The costs of alternatives are measured by their requisite estimated dollar expenditures. Effectiveness is defined by the degree of goal attainment, and may also (but not necessarily) be measured in dollars. Either the net effectiveness (effectiveness minus costs) or the cost-effectiveness ratios of alternatives are compared. The limited view of costs and effectiveness distinguishes this technique from **cost-benefit analysis,** which encompasses wider impacts of alternatives. For *cost-flow assumption,* see **flow assumption.** *Cost improvement* is any systematic approach to containing costs through more efficient and effective work methods. A *cost leader* is the company with the lowest prices for a product line in a given industry. The *cost method* is a way of reporting the investment (of less than twenty percent of voting stock) of one company in another. The initial investment is recorded at cost; subsequent dividends are treated as revenue. *Cost of capital* is what a company must pay for its financing. It is frequently used to determine the minimum desired rate of return for any investment and is the basis upon which investment projects are selected or rejected. See **hurdle rate** and **opportunity cost.** A *cost of living adjustment* is a wage increase automatically tied to the inflation rate. A *cost of living allowance* is extra pay or expenses for working in a high-cost living area. A *cost of living* (or *escalator*) *clause* is a provision in a contract, such as a **labor agreement** or a retirement plan, that gives an automatic wage or benefit increase tied to inflation as measured by a standard indicator, such as the **Consumer Price Index.** A *cost plus contract* is a **contract** that pays a **contractor** for the cost of labor and materials plus a fixed percentage of cost or a negotiated fee as profit. For *cost push inflation,* see **inflation.** *Cost reports* are **accounting** reports which show either in detail or summary form the essential cost data of production or distribution. These reports usually compare actual costs to both standard costs and budgeted costs. *Cost sharing* is a provision of a health insurance policy which requires the insured to pay some portion of covered medical expenses. Several forms of cost-sharing are employed, particularly **deductibles, coinsurance** and **copayments.** *Cost sharing* does not refer to nor include the amounts paid in **premiums** for the **coverage.** A *cost standard* is the **predetermined costs** of

direct labor, material, and **overhead** of an item, process, activity, or operation. *Cost standards* are established as a basis for control and reporting in a **standard cost system.** *Cost-volume-profit analysis* is an examination of the effect on profits of variations in costs and sales factors. *Costing out* is determining the actual cost of a contract proposal (wages, fringe benefits, etc).

Council of Economic Advisers A part of the Executive Office of the President, the CEA consists of three economists (one designated chairman) appointed by the president who formulate proposals to "maintain employment, production and purchasing power." The CEA is the president's primary source of economic advice.

Countercyclical Things, such as special monetary, fiscal, and program policies, that smooth out swings in economic activity are called *countercyclical.* **Automatic stabilizers** have a countercyclical effect without necessitating changes in governmental policy.

Counteroffer 1. A rejection of an **offer** and a new offer made back. A *counteroffer* sometimes looks like an **acceptance** with new terms or conditions attached, but if these terms or conditions have any substance at all, it is really a rejection, and no contract is made until the counteroffer is accepted. However, see the following for a contrast. 2. Under the **Uniform Commercial Code** a *counteroffer* for the sale of goods may be an acceptance with new terms proposed for the **contract.** 3. More generally, a *counterproposal* is any offer made in response to another offer.

Countersign Sign a document in addition to the primary or original signature in order to approve the validity of the document. A bank may ask a person to countersign his or her own check made out to "cash," and a company may require a supervisor to countersign all orders written by lower-ranking employees.

Countertrade An international trade transaction whereby the exporting country agrees to purchase products or services from the importing country so that the latter can offset some or all of the foreign exchange costs of the imports. In countertrade, the exporting party is usually a **First World** country and the purchaser either a communist state or a developing nation.

Countervailing duty A retaliatory extra charge that a country places on imported goods to counter the subsidies or bounties granted to the exporters of the goods by their home governments.

Coupon A **certificate** of interest or a **dividend** due on a certain date. The coupons are detached one by one from the primary document (bond, loan agreement, etc.) and presented for payment when due. *Coupon bonds* are bonds that have certificates attached to them representing the amount of interest due on the bond during its entire term. Each individual coupon represents an obligation on the part of the bond issuer to pay interest for a stipulated period, usually six months. Coupon bonds are usually **negotiable instruments** payable to the **bearer** and transferable by delivery without the necessity of **indorsement.** If a coupon is detached and lost by its owner and the finder or person purchasing from the finder receives payment on the coupon, the company would not be liable to the original owner for the amount of the coupon. *Coupon stripping* is the purchase of bonds by a **broker** who then repackages them so that the receipts to **interest** and **principal** payments can be separately sold.

Course Progress or passage. *Course of business* is what is normally done by a company. This is different from *custom* or *usage*, which is what is normally done in a particular *type* of company. *Course of dealing* is the prior history of business between two persons. *Course of employment* means directly related to employment, during work hours, or in the place of work.

Covenant A written promise, agreement, or restriction usually in a **deed.** For example, a *covenant for quiet enjoyment* is a promise that the seller of land will protect the buyer against a defective **title** to the land and against anyone who claims the land; and a *covenant running with the land* is any agreement in a deed that is binding for or against all future buyers of the land.

Cover 1. Make good. 2. Protect (for example, insurance **coverage.**) 3. Protect yourself from the effects of a business deal that falls through or isn't made good on; for example, buy what you need from a new company when the original one can't make good on a sale. 4. *Cover your ass (CYA)* is any bureaucratic technique that serves to hold a person harmless for policies or actions with which he or she was once associated.

Coverage 1. The amount and type of **insurance** on a person, an object, a business venture, etc. 2. The *ratio* of a company's income that is available to pay **interest** on its **bonds** (or to pay **dividends** on its preferred **stock**) to the interest itself (or the dividends).

Covered jobs All those positions that are affected and protected by specific labor legislation or union contracts.

Craft Any occupation requiring specific skills that must be acquired by training. For *craft guild,* see **guild.** A *craft union* is a labor organization that restricts its membership to skilled craft workers (such as plumbers, carpenters, etc.), in contrast to an **industrial union** that seeks to recruit all workers in a particular industry. A *craft unit* is a **bargaining unit** that consists only of workers with the same specific skill (such as electricians, plumbers, or carpenters).

Crash A shutdown in computer **hardware** caused by malfunction or a stop in computer operations caused by a bad **program** instruction.

Crawling peg The small daily changes in foreign exchange rates.

Creative financing Any financing (usually home-purchase) outside the normal pattern. It is used to complete a deal that would have failed otherwise. It may be risky.

Credentialing The recognition of professional or technical competence. The credentialing process may include registration, certification, licensure, professional association membership, or the award of a degree in the field. *Credentialism* is an emphasis on paper manifestations, such as college degrees, instead of an actual ability to accomplish the tasks of a job.

Credit *Credit* has several meanings, including the right to delay payment for things bought or used; money loaned; a record in an **account** book of money owed to you or money you have paid out; a deduction from what is owed. See **Consumer Credit Protection Act** and **tax credit.** A *credit agency* (or *bureau*) is an agency that gathers and distributes information about the credit used by individuals, firms and corporations and on their financial reliability. Specialized mercantile agencies and **Dun & Bradstreet, Inc.,** function in the business field; **retail credit bureaus** in the consumer field. See **credit interchange.** Specialized lending agencies that finance the consumer are also called

credit agencies. Credit allocation is the entire structure of
government laws, regulations, loan guarantees, subsidies,
and taxes that provide for or induce credit flows among
sectors of the economy which differ from flows that would
occur in a perfectly competitive financial economy. Credit
allocation policies are set to meet certain social priorities,
and may involve encouragement of certain sectors such as
housing, small business, and state and local governments,
or discouragement of other sectors, as when credit controls are applied. *Credit controls* are government restraints
on lending, expressed in terms of the volume of lending
permitted to certain sectors or through other limits on
lenders. Unlike credit restraint applied to the entire economy through restrictive **monetary policy,** *credit control* is
generally targeted at individual categories of borrowing
and lending, and may even apply to specific transactions.
Credit counseling is a formal effort to help overextended
consumers manage their personal debts. *Credit information interchange* is the exchange of customer credit information among businesses. It is made through the direct
interchange of **ledger** experience by individual firms, trade
group interchange, and retail *credit bureaus.* The information usually includes how long business has been done,
the greatest amount of credit recently given, the amount
owing, amount past due, terms of sale, and method of
payment. *Credit instruments* are cash, **bonds, notes,** and
all **negotiable instruments.** *Credit insurance* is insurance
that offers protection against unusual **bad debt** losses.
The insurance company agrees to reimburse the insured
when losses exceed a stated sum, known as the "normal
loss deduction" or primary loss. Credit insurance is issued
to manufacturers, distributors, and some service companies, especially advertising agencies. It is rarely available to retailers. *Credit life insurance* is insurance covering
the unpaid balance of a loan in the event of a borrower's
death. A *credit limit* is the maximum amount of *credit* a
business will give to a customer. This may be based on past
experience, on the customer's general *credit rating,* on other
factors, or on an arbitrary limit. For *credit line,* see **line
of credit.** *Credit management* is setting up and administering an organization's financial policies related to gaining,
giving and withdrawing credit. Important aspects of credit
management are the collection of **accounts receivable** and

the setting of *credit limits*. **Credit money** is all paper money; its value depends on general acceptance since it has no intrinsic worth. This contrasts with **commodity money.** A *credit rating* is an evaluation of the ability of a person or business to pay debts. Usually, a **credit bureau** makes an evaluation based on past payments and current finances, then uses the information in *credit reports* to businesses that are considering making a loan or offering other credit. *Credit rating* also helps determine an organization's ability to sell its **bonds.** This credit rating translates into a rating for each **issue** which in turn determines the level of interest the organization must pay to entice buyers. The two major bond rating services are **Standard and Poors Corporation** and **Moody's Investors Service.** *Credit risk* is the possibility of loss to a lender resulting from nonpayment by a borrower. A *credit union* is a state- or nationally chartered financial cooperative organization of individuals with a common bond (such as employment, labor union membership, or residence in the same neighborhood). *Credit unions* accept deposits of members' savings and transaction balances in the form of share accounts, pay dividends (interest) on them out of earnings, and primarily provide consumer credit to members. The federal regulator for credit unions is the National Credit Union Administration.

Example of Credit Term	*Meaning*
1. 2/10 net 30	A 2 percent discount from the invoice price may be taken if payment is made within 10 days; otherwise, the net invoice amount is due within 30 days.
2. net 45	The invoice amount is due within 45 days; no cash discount is given.
3. 1/10 net 45 EOM	A 1 percent discount may be taken for payment within 10 days following the last day of the current month (EOM or end of month); otherwise, the invoice amount is due within 45 days following the current month.
4. net 10 ROG	The net amount is due 10 days after receipt of the goods (ROG).

Credited service Employment time that an employee has for **benefit** purposes.

Creditor A person to whom a debt is owed. A *creditor beneficiary* is a person who financially benefits from a contract between other people in which one of those persons promises to do something for the creditor beneficiary. *Creditors' levies* (**attachments,** etc.) of **stock** can usually be made only in the state in which the corporation was organized, regardless of where the debtor resides or where the certificate of stock is actually located. In some cases, it has been held that a levy can be made upon stock of a nonresident in a foreign corporation if the stock is actually in the state. A *creditors' meeting* is the first meeting of persons to whom a **bankrupt** person owes money or who hold **security** interests in a bankrupt's property. The *creditor's position* is the part of a property's sale price that is put up by the **mortgage** lender.

Credits Records in an **account** book of money owed to you or money you have paid out. (The opposite of **debits.**)

Creditworthiness Past and prospective ability to repay debts.

Cremation certificate A sworn statement certifying that certain persons, usually representatives of corporate trust departments, transfer agents, or other appointed agents, in the presence of one another, destroyed, by burning, the cancelled or unused certificates of stock, stock purchase warrants, bonds, or other documents listed in the certificate.

Crisis bargaining Collective bargaining negotiations conducted under the pressure of a **strike** deadline.

Criterion (*plural*: **criteria**) A standard against which other things are measured; for example, a measure of job performance or other work-related behavior against which performance on a test or other predictor measure is compared. *Criterion contamination* is the influence on *criterion measures* of variables or factors not relevant to the work behavior being measured. If the criterion is, for example, a set of supervisory ratings of competence in job performance and if the ratings are correlated with the length of time the supervisor has known the individual people he or she rates, then the length of acquaintance is a contaminant of the criterion measure. Similarly, if the amount of production on a machine is counted as the criterion measure and if the amount of production depends in part on the age of the machine being used, then age of machinery is a contaminant of production counts. A *criterion-referenced test* is a test by which a candidate's performance is measured according to the degree specified criteria have been met. *Criterion relevance* is a judgment of the degree to which a *criterion measure* reflects the important aspects of job performance. Such a judgment is based on an understanding of the measurement process itself, of the job and worker requirements as revealed through **job analysis,** and of the needs of the organization involved.

Critical-incident method   Identifying, classifying and recording significant examples—*critical incidents*—of an employee's behavior for purposes of **performance evaluation.**

Critical path   See **CPA.**

Critical score   A **cutting score.**

Cross   Intersection. *Cross-check* is a procedure by which the National Labor Relations Board or an appropriate state agency compares union **authorization cards** to an employer's payroll to determine whether a majority of the employees wish union representation. *Cross picketing* is **picketing** by two or more **unions** that claim to represent the same workers. *Cross trades* are a maneuver, on the part of two or more parties, which results in the appearance of greater **market** activity. Such false activity is now outlawed under **securities** and **commodities** laws. See *crossing. Cross validation* is a process which seeks to apply the results of one validation study to another. As such, it is a check on the accuracy of the original validation study. *Crossing* is a **broker's** buying a **stock** or other **security** from one client and selling it to another without going through an **exchange.** See *cross trades*.

Crowding out   The displacement of private investment expenditures by increases in public expenditures financed by sales of government securities.

Crown jewels   Valuable properties or **assets** that make a company vulnerable to a **takeover** bid.

Culpeper Switch   A computerized Federal Reserve facility located in Culpeper, Virginia, which serves as a central relay point for messages transmitted electronically between Federal Reserve districts on the **Fedwire.** Messages moving billions of dollars of funds and securities daily are processed by Culpeper in electronically coded form.

Cum dividend A share of **stock** that is sold with a **dividend declared** but not yet paid. The buyer is entitled to receive the dividend when it is paid. See **ex dividend** for contrast.

Cum rights A **stock** that comes "with rights" to buy other stock at a specified price.

Cumulative preferred stock A class of **preferred stock,** which, if **dividends** are not paid in any given year or dividend period, entitles the owner to the **arrearage** in subsequent years. Ordinarily, if the **certificate of incorporation** does not specify whether the stock is to be cumulative or not, the law will hold the preferred stock to be cumulative. When the arrearage on cumulative stock is paid, it does not bear interest, nor does the arrearage become a liability of the corporation. Sometimes in order to enable a corporation to get on its feet before subjecting itself to the payment of dividend arrearages, stock is issued as non-cumulative and only becomes cumulative after the lapse of a few years. Some companies issue cumulative preferred stock but place a time limitation upon the cumulative feature. When arrearages become sizable enough to encumber the corporation's ability to procure additional financing, they are generally eliminated by settlement through a plan of readjustment. Cumulative stock is sometimes issued in order to protect stockholders from a manipulation of the corporate books that enables the corporation to adjust its profits figure so that it need not pay dividends on preferred stock in years that it pays no dividends on **common stock.**

Cumulative voting A system of voting for **directors** of a **corporation** under which each **stockholder** is entitled to a number of votes equal to the number of shares he or she owns multiplied by the number of directors to be elected. The votes may be cast for one candidate—cumulated—or distributed among the candidates in any way. This system enables the minority stockholders to elect one or more of the directors. *Cumulative voting* may be provided by statute, by the corporation's charter or by-laws, or by contract among all the stockholders, provided the agreement is not otherwise illegal. To determine how many shares you must own or control to elect a certain number of directors, use this formula:

$$\frac{\text{number of} \atop \text{voting shares} \ \text{x} \ \text{number of directors} \atop \text{you want to elect}}{\text{number of directors} + 1 \atop \text{to be elected}} + 1$$

Cure It is a *cure* when a seller delivers goods, the buyer rejects them because of some defect, and the seller then delivers the proper goods within the proper time.

Current 1. *Current* has many meanings; for example, immediately, within the same **accounting** period, within a year, within a few months, easily converted to cash, etc. 2. *Current assets* are a company's cash plus those things such as short-term **securities, accounts receivable,** and **inventory** that will probably be turned into cash in the next few months or at least within the same accounting period. *Current liabilities* are a company's debts, such as **accounts payable,** wages, short-term borrowing, and taxes that must be paid within the next few months or at least within the same accounting period. *Current liabilities to tangible net worth* is a ratio for evaluating a company's financial condition by comparing what's owed to what's owned. The *current ratio* is a company's *current assets* divided by its *current liabilities.* It is a measure of a company's relatively short-term financial strength. See also **working capital** and **quick assets.** 3. A *current account* is a checking account with a bank; or in the context of international trade, that part of the **balance of payments** that consists of exports and imports of goods and services, as well as inward and outward unilateral transfers. The *current account balance* is the amount by which a country's exports of goods and services and inward transfers exceed (current account surplus) or fall short of (current account deficit) its imports of goods and services and outward transfers. This balance, which includes services and transfers as well as merchandise, is more comprehensive than the trade balance, which includes only merchandise. See also **capital account.** *Current cost standards* are based on current operating rates and price levels for each cost item; they are the costs that are used in financial **statements** as the costs of manufacturing and, sometimes, for inventory costs. See *current value accounting. Current dollars* are the opposite of **constant dollars.** *Current return*

is the present income from an investment. The percentage
rate of current return on investments in **stock** is determined by dividing the current annual **dividend** payment
by the cost price. Changes in the dividend rate affect the
rate of current return; changes in the price of the stock do
not. The current return on **bonds** is determined by dividing the annual interest payment by the price paid for the
bond. See **return** and **yield**. *Current value accounting* is
reporting **assets** at their present replacement cost (or **net
realizable value**) if they are to be sold. The *current yield*
is the rate of annual return of an investment based on the
price actually paid for it.

CUSIP number A number given by the Committee on
Uniform Securities Identification Procedures of the American Bankers Association to identify each **issue** of **securities.**

Custom house The office where goods going into or out of
a country are inspected and registered, and where taxes
are paid. A *customhouse broker* is an individual or firm
licensed to enter and clear goods through **customs.**

Customs 1. Taxes payable on goods brought into or sent
out of a country. (Also called **duty** and **tariff**.) 2. The
branch of government that oversees and taxes goods
brought in and out of a country. 3. A *customs union* is a
group of nations that has eliminated trade barriers among
themselves and imposed a common tariff on all goods
imported from all other countries. The European **common market** is a *customs union*. *The Customs Valuation
Code* lays down international rules for uniform and equitable valuation for duty purposes for all classes of international trading. The primary method of valuation under
the code is transactional value.

Cutthroat pricing See **predatory intent.**

Cutting score A test score used as an employment requirement. Those at or above such a score are eligible
for selection or promotion; those below the score are
not.

Cycle billing A system of billing retail customers on successive dates throughout the month. Customer accounts
are grouped either numerically or alphabetically. A mailing date is scheduled for each group, and it remains the
same each month. The schedule provides for the mailing
of statements on successive dates rather than at the end of

the month. The number of cycles and billing dates correspond with the number of groups.

Cyclical stock   A **stock** that tends to respond to changes in the **business cycle;** for example, airline stocks tend to go down during recessions.

Cyclical unemployment   Unemployment caused by a downward trend in the **business cycle.**

D

D In newspaper financial tables, an indication, lowercase (d), that the price of a **security** has reached a new 52-week low; or that a bond is deeply **discounted;** or that a **mutual fund** is trading **ex-distribution;** or that a **dividend** has been paid by an **over-the-counter** stock that has not regularly paid them. 2. A **bond** in **default.**

DBA 1. Doctor of Business Administration 2. Doing business as.

DFC Development Finance Company.

DISC Domestic International Sales Corporation.

Daily rate Basic pay earned by an employee for a **standard** work day.

Daisy wheel A circular typehead for a letter-quality printer.

Damages Money that a court orders paid to a person who has suffered a loss or injury by the person whose fault caused it.

Data *Datum* is a single bit of information; *data* is the plural of *datum*. A *data bank (or base)* is information stored in a computer system so that any particular item or set of items can be extracted or organized as needed. *Data bank* (or *database*) is also used to refer to any data-storage system, or to the collection of information itself. A *database management system* is **software** that manages, updates, secures and gains computer access to these files.

Data processing A broad word for all manipulation of data: classifying it, sorting it, putting it in or taking it out of a computer, preparing reports, calculating answers, etc.

Date of issue The day a document is formally put out or takes effect. The day that shows on the document itself; *not necessarily* the day it actually appears. For example, the *date of issue* of an **insurance** policy is the first day the policy says it will take effect, *not* the day the insurance is agreed to or the day the document is delivered.

Day A *day book* is a book in which a merchant records each day's business as it happens. A *day certain* is a specific future date. For *day order,* see **order.** A *day wage* is earnings per day, for a set number of hours. *Daywork* is a regular day shift that is paid on the basis of time rather than **output.** A *day worker* is a casual, usually unskilled, worker hired by the day.

De facto In fact; actual; a situation that exists in fact whether or not it is lawful. For example, a *de facto corporation* is a company that has failed to follow some of the technical legal requirements to become a legal **corporation,** but carries on business as one in good faith.

De jure Of right; legitimate; lawful, whether or not true in actual fact.

Dead freight Money paid by a shipper for that part of a ship's or vehicle's capacity that is not filled.

Dead time Time on the job lost by a worker through no fault of his or her own.

Deadheading 1. Bypassing of more senior employees in order to promote a more qualified but more junior employee. 2. In the transportation industry, *deadheading* refers to either the movement of empty vehicles to a place where they are needed or the practice of providing free transportation for the company's employees.

Dealer 1. Any person (or firm) who buys and sells things as a business. 2. A financial firm engaged in the purchase and sale of **commodities** or **securities** for its own account and at its own risk rather than for customers, as does a **broker.**

Death and gift taxes Taxes imposed on transfer of property at death, on contemplation of death, or as a gift.

Death benefit A **benefit** provided under a **pension** plan that is paid to an employee's survivors or estate. Payments may be made in monthly installments or in a lump sum.

Debenture A corporation's obligation to pay money (usually in the form of a **note** or **bond**) that is not **secured** (backed up) by any specific property. The common use of the word includes only long-term bonds. [pronounce: de-*ben*-chur]

Debit card A plastic card, like a credit card, but which allows a person to make a purchase that is paid for by a direct subtraction from the person's bank account.

Debits Records in an **account** book of money you owe or of money paid to you. (The opposite of **credits**.)

Debt 1. A sum of money owed because of an agreement (such as a sale or loan). 2. Any money owed. 3. A *debt collector* is anyone, other than a **creditor** or creditor's attorney, who regularly collects debts for others. The *debt crisis* refers to the recurrent problem of **Third World** nations to repay their loans from, and service the **interest** owed to, free world commercial banks and international financial institutions. The *debt-equity ratio* is a **leverage ratio.** It is total *debt* divided by **stockholder's equity**. *Debt financing* is a company's raising money by **issuing bonds** or notes rather than by issuing **stock,** which is called **equity financing**. *Debt poolers* (or *debt adjusters* or *debt consolidators*) are persons or organizations who take a person's money and pay it out to **creditors** by getting the creditors to accept lower monthly payments. Unless these services are nonprofit credit counselling organizations, the chances are that the debtor will wind up paying much more than by making the arrangements him or herself. For *debt ratio,* see **leverage ratios.** *Debt relief* in an international context refers to methods for releasing **developing countries** from the obligations to repay loans. *Debt service* is regular payments of **principal, interest,** and other costs such as insurance made to pay off a loan.

Debtor A person who owes money.

Debtor nation 1. A nation that borrows more from other nations than it loans them. 2. A nation that receives more investments from foreign sources than from its own internal sources.

Debtor's position The part of a property's sale price that is put up by the person buying the property, rather than by the **mortgage** lender.

Debugging 1. A process of detecting, locating, and removing mistakes or imperfections from a computer **program** or any new system. 2. Removing unwanted electronic surveillance equipment. *Bugging* is putting it there in the first place.

Decapitalization A reduction of **capital stock.** It is sometimes accomplished by a **reverse split** having **stockholders** receive one share for a larger number of shares.

Deceptive pricing guides Formal guidelines promulgated by the Federal Trade Commission to prevent misuse of various price advertising methods.

Decision packages Mechanisms used in **zero-base budgeting** to look at the effects on programatic resource requirements, products and levels of performance of alternative levels of funding. *Consolidated decision packages* are packages prepared at higher organizational and program levels that summarize and supplement information contained in *decision packages* received from subordinate units. Consolidated packages may reflect different priorities, including the addition of new programs or the abolition of existing ones.

Decision rule Any directive established to make decisions in the face of uncertainty. For example, a payroll office might be given a *decision rule* to deduct one hour's pay from an employee's wages for each lateness that exceeds ten minutes but is less than one hour.

Decision tree A graphic method of presenting various decisional alternatives so that the various risks, information

DECISION TREES

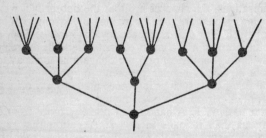

"BUSHY"

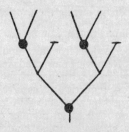

"PRUNED"

needs and courses of action are visually available to the decisionmaker. The various decisional alternatives are displayed in the form of a tree with nodes and branches. Each branch represents an alternative course of action or decision, which leads to a node which represents an event. Thus, a *decision tree* shows both the different courses of action available as well as their possible outcomes.

Declaration 1. An announcement of a set-aside of money. For example, a *declaration of dividends* is a corporation's setting aside part of its profits to pay stockholders; and a *declaration of estimated tax* is a statement and set-aside of money required by the **IRS** of persons who have income from which taxes have not been withheld. 2. A formal statement of fact.

Declining balance 1. The decreasing amount owed on a **debt** as monthly or other periodic payments are made. 2. A form of *accelerated* **depreciation** that takes a fixed percentage (125%, 150% or 200%) over the **straight line method** on a declining balance each year. *Double declining balance* (200%) takes twice the straight line rate.

Decrement The amount of decrease in a property's value.

Dedication 1. The gift or other transfer of land (or rights in land) to the government for a specific use, such as a park, and its acceptance for that use by the government. 2. Publishing a work without getting a formal **copyright** may be a *dedication* of that work to the public, and anyone may then publish, perform, duplicate, etc.

Deductible 1. That which may be taken away or subtracted. Something that may be subtracted from income for tax purposes. 2. That part of a loss that must be borne by a person with **insurance** before the insurance company will pay the rest. For example, a **policy** with a "$100 deductible" clause will pay nothing on a $100 loss, and pay $200 on a $300 loss.

Deduction 1. Subtractions from income for tax purposes. *Itemized deductions* are those nonbusiness expenses that may be subtracted from **adjusted gross income** by listing the amounts in the proper categories. 2. Any subtraction of money owed; for example, any amount for any reason that is withheld from an employee's pay and credited toward a legitimate purpose such as taxes or insurance.

Deed A document by which one person transfers the legal ownership of land (and what is on the land) to another person.

Deed of trust 1. A document by which a person transfers the legal ownership of land to independent **trustees** to be held until a debt on the land (a **mortgage**) is paid off. 2. A document that creates a **trust** of any kind.

Deep pockets The one person (or organization), among many possible defendants, best able to pay a **judgment** has *deep pockets*. This is the one a plaintiff is most likely to sue.

Deep Rock Doctrine 1. The principle that even if an **insider** has a better claim to the property of a company that is going out of business, a court may give the property to **creditors** if that is fairer. 2. See **instrumentality rule.**

Defalcation 1. Failure of a person to account for money trusted to his or her care. There is the assumption that the money was misused. 2. Setting off one claim against another; deducting a smaller debt one is owed from a larger debt one owes.

Default 1. A failure to perform a legal duty, observe a promise, or fulfill an obligation. For example, the word is often used for the failure to make a payment on a debt once it is due. 2. Failure to take a required step in a lawsuit; for example, to file a paper on time. This *default* leads to a default **judgment** against the side failing to file the paper.

Defeasance clause The part of a **mortgage** contract that says that the mortgage is ended once all payments have been made or once certain other things happen.

Deferred Delayed. A *deferred annuity* is an **annuity** that does not start until after a specified period or until the annuitant reaches a specified age. *Deferred charges* are a company's current spending for long-term needs such as research. It will be deducted from taxes over several years, not all at once. *Deferred compensation* is payments to employees, such as those made under a **pension plan** that satisfies **IRS** rules, that will not be taxed until the employee actually gets the money. *Deferred full vesting* is a pension plan that provides that an employee retains rights to accrued **benefits** if he or she is terminated after a specified age or after he or she completes a specified period of service in the organization. *Deferred graded* *vesting* is a pension plan that provides that an employee acquires a right to a specified percentage of accrued benefits when he or she meets the participation requirements stipulated by the plan. *Deferred income* is an account for monies received but not yet earned. Ordinarily, that portion of the income that has been earned is included in the profit-and-loss **statement,** and the unearned portion is shown as an item of deferred income in the liability section of the **balance sheet**. A *deferred life annuity* is an **annuity** that becomes effective at a specified future date. If death occurs before the specified date, no benefits are paid. Once the annuity has started, it continues only for the life of the insured. *Deferred stock* is stock on which no **dividends** are to be paid until after a certain other **class** of stock has received its dividends. Provisions of this sort are usually made in a corporate **reorganization** or *recapitalization*. A *deferred wage increase* is a negotiated pay increase that does not become effective until a specified future date.

Deficiency A lack or shortage. For example, the difference between a tax owed and a tax paid is a *deficiency*. A **deficiency** *judgment* (or *decree*) is a court's decision that a person must pay more money owed than the amount **secured** by property. For example, when an auto dealer repossesses (takes back) a car for failure to make payments and then sells the car for eight hundred dollars, if the debt owed is one thousand dollars, some states will allow the car dealer to sue for a two-hundred-dollar *deficiency judgment*. The same thing can happen in a mortgage **foreclosure.**

Deficit Something missing or lacking; less than what should be; a "minus" **balance.** For example, if a city takes in less money than it must pay out in the same time period, it is called *deficit financing* or *deficit spending*. *Deficit elimination* is the removal of a deficit **account** from the books of the corporation to permit the **declaration** of a **dividend.** A corporation may not declare a dividend if, at the time of the proposed distribution, the **balance sheet** of the corporation shows a deficit. A deficit may be wiped out in one of the following ways: by reappraising undervalued **assets;** by converting unnecessary **reserves** into **surplus;** or by reducing **capital** stock through a decrease in the **par value** per share or in the number of shares outstanding.

Deficit elimination by the **board of directors** must be honest and in good faith; and it must not be contrary to the provisions of the charter, or statutes or decisions of the state in which the company was incorporated.

Degrees Gradations used in the point-rating method of **job evaluation** to differentiate among job factors.

Dehiring Generally, any means of encouraging a marginal or unsatisfactory employee to quit as an alternative to being fired.

Del credere (Italian) An **agent** who sells goods for a person and also **guarantees** to that person that the buyer will pay in full for the goods. [pronounce: del *cred*-er-e]

Delectus personae (Latin) "Choice of person." The right of a **partner** to choose, approve, and disapprove of other partners.

Delinquency Failure, omission, or violation of duty; misconduct. For example, a debt that has fallen behind in payment is called a *delinquency*. A *delinquency ratio* is a ratio of the volume of outstanding delinquent accounts to sales for a specified period—a year, a quarter, or a month. This ratio reflects the strictness or laxity of a company's credit and collection policies. The lag factor that distorts the **bad debt ratio** and the **collection ratio** is less marked in the *delinquency ratio*, because the delinquency of a past-due account occurs sooner after the sale than collection of the account or its development into a **bad debt.**

Delinquent 1. Overdue and unpaid. 2. Willfully and intentionally failing to carry out an obligation.

Demand 1. A forceful claim that presupposes that there is no doubt as to its winning. 2. The assertion of a legal right; a legal obligation asserted in the courts. 3. "On demand" is a phrase put on some **promissory notes** or other **negotiable instruments** to mean that the money owed must be paid immediately when the **holder** of the note requests payment. These are called *demand notes*. A *demand deposit* is money given to a bank that may be taken out at any time; for example, a checking account. 4. The strength of buyer desire for and willingness to pay for a product. For *demand-pull inflation,* see **inflation.** A *demand schedule* is the varying amount of a good or service sought at varying prices, given constant income and other factors. A graph plotting these sales at different prices is a *demand curve*.

Demise 1. A **lease.** 2. Any transfer of property (especially land). *Not* "devise." 3. Death.

Demotion The reassignment of an employee to a job of lower status, responsibility, and pay. There are three basic kinds of demotions: *voluntary demotion* is usually the result of a reduction in force in which the employee takes a job of lower status and pay rather than being laid off; *involuntary demotion* results from a worker's inability to perform adequately on the job; and *disciplinary demotion* usually takes place after an employee has been repeatedly warned to stop some kind of misconduct or disruptive behavior.

Demurrage The amount charged for the use of railroad freight cars, ships, or pier facilities, over the allotted "free time" published in the carrier's **tariff** or agreed to by contract. *Demurrage charges* often increase progressively by periods, to encourage the holder to return the equipment to the carrier.

Dependent 1. An individual who relies upon another individual for a significant portion of support. In addition to the requirement for financial support there is often a requirement for a blood relationship. The Internal Revenue Code defines as dependents for the purposes of *tax deductions* many types of relatives (and some others) over half of whose support for the calendar year was received from the taxpayer. In **insurance** and other programs the specific definition is quite variable, often being limited to the individual's spouse and children. Other dependents of the kinds recognized by the IRS are sometimes known as *sponsored dependents*. 2. A *dependent variable* is a factor in an experimental relationship that has or shows variation which is hypothesized to be caused by another *independent factor* or *variable*.

Depletion **Amortization** of a natural resource. One possible example would be dividing the cost of coal properties by the estimated tonnage they contain to give the amount per ton to be used in charging depletion. Thus, if the coal properties, including original purchase, digging, and surveying, cost $500,000, and the estimated tonnage is 100,000 tons, the depletion is $5.00 per ton. Then if 10,000 tons of coal are mined in the fiscal period, the depletion charge (and the corresponding reduction in the value of the coal properties) is $50,000. A *depletion allowance* is a ta-

deduction for extractors of oil, minerals, and other natural resources because they are being used up.

Deposit 1. Place property in another's hands for safekeeping. 2. Give someone money as part payment, **earnest money** or **security** for a purchase. 3. Money placed in a bank or similar financial institution, often to earn interest. *Demand deposits* may be taken out at any time and *time deposits* must be left in for a certain time.

Depositary The person who receives a **deposit.** See **depository.**

Depository The place (such as a bank) where a **deposit** is kept. See **depositary.**

Depreciation 1. A reduction in the value of a **fixed asset** because of wear and tear from use or disuse, accident, inadequacy, or from **obsolescence.** Depreciation is distinguished from *deterioration*, which is the loss of quality or substance of facilities, materials, and products. 2. The amount of the fall in value in no. 1 that is "written off" or charged to a particular time period for tax **deduction** purposes. If an equal amount of depreciation is taken in each year of a property's useful life, it is called *straight line* depreciation. If more of the depreciation is taken early, it is called *accelerated* depreciation. Among these accelerated methods are various **declining balance** methods. *Depreciation* is a type of **amortization** of physical objects used in a business. Depreciation, as part of overhead in figuring manufacturing costs, has the effect of reducing stated earnings during any current accounting

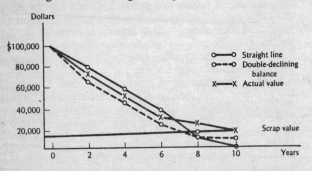

Declining Asset Value Compared to Depreciation Schedules

period, which in turn lowers income taxes, permitting a more attractive selling price for a firm's products. *Depreciation life estimates* are the estimated life expectancies of assets. These are key factors along with **salvage value** and choice of depreciation method in determining the annual charge of depreciation.

Deregulation A change in the philosophy of a government **regulatory agency** occasioned by new leadership or new laws calling for a reduction in the **regulation** of a particular industry.

Derivative action A lawsuit by a **stockholder** of a **corporation** against another person (usually an officer of the company) to enforce rights the shareholder thinks the corporation has against that person. Any financial recovery goes to the corporation, which then has the duty to reimburse the stockholder for expenses.

Desk The *Desk* is the trading desk at the New York Federal Reserve Bank, through which open market purchases and sales of government securities are made. The desk maintains direct telephone communication with major government securities dealers. A *foreign desk* at the New York Federal Reserve Bank conducts transactions in the foreign exchange market. *Desktop media* is the integration of sound, pictures and text for multi-media communications using a personal computer. *Desktop publishing* uses personal computers to produce documents that once had to be typeset.

Desk audit 1. A review of a job or jobs to see if the duties fit the assigned pay and rank and possibly to see if the person filling the job has the right qualifications. It usually includes an interview with the incumbent and the incumbent's supervisor made at the employee's desk or regular place of work. 2. The review of a federal tax return by an **IRS** employee who needs no additional information from the taxpayer.

Destination contract A deal in which the risk of loss or of damage to a shipment of goods passes from seller to buyer once the goods are offered up at their destination.

Destination control statement Statements that the U.S. government requires to be displayed on export shipments that specify the destinations for which export of the shipment has been authorized.

Destroy 1. With regard to contracts or other legal documents, *destruction* does not necessarily mean total physical destruction. You can *destroy* a document's *legal effect* by less extreme methods, such as tearing it in half or writing over it. 2. *Destruction* may mean many different things. For example, in an insurance contract, *destruction* may mean a total wreck or merely harm that makes something useless for its intended purpose.

Detail A temporary assignment of an employee to a different **position** for a specified period with the assumption that the employee will return to "normal" duties at the end of the detail. Technically, a position cannot be "filled" by a detail, as the employee continues to be the incumbent of the original position. A *detail person* is a sales representative of a pharmaceutical manufacturer who promotes prescription drugs for use by physicians, dentists, and pharmacists.

Determination 1. A final decision (usually of a court or other formal decision-maker such as a **hearing examiner**). 2. Any formal decision. For example, the **IRS** puts out *determination letters* to explain whether or not an organization has been given *tax exempt* status.

Devaluation Reducing the value of a country's money relative to other countries' money (or reducing its legal metallic content). It is usually an official recognition that the currency has in fact already irretrievably lost some of its value (depreciated) on international markets and is used as a last resort to correct a chronic **balance-of-payments** deficit.

Developed countries Countries with high per capita incomes and standards of living. Whether a country is termed "developed" or "developing" is determined by such factors as **GNP,** education, level of industrial development and production, health and welfare, and agricultural productivity. In general, the developed market economies of the **First World** together with the developed centrally planned economies of the **Second World** are considered the developed countries.

Developing countries Used interchangeably with **Third World,** "less developed countries," "underdeveloped countries," and "the South" to refer to those countries with low per capita incomes and standards of living. *Very* low-income developing countries are often referred to as the **Fourth World.**

Development 1. A piece of land subdivided into building lots and sold, or built upon and then sold. 2. Preparation of a mining site to make the minerals accessible by stripping, blasting, tunneling, etc.

Development finance companies (DFCs) Independent financial institutions in **developing countries** that are supported technically and managerially by the **International Finance Corporation** and supported financially by the **International Bank for Reconstruction and Development.**

Development-stage company A new company whose principal activities have yet to start or one which has yet to generate any significant revenue.

Devest See **divest.**

Deviation 1. A departure from usual conduct, such as an employee's use of work time for personal business. 2. A change from original terms or plans, such as a **contractor's** substituting one type of wood for another specified in building plans. 3. The amount by which a score differs from a reference value such as the **mean** or the **norm.**

Differential piece work (or rate) A wage program in which the money rate per piece is determined by the total number of pieces produced over a time period—usually a day. See **Taylor differential piece rate plan.**

Differential user charge Any user charge scaled to meet the requirements of different kinds of customers, levels of usage, time or season of use, etc.

Differentials Increases in wage rates because of **shift work** or other conditions generally considered to be undesirable.

Diffusion In marketing, the process (and the rate) by which new products are adopted by new users.

Dilution 1. The use of a **trademark** by a product so unlike the original that, while it will cause no confusion, it may still lower the trademark's value. 2. *Dilution* of **stock** occurs when the stock is **watered** or when more stock is sold than the value of the company can support.

Dilutive securities **Securities** such as warrants and options that can dilute the value of a company's stock by requiring the issuance of more shares, which would cause a concomitant drop in earnings per share or book value per share.

Diminishing value method Calculation of **depreciation** by applying a fixed percentage to the **net value** of the **asset** at the end of each **fiscal year.** With this method, an estimated residual or **surplus** value is always set, although it is not always deducted from original cost, because theoretically a true zero balance can never be reached. The chief value of this method is that it assigns greatest depreciation to the early years of the asset when maximum loss of resale value normally occurs.

Direct Immediate or straight. A *direct action* is either a lawsuit by a person against his or her own **insurance** company (instead of against the person who did the harm or against that person's insurance company) or a lawsuit by a stockholder to enforce his or her own rights against a company or its officers (rather than to enforce the **corporation's** rights in a **derivative actions**). A *direct cost* is a *cost* which is identifiable directly with a particular activity, service or product of the program experiencing the cost. Accuracy in **cost accounting** depends on the degree to which direct costs constitute the cost of the product. The higher the percentage of direct costs to total product cost, the more accurate the cost accounting will be. **Indirect costs** such as **overhead** assigned to products are less accurate because the assignment must be on an arbitrary basis that varies with the judgment of the accountant who does the assigning. *Direct labor* consists of work performed on a product that is a specific contribution to its eventual completion. (*Indirect labor* consists of all support activities that do not contribute directly to the completion of a product.) A *direct labor standard* is the predetermined costs of *direct labor* required for the manufacture of a product. It makes possible the determination of a **standard** labor cost per unit. *Direct materials* are the cost of materials entering directly into the finished product. For example, the steel used to make automobile bodies and the rubber used to make tires are considered direct materials. Certain low-cost materials such as glue, washers, screws, nails, etc., are also *direct materials* in the sense that they are part of the finished product but, for costing purposes, it is more efficient to classify such items as indirect materials and treat them in the same way as other *indirect costs*. The advantage of treating costs as direct is the increased accuracy of unit costs. A *direct materials budget* is a statement of estimated quantities of direct materials needed to meet specified production goals in the *production budget*. A *direct materials standard* is the predetermined cost of the materials entering directly into the item manufactured. *Direct placement* is a company selling its **stock** or **bonds** directly to a buyer, rather than to the public through underwriters. This is also called *private placement*. A *direct reduction mortgage* is a type of mortgage in which the payment size decreases with each payment because **interest** is paid on only the **principal** still owed. Contrast this with a **constant payment mortgage**. *Direct response* refers to advertising that asks the customer to respond directly to the advertiser by means of a coupon order form or telephone number. *Direct selling* is a manufacturer selling directly to a customer rather than through a wholesaler or retailer. A *direct writer* is an insurance **agent** who generally deals with only one insurance company.

Director 1. Head of an organization, group, or project. 2. A person elected by the shareholders (owners) of a **corporation** to make all **corporate** decisions such as the hiring of the persons who actually run the day-to-day operations. Directors as a group are a *board of directors*. Those who are also major stockholders, officers, or employees of the company are called *inside directors*; those with no such interest are *outside directors*; and those with business contracts with the corporation or any other personal financial interest are *interested directors*. Directors are personally liable for the following violations of their trust: for secret profits; for waste of corporate assets; for losses due to negligence; for acts beyond the corporate powers; and for fraudulent statements and acts. Directors are *not* liable for losses suffered by the corporation as a result of their poor judgment if they have acted honestly and within their powers, but they *are* presumed to know everything concerning corporate affairs that they might have learned by the use of reasonable care and diligence.

Disburse Pay out of a fund of money. In budget talk, *gross disbursements* represent the amount of checks issued and cash or other payments made less refunds received. *Net disbursements* represent gross disbursements less income collected and credited to the appropriation or fund account, such as amounts received for goods and services provided.

Disc See **disk**.

Discharge 1. See **dismissal**. 2. Release; remove; free; dismiss. For example, to *discharge* a contract is to end the obligation by agreement or by carrying it out.

Disciplinary action Any action short of **dismissal** taken by an employer against an employee for a violation of company **rule** or **policy.** This includes *disciplinary layoffs* and *suspensions.*

Disciplinary fine A fine that a union may levy against a member for violating a provision of the union's **bylaws.**

Discipline See **adverse action, preventive discipline, progressive discipline,** and **slide-rule discipline.**

Discipline clause A provision of a **collective bargaining** agreement that stipulates the means for disciplining workers who violate management or union rules.

Disclaimer The refusal to accept certain types of responsibility. For example, a *disclaimer clause* in a written sales contract might say "we give you, the purchaser, promises A, B, C, etc., but *disclaim* all other promises or responsibilities."

Disclosure Revealing something that is secret or not well understood. For example, the *disclosure* in a **patent** application is the statement of what the invention is, what it does, and how it works. In **consumer** law, *disclosure* refers to what information must be made available in a loan or other **credit** deal and how that information must be presented to make it clear.

Discount 1. A deduction or lowering of an amount of money; for example, a lower price. 2. Paying **interest** in advance. 3. See **discounting** and **loan discount.**

Discount rate 1. The percentage of the face value of a commercial **note, bill, mortgage,** etc., that is deducted from the payment by a buyer such as a bank. 2. The rate set by the **Federal Reserve Board** for the charge made by Federal Reserve Banks to other banks borrowing money from them. This greatly influences the banks' rate of borrowing. See **rediscount rate.** 3. See **discounting.**

Discount window The figurative expression for the **Federal Reserve** facility for lending directly to eligible **depository** institutions.

Discounted cash flow method See **profitability index.**

Discounting Calculating the present value of money to be paid or collected in a future payment or a series of future payments. The process involves answering the question: "How much money would I need to invest today at a certain interest rate to equal what will be paid or collected in the future?" The calculation is the reverse of

compounding interest, and the interest rate used is called the **discount rate** or the *capitalization rate*.

Discretion The power to act within general guidelines, rules, or laws, but without either specific rules to follow or the need to completely explain or justify each decision or action. For example, a *discretionary account* exists when a customer gives a stockbroker great leeway in deciding what stocks to buy and sell, when to buy, etc. *Discretionary income* is that which remains for spending after taxes and other necessities.

Discrimination 1. In the context of employment, the failure to treat equals equally. Whether deliberate or unintentional, any action that has the effect of limiting employment and advancement opportunities because of an individual's sex, race, color, age, national origin, religion, physical handicap, or other irrelevant criteria is *discrimination*. Because of the **EEO** and civil rights legislation of recent years, individuals aggrieved by unlawful discrimination now have a variety of administrative and judicial remedies open to them. See also **reverse discrimination.** 2. In the context of international trade, the inequity of trade treatment accorded one or more exporting nations by an importing nation. This may take the form of preferential **tariff** rates for imports from particular countries, or trade restrictions that apply to the exports of certain countries but not to similar goods from other countries. For comparison, see **most-favored-nation** treatment.

Discriminatory discharge The dismissal of an employee for union activity; an **unfair labor practice.**

Dishonor Refuse to accept or pay a **negotiable instrument** when it comes due.

Disinterested Impartial; not biased or prejudiced; or affected personally or financially by the outcome. (The word, however, does *not* mean "uninterested" and does *not* mean lacking an opinion.)

Disintermediation The process that occurs when large numbers of people take their money out of savings and similar accounts and put the money directly into investments that pay higher rates of interest (and that the savings banks might have invested in with the same money).

Disk A rotating circular magnetic storage device for computer data. A *disk drive* is the unit that "plays" the disk and allows **random access memory.** A *diskette* is a **floppy**

disk. Disks are either floppy or hard (with greater and more permanent storage). And a *disk operating system* is a set of **programs** on a disk that is copied by the computer to run basic functions.

Dismissal   Management's removal of an employee from employment. *Dismissal pay* is the same as **severance pay.**

Disorderly market   A securities exchange where prices are erratic and buyers and sellers are not easily available to each other.

Disparagement   The discrediting, belittling, or "talking down" of something or someone. Under some circumstances, you can be sued for doing it; for example, *disparagement* of **title** and *disparagement* of **property**. Also, a seller's disparagement of an advertised item may be part of prohibited **bait and switch** sales tactics.

Disparate effect   The tendency of employment screening devices or criteria to limit the appointment opportunities of women and minorities at a greater rate than for nonminority males.

Dispatch   An amount paid by a cargo ship's operator to a charterer if loading or unloading is completed in less time than stipulated in the **charter party.**

Disposable earnings   Gross or *total* pay, minus **deductions** required by law. This is *not* exactly the same as **take home pay,** since voluntary deductions may further reduce *take home.*

Dissolution   Ending or breaking up. For example, *dissolution* of a contract is a mutual agreement to end it and *dissolution* of a corporation is ending its existence.

Distress   Forced. A *distress sale* of goods might be a "going out of business" sale in which prices are low, and a *distress sale* of land might be due to a mortgage **foreclosure.**

Distribution   The sale of a large block of a corporation's **stock.**

Distribution channel   See **channel of distribution.**

Distribution upon dissolution   The apportionment, division and delivery of the portion of corporate **assets** to which each claimant is entitled on the **dissolution** of a corporation. The assets of a dissolved corporation belong to the stockholders. However, the corporate **debts** must be paid and its obligations discharged before the proceeds obtained in liquidating the assets may be distributed among the stockholders. Then, **preferred stock** is generally issued upon the agreement that it will be entitled to certain preferences in distribution upon dissolution. Also, if a stockholder has not paid in full for stock, he or she may share in the proceeds only in proportion to the amount actually paid.

Distributor 1. Wholesaler. 2. An **agent** who sells for a supplier directly and maintains an inventory of the supplier's products.

District council A level of **labor organization** below the national union but above the locals. The district council is composed of local unions in a particular industry within a limited geographic area.

Diversification 1. A company's adding new product lines or going into an entirely new business. 2. An investor's buying new types of stock or other **securities,** usually to reduce the risk of one stock's sudden fall in price.

Divestiture 1. Selling off or otherwise disposing of a major asset. 2. The court order to a company that it get rid of something (another company, stock, property, etc.) because of **antitrust** laws. The company's carrying out of the court order is also called *divestiture* (or *divestment*).

Dividend A share of profits or property; usually a payment per **share** of a **corporation's stock.** A few of the many different types of dividends include *asset (or property) dividend* (paid in the form of property instead of cash or stock; for example, a blivit manufacturer might give each owner a blivit); *consent dividend* (declared to avoid a personal **holding company** or **accumulated earnings tax,** but never actually paid; this dividend is then taxed to the owners as if paid and increases their **basis** of ownership); *constructive dividend* (unreasonable compensation paid to an owner that will be taxed like a dividend; this could be unusually high wages, bargain purchases of company property, etc.); *cumulative dividend* (if not paid regularly, usually on **preferred stock,** it accumulates and must be paid before any **common stock** dividends are paid); *deficiency dividend* (paid to make up for a missed one; often to avoid paying a personal holding company tax); *liquidating dividend* (the distribution of cash or property to stockholders during the dissolution of a business); *scrip dividend* (paid in **scrip,** in **certificates** of ownership of stock not yet issued, or in short-term loan **notes;** done to divide profits but delay paying them out); and *stock dividend* (not a real dividend, but a dividing up of the increased worth of a company by **issuing** more stock).

Dividend reinvestment plan A plan in which a corporation, at the request of a stockholder, automatically reinvests stock dividends in additional shares (and fractions thereof) of stock.

Dividend yield A **profitability ratio: dividends** paid per share in a given year divided by average **market** price for that year.

Division of labor A production process that has individual workers specializing in the varying aspects of a larger task.

Dock Deduct a part of an employee's wages as a penalty for tardiness, **absenteeism,** breakage, etc.

Dock receipt A receipt issued by an ocean carrier to acknowledge delivery of a shipment at the carrier's dock or warehouse facilities.

Docket A list of cases, usually with file numbers, set down for trial in a court or a list of specific actions taken in a court. For example, a *judgment docket* is a list of all final actions taken by a court. It is often used to give notice to the public of new **liens** on property.

Document of title A piece of paper that is normally accepted in business as proof of a right to hold goods; for example, a **bill of lading** or a **warehouse receipt.**

Documents against acceptance (D/A) Instructions given by a shipper to a bank indicating that documents transferring **title** to goods should be delivered only upon acceptance of the attached **draft.**

Doing business A general, flexible term meaning carrying on enough business for profit within a state so that another person can sue the company in that state. "Doing business" also means that the state itself can tax the company or otherwise claim **jurisdiction** over it.

Dollar (or dollar cost) averaging A long-term method of buying **securities** or other potentially volatile investment property to minimize risk. By regularly buying the same dollar amount, short-term price swings will not matter because you buy more **shares** when the price is lower. This works well unless the securities you choose are permanent losers.

Domestic 1. Relating to the state. For example, a *domestic corporation* is a corporation created under the laws of the state in question. 2. Relating to the country. 3. Relating to the home.

Domestic international sales corporation A U.S. company whose income comes primarily from foreign sales; a *DISC* may get special tax breaks.

Domicile A person's permanent home, legal home, or main residence. The words "abode," "citizenship," "habitancy," and "residence" sometimes mean the same as *domicile* and sometimes not. A *corporate domicile* is the *corporation's* legal home and usually its central office; an *elected domicile* is the place the persons who make a **contract** specify as their legal homes in the contract. [pronounce: *dom*-i-sill]

Donated stock (or surplus) Stock given back to a corporation by its shareholders.

Dormant "Sleeping," inactive, silent or concealed. For example, a *dormant partner* is a partner who has a financial interest but takes no control over the business and is usually unknown to the public.

Dot matrix The use of dot combinations to form, display and print characters such as letters and numbers.

Dotted-line responsibility 1. A customer's obligations after signing. Where? On the "dotted line." 2. An obligation that organizational members have to consult with, but not report to, each other. This is reflective of the "dotted-line" connections that exist on organizational charts.

Double Twice or dual. A *double-column tariff* lists two **duty** rates for some or all **commodities.** Imports may be taxed at a higher or lower rate depending upon the importing nation's trade relationship with the exporting nation. *Double entry* is a method of **bookkeeping** that shows every transaction as both a **debit** and a **credit** and by using both horizontal rows and vertical columns of numbers. If the total of the horizontal rows and the vertical columns is not the same, it is easier to find out where mistakes are than if the records were kept with only one "entry" for each item. *Double indemnity* is a double insurance payoff when something happens in a certain way; for example, a ten-thousand-dollar payment for a person's death and twenty thousand for an accidental death. *Double insurance* is insurance from more than one company on the same **interest** in the same thing. It is usually not possible to collect more than a thing is worth. *Double ordering* is the dubious practice of placing orders with two suppliers for the same product with the intention of cancelling one order when the other is delivered first. *Double taxation* is either the illegal imposition of two taxes on the same property by the same government during the same period for the same purpose, or it is any time the same money is taxed twice. A *legal* form of *double taxation* is taxing a **corporation** on its profits, then taxing its **stockholders** on their **dividends** from the corporation. *Double time* is a penalty or **premium** rate of pay for **overtime** work, for holiday or Sunday work, etc., amounting to twice the employee's regular hourly wage.

Dovetail seniority The combining of two or more **seniority** lists (for example, when different companies merge) into a master seniority list. Each employee retains previously earned seniority even though thereafter employed by a new employer.

Dow Jones (Industrial Average) The average price of stocks of a selected number of the largest U.S. industrial corporations. Dow-Jones (which publishes, among other things, the *Wall Street Journal*) also produces a variety of other **averages.** *Dow theory* is a method of forecasting securities prices premised upon an analysis of average prices over time.

Down Not in operation.

Down payment The cash that must be paid at the time that something is bought by **installments** (on time).

Down time Periods of inactivity while waiting for the repair, setup or adjustment of equipment. *Down time pay* is payment for time spent idle because of equipment failure (or routine maintenance) that is clearly beyond the responsibility of the employee.

Downgrading The reassignment of an employee to a **position** having a lower rate of pay or lesser responsibilities.

Downsize To make a smaller version of a product.

Downtick See **uptick.**

Draft A **bill** of exchange or any other **negotiable instrument** for the payment of money **drawn** by one person on another. To use an ordinary personal check as an example: one person (the **drawer**) writes the check to pay money from a bank (the **drawee**) to another person (the **payee**). An *overdraft* is writing a check for more money than there is in the account; a *sight draft* is payable on demand; and a *time draft* is payable after a certain number of days. A *date draft* matures in a specified number of days after the date it is issued without regard to the date of **acceptance;** a *documentary draft* has documents attached.

Dragnet clause   A provision in a mortgage or similar document in which **security** is given not only for the present debt, but for past and future debts.

Drago doctrine   The principle that one country should not intervene militarily in another country to force or secure payment of debts owed by the second country to citizens of the first.

Draw   1. Write out and sign a **bill** of exchange or make a **note** (see those words).   2. Take money out of a bank account.   3. Prepare a legal document.   4. See **drawing account**.

Drawback   The refund of taxes or duties that have been paid on imported merchandise that is re-exported. The *drawback* may be on raw materials that are used in the manufacturing process or it may be on goods that are only partially altered, and then exported. The drawback is essentially a form of subsidy that attempts to put the domestic producer on an equal footing with foreign competitors.

Drawee   1. A person to whom a **bill** of exchange is addressed, and who is requested to pay the amount of the bill.   2. A bank that has a **deposit** withdrawn from it.

Drawer   The person drawing a **bill** of exchange or signing a check.

Drawing account   A fixed sum advanced to sales personnel at regular time intervals (weekly or monthly) or a limited amount against which the sales person can draw as needed during a predetermined time period so long as the outstanding balance does not reach a predetermined limit. Amounts so drawn must be paid back to the company out of **commission** earnings during the same time period.

Drop shipment   The delivery of goods directly from manufacturer to retailer or to **consumer** even though a **wholesaler** earns a profit for placing the order.

Dual   Double. A *dual career couple* is a husband and wife pursuing professional careers that both feel are equally important. This has important implications for recruitment and transfer policies; for example, one spouse may be unwilling to accept a move unless an appropriate job is also found for the other. A *dual ladder* (or *parallel* *ladder*) is a variant of a **career ladder** that provides separate career hierarchies so that both technical and managerial employees can have appropriate career advancement. A *dual pay system* is a wage program that allows employees to select the more advantageous of alternative means of computing earnings. For example, transportation employees might have the option of being paid on the basis of miles traveled or on the basis of hours worked. *Dual pricing* is the selling of an identical product for different prices in different markets. The practice of dual pricing may often relate to export subsidies or **dumping.** The *dual system* is the **chartering** and **regulating** of banks, savings and loan associations, credit unions, etc., by either state or the federal government (through the **Comptroller of the Currency.**) *Dual unionism* is the situation in which two rival unions claim the right to organize workers in a particular industry or locality.

Due 1. Owing and payable. For example, a *due bill* is an I.O.U., especially a company's I.O.U., that can be sold by the person to whom money is owned to another person, and then cashed in for goods or services. And a *due date* is the day a tax or debt must be paid. *Due on sale* is a contract clause which gives the lender the right to require immediate repayment of the balance owed if the property changes hands. While *due on sale clauses* have long been included in **mortgage** contracts, they are being increasingly enforced by lenders when buyers try to assume sellers' existing low-rate mortgages. In these cases, the courts have frequently upheld the lender's right to raise the interest rate to the prevailing market level. 2. Just, proper, regular, lawful, sufficient, or reasonable. For example, *due care* means proper or reasonable care for the situation. And the *Due Process Clause* of the U.S. Constitution requires that no person shall be deprived of life, liberty, or property without due process of law. The requirements of *due process* are regularly changed by the Supreme Court. The central core of the idea is that a person should always have **notice** and a real chance to present his or her side in a legal dispute and that no law or government procedure should be **arbitrary** or unfair.

Dues 1. Fees that must be periodically paid by **union** members in order for them to remain in good standing with their union. The dues are used to finance all of the

activities of the union and its affiliates. 2. The experiences that one must have before being ready for advancement. In effect, "you have to pay your dues" before you
can be perceived as a legitimate occupant of a higher
position.

Dumb terminal A typewriter, **VDT,** printer, etc., that can
operate only when connected to a computer.

Dummy 1. Sham; make believe; set up as a "front." For
example, *dummy* incorporators are persons who initially
set up a corporation to meet the formal requirements of a
state's corporation laws and then drop out. It is perfectly
proper in most cases. 2. A model of a proposed new
product.

Dump 1. Sell something in other countries for less than it
is sold at home. Federal law prohibits some sales of this
sort by foreign companies, international trade agreements
prohibit others, and antidumping **duties** discourage many
more. 2. Unload large quantities of goods regardless of
price. 3. Data transfer, data printout, or a listing of data
stored by a computer. 4. A power cut-off.

Dun Demand payment on an overdue debt.

Dun and Bradstreet A major supplier of business credit
ratings.

Dunnage Material used to brace and protect a shipment in
a carrier's vehicle. It may consist of blocking, special
flooring, lining, racks, bulkheads, etc.

Duopoly Only two sellers of a product or service.

Duties Taxes imposed on the export or import of goods.
The term *duty* is distinguished from the term **tariff** solely
by the fact that the *duty* is the *actual tax* imposed or
collected, while the tariff, technically speaking, is the
schedule of duties. However, in practice the words are
often used interchangeably. Various types of *duties* include: 1. *Import duties* are imposed on goods entering a
nation or political unit. 2. *Export duties* are imposed on
goods leaving a nation or political unit. Export duties are
expressly forbidden in the United States by our Constitution which provides that "no tax or duty shall be laid on
articles exported from any state." Other countries, however, lay export duties even on their chief exports for
revenue purposes, to bolster domestic manufacture of
some article, or to encourage the keeping of scarce raw
materials within the country for home use. 3. *Transit*

duties are imposed by a country simply for allowing goods to pass through its territory en route from one country to another. The United States does not levy transit duties. 4. *Ad valorem duties* are imposed on goods on the basis of value. The advantage of ad valorem duties is that they fluctuate with economic conditions—that is, the duty rises and falls in relationship to prices. The disadvantage of the ad valorem system is that it presents a valuation problem, is an expensive system to maintain, and opens the doors to corruption. 5. *Specific duties* are imposed on the basis of some unit of measurement as, so much per pound, per bushel, per dozen, etc. Specific duties avoid the problems of appraisement involved in the collection of ad valorem taxes. The disadvantages of specific duties are that they require a minute detailing of rates for the many products imported and that they do not reflect changes in economic conditions. 6. *Compound duties* have the combined attributes of ad valorem and specific duties. Fifty cents per pound, plus 10 percent ad valorem is the way that a combined duty would be imposed. 7. *Subsidies and bounties* are amounts paid by governments, on the export of certain goods from their countries, for the purpose of stimulating the export of those goods. A *bounty* is given gratuitously. A *subsidy* is given in exchange for the meeting of some condition or other. Subsidies and bounties may be given either in the form of direct cash payments based on the number of units of the product exported, or they may take the form of especially low freight rates on the particular article, or of special tax exemption or low-interest government loans, etc. 8. *Countervailing duties* are imposed in addition to the regular duty, for the purpose of counteracting the effect of a bounty or subsidy in another country. 9. *Anti-dumping duties* are calculated to offset the advantage gained by exporters when they sell their products in a foreign country at a price lower than that at which the same article sells at home, or at a price even lower than the cost of production.

Duty 1. A tax on imports or exports. In addition, *duty of tonnage* is a governmental port charge or port tax on a boat. See **duties** for information on different types. 2. A large segment of the work done by one individual. A job is made up of one or more duties. 3. An obligation to obey a law or a legal obligation to another person. For example, the *duty of fair representation* is the obligation of a labor union to represent all of the members in a **bargaining unit** fairly and without **discrimination.** And the *duty to bargain* is the obligation under various state and federal laws that employers and employees bargain with each other in **good faith**.

E

E 1. In a newspaper **stock** transaction table, an indication that a stock **dividend** was declared and paid in the previous year. 2. **Standard & Poor's** ranking of the covenant language of **investment-grade bonds.** Rankings from E-1 (highest) to E-5 (lowest) indicate the degree of protection offered bondholders.

ECU European Currency Unit.

EDP Electronic data processing.

EEC European Economic Community. See **Common Market.**

EEO Equal employment opportunity.

EEOC Equal Employment Opportunity Commission.

EFTS Electronic fund transfer system.

EMS 1. **European Monetary System.** 2. Electronic message system (or service).

EMU European Monetary Union.

EOM End of month.

EPA Environmental Protection Agency. A U.S. agency that enforces pollution control, does environmental research, etc.

EPS Earnings per **share.**

ERISA Employee Retirement Income Security Act.

ESOP Employee stock ownership plan.

ESOT Employee stock ownership trust. A **trust fund** set up to fund an employee stock ownership plan, giving tax benefits to employer and employee.

Earlier maturity rule Bonds that come **due** first get paid off first even when the company must make unusual debt payments.

Earned income 1. Money or other compensation received for work. It does not include the profits gained from owning property. 2. The *earned income credit* is a tax break given to some low-income workers.

Earned surplus Retained earnings.

Earnest money A **deposit** paid by a buyer to hold a seller to a deal and show the buyer's **good faith; a binder.**

Earnings 1. The total remuneration of an employee or group of employees for work performed, including **wages, bonuses, commissions,** etc. 2. A company's profit, usually as related to its **stock dividends.** An *earnings multiple* is the number by which an annual stock **dividend** must be multiplied to equal the stock's selling price. *Earnings per share* is a company's profits available to pay **dividends** on its **common stock** divided by the number of **shares** of stock owned by investors. *Primary earnings per share* and *fully diluted earnings per share* divide the available profits by not only the shares of common stock, but by everything that can be turned into common stock (**convertible** stock and bonds, **options, warrants,** etc.). For *earnings report,* see **statement** of income.

Easement An *easement* on a piece of land is the right of a specific nonowner such as a next-door neighbor, the government, or the general public to use part of the land in a particular way. This right usually stays with the land when it is sold. Typical *easements* include the right of the owner of a piece of land with no streetfront to use a specific strip of another person's land to reach the street, or the right of a city to run a sewer line across a specific strip of an owner's land.

Economic *Economic analysis* is a systematic approach to the problem of choosing how to employ scarce resources and an investigation of the full implications of achieving a given objective in the most efficient and effective manner. The determination of **efficiency** and **effectiveness** is implicit in the assessment of the cost effectiveness of alternative approaches. *Economic determinism* is the theory that economic concerns are the primary motivating factors of human behavior. *Economic efficiency* is that mix of alternative **factors of production** which results in maximum outputs, benefits, or utility for a given cost. Also, that mix of productive factors which represents the minimum cost at which a specified level of output can be obtained. *Economic imperialism* is the indirect domination of a country by *de facto* control of its economy. *Economic indicators* are measurements of various economic and business movements and activities in a community, such as employment, unemployment, hours worked, income, savings, volume of building permits, volume of sales, etc., whose fluctuations affect and may be used to determine overall economic trends. *Economic man* is a historical concept that finds humans motivated *solely* by economic factors—always seeking the greatest reward at the least possible cost. Any management philosophy assuming that workers are motivated by money and can be further motivated only by more money is premised on the *economic man* concept. An *economic order quantity* is the optimal amount of stock to order (or reorder) so that the costs of ordering and storing will be minimal. Also called *economic lot size* or *optimal lot size. Economic policy* is the process by which a government manages its economy. For *economic rent,* see **ground rent.** An *economic strike* is a refusal to work because of a dispute over wages, hours, working conditions, etc. It is different from an **unfair labor practice** strike and may result in the loss of a job. An *economic time series* is a set of quantitative data collected over regular time intervals (e.g., weekly, monthly, quarterly, annually) which measures some aspect of economic activity. The data may measure a broad aggregate such as the **gross national product,** or a narrow segment such as the sale of tractors or the price of copper.

Economies of scale   Cost savings resulting from aggregation of resources or mass production. In particular, it refers to decreases in average cost when all **factors of production** are expanded proportionately.

Economy and efficiency audits   **Audits** which seek to determine whether an organization is managing its resources (such as personnel, property, space) economically and efficiently, the causes of inefficiencies or uneconomical practices, and whether the entity has complied with policies and regulations concerning matters of economy and efficiency.

Edge corporation   A corporation chartered by the **Federal Reserve** to engage in the business of international banking or other international and foreign financial operations.

Effective labor market   A labor market from which an employer actually draws applicants, as distinct from the labor market from which an employer attempts to draw applicants.

Effective rate   See **tax rate.**

Effectiveness Traditionally, the extent to which an organization accomplishes some predetermined goal or objective; more recently, the overall performance of an organization from the viewpoint of some strategic constituency.

Efficiency (or efficiency ratio) Productive *efficiency* is generally determined by seeking the ratio of output to input, which is called the *efficiency ratio*. Generally speaking, *efficiency* refers to the promotion of administrative methods that will produce the largest store of results for a given objective at the least cost; the reduction of **material** and **personnel** costs while maximizing precision, speed, and simplicity in administration. *Efficiency expert* is the mildly perjorative and decidedly dated term for a management or **systems** analyst. *Efficiency rating* is the dated term for **performance appraisal.**

$$\text{efficiency} = \frac{\text{output}}{\text{input}}$$

Efficient market A **stock, commodity,** etc., trading place or method that immediately gets and uses all available information, so that prices reflect full and current information.

Elasticity A numerical measure of the responsiveness of one **variable** to changes in another. For example, *elasticity of demand* is the amount that **demand** for a product will change in response to a change in price, consumer income, promotional activity, etc. *Price elasticity of demand* is the most commonly used elasticity measurement. Demand is elastic if lowering an item's price will stimulate enough sales to bring in more total revenue.

Electronic data processing (EDP) Computer manipulation of data. The term is gradually being supplanted by **management information systems.**

Electronic fund transfer systems A variety of systems and technologies for the transferring of payments and credit electronically. See **automated clearing house; automated teller machine; point-of-sale terminal systems; remote service unit;** and **wire transfer.**

Electronic mail (or message systems) Primarily the transmission of messages from computer to computer, but also telex, **electronic funds transfer systems,** computer conferencing, facsimile transmission, etc.

Element (or job element) The smallest unit into which a **job** can be divided without analyzing the physical and mental processes necessarily involved.

Eligible commercial paper **Negotiable instruments** which, because they meet certain requirements, are qualified for **rediscounting** at a special rate by banks that are members of the **Federal Reserve System.**

Embargo 1. A government's refusal to allow the transportation of certain things in or out of the country. 2. A government's stopping the ships or planes of another country from coming in or going out.

Embezzlement The **fraudulent** and secret taking of money or property by a person who has been trusted with it. This usually applies to an employee's taking money and covering it up by faking business records or **account** books.

Emeritus director A non-voting ex-director of a corporation who continues to sit in at all board meetings, receives directors' fees, and has the right to express opinions.

Eminent domain The government's right and power to take private land for public use by paying for it.

Emolument Any financial or other gain from employment. This is broader than wages or salaries.

Employee A general term for all those who work for hire. An *employee assistance program* is a formal program designed to assist employees with personal problems through both internal counseling and aid, and a referral service to outside counseling resources. The thrust of such programs is to increase **productivity** by correcting distracting outside personal problems. *Employee development* may include **career development** and upward mobility. It may be oriented toward development for better performance on an employee's current job, for learning a new policy or procedure, or for enhancing an employee's potential for advancement. An *employee discount* is a reduction in the price of goods or services offered by an employer to employees as a **benefit.** The *Employee Retirement Income Security Act* is a federal law that established a program to protect employees' pension plans. The law set up a fund to pay pensions when plans go broke and **regulates** pension plans as to *vesting* (when a person's pension rights become permanent), nondiversion of benefits to anyone other than those entitled, nondiscrimination against lower-paid employees, etc. See **pen-**

sion plan, vested, and **annuity.** Popularly known as *ERISA* or the **Pension Reform Act** of 1974. An *employee stock ownership plan* is an employee benefit plan that uses company stock to provide **deferred compensation.**

Employer A person who hires others. An *employer association* is a voluntary organization of employers whose purpose is to deal with problems common to the group. Such associations have frequently been formed primarily to present a united front in dealing with the representatives of their respective organized workers. *Employer liability acts* are federal and state laws defining under what circumstances an employer must pay for an employee's injuries and illnesses. These laws commonly abolish employer's defenses such as the fellow servant rule and contributory negligence. Many of these laws are now called **workers' compensation laws,** especially when they set up a fund for payments. An *employer unit* is any **bargaining unit** that holds all of the eligible employees of a single employer.

Employment Any occupational activity, usually, but not necessarily, for pay. An *employment agency* provides brokerage services between employers and individuals seeking work. Fees or commissions are usually charged to the employer, the worker, or both. *Employment manager* is the job title sometimes given to managers who function as **personnel directors**. The *employment-population ratio* or *E-P ratio* or *employment ratio* is the ratio of employment to working-age population. Some economists think that the E-P ratio is more useful for diagnosing the severity of an economic slowdown than is the unemployment rate. An *employment practice,* in the context of **equal employment opportunity,** is any screening device operating at any point in the employment cycle. If an employment practice is not related to job performance, it will not be able to withstand a court challenge. *Employment relations* is a general term for all relationships that occur in a worker-manager context. While used synonymously with **labor relations** and **industrial relations,** it is often applied in non-union situations in order to emphasize "non-union." An *employment standard* is a specific requirement for employment. An employment **standard** can be based on a wide variety of things. For example, if assessment is based on tests, the standard might be a specific **cutting score.** If education is assessed, the standard might be a specific class standing, or grades of B or better in certain courses of study. The *Employment Standards Administration* is an agency of the Department of Labor that administers laws and regulations setting **employment standards,** providing **workers' compensation** to those injured on their jobs and requiring federal contractors to provide **equal employment opportunity.** Its major divisions include the Wage and Hour Division, the **Office of Federal Contract Compliance,** and the Office of Workers' Compensation. *Employment taxes* are any of a variety of taxes levied by governments on an employer's payroll. The most common employment tax is the employer's contribution to **social security** known as FICA taxes (after the Federal Insurance Contribution Act). There are also FUTA taxes (after the Federal Unemployment Tax Act) and sometimes other **unemployment insurance** contributions required by state law.

Enabling clause 1. The part of a **statute** that gives officials the power to enact and enforce it. 2. That part of **GATT** which permits **developed country** members to give more favorable treatment to **developing countries,** and special treatment to the least-developed countries, notwithstanding the **most-favored nation** provisions of GATT.

Encumbrance A **claim, charge,** or **liability** on property, such as a **lien** or **mortgage,** that lowers its value.

End balance method Charging a full month's **interest** on all bills unpaid at the end of each monthly billing period. (If a purchase is made on the last day of the month and payment made one day later, "1 percent interest" could turn into a true **annual percentage rate** of over 300 percent by this method.)

End position The legal and financial status of a person at the end of a **contract,** such as the options available to someone who has **leased** equipment (renew the contract, return the equipment, pay for damages, etc.).

End-testing Examining individuals who have just completed a course of training on the subject in which they were trained in order to measure the individual's attainments or the effectiveness of the training.

Endowment An insurance policy that pays a set amount at a set time or, if the person insured dies, pays the money to a **beneficiary.**

Engineering estimate   An estimate of costs or results based on detailed measurements or experiments and specialized knowledge and judgment. Also referred to as the *engineering method of cost estimating.*

Engineering management   A loose term for the **management** of work that is predominately technical.

Enlightened self-interest   The concept that if a business behaves in a socially responsible way it will further its own long-term profitability.

Enterprise   1. A business. A *manufacturing enterprise* is one that makes products prior to their sale. A *merchandising enterprise* is one that buys products ready to be resold.   2. A quality of management associated with initiative, resourcefulness, and daring.   3. An *enterprise zone* is an area of high unemployment and poverty which is granted business tax reductions by a state in order to lure industry and concomitant prosperity.

Entry   1. The act of making or *entering* a formal record by writing it down; also the thing itself written down.   2. In international trade, the documents that must be filed with **customs** authorities upon the arrival of imported goods, filing and accepting of such documents, and actual passing of goods through customs.   3. An *entry level* is the lowest position in any job promotional line, as defined locally by **collective bargaining** agreements, past practice, or applicable personnel rules.

Environmental impact statements   Documents required by federal and state laws to accompany proposals for projects or programs that might harm the environment.

Equal Credit Opportunity Act   A federal law prohibiting discrimination based on race, color, religion, sex, national origin, or age of any **credit** transaction.

Equal employment opportunity   A set of employment procedures and practices that effectively prevent any individual from being adversely excluded from employment opportunities on the basis of race, color, sex, religion, age, national origin, or other factors that cannot lawfully be used in employment efforts. The *Equal Employment Opportunity Commission* was created by the **Civil Rights Act** of 1964 to make equal employment opportunity an actuality. An *equal employment opportunity counselor* is an individual within an organization who provides an open and systematic channel through which employees may raise questions, discuss real and imagined **grievances,** and obtain information on their procedural rights. Counseling is the first stage in the discrimination complaint process. An *equal employment opportunity officer* is an official within an organization whose designated responsibility is monitoring EEO programs and assuring that both organizational and national EEO policies are being implemented.

Equalization 1. The process of adjusting **assessments** and taxes on real estate in order to make sure that properties are properly valued and are taxed fairly according to value. 2. A wholesaling service involving the acquisition of products for dispersement of the quality and quantity demanded by the market. This involves the accumulation of the products demanded seasonally, the storage and dispersement of products produced seasonally, and the taking up of the slack between currently changing volumes of output and consumption. It is the adjustment of supply to demand on the basis of time, quality, and quantity.

Equalizing dividend A special **dividend** declared and paid in order to correct unequal dividend benefits among stockholders which occurred because of changes in the regular dividend rates, such as those that occur in a merger of two corporations.

Equilibrium In balance; the stable condition of a management or an economic system which will continue until a **variable** is altered. The *equilibrium of the firm* exists when the forces in the environment that bear upon its profitability are in a state of balance such as when there is no further possibility of increasing profits. The *equilibrium of the industry* exists when conditions are such that no firm, either inside or outside of the industry, has any reason to challenge present arrangements. The *equilibrium price* exists when quantity offered is equal to quantity demanded.

Equipment trust The method of financing business equipment in which **title** to the property is held by **trustees** until paid for.

Equitable Just, fair, and right for a particular situation. For example, an *equitable mortgage* is a court's deciding that a **deed** transferring property was really given to **secure** a debt, so that a **mortgage,** not a complete transfer of property, exists.

Equity 1. Stock. Sometimes **common stock** only. For example, *equity capital* is that portion of the total **capital** of a business which has been furnished by the stockholders (as opposed to *borrowed capital*, which is furnished by corporate creditors). *Equity financing* occurs when a corporation raises money by selling stock rather than by *debt financing*, which is selling **bonds** or borrowing. Stocks, and other stocklike **securities,** are called *equity securities* or *equity shares*. The capital invested is received by the corporation as *risk capital* or **venture capital,** and invested subject to the hazards of the particular type of business. It creates no debt to burden the business, because returns **(dividends)** to common-stock owners are contingent upon satisfactory earnings and the discretion of the board of directors; and dividends to **preferred stock** owners, though fixed, are not an absolute charge against the corporation, and must be paid only if earnings warrant such payment. *Equity method* is a way of reporting the investments (of at least twenty percent of voting stock of an **unconsolidated** company) of one company in another. The initial investment is recorded at cost; subsequent earnings increase (or decrease) long-term investment in the accounts of the owner company. **Dividends** paid by the partially owned company reduce long-term investment. The investing company's earnings (or losses) from such transactions usually appear on a **statement** as a single amount called a *one-line consolidation*. For a contrast, see **cost method.** *Equity theory* is the basis upon which **consolidated statements** are prepared when they present in an equal manner the proprietary rights of both majority and minority stockholder interests. 2. The value of property after all charges against it are paid. This is also called *net worth* or *net value*. An *equity investor* exists if Jay borrows money from Elizabeth to buy equipment that is then **leased** to Charles in a deal with special tax advantages. Jay is called the *equity investor*. *Equity of redemption* is the right of a person who has lost property through a mortgage **fore closure** to get it back by paying all money owed, interest, and costs within a state-specified time period. 3. Fairness in a particular situation. In this context, *equity* also refers to a court's power to "do justice" where specific laws do not cover the situation.

Escalator clause 1. A **contract** term that allows a price to rise if costs rise. Or, in the case of a maximum payment **regulated** by the government (such as rent controls), for the price to rise if the maximum is raised or eliminated. 2. See **cost of living clause.**

Escape clause A **contract** provision that allows a person to avoid doing something or to avoid **liability** if certain things happen. For example, an *escape clause* in a maintenance-of-membership-shop union contract may provide for a period of time during which union members may withdraw (escape) from the union without affecting their employment.

Escrow Money, property, or documents belonging to person A and held by person B until person A takes care of an obligation to person C. For example, a mortgage company may require a homeowner with a mortgage to make monthly payments into an *escrow account* to take care of the yearly tax bill when it comes due.

Estate building That part of an executive-compensation program concerned with turning portions of an executive's salary and fringe benefits into **assets** that will benefit heirs after the executive's death.

Estate planning Carrying out a person's wishes for property to be passed on at his or her death and gaining maximum legal benefit from that property by best using the laws of wills, **trusts, insurance, property,** and **taxes.**

Estate tax A federal or state tax paid on the property left by a dead person. It is paid on the property as a whole before it is divided up and handed out. This is the opposite of an inheritance tax, which is based on the money each individual inherits and is paid by each heir separately.

Estimated tax Some persons with income other than salaries must estimate, "report," and pay income tax four times a year.

Estoppel 1. Being stopped by your own prior acts from claiming a right against another person who has legitimately relied on those acts. For example, if a person signs a **deed,** that person may be *estopped* from later going to court claiming that the deed is wrong. 2. Being stopped from proving something (even if true) in court because of something you said before that shows the opposite (even if false).

Estoppel certificate A **mortgage** company's written statement of the amount due on a mortgage as of a particular
date.

Eurocurrency A deposit in the bank of one country, but in
the currency of another country. For example, a deposit
in French francs in a British bank is a *Eurocurrency
deposit*. About 75 percent of Eurocurrency deposits are
Eurodollars. *Eurocurrency liabilities* are, in general, money
owed by U.S. banks, or U.S. branches of foreign banks,
to foreign affiliates. The **Federal Reserve** has a more
complex definition.

Eurodollars A deposit in U.S. dollars held in commercial
banks outside the United States. The international trade
in Eurodollars is a source of international short-term **capital**
which tends to flow to countries offering the highest interest rates. Other currencies that have filled this role are
called **Eurocurrencies.** The *Eurodollar market* is a global
network of foreign banks, including foreign affiliates and
branches of U.S. banks, that make loans and accept deposits in dollars.

European Monetary System The monetary system established by the European **Common Market** to create a zone
of monetary stability. The *European Currency Unit* is the
denominator of the EMS exchange-rate mechanism; each
national currency is related to the ECU and to the other
EMS currencies in a **parity** grid. The Common Market's
long-term goal is a *European Monetary Union*, a single
currency.

Evasion Eluding or dodging. *Tax evasion* is the illegal
nonpayment or underpayment of taxes due, while *tax
avoidance* is the legal reduction or nonpayment of taxes
by using **deductions, exemptions,** etc.

Evergreen contract An agreement that automatically re-
news itself each year unless one side gives advance notice
to the other side that it will end.

Ex (Latin) A prefix meaning many things, including out
of, no longer, from, because of, by, and with. When used
in pricing terms, such as "ex factory" or "ex dock," it
signifies that the price quoted applies only at the point of
origin. *Ex-distribution* refers to a stock that no longer has
the rights to benefits it had at an earlier date. *Ex-dividend
stock* is shares of *capital stock* the sale of which does not
include the right to a previously declared **dividend.** Divi-

dends are declared payable only to stockholders of **record** on a specific date, known as the *record date*. Buyers who have stock transferred to their names after the record date do not receive the declared dividend. In order to reserve the dividend for the seller, stock is sold *ex-dividend* several days prior to the record date. The exact day on which stock is sold ex-dividend depends on the delivery rules of the securities exchange on which the stock is traded. *Ex officio* is a Latin phrase meaning "by virtue of the office." Many individuals hold positions on boards, commissions, councils, etc., because of an office that they temporarily occupy. For example, the mayor of a city may be an *ex officio* member of the board of trustees of a university in the city. *Ex parte* (Latin) means with only one side present. For example, an *ex parte order* is one made at the request of one side in a lawsuit when (or because) the other side does not show up in court. *Ex rights stock* is a stock sold without its special right to buy a new stock issue. It operates like *ex-dividend stock*.

Examination 1. An investigation; for example, the search through **title** records for any problems before buying property or the inquiry by the **patent** office into the novelty and usefulness of an invention. 2. A questioning; for example, the questioning of a witness under oath or the questioning in a hearing of a bankrupt about his or her full financial situation. 3. An employment test.

Excess capacity **Production** capability over what is needed to meet **market** demand.

Excess policy **Insurance** that pays only for losses greater than those covered by another policy.

Excess profits tax A tax on business profits over what is considered reasonable (calculated by return on investment or past yearly averages) and usually imposed in time of war.

Excess reserves The excess of **reserves** against bank **deposits** over the legally required reserves (usually expressed as a percentage of deposits). Within limits, the **Federal Reserve Board** has the power to alter the reserve requirements of member banks and to control the amount of **credit** expansion or contraction. When there are large *excess reserves*, there is a period of "easy" money, and funds are readily available at comparatively low interest rates.

Exchange   1. A swap or **barter;** a transaction that involves no money and in which no price or value is set for any item involved. *Exchange theory* is the notion that people, especially those in formal organizations, are motivated by an expectation that favors will in some way at some later time be returned. The everyday expression "You owe me one!" is a succinct summary of the importance and pervasiveness of exchange theory.   2. An organization set up to buy and sell **securities** such as stocks. An *exchange acquisition* is a method of acquiring a large block of stock on the floor of the exchange. A member **broker** will solicit orders to sell, and then the sell orders are lumped together and crossed with the buy orders in the regular market. Exchange acquisition is the counterpart of *exchange distribution*, which is the same process for selling a large block of stock.   3. The payment of debts in different places by a transfer of **credits** such as by **bill** of exchange.   4. *Foreign exchange;* for example, *exchange controls* are the attempt by countries facing acute **balance of payments** difficulties to conserve foreign currencies that come under their control by rationing them to importers who will bring in designated amounts and types of goods specifically approved by the government. They are sometimes considered a **non-tariff barrier** to trade. The *exchange rate* is the price of one currency in terms of another currency. For example, if $1 = 2 Deutsche Marks, the DM exchange rate for the dollar is DM 2, while the dollar exchange rate for the DM is $.50.

Excise   A federal, state or local tax on the manufacture, sale, or use of goods or on the carrying on of an occupation or activity. Technically, **excise taxes** are imposed on *acts* rather than on property. For example, excise taxes are levied on the *sale* of gasoline and tobacco, when *recording* certain documents, and on the *transfer* of stock, rather than on the items themselves. Excise taxes may be levied either against the seller or the purchaser, but if paid by the consumer are usually collected by the seller and then remitted to the taxing authority.

Exclusion   Not counting something. For example, a certain amount of money may be given away each year without paying a tax on giving it away. This is called an *exclusion*. See **deduction, exemption,** and **credit.**

Exclusionary clause A part of a **contract** that tries to restrict the legal **remedies** available to one side if the contract is broken.

Exclusive 1. Shutting out all others; sole; one only. An *exclusive economic zone* is the right of coastal states to control the living and nonliving resources of the sea for 200 miles off their coasts while allowing freedom of navigation to other states beyond 12 miles. For *exclusive agency listing* or *exclusive authorization listing,* see **listing.** For *exclusive contract,* see **output contract.** *Exclusive recognition for bargaining rights* in the private sector is the only form of recognition available to a union representing a specific **bargaining unit.** An employer is required to negotiate in **good faith** and to give exclusive bargaining rights to a union holding such recognition. In fact, a private employer may not bargain or consult with a union that does not hold exclusive recognition without committing an **unfair labor practice.**

Execution 1. Carrying out or completion. 2. Signing and finalizing a document such as a **contract.** 3. An official carrying out of a court's **order** or **judgment.** For example, a *writ of execution* orders a court official to take a debtor's property to pay a court-decided debt, usually by then holding an *execution sale*.

Executive 1. The branch of government that carries out the laws (as opposed to the judicial and legislative branches); the administrative branch. 2. Any high official in a branch of government, a company, or other organization. See **group executive** and **plural executive.**. An *executive committee* is empowered to exercise all the powers of the **board of directors** of a corporation in accordance with the policy of the corporation during intervals between board meetings. It does not have authority to inaugurate radical reversals of, or departures from, fundamental policies and methods of conducting the business prescribed by the full board. For example, an executive committee that has the powers of the board when the board is not in session may not assume sole control of the corporation for an indefinite period, amend **by-laws** that only the directors are by statute permitted to amend, change the number of members of the committee, remove a member by a majority vote, or appoint or remove officers and fix their salaries. Nor may such an executive committee execute a contract upon which the corporation is about to act. The calling of a meeting of the board of directors suspends the power of the executive committee to act in place of the board. For *executive development*, see **management development.** An *executive officer* is one of several top officials of a company or one particular official. An *executive order* is a law put out by the president or a governor that does not need to be passed by the legislature. *Executive salary continuation* is an extra **annuity** for an employee (beginning at retirement but in addition to all other retirement benefits) wholly funded by the employer. An **executive session** is a closed meeting of a committee, a **board,** etc. An *executive stock acquisition plan,* sanctioned under Section 423 of the Internal Revenue Code, allows executives **options** to buy company stock at a price equal to the lesser of 85 percent of the market price on the date of the option grant or 85 percent of the market price at the time the option is exercised. Executives participating in such a plan authorize payment deductions over a predetermined period of time (usually a year or more) which pay for all or part of the optioned stock at the end of the purchase period. *Executive supplemental compensation* is a type of **nonproduction bonus** that is based upon an estimate of an executive's contribution to the profitability of the company over a given time period. 3. Any **manager.**

Executor A person selected by a person making a will to **administer** the will and to hand out the property after the person making the will dies.

Executory Still to be carried out; incomplete; depending on a future act or event. The opposite of *executed.*

Exempt employees Employees who, because of their administrative, professional or executive status, are not covered by the overtime provisions of the **Fair Labor Standards Act.** In consequence, their employing organizations are not legally required to pay them for **overtime** work.

Exemption 1. Freedom from a general burden, duty, service, or tax. 2. The subtraction from income for tax purposes of a certain amount of money for each family member. Each *exemption* lowers the income on which a person must pay taxes. See also **credit, deduction,** and **exclusion.** 3. Property that may be kept by a debtor when property is taken away from the debtor by a court order such as in a **judgment** debt or **bankruptcy.**

Exercise Make use of. For example, to *exercise a purchase option* is to make use of a right to buy something by buying it. An *exercise price* is a *striking price*.

Eximbank See **Export-Import Bank.**

Exit interview A tool to monitor employee terminations that seeks information on why the employee is leaving and what he or she liked or disliked about his or her job, working conditions, company policy, etc. When interviews are not possible, *exit questionnaires* seek to gather the same information.

Exoneration 1. The right of a person who pays a debt for another person to be reimbursed by that person. 2. The right to be paid off on a **negotiable instrument**.

Expansion The enlargement of a company, either internally through addition to its own facilities and activities, or externally by purchase of another company or by **merger.** The relation of the company's expanded activities to its former business is classified as vertical, horizontal, or circular. A *vertical expansion* occurs when a company continues its present products but also undertakes directly related activities previously performed by others outside the business. An oil refinery expands vertically "downward" when it acquires oil wells; a manufacturer of small-tool parts expands vertically "upward" by making the complete tool. A *horizontal expansion* occurs when a company does more of what it is already doing. For example, it may build another wing to enlarge its capacity for producing products currently produced or closely related products. A *circular expansion* embraces supplementary products rather than present products or closely related ones. The manufacturer of cigarette lighters may decide to produce lighter fluid as a supplementary product, or a company may add a product it does not make itself as a supplementary product to be sold by its sales force.

Expense The cost of resources (*assets*) used in producing revenue. A *cost* is not an *expense* until the purchased good or service is used up in whole or in part. An *expense account* is a general ledger account for all operating expenses. It also refers to the advance or reimbursement of monies to an employee who incurs expenses in the ordinary **course of business.** For *expense center*, see **cost center**.

Expensing Taking a tax **deduction** for the cost of an **asset** rather than taking **depreciation** for that cost.

Experience rating A change in an insurance policy's cost due to an unusually high or low number of claims made, or a general review to establish new rates.

Export To send abroad. An *export broker* is an individual or firm that brings together buyers and sellers for a fee but does not take part in actual sales transactions. An *export commission house* is an organization which, for a commission, acts as a purchasing agent for a foreign buyer. An *export license* is a government document that permits the licensee to engage in the export of designated goods to certain destinations. A *validated export license* authorizes the export of only specific commodities during a specific time. An *export management company* is a private firm that serves as the export department for several manufacturers, soliciting and transacting export business on behalf of its clients in return for a commission, salary, or retainer plus commission. For *export processing zones,* see **foreign trade zones**. *Export quotas* are specific restrictions or target objectives on the value or volume of exports of specified goods imposed by the government of the exporting country. Such restraints may be intended to protect domestic producers and consumers from temporary shortages of certain materials, or as a means to moderate world prices of specified commodities. **Commodity** agreements sometimes contain explicit provisions to indicate when export quotas should go into effect among producers. Export quotas are also used in connection with **orderly marketing agreements** and **voluntary restraint agreements**. An *export trading company* is a company whose function is to provide export services, such as market research, transportation, warehousing, after-sales service, and trade finance, to importers and exporters. *Export subsidies* are direct government payments or other economic benefits given to domestic producers of goods that are sold in foreign markets. The *Export-Import Bank (Eximbank)* is an autonomous agency of the U.S. government created to facilitate export-import trade. Under various programs, the *Eximbank* provides export **credits** and direct loans to foreign buyers and sells **insurance** and export **guarantees** to U.S. manufacturers.

Exported tax A tax paid by nonresidents of a community.

Express Clear, definite, direct, or actual (as opposed to **implied**); known by explicit words.

Extender A contract clause that preserves some rights or duties after the main part of the contract expires or is otherwise completed.

External Outside. An *external alignment* relates positions within an organization to similar positions in the near environment. In theory, the most desirable external alignment calls for compensation programs similar to those provided by other employers in the local labor market. An *external audit* is an examination of the accounting records and the underlying internal controls of a business or other entity, usually performed by a certified public accountant. It forms the basis for an expression of opinion regarding the fairness, consistency, and conformity with accounting principles of financial statements prepared by the corporation or other entity (not the accountant) for publication. For *external economy* (or *diseconomy*), see externality. *External equity* is a measure of the justice of an employee's wages when the compensation for the position is compared to the labor market as a whole, within a region, profession, or industry. *Internal equity* is a measure of the justice of an employee's wages when the compensation for the position is compared to similar positions within the same organization. *External financing* is a corporation's raising money by selling stock or by borrowing. The *external labor market* is the geographic region from which employers reasonably expect to recruit new workers.

Externality Something that results from an encounter between a consumer and provider, which confers benefits or imposes costs on others, and is not considered in making the transaction (its value, the external cost, not being reflected in any charge for the transaction). Pollution is the classic example. *Externalities* are sometimes referred to as *spillovers*.

Extra expense insurance An insurance that protects a business against the extra expenses necessary to prevent a business stoppage following damage by fire or other named peril. Businesses whose customers depend on them for uninterrupted service, such as newspapers, laundries, and dairies, commonly need this insurance.

Extraordinary items Unusual and infrequent gains (or losses) unrelated to the normal business of a company which must be reported separately on a financial statement.

Extrapolation Predicting future events based on a continuation of past trends; extending the curve of a graph beyond the known data points.

F

FAS "Free along side" (a named destination). This provision means that the seller is to pay for the costs and assumes all risks in transporting the contracted items to a position alongside the vessel or plane the buyer has identified to transport the goods. In this shipping arrangement, the seller is only responsible to deliver the goods to a designated loading area and the buyer is responsible from that point. The seller must also provide the buyer with the required shipping documents.

FASB   Financial Accounting Standards Board.

FCC   Federal Communications Commission. A federal agency that regulates interstate and foreign communications by radio, television, wire, and cable.

FDA   Food and Drug Administration. The federal agency that **regulates** the safety of food, drugs, cosmetics, etc.

FDIC   Federal Deposit Insurance Corporation.

FHA   1. Federal Housing Administration. It insures housing loans through approved lenders on approved homes.
2. Farmers Home Administration. A federal agency that provides rural housing and other loans.

FI   "Free in"; a pricing term indicating that the charterer of a vessel is responsible for the cost of loading and unloading goods from the vessel.

FICA   Federal Insurance Contributions Act. The **social security** tax.

FIFO   "First in, first out." A method of calculating the worth of **inventory.** Under this **accounting** method, if a merchant buys a blivit for a dollar, then buys another for two dollars, then sells either blivit, the remaining blivit is worth two dollars. This procedure makes the value of inventory on hand closely conform to prevailing prices. And if procurement prices are changing, it strongly influences stated profits. See **LIFO** and **NIFO.**

FLSA　Fair Labor Standards Act.

FMCS　Federal Mediation and Conciliation Service.

FNMA　Federal National Mortgage Association.

FO　"Free out"; a pricing term indicating that the charterer of a vessel is responsible for the cost of loading goods from the vessel.

FOB　"Free on board." The selling price of goods includes transportation costs and all risks to the FOB point, which is a specific place named in the contract. *FOB factory* means that the seller's obligation is to tender delivery to the buyer by notifying the buyer, or the buyer's designated freight forwarder, that the goods are packaged, packed and ready for shipment from the seller's facility. The buyer usually has the burden for all costs and risks involved in transporting the goods as soon as the buyer or the freight forwarder takes control of the goods. *FOB named destination* means that the seller must at his or her risk (insurance) and cost (transportation) deliver the goods to the named destination, such as an airport, shipyard or the buyer's facility. The buyer then assumes costs and risks, even before reloading.

FTZs　Foreign trade zones.

FY　Fiscal year.

FYI　For your information.

Face　1. The language of a document including everything in it (not just the front page), but excluding things about the document that do not appear in it. For example, a **contract** can be valid "on its face" even though a person was forced to sign it at gunpoint and no court would uphold it. 2. *Face amount*, in life insurance, is the amount, stated on the front of the **policy,** that is payable upon the death of the insured. The actual amount payable to the beneficiary may differ according to the policy's specific provisions, such as double **indemnity** or subsequent **riders.** 3. *Face value* is the formal cash-in value written on a **note** or other financial document. It does not include anything more for **interest** or other charges normally added on. Face value is not the note's fluctuating value in the marketplace.

Facility of payment clause　An agreement in an insurance contract allowing the insurer to make payments to a particular person to hold for the person ultimately entitled to the money.

Facsimile Exact copy. For example, *facsimile signatures* are mechanically imprinted signatures on checks, stock certificates, and bonds. These signatures can be imprinted on checks with checkwriting machines. Banks have certain stipulations that must be complied with before they will honor them such as the company's releasing the bank from the responsibility for determining how the facsimile was imprinted on the check. See *fax.*

Factfinding An impartial review of the issues in a labor dispute by a specially appointed third party, whether it be a single individual, panel, or board. The *factfinder* holds formal or informal **hearings** and submits a report to the **administrative agency** or the parties involved. The factfinder's report, usually considered advisory, may contain specific recommendations.

Factor 1. A person who is given **goods** to sell and who gets a **commission** for selling them. *Factor's (or agent's) acts* are state laws that protect **buyers** of goods sold by **agents,** whether or not the owner approved the sale. 2. A specialized privately owned finance company that purchases **accounts receivable.** The *factor* offers some combination of the following services: purchases accounts receivable for immediate cash; maintains the ledgers and performs the other bookkeeping duties relating to the accounts receivable; collects the accounts receivable after having notified the customer of the transfer of the account from the seller to the factor; assumes the losses which may arise from a customer's financial inability to pay; furnishes loan funds to its clients on a seasonal or term basis, secured or unsecured, depending on the situation and the credit rating of the client; and offers advisory services, marketing surveys, and management and production counseling. *Factoring* began in the textile industry but has expanded into many other areas. Many factoring companies specialize in one industry or maintain separate departments for specific industries. *Factoring* is the practice of one individual or organization selling its accounts receivable to a second at a discount. A *factor's lien,* in connection with the lending of money mentioned earlier, is a claim against the **pledge** of raw materials, goods in process, finished goods, and any other materials that the borrower may own in connection with the operation of the business. The lien is a continuing one and applies to the entire **inventory** that may be on hand at the time of the necessity of enforcement. It must be placed on public record and usually requires that the borrower will report to the lender at specified intervals the nature and value of the inventory on hand. The borrower agrees, upon reduction of inventory, to pay the lender an amount equal to or greater than the reduction inventory. The lender usually requires a margin of inventory values against its advances, inspects the inventories frequently, and generally maintains a close watch over the investment.   3. *Factors of production* are the resources used to produce goods and services. There are three traditional factors: land, labor, and capital. Recently, **management** or entrepreneurship has come to be considered a factor as well. *Factor demand* is the aggregate need for a factor of production. *Factor earnings* are payments made to factors for their use as production inputs. *Factor incomes* are the proportion of total payments to factors that go to any one factor. *Factor markets* are the totality of the interactions between buyers and sellers of the four factors. *Factor mobility* is the relative freedom by which factors can move among uses; for example, if a specific plot of land can only be used for farming, its mobility is restrained because, among other things, it cannot be used as a factory site. *Factor payments* are the prices for the use of factors; for example, rent for land, wages for labor, and interest for capital.

Factory ledger   A subsidiary **ledger** containing manufacturing cost **accounts**, such as **raw materials, direct labor, overhead,** and **inventory.** A factory ledger is maintained when the number of manufacturing accounts becomes inconveniently large for inclusion in the company's general ledger. Factory ledgers are also used when manufacturing operations are scattered among several plants.

Failure of consideration   The situation that exists when something that is offered as part of a deal becomes worthless or ceases to exist before the deal is completely carried out.

Fair   Just. The *Fair Credit Billing Act* is a federal law **regulating** billing disputes and making credit card companies partially responsible for items bought by **consumers.** *Fair Credit Reporting Acts* are federal and state laws **regulating** the organizations that investigate, store, and give out **consumer credit** and information, organizations that collect bills, etc. Consumers are given rights to know about investigations, see and dispute their files, etc. A *fair day's work* is, generally, the amount of work produced in a work day by a qualified employee of average skill exerting average effort. *Fair Employment Practice Commission* is a generic term for any state or local government agency responsible for enforcing laws prohibiting employment **discrimination** because of race, color, sex, religion, national origin, or other factors. A *fair game* is a game (or real-world situation) in which the cost of each "trial" or "move" equals the expected gain from each trial. A game may be "fair" in this mathematical sense while being "unfair" if engaged in by opponents with unequal "playing" resources. The term also refers to a company ripe for a **takeover**. The *Fair Labor Standards Act* (also called the **Wages and Hours Act**) is a federal law that establishes minimum-wage, overtime-pay, equal-pay, recordkeeping, and child-labor standards affecting more than 50 million full-time and part-time workers in industries affecting interstate commerce. For *fair market value,* see **market value.** For *fair representation,* see **duty of fair representation.** A *fair-share agreement* is an agreement in which both the employer and the union agree that employees are not obligated to join the union, but that all employees must pay the union a prorated share of **bargaining** costs as a condition of employment. *Fair trade* is the fixing of a retail price for an item by the manufacturer. This is now illegal in most cases where the manufacturer is not the retailer. *Fair use* is the limited use that may be made of something **copyrighted** without infringing the copyright. For the primary meaning of *fair value,* see **market value.** *Fair value* is also the reference price against which U.S. purchase prices of imported merchandise are compared during an **antidumping** investigation. It is generally expressed as the weighted average of the exporter's home market prices or prices to third countries during the period of investigation.

Family Social group. A *family allowance* is a payment to a worker, in addition to regular wages, based on the number of dependent children that a worker may have. Many of the major industrial countries have family-allowance programs financed by their governments. A *fam-*

ily corporation (or *partnership*) is a **corporation** (or **partnership**) set up to spread income among family members, reducing the total tax bill. A *family-expense policy* is a **health insurance** policy that insures both the individual policyholder and his or her immediate dependents (usually spouse and children). *Family policy* is a vague term for the totality of current or future legislation (or corporate policies) aimed at reconciling the role of women as both mothers and members of the work force. Family policies seek to help working mothers better cope with their family responsibilities through paid maternity leave, subsidized or free day care for children, and so on. A *family T-group* is a work team that undertakes a **T-group** effort as a unit.

Fannie Mae See **Federal National Mortgage Association.**

Farm Credit Administration A federal agency that supervises the Farm Credit System of federal land banks and associated banks and **cooperatives.**

Fast track Rapid movement up the **corporate ladder** by means of a formal company-sponsored **management development** program, through one's individual initiative and aggressiveness, or through the help of a **mentor.**

Fatigue Weariness caused by physical or mental exertion that lessens the capacity to, and the will for, work. A *fatigue allowance,* in production planning, is that addi-

TYPICAL FATIGUE CURVE

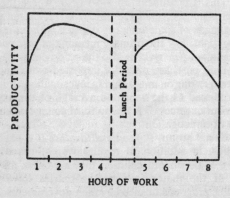

tional time added to "normal" work time to compensate for the factor of *fatigue*. **Fatigue curves** and **monotony curves** are graphic representations of **productivity** increases and decreases. As workers "warm up" or practice their tasks, productivity increases; thereafter fatigue sets in and productivity decreases. After lunch or coffee breaks, productivity should rise again slightly but thereafter continuously decline until the end of the day. This pattern varies with differing kinds of work. Fatigue curve measurements are essential in establishing realistic work **standards**. A *monotony curve* is characterized by a drop in productivity in the middle of the work period, great variability in the rate of productivity, and a tendency to "end spurt"— show an increase in productivity at the end of the work period due to a feeling of relief that the work period is almost over.

Fault 1. Negligence; lack of care; failure to do a duty. 2. Defect or imperfection. 3. According to the **Uniform Commercial Code,** *fault* means a "wrongful act, omission, or breach."

Fax To send a document from one location to another via a telephone by means of a facsimile (fax) machine.

Featherbedding Any labor practice that requires an employer to pay for more workers than are truly needed for a job, or to pay for work that is not performed.

Fed Federal Reserve System.

Federal Deposit Insurance Corporation A government corporation that provides deposit insurance to commercial banks and state mutual savings banks. Its insurance is required for national banks and state member banks of the **Federal Reserve System,** but is voluntary for other state banks which, if it insures, it also regulates.

Federal funds rate The interest rate at which depository institutions such as banks lend each other **reserve** funds on an overnight or temporary basis.

Federal Home Loan Bank Board The regulatory and supervisory agency for federally chartered savings and loan associations. Through its Federal Savings and Loan Insurance Corporation (FSLIC), it provides deposit insurance to all federal and many state savings and loan associations. Through 12 Federal Home Loan Banks (Federal Home Loan Bank System), it extends loans (advances) to, and provides other services for, insured savings and loan associations and a few other financial firms. It charters, insures, and supervises federal mutual savings banks.

Federal Home Loan Mortgage Corporation Under the supervision of the **Federal Home Loan Bank Board,** this corporation maintains a secondary market principally for **conventional mortgages**—those not guaranteed by the government. It purchases mortgages from primary lenders, including members of the Federal Home Loan Bank System and large mortgage bankers, for packaging into various sorts of **securities.** These securities are bought primarily by private investors such as pension funds, insurance companies, bank trust funds and thrift institutions. Also called *Freddie Mac.*

Federal Mediation and Conciliation Service Created by the **Labor-Management Relations Act,** FMCS helps prevent disruptions in the flow of interstate commerce caused by labor-management disputes by providing **mediators** to assist disputing parties in the resolution of their differences. FMCS can intervene on its own motion or by invitation of either side in a dispute. Mediators have no law-enforcement authority and rely wholly on persuasive techniques.

Federal National Mortgage Association (Fannie Mae) A federally chartered, but private, for-profit corporation owned by **stockholders** and regulated by the Department of Housing and Urban Development, *Fannie Mae* purchases government-guaranteed and other **mortgages** to add to its own **portfolio** and for limited resale. Fannie Mae issues its own **securities**, which are treated in financial markets as if they were those of a government agency, rather than a private entity.

Federal Open Market Committee The seven members of the Federal Reserve Board and five of the twelve Federal Reserve Bank Presidents. They meet every four to six weeks to set Federal Reserve guidelines regarding purchases and sales of government securities in the open market as a means of influencing the volume of credit and money. The FOMC also sets Federal Reserve policy relating to foreign-exchange markets.

Federal Register The first place that the rules and **regulations** (and *proposed* rules and regulations) of all U.S. **administrative agencies** are published. Abbreviated "Fed. Reg."

Federal Reserve System The central monetary authority of the United States created by Congress and consisting of a 7-member Board of Governors in Washington, D.C., 12 regional Federal Reserve Banks, and about 5,400 commercial banks that are members of the System. All national banks are members; state-chartered banks may elect to become members, in which case they are subject to Federal Reserve regulation. The *Fed*, as it is called, also interacts directly with all other U.S. depository institutions. It issues *federal reserve notes* (dollar bills, fives, etc.), lends money to banks and supervises them. Three major **monetary** tools are available to the *Federal Reserve System* to control the economy's supply of money and credit: open market operations which, through the purchase or sale of government bonds, increase or decrease the availability of dollars to member banks; **discount rate** adjustments which increase or decrease the interest rate charged to member banks for the money they borrow; and **reserve** requirements which, through changes in levels of reserves, increase or decrease the number of dollars a bank may make available for loan. Two less significant tools—moral suasion and selective controls over stock purchase **margin** requirements—are also used to help manage the economy.

Federal Savings and Loan Insurance Corporation See **Federal Home Loan Bank Board.**

Federal Trade Commission An independent agency that enforces prohibitions against **unfair competition** in business and "unfair or deceptive acts or trade practices"; it also enforces federal laws such as **Truth-in-Lending.**

Fedwire The **Federal Reserve** Communications System. An electronic communications network interconnecting Federal Reserve offices, the Board, depository institutions, the Treasury, and other government agencies. Fedwire is used for transferring **reserve** account balances of depository institutions and government securities, as well as for transmission of Federal Reserve administrative, supervisory, and **monetary policy** information.

Fidelity bond Insurance on a person against that person's dishonesty. A company must often buy this type of insurance when an employee is in a position of trust, handles large sums of money, and is seldom checked on by others.

Fiduciary 1. A person who manages money or property for another person and in whom that other person has a right to place great trust. 2. A relationship like that in no. 1. 3. Any relationship between persons in which one person acts for another in a position of trust; for example, lawyer and client or corporate director and stockholder. 4. *Fiduciary money* is currency backed only in part by precious metal.

Field 1. A set of data-holding positions in computer storage that are treated as one "unit" of information. 2. A *field examiner* is an **administrative agency** employee who conducts **certification elections** and investigates charges of **unfair labor practices.** *Field review* is a method of **employee** appraisal in which a representative of the **personnel** department visits an employee's work site in order to gather the information necessary for a written evaluation.

Field warehousing 1. An arrangement by which a lender takes formal control of goods stored in the possession of a borrower. The borrowing merchant, wholesaler, or manufacturer gets access to the goods, and the lender gets a **security** interest and close watch over the goods. 2. An arrangement in which goods are stored on either the seller's or the buyer's premises, under the supervision of a **bonded** warehouse representative, who assumes "possession" of the area. The warehousing firm physically segregates the goods under its control from other merchandise, and gives the seller a warehouse receipt, which serves as **collateral** for a bank loan. The seller then releases the goods to the buyer according to whether terms have been set up, usually as the buyer is able to pay for them or within certain credit limits. 3. See **factor's lien.**

Final offer arbitration A negotiating stratagem that has an **arbitrator** choose between the disputing parties' final or last offers.

Finance The manipulation of money and credit. This includes the fields of banking, taxes, insurance, and the money, foreign exchange, and investment markets; and directly involves other fields such as accounting, marketing, and production. It is an integral part of both public and private management. As a broad managerial field, it is the art (some would say science) of obtaining and managing funds. A *finance charge* is the **interest** or other payment made in addition to the price of goods or services paid off in **installments** or "on time." This does not include late charges, collection expenses, etc. In a **consumer** transaction, it must be expressed as an **annual percentage rate** and includes such things as interest, service charges, **points,** appraisal fees, and credit insurance premiums if required by lenders. *Finance companies* lend money to businesses and their customers in a wide variety of ways involving such things as **secured** and **unsecured** loans, purchase of **accounts receivable, field warehousing, factor's liens,** etc. See **financial,** which follows.

Financial   Concerning finance. *Financial accounting* is accounting for **assets, liabilities, revenues** and expenses to determine **net worth** and produce summary financial **statements.** The *Financial Accounting Standards Board* is a private organization that sets standards for financial accounting and reporting and promulgates **generally accepted accounting principles.** Its pronouncements are officially recognized as authoritative by the American Institute of Certified Public Accountants and the Securities and Exchange Commission. A *financial audit* is a determination of whether financial operations are properly conducted, whether the financial reports of an audited entity are presented fairly, and whether the entity has complied with applicable laws and regulations. A *financial claim* is documentary evidence of money owed. A *financial institution* is a **bank, trust company, credit union, savings and loan association,** or similar organization **licensed** by a state or the U.S. government to do financial business. A *financial lease* is a long-term property **lease** that cannot be cancelled and that provides no maintenance or other services. *Financial non-callability* refers to a provision in an agreement under which bonds are issued, which states that the debt can be paid out of excess cash, earnings, or cash available from selling stock, but not out of the proceeds of other borrowings. For *financial ratios,* see **ratio analysis.** A *financial report* or *statement* is a summary of what a company or other organization owns and what it owes. It may be in the form of a **balance sheet,** a profit and loss statement, or an **annual report.** Sometimes the word is used broadly to include any report in terms of money, even operating reports, but more strictly, it shows the financial status of the company at a given time. Financial reports are static, as they do not show how that status was achieved. See **statement** for examples. Note: This is *not* a **financing statement**. A *financial service* is a company that provides investment advice and publications. A *financial transaction* exchanges money for **assets** such as stocks and bonds.

Financing 1. The function of providing a business with the funds needed for operation, often through stocks, bonds, and short-term borrowing. 2. Obtaining something on **credit.**

Financing statement A paper, filed on the proper public records, that shows a **security** interest in goods. This is *not* a **financial statement.**

Finder A person who brings together two companies for a **merger,** who secures a **mortgage** for a borrower, who locates an **underwriter** for a company issuing **stock,** etc., usually for a fee.

Fire sale A sale at reduced prices due to fire or water damage or, sometimes, any emergency. Fire sales often require special licenses and are regulated to protect consumers.

Firm 1. A business. 2. A price or demand that is stable.

Firm offer A formal, usually written **offer** by a merchant that will be held open for a certain length of time. It is a type of **option** that requires no **consideration** to be valid.

First Initial. *First-dollar coverage* is insurance coverage which begins with the first dollar of expense incurred by the insured for the covered benefits. Such coverage, therefore, has no **deductibles** although it may have **copayments** or **coinsurance.** See also **last-dollar coverage.** For *first in first out,* see **FIFO.** *First-line management* is the level of management that is just above the workers (for example, a **foreman**). A *first mortgage* (or *lien*) is the mortgage (or lien) that has the right to be paid off before all others. This is not necessarily the first in time. For *first option,* see **right of first refusal.** *First world* refers to the rich, industrialized countries such as the United States, Canada, Western Europe, Australia, New Zealand, and Japan. These countries are often referred to as the **developed countries.** See also **Second, Third** and **Fourth Worlds.**

Fiscal Concerning **finance.** For example, the *fiscal year* is a period of time, equal to a calendar year, but starting on the day that the state or company uses as "day one" for its business records. This is often January, April, July, or

October first. *Fiscal policy* involves the manipulation of
government finances, by raising or lowering taxes or levels of spending to promote economic stability and growth.

Fishy-back service   The transporting of loaded truck trailers on ships.

Fitness for a particular purpose   The rule that if a merchant
knows or should know that an item is used for a particular
purpose, the merchant is responsible to buyers for that
item's fitness for the purpose. This is an **implied warranty.**

Fixed   Unchanging. *Fixed assets* are property such as land
and machinery used in a company's business. They are
not part of the company's merchandise; are used up slowly,
if at all; and are sometimes summarized as "property,
plant, and equipment." *Fixed asset turnover* is an activity
ratio: sales divided by total net value of plant and equipment. A *fixed benefit plan* is a pension plan or other
employee benefit plan with **benefits** that depend on a set
percentage of wages or with amounts or benefits that are
precisely named. *Fixed capital* represents investments in
assets intended for long continued use. *Fixed charges* (or
costs) are business costs that continue whether or not
business comes in; for example, rent, bond interest, property taxes, administrative salaries, etc. *Fixed-charge
coverage* is a **leverage ratio:** total fixed charges divided by
income available for paying them. A *fixed exchange rate*
is a system in which, by international agreement, the
exchange rate of each currency is fixed in terms of another currency, gold, or some artificial standard, and each
country is obliged to maintain its currency at or near this
fixed exchange rate. A *fixed price contract* is technically a
contract in which a named, exact price is specified for
goods or services, but there are so many variations (such
as *escalators* or *redeterminations* for increased costs or
incentives for meeting various goals) that the term is practically meaningless. A *fixed rate mortgage* is a loan **secured**
by property, whose interest rate is fixed for its life. Fixed
rate mortgages are not as readily available as in the past.
Because the market is highly changeable, many lenders
are reluctant to lock themselves into rates that cannot
adapt to new conditions. They are beginning to be replaced by **adjustable, renegotiable** and **variable** rate mortgages. A *fixed shift* is a work shift to which an employee
is assigned indefinitely. *Fixed* (or *created*) *work,* under

copyright law, is a new work that is put in stable, tangible form, such as written on paper, recorded on film, sculpted in clay, etc. This "fixation" gives the work an automatic copyright, whether or not the formalities of copyright are followed (although registering the work with the Copyright Office and putting a copyright notice on it gives the work many added protections).

Fixture Anything attached to land or a building. The word is sometimes used to mean those attached things that, once attached, may *not* be removed by a tenant and sometimes means those things attached that *may* be removed.

Flack A disrespectful term for a publicist.

Flag of convenience A merchant ship **registered** in a country that has low fees, low safety requirements, etc., rather than in the country where it is owned or does most of its business, flies a *flag of convenience*. This is different from *reflagging*, which is a diplomatic undertaking designed to qualify previously ineligible merchant ships for naval protection from friendly powers—whose flag they then fly.

Flagged rates Compensation rates paid to employees whose positions warrant lower rates.

Flash report A preliminary or estimated earnings report issued to top management as soon as possible after the close of the **accounting** period. It is a top-level report and indicates an overall trend since the details upon which it is based are not yet available.

Flat Level. A *flat benefit plan* is a **pension plan** or other employee **benefit** plan that is unrelated to salary level (pays the same to everyone, pays more by years of service, etc.). *Flat bonds* are those traded without interest. They are usually in default of interest and are sold without including the accrued interest in the price. A *flat organization* is one whose structure has comparatively few levels. In contrast, a *tall organization* is one whose structure has many levels. A *flat rate* is either a fixed amount of money paid each time period rather than paying at fluctuating levels (for electricity used, for services used, for changeable prices, etc.), or a pay structure offering only one rate of pay for each pay level. *Flat stock* is stock borrowed without any interest charge.

Flexday A company policy which allows employees to take off portions of workdays to attend to family emergencies.

Flexible budget A budget which provides for differing expense allowances for various levels of output. The levels function as guides as to what costs should be at given levels of output. Flexible budgeting is a cost-control technique which can be used with or without a formal **standard cost** system. The *variable* or *flexible budget* is used in companies where forecasting techniques have not been highly developed or where the demand for the company's products and services is especially volatile.

Flexible rate loan (or **mortgage**) See **adjustable rate mortgage.**

Flexi-time A flexible work schedule in which workers can, within a prescribed *band of time* in the morning and again in the afternoon, start and finish work at their discretion as long as they complete the total number of hours required for a given period of a day, week, or month. In most cases the workday can vary from day to day in its length as well as in the time that it begins and ends. The morning and evening bands of time are often designated as *quiet time*. Telephone calls and staff meetings are confined to *core time*, which generally runs from midmorning to midafternoon.

Flight of capital A fleeing of funds from one country to others to avoid high taxation, high inflation or a highly unstable political regime.

Flipping 1. A popular word for refinancing **consumer** loans, often at higher rates of interest. 2. Buying a large block of shares of a new offering of stock; then, if the price rapidly starts up, dumping all of the stock back on the market. This allows for the taking of quick profits and possibly buying the same stock again at a lower price.

Float 1. The time between the deposit of a check in one bank and its subtraction from an account in another bank. This is "free" use of the money by the person who wrote the check. It can also be looked at as that portion of a deposit, a bank account balance, or of the total deposits of a bank that is represented by uncollected funds. 2. To let a national currency's value against other currencies change freely depending on supply and demand rather than by one or both countries' fixing or **pegging** the **exchange** rate by law or otherwise. 3. That portion of a new **issue** of **securities** that has not yet been purchased by the public and is still to be absorbed by the market.

Floating Changeable. *Floating debt (or capital)* is short-term debt (or money available to *pay* short-term debt and other current expenses). A *floating exchange rate* is a system in which the **exchange** rate of each national currency in terms of every other currency is determined solely by market supply and demand for that currency. Factors affecting the demand and supply of each currency include trends in the current **balance of payments, inflation** and **interest** rates relative to those abroad, and expectations regarding future changes in exchange rates. *Floating interest* is an interest rate that varies with the general interest rate market. A *floating lien* is an arrangement in which property purchased by someone with a **secured** debt or **lien** on previously purchased property becomes subject to that debt or lien, and the original property remains subject to the lien until all debts are paid. A *floating (or floater) policy* is a supplemental insurance policy to cover items that frequently change location or quantity. *Floating securities* means issuing and selling **stocks** or **bonds.** This marketing process is called *flotation*.

Floor 1. The trading area of an organized **exchange** in the **securities** and **commodities markets.** A transaction on the floor is made in open trading as distinguished from one made by private negotiation off the floor. A *floor broker* makes trades for self or others. 2. A lowest limit. 3. *Floor plan financing* is a loan to a retail seller that is **secured** by the items to be sold and that is paid off as each sells.

Floppy A small, cheap, flexible plastic **disk** for a storage of computer data.

Flow assumption An assumption of the cost of an **inventory** withdrawal if there is not a specific identification of goods. The usual flow assumptions are: **first in, first out; last in, first out; next in,** and **first out.**

Flowchart A graphic representation of an analysis of, or solution to, a problem that uses symbols to indicate various operations, equipment, and data flow.

Fluctuating clause An **escalator clause.**

For cause For a sound legal reason, as opposed to merely a stated reason. To remove a person from a job *for cause* may require a better reason than "because we didn't like certain actions he took or like the way he handled his job." It usually requires proof that the person lacked the ability or fitness to do the job right.

Forbearance Holding off demanding payment on a debt that is due.

Force-field analysis A procedure for determining what factors, or forces, seem to be contributing to a problem.

Force majeure 1. Compelling circumstances. 2. The title of a standard clause in some contracts exempting the parties from nonfulfillment of their obligations as a result of conditions beyond their control, such as earthquakes, floods, or war.

Forced-distribution method A **performance appraisal** technique that predetermines the percentage of rates to be placed in the various performance categories.

Forced loan 1. A loan made by a bank when an **account** is overdrawn. 2. Any **draft** honored by a bank on uncollected funds; it is assumed that the funds will clear. 3. A loan that is in default and thus extended by necessity. 4. A loan required by a government of its citizens; for example, a withholding tax or payment for goods by **scrip.**

Forced sale A sale made to pay off a court's **judgment,** ordered by that court, and done according to rules set by that court. A **judicial sale.**

Forecasting An attempt to evaluate observable or known facts, and from them predict a future environment, or project a range of future possibilities or happenings.

Foreclosure An action by a person who holds a **mortgage** to take the property away from the mortgagor (such as the homeowner), end that homeowner's rights in the property, and sell the property to pay off the mortgage debt. Both the process (which is usually but not always done by lawsuit) and the result are called *foreclosure*.

Foreign Belonging to, coming from, or having to do with another country (or another state; for example, a Maine court would call a corporation incorporated in and based in Ohio a *foreign corporation*). A *foreign agent* is a person who must register with the federal government as a lobbyist, advertising agency, or other representative of a foreign country or company. *Foreign aid* usually consists of all official grants and concessional loans (i.e., loans made on "softer" than commercial terms), in currency or in kind, which are broadly aimed at transferring resources from developed to less developed countries for the purposes of economic development or income distribution. The *Foreign Credit Insurance Association* is a voluntary association of some 50 U.S. insurance companies that provides insurance coverage for credits extended by U.S. exporters to foreign purchasers. Commercial risks are insured equally by FCIA and the **Export-Import Bank**, and political risks are insured solely by the *Eximbank*. *Foreign exchange* is the currencies of foreign countries. For example, Deutsche Marks and Japanese yen are foreign exchange in the United States, while the U.S. dollar and the Japanese yen are foreign exchange in Germany. *Foreign exchange controls* are regulations aimed at rationing the available supply of foreign exchange according to a predetermined set of priorities. In their most severe form, domestic residents are required to sell all foreign exchange acquired from exports and other international transactions to the government at a specified exchange rate which permits the foreign exchange to be used only for approved purposes. The *foreign exchange desk* is the foreign exchange trading desk at the New York **Federal Reserve Bank.** The desk undertakes operations in the exchange markets for the account of the Federal Open Market Committee, as agent for the U.S. Treasury and as agent for foreign central banks. The *foreign exchange market* is where one currency is ex changed for another. It has no central location, but is instead a network of commercial banks, brokers, central banks and customers who communicate easily and quickly with each other by telephone and telex throughout the financial cities of the world. *Foreign exchange rates* refer to the number of units of one currency needed to purchase one unit of another, or the value of one currency in terms of another. A *foreign sales agent* is an individual or firm that serves as the foreign representative of a domestic supplier and seeks sales abroad for the supplier. A *foreign substance* is something not naturally occurring, such as a nail in a can of beans. A *foreign trade zone* is a designated area, usually near a port of entry, considered to be outside the **customs** territory of the U.S.; foreign and domestic merchandise may be moved into these areas for storage, exhibition, assembly, manufacturing, or processing without incurring any state or federal duties and without involving any quota restrictions. If the finished product is exported, no U.S. **duty** is paid; if the product is to be sold in the United States, no duty is paid until the product is ready to leave the zone. Outside the United States, such areas are called "free trade zones." See **free port.**

Foreman A first-line supervisor—the first level of management responsible for securing adequate **production** and the managerial employee who supervises the work of nonmanagerial employees. Present-day foremen work under a fading occupational title. It has fallen victim to the Department of Labor's effort to '"de-sex" the nature of work and has been retired as an officially acceptable job title by the fourth edition of the *Dictionary of Occupational Titles (1977).*

Form utility The ability of a product to satisfy a human want or need, usually because of the **value added** to it in the production process. See also **place, possession** and **time utility.**

Forms control A set of procedures or a program for improving the use, work flow, storage, and final disposition of forms.

Fortune 500 A directory of the 500 largest U.S. corporations published each year by *Fortune* magazine. These organizations are frequently described according to their rank in the directory, particularly in recruiting advertisements. A *Fortune 500 company* is any company on the list; a *Fortune 100 company* is one of the 100 largest.

Forty-Plus Club An organization of unemployed executives over 40 who band together to help each other find jobs.

Forward 1. Set a rate (such as an **interest** or **exchange** rate) today for a future transaction. 2. *Forward buying* is providing material for future needs, expanded business activity, or increased requirements by replenishing inventories in excess of short-term needs. Forward buying assures that material is on hand when it is needed, and that there are no production delays or stoppages due to lack of material. It also allows consolidation of known material requirements in a long-range purchasing program. A *forward contract* is a **futures** contract.

Foul bill A **bill of lading** that says that the goods are damaged or partly missing.

Founders' shares **Stock** designed to give its holders a residual share in the profits of the company, and to facilitate a concentration of corporate control. Founders' shares are usually issued in smaller amounts than other classes of stock, and generally carry dividend provisions that encourage the directors or *founders*, who are the holders of such shares, to increase the earnings of the corporation. Sometimes *founders' stock* is the only class of stock entitled to vote unless *dividends* on other stock are not paid. These shares are more frequently used by foreign than by American corporations. *Founders' shares* are also known as *management shares*.

Four-day workweek A reallocation of the standard forty-hour workweek over four days instead of five. By lengthening the workday, employees get a three-day weekend every week with no loss of pay. This concept differs from the 4-day/32-hour workweek that some union leaders advocate.

401(K) A tax-deferred retirement savings plan authorized by section 401(K) of the IRS code.

Four P's The four most basic variables in **marketing:** Product, Place, Promotion, and Price.

Fourth market An unlisted **securities** market where investors buy and sell directly to each other.

Fourth World Those **developing countries** with very low per capita incomes, little expectation of economic growth, and few natural resources. See also **First, Second,** and **Third Worlds.**

Fractional Fragmented. *Fractional money* consists of currency smaller than the standard unit. As the dollar is the standard, all coins worth less are *fractional*. A *fractional reserve* is the **Federal Reserve System's** requirement that member banks hold only a part of their demand deposits in **reserve.** A *fractional share* is less than a share of stock; used mainly in **dividend reinvestment.** *Fractionation* is the practice of having separate prices for services that were previously subject to a single overall charge to increase a customer's final costs.

Franchise 1. A business arrangement in which a person buys the right to sell, rent, etc., the products or services of a company and use the company's name to do business. 2. A special right given by the government, such as the right to vote or to form a corporation. A *franchise tax* is a tax on the right of a company to do business in a state. The tax may be based on a fixed fee, on the amount of business done, on assets, etc.

Fraudulent   Cheating. For example, a *fraudulent conveyance* is a debtor's transfer of property to someone else in order to cheat a creditor who might have a right to it.

Freddie Mac   See **Federal Home Loan Mortgage Corporation**.

Free   Unrestricted. A *free and open market* is a **market** in which supply and demand are expressed without restraint in terms of price. A market in which supply, demand, or price is regulated is called a *controlled market*. A *free astray* is a shipment that was lost and is later found and forwarded without further charges. *Free currency* is money that can be converted to foreign currency without restrictions. *Free enterprise* is a political and economic system in which most of the society's goods and services are provided by the private sector. A *free good* is a good or service that is so abundant, in relation to the demand for it, that it can be obtained without exertion or paying money or exchanging another good. A *freelancer* is an independent worker with some particular skill who takes assignments from various employers. A *free list* is a list of goods not subject to import licensing in a particular country. A *free market commodity* is one whose price is set by the supply of it and demand for it. A *free market price* occurs when prices are established by a market without government intervention. For *free on board*, see **FOB**. A *free port* is an area of a country (usually a marine port, but sometimes a railroad crossover, airport, etc.) set aside for bringing in and selling foreign goods without paying import taxes. See **foreign trade zone**. *Free reserves* refers to the unused lending ability of **Federal Reserve** member banks. A *free ride* is the possibility of a riskless profit. In a labor context, *free rider* is a derogatory term for a person working in a **bargaining unit** and receiving substantially all of the benefits of union representation without belonging to the union. *Free trade* is a theoretical concept to describe international trade unhampered by governmental barriers such as **tariffs** or nontariff measures. *Free traders* favor the reduction or elimination of tariff and nontariff barriers. A *free trade protectionist* is a member of the U.S. Congress who believes in free trade "in principle" but seeks **protectionist** legislation on a "temporary" basis for industries in his or her district which have been adversely affected by foreign imports. For *free trade zone*, see **foreign trade zone**.

Freedom of contract The constitutionally protected right to make and enforce contracts, limited only by reasonable health, safety, and consumer protection laws.

Freehold Ownership of land, either unrestricted or restricted by no more than a time limit.

Freeze-out The use of corporate power by a majority of the shareholders (owners) or of the **board of directors** to either get rid of **minority** shareholders and board members or to strip them of all power. See also **squeeze-out.**

Freight forwarder A shipper who collects less-than-carload/truckload lots from different consignors and combines the shipments into carloads or truckloads.

Frictional unemployment Unemployment that is due to the inherent time lag needed for the re-employment of labor.

Friendly takeover One company gaining control of another with the approval of the second company's **board** and officers.

Fringe benefits Things besides salary that either compensate a person for working (such as paid medical insurance or profit-sharing plans) or make it pleasant to work (such as on-site recreational facilities).

Front end load Charging a large part of the administrative costs, of **commissions**, etc., at the start of a deal to buy insurance, to lease property, etc. *Front loaded* refers to a labor agreement that provides for a greater wage increase in its first year of effect than in subsequent years.

Front money The initial **capital** needed to get a business started.

Front name See **street name**.

Frontage assessment A tax to pay for improvements (such as sidewalks or sewer lines) that is charged in proportion to the *frontage* (number of feet bordering the road) of each property.

Frozen account An **account** (usually a bank account) from which no money may be removed until a court **order** is lifted.

Frozen assets The property of a business that cannot be easily sold without damaging the business. This includes financial assets which, if sold, will hurt the company's financial structure. The opposite is **liquid assets**.

Frustration Blockage. *Frustration of contract* occurs when carrying out a bargain has become impossible because of some change or occurrence that is not the fault of the persons making the deal. The change must remove something (or change some condition) that the persons who made the contract knew from the beginning was necessary for the contract to be carried out. *Frustration of purpose* occurs when, even if a bargain can be carried out, some change has wiped out the real reasons for the contract. In some cases, promises need not then be carried out.

Full Total. *Full costing* means dividing up all **costs** for a time period, whether **direct** or indirect (overhead, etc.), product by product. *Full coverage* is insurance that pays for every dollar of a loss with no maximum and no **deductible** amount. A *full-crew rule* is a safety regulation requiring a minimum number of workers for a given operation. *Full disclosure* is the Securities and Exchange commission requirement that a public corporation must disclose (via annual and other reports) all pertinent financial and other data about a company's operations. *Full employment* is an economic situation in which all those who want to work are able to. In recent years, economists have been telling the public that "full" employment really means from 3 to 6 percent **unemployment**. *Full faith and credit,* in the context of government debt, refers to those obligations, usually **bonds,** that have first claim upon the resources of a jurisdiction. *Full-time workers*, according to the **Bureau of Labor Statistics,** are those employed at least 35 hours a week, and *part-time workers* are those who work fewer hours.

Fully diluted earnings per share The per **share** earnings of **common stock** after **common stock equivalents** and any other potential shares of stock have been issued. The difference between *primary earnings per share* and *fully diluted earnings per share* is that the former considers only common stock and equivalents while the latter considers all possible combinations of **potentially dilutive securities.** See also **anti-dilutive**.

Fully funded pension plan A **pension** plan whose **assets** are adequate to meet its obligations in the foreseeable future.

Fully paid stock Legally issued **stock** for which the issuing corporation has received at least **par value** in money, goods or services. See **corporation.**

Functional Effective. *Functional authority* is the authority inherent to a job or work assignment. A *functional illiterate* is an individual whose reading and writing skills are so poor that he or she is incapable of functioning effectively in the most basic business, office, or factory situations. *Functional job analysis* is a method of work analysis that measures and describes a position's specific requirements. Functional job analysis can discard traditionally restrictive labels for positions. In their place, a variety of component descriptions are used to more accurately illustrate the specific and varied duties actually performed by an incumbent. Functional job analysis data readily lend themselves to computerized **personnel management information systems.** *Functional leadership* is a concept holding that leadership emerges from the dynamics associated with the particular circumstances under which groups integrate and organize their activities, rather than from the personal characteristics or behavior of an individual.

Functus officio (Latin) A person whose official job is finished and who has no further authority to act. **Arbitrators** are said to be *functus officio* concerning a particular case after they have declared their **awards** on it.

Fund 1. A sum of money set aside for a particular purpose. See also **reserve.** 2. Money and all other **assets** (such as stocks or bonds) on hand. The *funds flow* refers to the management and movement of working **capital**.

Fundamental analysis Deciding whether to buy or sell a particular **stock** or other **security** based on the company itself, the industry in general, etc. See also **technical analysis.**

Funded Having enough funds to meet future **liabilities** or anticipated needs. *Funded debt* refers to either state and local debts that have a fund of money or a specific tax plan set aside for payment, or to a company's long-term debt, such as a **bond issue,** which may replace other short-term debts. A *funded pension plan* is a **pension** plan that provides for the periodic accumulation of money to meet the pension plan's obligations in future years.

Funeral (or bereavement) leave Paid time off for an employee at the time of a death in his or her immediate family. The biggest problem with administering such a benefit is defining "immediate" family.

Fungible Things that are easily replaced one for another. For example, pounds of identical rice are *fungible* because one may be substituted for another, but different paintings are not fungible. [pronounce: *fun*-ji-ble]

Furlough A period of **absence** from work, initiated either by the employer as a **layoff** or the employee as a leave of absence.

Future A time to come. *Future acquired property* is property that is made part of a **mortgage** on presently owned property. *Future advances* are funds lent on the same **security** as a previous loan. Some open-ended **credit** and **mortgage** contracts allow additional loans like this. *Future earnings* is the estimated money that would have been made in the future if an injury had not occurred. *Future interests* are present rights in property that give the right to future possession or use; for example, the right to own property and use it after ten years go by.

Futures Contracts promising to buy or sell standard **commodities** (rice, soybeans, etc.) or **securities** at a future date and at a set price. These are "paper" deals and involve profit and loss on promises to deliver, not possession of the actual commodities.

G

GAAP Generally accepted accounting principles.

GAAS Generally Accepted Auditing Standards, put out by the American Institute of **Certified Public Accountants**.

GAO General Accounting Office. See **general**.

GATT General Agreement on Tariffs and Trade. See **general**.

GIGO Garbage in, garbage out.

GMAT Graduate Management Admission Test. The GMAT, administered by the Educational Testing Service of Princeton, N.J., is required for admission to most graduate schools of business and management.

GNMA Government National Mortgage Association.

GNP Gross National Product.

GPM Graduated payment mortgage.

GTC Good till cancelled.

Gain sharing Any of a variety of wage payment methods in which the worker receives additional earnings due to increases in **productivity**.

Game theory A mathematical approach to decisionmaking in situations involving two or more players with presumably conflicting interests. Because the theory of games assumes rationality on the part of the players, the strategies and decisions of one player are heavily dependent upon the anticipated behavior of the opposition. The possible outcomes of a two-person game are frequently presented in a *payoff matrix* consisting of numbers arranged in rows and columns with the degrees of preference that each player assigns to each outcome. Of course, a player's overall strategy is a *game plan*. See **maximax, maximin, minimax,** and **zero-sum game**.

Gaming simulation A model of reality with dynamic parts that can be manipulated to teach the manipulator(s) how to better cope with the represented processes in real life.

Gantt Chart Any chart which uses straight lines to compare planned and actual progress over time, usually used to coordinate overlapping production activities with parallel lines and bars.

Activity	Time				
	Mon.	Tues.	Wed.	Thurs.	Fri.
scrape & sand bad spots	～～ Planned (Mon–Tues) / ▬▬ Actual (Mon–Tues)				
prime bare spots		～～ Planned (Tues) / ▬▬ Actual (Tues–Wed)			
paint house			～～ Planned (Wed–Thurs) / ▬▬ Actual (Thurs–Fri)		
trim house					～～ Planned / ▬▬ Actual

Gantt Chart of Painting a House   ～～～～ Planned   ▬ ▬ ▬ ▬ ▬ Actual

Garnishee A person who holds money or property belonging to a debtor and who is subject to a **garnishment** proceeding by a creditor.

Garnishment A legal proceeding taken by a **creditor** after a **judgment** is received against a **debtor**. If the creditor knows that the debtor has money or property with someone else (such as a bank account or wages paid by an employer), the creditor first has the money tied up by legal process and then takes as much of it as state laws allow to pay off the debt. The amount of wages that may be *garnished* also is limited by the *Federal Wage Garnishment Act* which, in addition, gives some protection from dismissal due to garnishment.

General A whole group, as opposed to only a part of the group or only one individual in the group; applying to all, as opposed to only some or only one; broad or unlimited. The opposite of *general* is often **special** or **limited**. For those *general* words (such as *general partner*) that are not listed among the following words, see the main word (such as **partner**). The *General Accounting Office* assists the U.S. Congress in financial matters; **audits** and investigates federal programs; settles claims against the U.S.; etc. The *General Agreement on Tariffs and Trade* is a multilateral trade agreement containing guidelines for conduct of international trade based on three basic principles: nondiscriminatory treatment of all signatories in trade matters; eventual elimination of **tariff** and **non-tariff barriers** to trade, mostly through negotiations; and resolution of conflicts or damages arising from trade actions of another signatory through consultation. The agreement, however, contains many practical exceptions to these principles and no sanctions for their violation. For *general asset currency,* see **asset currency.** A *general assignment for creditors* is a transfer of all rights to a debtor's property to a **trustee** who settles the debtor's affairs and distributes money to the creditors. A *general average loss* is a loss at sea that will be shared by the shipowner and all owners of cargo shipped. This happens if the lost or damaged items (often thrown overboard) were intentionally lost to save the ship and the rest of the cargo. A *general building scheme* is the division of a piece of land into separate building lots that are sold with identical restrictions on each as to how the land may be used. A *general cash issue (or offer)* is a sale of stock or other **securities** open to all buyers. A *general (or prime) contractor* is a person who **contracts** for a whole project (such as a building job) and hires subcontractors (such as plumbers) to do specialized work. A *general creditor* is a person who is owed money, but who has no **security** (for example, a mortgage) for the debt. A *general labor union* is any labor organization that accepts as members workers in every skill category. A *general manager* is a person authorized to manage and control all the general business of a corporation or organization; one empowered by a corporation to direct and control its day-to-day affairs; and to do everything that the corporation itself could do in transacting business. Whether a general manager is considered an **officer** or a mere employee of the corporation is of little importance in determining his or her powers. *General obligation bonds* are **municipal bonds** which are backed by the **full faith and credit** of the issuing state or local government to the extent of its taxing power and whose principal and interest are paid for out of general revenues. *General price-level accounting* is reporting financial statements in **constant dollars.** A *general strike* is a work stoppage by a substantial portion of the total workforce of a locality or country. A *general tariff* is a **tariff** that applies to countries that do not enjoy either preferential or **most-favored-nation** tariff treatment.

Generally accepted accounting principles The totality of the conventions, assumptions, rules, standards, and procedures which collectively define the responsible practice of **accounting.** The **Securities and Exchange Commission** has allowed the accounting profession to establish its own guidelines, first through the Committee on Accounting Principles (from 1939 to 1959), and later through the Accounting Principles Board (from 1959 to 1973)—both of the American Institute of Certified Public Accountants. In 1973 the Accounting Principles Board was superseded by the **Financial Accounting Standards Board.**

Generic management 1. **Management** practices that are equally applicable to the public, private, and not-for-profit sectors. 2. Academic programs that offer substantially the same content for degrees in either public, private, or not-for-profit management.

Generic name The non-trademark name of a product.

Gentlemen's agreement A dated phrase for a deal that cannot be enforced in court and that depends solely on the **good faith** of the persons making it. *Informal agreement* is a better phrase for this type of deal.

GERT *Graphical Evaluation and Review Technique.* An offshoot of **PERT** that aids project planning when all activities to be performed are not known in advance and when it is not known whether all prior tasks must be completed before subsequent ones may start.

Ghost profits See **inventory profits.**

Gilt edge A popular term for a **stock, bond,** or other **security** with the highest rating (for safety of investment) or for a **negotiable instrument** with similar safety.

Ginnie Mae See **Government National Mortgage Association.**

Give-up A **securities** term for a **commission** split among brokers or the share of the commission "given-up" to another broker.

Giveback   Management's demand that a union negotiate a new contract with lower salaries or benefits, usually to preserve jobs.

Glamour stock   A heavily traded **security** whose price consistently rises. But *glamour* is a fickle thing; it tends to leave a stock when its price gets depressed.

Glass-Steagall Act   The Banking Act of 1933 which forced a separation between banking and the securities business.

Global office   1. An office with various units in different countries. 2. The movement of office jobs abroad to take advantage of lower wage and other costs made possible by electronic communications and rapid air freight services.

Global village   The notion that because of modern electronic communications the people in the whole world will become as closely linked as the people in a pre-modern archtypical village.

Gnomes of Zurich   The secretive Swiss financial and banking institutions.

Go-go fund   A 1960s term for a very speculative **mutual fund** that sought big gains in short time.

Go long   Buying a security. See **long**.

Go private (or public)   See **going private (or public)**.

Go short   Selling a **security** that is not owned (or owned but not delivered). See **short sale**.

Goal   In the context of **equal employment opportunity** a *goal* is a realistic objective which an organization endeavors to achieve through **affirmative action**. A **quota,** in contrast, restricts employment or development opportunities to members of particular groups by establishing a required number or proportionate representation which managers are obligated to attain without regard to "equal" employment opportunity. To be meaningful any program of goals or quotas must be associated with a specific *timetable*—a schedule of when the goals or quotas are to be achieved.

Going   Moving or active. The *going and coming rule* says that a person going to or coming from work is usually not covered by **workers' compensation** laws. A *going concern* is a company that is transacting its usual business in its usual way (even if in a weak financial condition). *Going concern value* is either **book value** or the cost of establishing a business. *Going private* is either a company's taking its **stock** off a stock exchange or a company's rebuying its own stock or otherwise rearranging its financial affairs so that it is no longer owned by many persons (for example, by **merging** with or being bought by a larger company). *Going public* is selling **shares** in a corporation to the general public for the first time. The *going rate* is the wage rate most commonly paid workers in a given occupation.

Gold certificates Credits held by **Federal Reserve Banks**. Except for some actual gold certificates used for educational displays, all *gold certificates* are Federal Reserve bookkeeping credits.

Gold-circle rate A pay rate that exceeds the maximum of an employee's evaluated pay level.

Gold fixings The manner in which the price of gold is established each business day; when a price emerges among buyers and sellers that nearly equates gold demand with supply, that price is said to be "fixed" by the bullion houses involved. The most influential gold market is in London.

Gold standard A monetary system in which all forms of money, paper and otherwise, are held at a parity with a coined monetary unit defined by its gold content and are convertible into this gold coin on demand.

Goldbricking A "goldbrick" was a slang term for something that had only a surface appearance of value well before it was adopted by the military to mean shirking or giving the appearance of working. The word has now come to imply industrial work slowdowns whether they be individual initiatives (or the lack of individual initiative) or group efforts (organized or otherwise).

Golden handcuffs The feeling of being bound to remain in a job because financial benefits would be forfeited upon resignation.

Golden handshake Dismissing an employee while at the same time providing him or her with a large cash **bonus.**

Golden parachutes 1. No-cut contracts with wonderful **fringe benefits** given to (and usually by) executives of a company facing a **takeover** bid. Their declared purpose is to give the executives a free hand in fighting the takeover by not being intimidated by loss of jobs, but these benefits have been called "executive incompetence insurance." 2. Being able to leave an organization with a substantial financial benefit.

Goldfish-bowl bargaining   Same as **sunshine bargaining.**

Good faith   1. Honest; honesty in fact. For example, in the context of equal employment opportunity, *good faith* is the absence of discriminating intent.   2. For a merchant, *good faith* also means "the observance of reasonable commercial standards of fair dealing in the trade," according to the **Uniform Commercial Code**   3. A *good faith purchaser* is a person who buys something (usually a **negotiable instrument**) without knowing any facts that should make a person suspicious of the seller's **title** to the thing.   4. *Good-faith bargaining* is a requirement of Section 8(a) (5) of the **National Labor Relations Act** which makes it illegal for an employer to refuse to bargain in good faith about wages, hours, and other conditions of employment with the representative selected by a majority of the employees in a unit appropriate for **collective bargaining.**

Goods   A general word that can have a meaning as broad as all property (excluding land) or as narrow as items for sale by a merchant. *Durable goods,* such as refrigerators, have a long life; *fungible goods,* such as a pound of rice, are interchangeable; *hard goods* are durable goods sold to consumers; and *soft goods* are things like clothing.

Goodwill   The reputation and built-up business of a company. It can be generally valued as what a company would sell for over and above the value of its physical property, money owed to it, and other **assets.**

Government corporation   A government-owned corporation or an agency of government that administers a self-supporting enterprise. Such a structure is used when an agency's business is essentially commercial, when an agency can generate its own revenue, and when the agency's mission requires greater flexibility than government agencies normally have. Examples of federal government corporations include the Saint Lawrence Seaway Development Corporation, the Federal-Deposit Insurance Corporation, the National Railroad Passenger Corporation (AMTRAK), and the Tennessee Valley Authority. At the state and municipal levels, corporations, often bearing different names, such as "authorities," operate enterprises such as turnpikes, airports and harbors (such as the Port of New York Authority).

Government National Mortgage Association   This federal
corporation assists the financing of federally guaranteed
mortgages. It guarantees payments on bonds backed by
pools of Federal Housing Administration and Veterans
Administration mortgages assembled by lenders. The payments of **principal** and **interest** on the mortgages are
passed through to the holders of the bonds. This Association also purchases mortgages at above-market prices (low
interest rates) from their originators, for sale to the **Federal National Mortgage Association** and other investors,
absorbing the loss incurred in this tandem program.

Government securities   See **Treasury.**

Grace   1. A favor.   2. A holding off on demanding payment of a debt or enforcing some other right. Often
called *grace days*, these days may be truly a favor or they
may be a legal requirement.

Gradual pressure strike   A concerted effort by employees
to influence management by gradually reducing **production**
until their objectives are met.

Graduated   By degrees. A *graduated lease* is a commercial
lease with payment that varies according to the money
made by the renter or by some other standard such as the
number of people who enter the store. A *graduated payment mortgage* is a **mortgage** in which payments go up by
a set formula over the years. See **variable rate mortgage.**
They are designed for home buyers who expect to be able
to make larger monthly payments in the near future.
During the early years of the loan, payments are relatively low. They are structured to rise at a set rate over a
set period (5 or 10 years). They then remain constant for
the duration of the loan. Even though the payments change,
the interest rate is usually fixed, so during the early years,
payments are lower than the amount dictated by the
interest rate. During the later years, the difference is
made up by higher payments. One variation is the *graduated payment, flexible rate mortgage*. This loan also has
graduated payments early in the loan. But, like other
flexible rate loans, it ties the interest rate to changes in an
agreed-upon index. If interest rates climb quickly, greater
negative **amortization** occurs during the period when payments are low. If rates continue to climb after that initial
period, the payments will, too. This variation adds in-

creased risk for the buyer. But if interest rates decline during the life of the loan, payments may as well. For *graduated tax,* see **tax rate.**

Grandfather clause   An exception to a restriction or requirement that allows all those already doing something to continue doing it even if they otherwise would be stopped by the new restriction or obligated to meet the new requirement. For example, if a company were to establish a policy that all managers had to have a master's degree as of a certain date, it might exempt managers without such degrees who were hired prior to that date.

Grantor-grantee index   County records with the volume and page numbers of all recorded documents such as **deeds** and **negotiable instruments.** The records are kept by the names of the person transferring the property and the person to whom it was transferred. See **tract index.**

Graphic rating scale   A **performance appraisal** chart that lists traits (such as promptness, knowledge, helpfulness, etc.) with a range of performance given for each (unsatisfactory, satisfactory, etc.)

Graveyard shift   A slang term for the tour of duty of employees who work from 11 P.M. or midnight until dawn.

Great Depression   The period between the stock market crash of October 29, 1929, and World War II, when the United States and the rest of the Western world experienced the most severe economic decline in this century.

Green card   A small document which identifies an alien as a permanent resident of the U.S. entitled to legally find employment.

Greenback   U.S. Treasury notes during the Civil War; now any paper money.

Green(or blue-)-circle rate   A pay rate that is below the minimum rate of an employee's evaluated pay level.

Greenmail   Buying off a potential **raider** by paying him more than the market price for his shares in order to stop a **hostile takeover.** The usual purpose of the *greenmail* is to save the jobs of the company's executives who would expect to be fired if the takeover attempt succeeded.

Green river ordinance   A local law that protects residents against peddlers and door-to-door salespersons.

Gresham's Law   Bad (or cheap) money will drive good (or dear) money out of circulation.

Grey-collar workers Technicians and others whose jobs have elements of both blue and white collar work.

Grey market Business transactions that are certainly legal, but hardly ethical.

Grievance While a *grievance* may be any dissatisfaction felt by an employee in connection with his or her employment, the word generally refers to a formal complaint initiated by an employee, by a union, or by management concerning the interpretation or application of a **collective bargaining** agreement or established employment practices. A *grievance (or rights) arbitration* is concerned with disputes that arise over the interpretation or application of an existing collective bargaining agreement. The *grievance arbitrator* interprets the contract for the parties. A *grievance committee* consists of those union and management representatives who are formally designated to review grievances left unresolved by lower elements of the *grievance machinery* (which is the totality of the methods, usually enumerated in a collective bargaining agreement, used to resolve the problems of interpretation arising during the life of an agreement). Grievance machinery is usually designed so that those closest to the dispute have the first opportunity to reach a settlement. A *grievance procedure* is the specific means by which grievances are channeled for their adjustment through progressively higher levels of **authority** in both an organization and its union. Grievance procedures, while long considered the "heart" of a labor **contract,** are increasingly found in non-unionized organizations as managers realize the need for a process to appeal the decisions of supervisors that employees consider unjust.

Grievant A person who files a formal **grievance.**

Gross 1. Great or large. 2. Flagrant or shameful. 3. Whole or total. *Gross income* is money taken in (as opposed to **net** income, which is money taken in minus money paid out). Under the federal tax laws, *gross income* is money taken in minus **exclusions** (such as gifts or interest on tax-free bonds). It is formally defined as "all income from whatever source derived" in the Internal Revenue Code. A *gross lease* is a **lease** in which the landlord pays all ownership and maintenance expenses, and the tenant pays rent. Contrast this with a **net lease.** The *gross national product* is a single figure that sums up the yearly value of goods and services produced by a country, plus breakdown on these and on income, investment, savings, prices, etc. It is usually measured as the sum of expenditures on the final **market value** of goods and services or as the income earned in producing the goods and services. *Gross private domestic investment* is a measure of the value of purchases of new **capital** goods plus the value of the increase (or decrease) in the physical stock of goods held by business. It includes all new housing and is, essentially, the total of **fixed investment** and **change in business inventories**. *Gross profit margin* is a **profitability** ratio: sales minus the costs of goods sold all divided by net sales. To *gross up* is to add back into the value of property or income the amount that has already been deducted or paid out (usually for taxes).

Ground rent Rent paid for land when the tenant has put up the building.

Group Collective. A *group annuity* is any of a variety of **pension** plans designed by insurance companies for a group of persons to cover all of those qualified under one contract. *Group dynamics* is the study of the nature of groups, how they develop, and their relationships to individuals, other groups, and larger institutions. A *group executive* is a manager responsible for the work of two or more organizational divisions. *Group insurance* is any insurance plan that covers individuals (and usually their dependents) by means of a single policy issued to the employer or association with which the insured individuals are affiliated. The cost of group insurance is usually significantly lower than the costs for equivalent individual policies. Group insurance policies are written in the name of the employer so that individual employees are covered only as long as they remain with the insuring employer. Sometimes group insurance policies provide that an employee can continue coverage upon resignation by buying an individual policy. The most common kinds of group insurance are *group health insurance* and *group life insurance*. Many employers pay a substantial portion or all of the cost of group insurance. A *group of classes* is two or more closely related job classes having a common basis of duties, responsibilities, and qualification requirements but differing in some particular (such as the nature of specialization) that is essential from the standpoint of recruitment and selection and requires that each **class** in the group be treated individually. Such classes have the same basic title but may be distinguished by a parenthetic. For example: Engineer (Chemical), Engineer (Electrical), etc. *Groupthink* is the psychological drive for consensus, at any cost, which tends to suppress both dissent and the appraisal of alternatives in small decisionmaking groups.

Growing equity (or rapid payoff) mortgage A **mortgage** which combines a fixed **interest** rate with a changing monthly payment. The interest rate is usually a few percentage points below market. Although the mortgage term may run for 30 years, the loan will frequently be paid off in less than 15 years because payment increases are applied entirely to the **principal.** Monthly payment changes are based on an agreed-upon schedule of increases or an index. For example, the plan might use the U.S. Commerce Department index that measures after-tax, per capita income, and payments might increase at a specified portion of the change in this index, possibly 75 percent. With this approach, income must be able to keep pace with the increased payments. While the plan does not offer long-term tax deductions, it does permit the borrower to pay off the loan and acquire equity rapidly.

Growth stock A stock invested in primarily for an increase in value (**capital** gains) rather than for income payments (**dividends.**) A *growth fund* specializes in growth stocks.

Guarantee Same as guaranty.

Guaranteed Assured. A *guaranteed annual wage* is any of a variety of plans in which an employer agrees to provide employees with a predetermined minimum number of hours of work or salary each year. *Guaranteed dividends* are **dividends** payable on *guaranteed stock.* For example, a **parent** company may guaranty dividends on the stock of a **subsidiary,** and in that event the guarantee amounts to a debt owed by the parent company to the stockholder of the subsidiary conditioned on the failure of the subsidiary to pay its own dividends. As dividends may be paid only out of **surplus,** a corporation may not properly guaranty payment of dividends on its own shares. Otherwise dividends might be paid out of **capital** if no surplus were available. Use of this term in corporate stock **certificates** usually is interpreted to mean only that dividends will be **preferred** and **cumulative,** and that dividends will be

declared when a surplus is available. Where statutes expressly permit the guaranty of dividends payable out of **net profits,** and a fixed rate and time of payment appear in the contract of issuance of the stock, many courts consider stockholders thus preferred to be **creditors.** In such cases the directors' usual discretion in declaring dividends is waived, in effect, and the stock certificate amounts to a note or evidence of debt rather than a true share certificate. *Guaranteed earnings* is a provision in some union contracts stating that employees will be paid (guaranteed) a specified minimum wage, even when production must cease because of a machinery breakdown or some other cause beyond the control of the employees. A *guaranteed mortgage* is a mortgage made by a mortgage company that then sells the mortgage to an investor, guarantees payments to the investor, and manages the mortgage for a fee. A *guaranteed (base) rate* is a minimum wage guaranteed to an employee working under an **incentive pay** program. *Guaranteed stock* is corporation stock, usually **preferred stock,** which is assured of receipt of a certain amount of dividends periodically or of a preference in the distribution of any dividends, at fixed rates, by the terms of its contract of insurance. The payment of the amounts thus established is guaranteed by a third party, usually a **parent** company. See *guaranteed dividends* for more information. A *guaranteed workweek* is a provision in some union contracts that an employee will be paid a full week's wages even when there is not enough actual work available to otherwise warrant a full week's pay.

Guaranty   1. The same as a merchant's **warranty** (promise) that goods are of a certain quality, will be fixed if broken, will last a certain time, etc.   2. A promise to fulfill an obligation (or pay a debt) if the person who has the obligation fails to fulfill it. For example, John contracts with Ron that if Ron lends Don five dollars and Don fails to pay it back in a week, John will pay it.   3. Any promise.

Guest worker   A European term for foreign workers allowed to enter and work in a country for a temporary period.

Guideline method   A job evaluation technique that determines the value of a position in an organization not by an analysis of the position's content, but by what the **labor market** says it is worth.

Guidelines (or guideposts) 1. General standards, usually expressed as a percentage, by which the federal government may measure wage and price increases to determine if they are consistent with the national economic interest. 2. Published outlines for action or suggested courses of conduct that many federal agencies issue for the guidance of their clients.

Guild A medieval Western European association for mutual aid or for the furtherance of religious and business interests. Merchant guilds date from the 11th century. The modern **union** movement usually traces its lineage to the craft guilds of the Middle Ages, which paralleled the merchant guilds of the time. *Craft guilds* were associations of individual workers who sought to regulate production, establish standards, and fix prices. These craft guilds gave us the now familiar rankings for their classes of membership —**apprentice, journeyman,** and **master.**

Gypsy A slang term for an independent operator of a truck, taxi, etc., who owns his or her own vehicle.

H

H 1. In newspaper stock transaction tables, an indication that the most recent **dividend** of an **over-the-counter stock** has been omitted. This indicator is always lowercase (h) and follows the previous year's dividend. 2. In newspaper stock transaction tables, an indication of a new 52-week high price for a stock.

HDC Holder in due course.

HMO Health maintenance organization.

HOW Homeowners warranty.

HR 10 Plan See Keogh Plan.

HUD Department of Housing and Urban Development. The U.S. cabinet department that coordinates federal housing and land-use policy and funds housing construction through a variety of programs.

Habitability The requirement that a rented house or apartment be fit to live in, primarily that it pass building and sanitary code inspections.

Halo effect Bias in ratings arising from the tendency of a rater to be influenced in rating specific traits by his or her general impression of the person being rated.

Halsey plan An **incentive** pay system in which workers are allowed to use their individual past performance as a **standard,** with the value of any increased output divided between the employee and the employer.

Hammer Either a **forced sale** or any sale by auction.

Handicapped individual Any person who has a physical or mental impairment which substantially limits one or more of such person's major life activities. A *qualified handicapped individual,* with respect to employment, is one who, with **reasonable accommodation,** can perform the essential functions of a job in question.

Harassment Words and actions that unlawfully annoy or alarm another. *Harassment* may include anonymous, repeated, offensively coarse, or late-night phone calls; insulting, taunting, or physically challenging approaches; words or actions by a debt collector that serve no legitimate purpose; etc. See **sexual harassment.**

Hard copy Typed-out or printed information as opposed to computer-stored, computer tape or disk-stored, etc.

Hard-core unemployed Those individuals who, because of racial **discrimination,** an impoverished background, or the lack of appropriate education, have never been able to hold a job for a substantial length of time.

Hard funding Money that is annually budgeted for an organization's activities, in contrast to *soft funding,* which implies that the money comes from a grant or some other source that will not continue indefinitely.

Hardhat A construction worker.

Hardship allowance Additional money paid to an employee who accepts an assignment that offers difficult living conditions, physical hardships, unattractive climate, or a lack of the usual amenities found in the United States.

Hardware Formally, the mechanical, magnetic, electrical, and electronic devices or components of a computer. Informally, any piece of computer or automatic-data-processing equipment. See **software.**

Harmonization Cutting **tariffs** in a way that will tend to make tariffs on most items more nearly uniform within each individual country's tariff schedule.

Hatch Act A collective popular name for two federal statutes. The Hatch Act of 1939 restricted the political activities of almost all federal employees, whether in the competitive service or not. A second Hatch Act in 1940 extended these restrictions to positions in state employment having federal financing.

Hawthorne Studies Conducted at the Hawthorne Works of the Western Electric Company near Chicago, these are probably the most important management experiments yet reported. Beginning in the late 1920s, a research team from the Harvard Business School started a decade-long series of experiments aimed at determining the relationship between work environment and **productivity.** The experimenters, because they were initially unable to explain the results of their findings, literally stumbled upon what today seems so obvious—that factories and other work situations are first of all social situations. The Haw-

thorne Studies are generally considered to be the genesis
of the **human relations** school of management thought.
The Studies are also famous for their discovery of the
Hawthorne Effect: any production increase due to the
known presence of benign observers.

Hazard Any risk or danger of loss or injury; for example,
hazard pay is compensation paid to an employee above
regular wages for work that is potentially dangerous to his
or her health. In **insurance** law, *hazard* is the probability
that something may happen, and *moral hazard* is the risk
of fire or similar destruction as measured by the careful-
ness, integrity, etc., of the person whose property is insured plus the loss (or gain) the person would suffer from
the destruction of the insured property.

Headhunter A slang term for executive recruiter.

Health Well-being. The *Department of Health and Human Services* is a federal, cabinet-level department most
concerned with health, welfare and income security plans,
policies and programs. *Health benefits* are the total health
services and **health insurance** programs that an organization provides for its employees. A *health maintenance
organization* is an organized system for providing health
care in a geographic area, which delivers an agreed upon
set of basic and supplemental health maintenance and
treatment services to a voluntarily enrolled group of persons. The *HMO* is reimbursed for these services through
a predetermined, fixed periodic prepayment made by or
on behalf of each person or family unit enrolled in the
HMO without regard to the amounts of actual services
provided. The HMO then hires or contracts with health
care providers. A federal law requires that employers of
25 or more who currently offer a medical **benefit** plan
offer the additional option of joining a qualified HMO, if
one exists in the area.

Hearing 1. A court proceeding. 2. A trial-like proceeding that takes place in an **administrative agency** or other
non-court setting. A *hearing examiner* is a judgelike official in an administrative agency. Also called an **administrative law judge.** 3. A meeting of a legislative committee
to gather information.

Hedging Safeguarding a deal or speculation by making
counterbalancing arrangements. For example, if a dealer
contracts to deliver a hundred ounces of gold at a future

time, then thinks that the price of gold may go up, the dealer might contract to *buy* fifty, or even a hundred, ounces of gold for that same future delivery date. A *hedge fund* is a *mutual fund* that seeks **capital gains** as a hedge against inflation.

Heterogeneous shopping goods   Goods perceived by the customer to be different enough to warrant inspection to determine quality and suitability. For a contrast, see **homogeneous shopping goods.**

Heuristic   1. A short-cut process of reasoning that searches for a satisfactory, rather than an optimal, solution to a very large, complex or poorly defined problem.   2. Any systematized trial-and-error problem solving technique. Contrast **algorithm.**

Hiccup   A quick temporary decline in the stock market.

Hidden agenda   Unannounced or unconscious goals, personal needs, expectations, and strategies that each individual brings with his or her participation in a group. Parallel to the group's open agenda are the private or hidden agendas of each of its members.

Hidden asset   An **asset** with a much higher value than the value stated in a company's financial records.

Hidden inflation   See **inflation.**

Hierarchy   An ordering of persons, things, or ideas by rank or level, with more at the bottom than at the top. A typical *hierarchy* is the army (many privates, some majors, very few generals, etc.) Most **bureaucracies** whether in the public or private sector are arranged this way.

High flyer   A highly speculative **stock** whose price varies greatly compared to other stocks.

Highest and best use   The use of land or facilities that would bring in the most money. For example, a real estate **assessor** valuing a piece of farm land inside an urban area might say that it should be taxed as if an office building could go up on the site.

Hire purchase   Installment buying in the United Kingdom.

Hiring hall   An employment office usually run by the **union** to coordinate the referral of its members to jobs. Sometimes *hiring halls* are operated jointly with management or state government assistance. Hiring halls are especially important for casual or seasonal trades (such as construction and maritime work).

Hiring rate   See **accession rate.**

Historical cost   See **actual cost.**

Hit the bricks   A slang phrase for going out on **strike.**

Hobby loss   A non-**deductible** loss from a hobby, rather than a loss from a profit-making activity. One test of a *hobby loss* is whether or not the activity made a profit in two of the last five years.

against another person.

Hold over   Keep possession as a tenant after the **lease** period ends.

Holder   1. A person who has legally received possession of a **negotiable instrument,** such as a check, and who is entitled to get payment on it.   2. The *holder of record* is the person who owns a given stock on a given date for the purposes of receiving **dividends** or other benefits of ownership.

Holder in due course   A **holder** who buys a **negotiable instrument** thinking that it is **valid,** and having no knowledge that any business involving it is shady. The **Uniform Commercial Code** defines it as "a holder who takes the instrument for value, in good faith and without notice that it is overdue or has been dishonored or of any defense against or claim to it." But this definition is limited to the "usual course of business" and does not usually include **judicial sales,** inheritance, etc. A *holder in due course* has more rights than a mere *holder.* For example, except in **consumer** sales and credit, a holder in due course of the financial paper involved in a sale of goods cannot be sued for defective goods by the buyer of those goods.

Holding company   A company that exists primarily to control other companies by owning their stock. A *personal holding company* is formed by a few persons to avoid taxes. This type of company is subject to a special federal income tax.

Holding gain (or loss)   The difference in the value of an **asset** from the time it was bought to any other subsequent time period (usually when it is sold or otherwise disposed of). See **capital gain tax.**

Holding period   The length of time a **capital** asset must be owned to make the federal taxation more favorable as a **capital gain.**

Hollerith cards   Punched cards used to input data and instructions into data-processing machines and computers.

Home port doctrine   1. A ship in interstate or foreign commerce may be taxed only in its home port.   2. A provider of repairs for a ship anywhere other than in the home port can get a **lien** for these repairs, but in the home port, local law decides whether a lien is allowed.

Homeowners policy   A standard type of **insurance** that covers fire, water, theft, **liability,** and other losses.

Homeowners warranty   The protection of a new home against major defects for several years either under a **warranty/insurance** program run by a national builders' associaton or under state laws.

Homestead exemption   State laws allowing a head of a family to keep a home and some property safe from **creditors** or to allow certain persons (such as those over a certain age) to avoid paying real estate or inheritance taxes on their homes.

Hometown plan   A voluntary **affirmative action** plan for the construction crafts and trades developed by a local construction industry, usually in cooperation with the Department of Labor.

Homogeneity principle   The principle of **administration** that advises the executive to group the major functions of an organization together according to their purpose, the process used, the persons served, or the places where it takes place, with each constituted as a single unit under the direction of a single administrator guided by a single plan of action.

Homogeneous shopping goods   Goods perceived by the customer to be basically the same; price then becomes the prime criterion for purchase. For a contrast, see **heterogeneous shopping goods**.

Honor   To **accept** (or pay) a **negotiable instrument,** such as a check, when it is properly presented for acceptance (or payment).

Horizontal   Parallel. *Horizontal analysis* is the year-to-year comparison of financial **statements**. For *horizontal loading,* see **job loading**. A *horizontal merger* is one company acquiring another that produces the same or similar products for sale in the same geographic area. *Horizontal price-fixing* is an agreement among competing producers, wholesalers, or merchants to set the price of goods. These agreements are prohibited by law. A *horizontal promotion* is advancement for an employee within his or her basic job category. For example, a promotion from Window Washer I to Window Washer II or from Junior Accountant to Intermediate Accountant. A *horizontal property act* is a law dealing with **cooperative** housing or **condominiums.** For *horizontal union,* see **craft union.** A *horizontal work group* is a work group that contains individuals whose positions are essentially the same in terms of rank, prestige, and level of skill.

Hospitality management   A loose term which encompases the food service and lodging industry; basically hotel or restaurant management.

Hospitalization   A **group insurance** program that pays employees for all or part of their hospital, nursing, surgical, and other related medical expenses due to injury or illness to them or their dependents.

Hourly rate workers   Employees whose weekly pay is determined solely by the actual number of hours worked during a week.

House   Internal. A *house account* is an account serviced by branch or home office executives. Usually no credit is given nor **commissions** paid when sales are made to such accounts. A *house counsel* is a lawyer who is an employee of a business and does its day-to-day legal work. A *house organ* is any publication—magazine, newspaper, newsletter, etc.—produced by an organization to keep its employees informed about the activities of the organization and its employees. *Internal house organs* are directed primarily to an organization's employees; *external house organs* find a wider distribution as part of the organization's **public relations** program. Neither takes outside advertising.

Housekeeping agency   An **auxiliary agency**.

Housing allowance   1. Special compensation, consisting of a **flat rate** or a salary percentage, for the purpose of subsidizing the living expenses of an employee; usually paid only to employees sent overseas.   2. A subsidy paid directly or indirectly to citizens whose incomes are below a certain standard in order to enable them to live in conventional, nonpublic, housing.

Human   People. *Human capital* is a concept that views employees as **assets** in the same sense as financial **capital.** It presupposes that an investment in human potential will yield significant returns for the organization. *Human-factors engineering,* also called *ergonomics,* is design for human use. The objective is to increase the effective use of physical objects while at the same time attending to concerns such as health, safety, **job satisfaction,** etc. These objectives are sought by the systematic application of relevant information about human behavior to the design of the things (usually machines) that people use and to the environments in which they work. *Human relations* is the discipline concerned with the application of the **behavioral sciences** to the analysis and understanding of human behavior in organizations. *Human resource accounting* is a concept that views the employees of an organization as **capital** assets similar to plant and equipment. While the concept is intuitively attractive, calculating the value, replacement cost, and **depreciation** of human assets poses significant problems. Consequently, it is viewed with considerable skepticism by managers and accountants. *Human resources* (originally called *manpower*) is a general term for all of the employees in an organization or the workers in a society. See also **personnel.** *Human resources administration* is an increasingly popular euphemism for the management of social welfare programs. Many jurisdictions that had Departments of Welfare have replaced them with Departments of Human Resources. *Human resources development* is a comprehensive approach to **training** which includes **needs analysis,** training, **management development,** and training evaluations. *Human resources management,* although often used synonymously with **personnel** management, transcends traditional personnel concerns. Instead of viewing the personnel function as simply that collection of duties necessary to recruit, pay, and discharge employees, an HRM approach assumes that personnel's appropriate mission is the optimal use of its organization's human resources. *Human resources planning* (originally *manpower planning*) has no universally accepted definition or consensus on what activities should be associated with it. Organizations claiming that they do such planning appear to use a wide variety of methods to approach their own unique problems. At the macro level, this means projecting what skills will be in demand to service the economy. At the micro level, this entails projecting specific requirements for the work force of the organization, or what quantities and qualities of personnel will be needed to carry out organizational objectives. Both levels are concerned with future supply aspects.

Hurdle rate The minimum acceptable rate of profit expected on a project for it to be started. See **opportunity cost.**

Hybrid state (or **hybrid theory justification**) A state in which a **mortgage** is considered a cross between a lien and a transfer of **title.** In a *hybrid state* the **creditor** must use **foreclosure.** One example is a state in which **trustees** hold title to the property during the mortgage.

Hype Extreme advertising and **public relations** promotion of a product, person or event.

Hyperinflation See **inflation.**

Hypothecate 1. To **pledge** or **mortgage** a thing without turning it over to the person making the loan. 2. Securing repayment of a loan by holding the stock, bonds, etc., of the debtor until the debt is paid, with the power to sell them if it is not paid.

I

I   In newspaper **stock** transaction tables, an indication, lower-case (i), that a **dividend** was paid after a regular dividend or **split**.

IBRD   **International Bank for Reconstruction and Development.**

ICC   **Interstate Commerce Commission.**

IFC   **International Finance Corporation.**

ILO   **International Labor Organization.**

IMF   **International Monetary fund.**

IMM   International Money Market. The part of the Chicago Mercantile Exchange that deals in financial **futures** such as **treasury bill** futures contracts.

I/O   1. Input/Output. 2. For I/O psychology, see **industrial psychology.**

IOU   "I owe you." A written acknowledgment of a debt.

IRA   **Individual retirement account.**

IRC   **Internal Revenue Code.**

IRS   Internal Revenue Service. The U.S. tax collection agency.

Iceberg principle   Important business and marketing information is often hidden in summary data. See **organizational iceberg.**

Ideal capacity   A company's theoretical ability to produce its products if absolutely nothing goes wrong, breaks down, etc.

Identity   In patent law, *identity of invention* means exact sameness as to looks, parts, method of operation, and results.

Idle capacity cost   Those **fixed costs** inherent in the ownership of **fixed assets** or other types of productive facilities even when they are not being used at their full capacity. **Depreciation** charges on machinery, rent on unused portion of a factory, and under-use of permanent employees

249

are typical examples. *Idle capacity costs* often enter into managerial decisions to accept orders at the **break-even point** or at lower than normal profit margins.

Idle time Time for which employees are paid but not able to work because of mechanical malfunctions or other factors not within their control.

Illegal *Illegal* usually means contrary to the criminal law, but is sometimes used as a synonym for *unlawful*, contrary to any (even **civil**) law. *Illegal aliens* are individuals from other countries who are living or working in the United States unlawfully. The Department of Labor prefers to call them "undocumented workers." An *illegal bargaining item* is any proposal made during the **collective bargaining** process that is expressly forbidden by law; for example, a **union** shop in a **right-to-work** state. An *illegal dividend* is a **dividend** that impairs the **capital** of the corporation. Under **statutes** in most states, **directors** who declare and pay dividends unlawfully are personally **liable** to the corporation and to affected creditors. In a few states they may be punished under criminal law. If there is no specific statute on this subject in a particular state, they are personally liable for the amount unlawfully paid out except if the corporation was **solvent** and was not rendered **insolvent** by their action, and their action was due to an honest mistake of judgment. In most jurisdictions illegally declared dividends must be returned only by shareholders who knew of the illegality when they received them, and by all shareholders if the corporation was insolvent at the time, or thereby became insolvent. Shareholders who transfer their shares after receiving an illegal dividend do not escape liability for return of the amounts due back. An *illegal strike* is a strike that violates existing law. While most public sector strikes are illegal, so are strikes that violate a **contract,** that are not properly authorized by the union membership, and that violate a court injunction.

Image consultant A **public relations** practitioner who specializes in teaching executives how to project a more impressive image (both inside and outside of the employing company) by dressing, speaking, socializing, drinking, and cavorting in a more "executive-like" manner.

Imitation Something made intentionally to resemble something else. In **trademark** law, if a use of words, letters, signs, etc., is close enough to a trademark to fool the general public (not necessarily when placed side by side, but when there is no chance to compare the two), it is an *imitation* and usually forbidden.

Immediate full vesting A **pension** plan that entitles an employee to all of the retirement income—both his or her contributions as well as those of the company—**accrued** during participation in the plan.

Impaired capital A reduction in a company's stated **capital** brought about usually by losses.

Impasse A condition that exists during labor-management negotiations when either party feels that no further progress can be made toward reaching a settlement. Impasses are resolved either by **strikes** or the helpful intervention of neutral third parties.

Implicit price deflator A price **index** for the **gross national product;** the ratio of GNP in current prices to GNP in constant prices.

Implied Known indirectly. Known by analyzing surrounding circumstances or the actions of the persons involved. The opposite of **express.** *Implied authority* is the authority one person gives to another to do a job even if the authority is not given directly (such as an employee's authority to buy and charge gas if the van runs out while making a delivery). *Implied terms* are parts of a **contract** that do not exist on paper, but are part of the contract nonetheless (because the law requires them, because usual contracts in that business have them, etc.). An *implied trust* is one that comes about by **operation of law** or by judicial **construction** as opposed to one that is deliberately created. An *implied warranty* is the legal conclusion that a merchant promises that what is sold is fit for normal use, or, if the merchant knows what the buyer wants the thing for, that it is fit for that particular purpose. Unless these *implied warranties* are expressly excluded (for example, by clearly labeling the item sold **as is,**) a merchant will be held to them.

Import To bring things from elsewhere. The *import-export clause* is the constitutional provision that no state of the United States may tax imports and exports of other states unless the tax is absolutely necessary for inspection laws or otherwise permitted by Congress. An *import license* is a document required and issued by some national governments authorizing the importation of goods into their individual countries. An *import quota* is a means of restricting imports by the **issue** of licenses to importers, and assigning to each a quota after determination of the amount of any commodity which is to be imported during a period. Such licenses may also specify the country from which the importer must purchase the goods. An *import restriction* might be a **tariff** or *import quota,* a limit on the amount of foreign currency available to imports, an import deposit requirement, import surcharges, or prohibitions on various categories of imports.

Impossibility That which cannot be done. A contract is not binding and cannot be enforced if it is *physically impossible* (for example, to be in two places at once); *legally impossible* (for example, to make the contract at age four); or *logically impossible* (for example, to sell a car for one thousand dollars when the buyer pays two thousand for it). These are all examples of *objective impossibility*. However, *subjective impossibility* (such as not having enough money to pay for something you have contracted to buy) will not get you out of a contract.

Imprest A loan or advance. An *imprest fund* is petty cash.

Improper accumulation Too much profit that is kept by a business to shield the owners from personal taxes. See **accumulated earnings tax.**

Improvement An addition or change to land or buildings that increases the value; more than a repair or replacement. See **repair** for the *tax* difference. In the case of machinery, a repair that *increases* a machine's usefulness or efficiency may be considered an improvement also.

Impulse goods Products bought on the spur of the moment as opposed to planned purchases.

Imputations Estimates which make possible the inclusion of data for **variables** which are difficult to measure or do not take measurable monetary form. The general procedure for counting these nonmonetary variables is to value them as if they were paid for.

Imputed Credited. *Imputed cost* is a cost not recognized as an actual cost by accountants. These costs may figure in management decisions but do not result in transfers of cash; for example, the cost of services given or received without charge. For *imputed income,* see **income.** *Imputed negligence* exists if, for example, David is **negligent**

and Paul is responsible for David's actions. David's negligence is *imputed* (carried over or attributed) to Paul. And *imputed notice* occurs if, for example, Todd is given **notice** of something (a fact, a lawsuit, etc.) and Todd is Noah's **agent** (lawyer, manager, etc.). Then notice to Todd can be *imputed* (treated as if given) as notice to Noah.

In-basket exercise A training technique and type of test frequently used in management **assessment centers** to simulate managerial problems by presenting the subject with an array of written materials (the kinds of items that might accumulate in an *in basket*) so that responses to the various items and problems can be evaluated.

In the black (red) Making a profit (taking a loss).

In blank Without restriction. Signing a **negotiable instrument,** such as a check, without making it payable to anyone in particular (leaving the "pay to" space empty).

In kind 1. The same type of thing. For example, a loan is returned *in kind* when a closely similar, but not identical object is returned. 2. *In kind payments* are noncash payments for services rendered. 3. An *in-kind (or soft) match* is a grant recipient's fulfilling of its cost-sharing obligation by a contribution other than cash, such as the rental of space or equipment or staff services.

In-and-out The purchase and sale of the same **security,** by a speculator or trader, within a comparatively short period of time.

Inactive stock When the volume of trading in a particular stock is no more than a few hundred shares a week, the stock is said to be *inactive*. Inactive stocks are generally traded in lots of ten shares rather than the customary hundred.

Inc. Incorporated: for example, "Pink Ink, Inc." is the Pink Ink Corporation.

Incentive A reward, whether monetary or psychic, that motivates or compensates an employee for performance above **standard.** This may be through *incentive awards* (a formal program to motivate individual or group effort or efficiency) or an *incentive wage, pay* or *rate* (a wage system that rewards above-standard work by an individual or a group). This may be built into an individual or union *incentive contract*.

Incident of ownership An indication that a right or some property has been kept rather than fully given away; some measure of control kept over something.

Income 1. Money gains from business, work, or investments; sometimes, more broadly, any financial gain. *Accrued income* is earned, but not yet received. *Earned income* is from work or a business, rather than from investments; *gross income* is what is taken in before **deductions**; *imputed income* is a benefit that will be taxed as income even though it doesn't look like income; and *ordinary income* is from wages, interest, etc. (everything except **capital** gains, such as stocks that go up, etc.). For more details on these words and for other types of **income,** see the individual words. 2. *Income averaging* is reducing taxes by showing that income in prior years was far lower and by paying tax on the basis of average income for several years. *Income basis* is a way of figuring out the *rate of return* (payoff) of a **security** (such as a stock or bond) by dividing the price paid for it by the income (**interest** or **dividends**) paid that year. *Income bonds* are **bonds** on which the interest is to be paid only when the company has earnings to pay it. Income bonds are rarely issued for public subscription; they result primarily from **reorganizations,** so the term *adjustment bond* is often used to describe them. While income bonds are bonds in name, the interest on them is contingent upon earnings and may require a **declaration** by the **board of directors,** much like **preferred stock.** They are often secured by a mortgage. The *income effect* refers to the change in the demand for a product as a change in its price increases (or decreases) the ability of consumers to buy it. An *income fund* is a **mutual fund** whose prime objective is to maximize current income. *Income-in-kind* is the receipt of goods or services as payment for something. *Incomes policy* is a general term for the totality of the federal government's influence upon wages, prices and profits. *Income property* is bought more (or as much) for current income than for **capital** appreciation. *Income return* is either the annual gain from an investment or the percentage figure found by dividing the annual gain by initial price. *Income splitting* is reducing total family taxes by giving income-producing property (such as stocks) to a family member who pays taxes at a lower rate. For *income statement,* see **statement** of income. An *income tax* is a tax on profits from business, work, or investments, but not on the growth in value of investments or property. For **income tax return,** see **tax return.**

Incontestability clause   A provision in a life or health insurance **policy** that after a certain number of years the insurance company cannot get out of the contract by claiming that statements made in the original application were wrong.

Incorporate   Formally create a **corporation.** The persons who do this initially are called *incorporators,* and the process *incorporation.* It sometimes takes place (after the paperwork is completed) at an *incorporators' meeting* and sometimes by the filing of a *certificate of incorporation* with the directors' names. For *incorporated partnership* see **closed corporation.**

Increment   1. One piece or part of a piece-by-piece increase. For example, in a salary structure, an *increment* is an established salary increase between steps of a given salary **grade,** marking a steady progression from the minimum of the grade to the maximum.   2. Anything gained or added.   3. The process of gaining or adding to something. *Incremental budgeting* is a method of budget review focusing on the increments of increase or decrease in the budget of existing programs. See **zero-base budgeting.** An *incremental cost* is the cost associated with a change in the level of output. For example, if presently the total cost of production is $100,000 and under a planned increase in volume the total cost would be $125,000. The *incremental cost* would then be $25,000. For *incremental product,* see **marginal product.** For *incremental revenue,* see **marginal revenue.** *Incrementalism* is an approach to decisionmaking in which executives begin with the current situation, consider a limited number of changes in that situation based upon a restricted range of alternatives, and test those changes by instituting them one at a time.

Incubator   A program to nurture new businesses by subsidizing selected start-up costs, providing technical help, etc.

Incur   1. Get.   2. Get something bad, such as debt or **liability,** because the law places it on you. For example, you *incur a liability* when a court renders a money **judgment** against you, and you *incur a debt* for a purchase when all events have occurred giving the seller a right to payment under a **contract.**

Indebted stockholder   A stockholder of a corporation who owes money to the corporation.

Indemnify Compensate or reimburse a person who has suffered a loss.

Indemnity 1. A contract to compensate or reimburse a person for possible losses of a particular type; a type of **insurance;** sometimes a type of **bond.** 2. An *indemnity letter* is a letter sent to the **stockholder** concerned in the case of a lost **dividend** check, with an agreement for signature, which will protect the company from double **liability** if it issues a duplicate check and the first check also is cashed by someone.

Indent In international trade, a **contract** or an **order.**

Indenture 1. An old word for a formal paper, such as a **deed,** with identical copies for each person signing it. 2. The written agreement of sale for **bonds** that contains the **maturity** date, **interest** rate, etc. 3. Any **mortgage** or similar agreement in which there is a **lien** or similar **security interest.** 4. An **apprenticeship** agreement.

Independent An *independent agency* is a federal **agency, board** or **commission** that is not part of one of the cabinet departments or of the Executive Office of the President; for example, the **Federal Trade Commission** or the **Federal Reserve Board.** An *independent contractor* is a person who contracts with an employer to do a particular piece of work by his or her own methods and under his or her own control. An independent contractor is neither an **agent,** nor an employee, and this fact is important in labor law, tort law, tax law, etc. An *independent union* is a union that is not affiliated with the **AFL-CIO.**

Index 1. A measure of relative value, such as the **Consumer Price Index.** 2. A measure of market trends such as the **Standard & Poor's** index of 500 stocks. For *index arbitrage,* see **program trading.** An *index fund* is a **mutual fund** that seeks to match the performance of a stock index by owning the same stocks in the same proportions as the index. An *index number* is a measure of relative value compared with a base figure for the same series. In a **time series** in index form, the base period usually is set equal to 100, and data for other periods are expressed as percentages of the value in the base period. An *index option* is an **options contract** based on an index instead of an individual stock.

Indexing Linking the level of payments (on bonds, wages, pension benefits, etc.) or of taxes to an *index,* such as the **Consumer Price Index,** to account for **inflation.**

Indicia Indications: pointers; signs; circumstances that make a certain fact probable, but not certain. For example, *indicia of partnership* are those facts that would make you believe that a person is a **partner** in a business even if it doesn't seem so on the surface, and *indicia of title* are documents, other than original legal proofs, that something is owned (a copy of a bill of sale, etc.). [pronounce: in-*dish*-i-a]

Indictment A formal accusation of a crime, made against a person by a grand jury upon the request of a prosecutor. [pronounce: in-*dite*-ment]

Indirect Not **direct.** *Indirect business taxes and nontax liabilities* are those tax liabilities paid by business other than employer contributions for **social insurance** and corporate income taxes. Sales, excise, and real property taxes are the principal types of *indirect taxes.* Nontax liability consists of payments for such things as fines, charges for government services, special assessments, etc. *Indirect costs* are **fixed charges.** *Indirect labor costs* is a loose term for the wages of nonproduction employees. *Indirect materials* is an **accounting** term used to classify certain low-cost materials, such as glue, washers, and thread, for costing purposes. Such items are part of the finished product but it is more efficient for accounting purposes to classify them as *indirect materials* and treat them in the same way as other **fixed charges.** An *indirect tax* is a tax on a right, privilege, or event (such as the granting of the right to **incorporate**) rather than a tax on a thing, on income, etc. See **direct tax.** *Indirect wages (or income or compensation)* are the nonfinancial benefits employees receive from their work situations—favorable organizational environment, nontaxable benefits, **perquisites,** and the **authority, power,** or status that may come with their jobs. See **direct** for other words.

Individual Single. An *individual agreement* **(or** *contract***)** is a formal agreement between a single employee and employer that determines the employee's conditions and terms of employment. It is reached through *individual bargaining.* Before the advent of modern **collective bargaining,** individual bargaining prevailed, and the employee was usually bargaining from a position of slight strength. An *individual contract pension trust* is a **pension** plan that creates a **trust** to buy and hold **title** to employees' individual insurance or **annuity** contracts. The employer makes payments to the trust, which then pays the insurance **premiums** on its various contracts. An *individual development plan* is a periodically prepared schedule of career development experiences, including both work assignments and formal training, designed to meet particular developmental objectives needed to improve current performance or to prepare the individual for positions of greater responsibility. *Individual Retirement Accounts* allow individuals to set up retirement programs into which they can put aside a limited amount of money that builds up tax free until retirement. Individuals *may* start withdrawing funds from these accounts at age 59½ and *must* begin withdrawals by age 70½. Funds are taxed in the year they are withdrawn. See also **Keogh Plan.**

Indorsement 1. Signing a document "on the back" or merely signing it anywhere. 2. Signing a **negotiable instrument,** such as a check, in a way that allows the piece of paper, and the rights it stands for, to transfer to another person. A *qualified indorsement* limits rights (for example, signing "without **recourse**") and a *restrictive indorsement* limits its purpose or the person who may use it (for example, signing "for deposit"). See **accommodation, blank,** and **conditional indorsements.**

Industrial Having to do with business or manufacturing. For *industrial accident insurance,* see **workers' compensation.** For *industrial classification,* see **standard industrial classification system.** *Industrial democracy* is any of a variety of efforts designed to encourage employees to participate in an organization's decisionmaking processes by identifying problems and suggesting solutions to them in a formal manner. *Industrial democracy* connotes joint action by management and workers' representatives while *participative management* connotes cooperative programs that are unilaterally implemented from on high. *Industrial design* is that aspect of **production** concerned with the styling of, and human/machine interface with, products made by machine. While engineering is concerned with the mechanics of a product and marketing is concerned with selling it, *industrial design* is concerned with how easy, comfortable and desirable it is for people to use the product. *Industrial distributors* are sellers of industrial supplies and equipment, the goods used by factories, railroads, mines, etc., in the normal operation of business exclusive of raw materials. *Industrial engineering* is a broad engineering field that generally involves **work measurement, job design, statistical quality control, job evaluation, materials** handling and **operations research.** In most cases, the industrial engineering department is responsible to a production executive. In many plants, the industrial engineering unit is primarily responsible for devising better work procedures, and may be known as the **methods engineering** department, the time study department, or the methods and standards department. There is no common assignment of responsibilities to industrial engineers. *Industrial hygiene* is that branch of preventive medicine devoted to protecting the health of industrial workers. *Industrial medicine* is that branch of medicine that is concerned with protecting workers from hazards In the workplace and with dealing with health problems and emergencies that may occur during working hours. *Industrial policy* is government regulation of industrial planning and production through law, tax incentives, and subsidies. *Industrial psychology* has traditionally been concerned with those aspects of human behavior related to work organizations; its focus has been on the basic relations in organizations between employees and their co-workers, employees and machines, and employees and the organization. Because the term *industrial psychology* holds a restrictive connotation, the field is increasingly referred to as *industrial and organizational psychology* or *I/O psychology*. *Industrial relations* is generally used to refer to all matters of mutual concern to employers and employees and their representatives. In a more technical sense, its use should be limited to labor-management relationships in private sector manufacturing organizations. For *industrial relations common law,* see **common law of the shop.** An *industrial revenue bond* is a tax-exempt local government **issue** to pay for a plant formally owned by the local government but leased to a firm on a long term basis. A locality uses these **bonds** to attract new industry. See **municipal bonds.** *Industrial revolution* is a very general term that refers to a society's change from an agrarian to an industrial economy. The Industrial Revolution of the Western world is considered to have begun in England in the 18th century. *Industrial standardization* is the systematic development, adoption, implementation, and adjustment of industrial **standards** to facilitate the interchangeability needed for **mass production,** the acceptance of new technology, and safety. Industrial standardization is an example of the self-regulation of business. The American National Standards Institute has promulgated over 12,000 American National Standards in common use by industry and government. An *industrial* **(or** *vertical***)** *union* is a **union** whose members work in the same industry and encompass a whole range of skilled and unskilled **occupations.**

Industry   Any type of trade or business. In economics the term used to identify a segment of productive enterprise; for example, the steel industry, the chemical industry, etc. *Industry-wide bargaining* is **collective bargaining** that results in a single **master agreement** negotiated by all of the major employers in an industry and one or more unions who represent workers throughout the industry. An *infant industry* is one that is just starting and has not yet reached its full potential for **economies of scale;** such industries often seek **tariff** protections so that they do not have a price disadvantage with established foreign firms.

Inflation   A rise in the costs of goods and services which is equated to a fall in the value of a nation's currency. *Deflation* is the reverse, a fall in costs and a rise in the value of money. *Cost-push inflation* is inflation caused by increases in the costs of production which are independent of the state of **demand.** *Demand-pull inflation* is

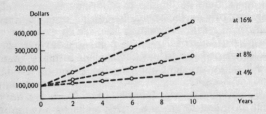

Changes in Residual Value on $100,000 Asset as a Function of Expected Rate of Inflation

inflation caused by increased demand rather than by increases in the costs of production. *Hidden inflation* is a price increase achieved by selling smaller quantities (or a poorer quality) of a product for the same price as before. *Hyperinflation* is inflation so extreme that it practically destroys the value of paper money. *Inflation accounting* is using either current costs to measure the impact of inflation or **constant dollars** to eliminate the effect of inflation on financial reports.

Information management See **records management.**

Infomercial A five- to thirty-minute television commercial using a talkshow format.

Infrastructure 1. The core of an organization's effectiveness, whether expressed as physical plant or human resources, that is essential for continuing operations. 2. Those physical **assets** of a nation that relate to its industrial productivity such as roads, dams, bridges, power plants, etc.

Infringement 1. A **breach** or violation of a right. 2. The unauthorized making, using, selling, or distributing of something protected by a **patent, copyright,** or **trademark.** If a patent is *infringed,* the patent holder may sue for relief in the appropriate federal court. He or she may ask the court for an injunction to prevent the continuation of the infringement, and may also ask the court for an award of damages because of the infringement. In such an infringement suit, the defendant may raise the question of the validity of the patent, which is then decided by the court.

Innocent 1. Not guilty. 2. Not responsible for an action or event. 3. In **good faith,** or without knowledge of legal problems involved.

Input Raw material of any process; especially computer data.

Insecurity clause A section of a **contract** that allows a creditor to make an entire debt come due if there is a good reason to think that the debtor cannot or will not pay.

Insider A person who has business knowledge not available to the general public. This could be anyone from a **corporate officer** to the brother-in-law of a company's outside **accountant** (see **tippee**). There are federal rules about stock trading and other actions by *insiders* and monthly reports required on *insider trading* (usually by those owning 10 percent or more of a company). *Insider loans* are loans between a corporation and its stockholders, directors and officers. In general, an insider may lend money *to* a corporation on the same commercial basis as any lender if it is clear that the company needs the funds and that no attempt has been made to improperly **secure** a debt in preference to other creditors. In some states, an insider may not borrow money *from* a corporation under any circumstances and a corporation may not even secure or guarantee debts for insiders. Even in those states where such loans are permitted, courts will look closely at them to be sure they are on proper commercial terms, especially in cases where insider knowledge, mentioned above, is combined with a corporate loan to take advantage of the knowledge.

Insolvent The condition of some persons (or organizations) who either cannot pay debts as they come due or whose **assets** are less than **liabilities.**

Inspection 1. Laws on such subjects as on-site examinations of cleanliness in serving, storing, or shipping food; safety of medical machines, buildings, work conditions, etc. 2. In **quality control,** the *inspection* function helps to ensure that products meet selected quality **standards** by rejecting all work that falls below standard and analyzing production to make possible the location and correction of deficiencies. Inspection must determine the quality of incoming parts and materials, the quality of final assemblies, and any flaws in the manufacturing process. 3. *Inspection of books* is the examination of corporate books and records. **Stockholders** have this right for proper purposes by virtue of their ownership of an interest in the company. **Directors** are entitled to an unqualified right to inspect the books and records at all reasonable times. **Creditors** and other persons may have a right of inspection for some purposes. 4. *Inspector general* is a job title (of military origin) for the administrative head of an inspection/investigative unit.

Installment 1. A separate delivery or payment. An *installment contract* usually includes the delivery of goods in separate lots with payments made for each. 2. A regular, partial payment of a debt. *Installment credit* is an arrangement in which a buyer pays the price (and, usu-

ally, interest and other finance charges) in regular (usually monthly) payments. Installment sales, loans, etc., are
usually subject to laws such as interest rate maximums
and the **Truth-in-Lending Act.**

Instant interest Advance payment of **interest** on a bank
account; that is, paid when the deposit is first made rather
than when it would normally be posted.

Institutional advertising Advertising designed more to improve a company's image than to sell its products.

Institutional discrimination Practices contrary to **EEO** policies that occur even though there was no intent to
discriminate.

Institutional investors Institutions whose investment of funds
is most important to their operations, although they
are formed principally for purposes other than investment.
These institutions include pension funds, insurance companies, trusts, and charitable organizations. Their investments constitute a substantial portion of the market for
investment **securities.** See **investing instrument.**

Instrument 1. A written document; a formal or legal document such as a contract or a will. 2. Short for **negotiable
instrument.**

Instrumentality A **corporation** that is totally controlled by
another corporation. The **instrumentality rule** is the
legal rule that a **subsidiary corporation** must be an
independent entity, and not a mere instrument or tool of
its **parent corporation,** if the separate corporate entity
of the subsidiary is to be recognized. If it is not an independent entity, the parent corporation may be liable for
its debts.

Insurable interest A person's real financial interest in another person or in an object. The *interest* is, for example,
the fact that a person will suffer financially if the insured
person dies or the insured object is lost. An **insurance**
contract must involve an *insurable interest,* or it may be a
form of gambling and unenforceable.

Insurable risk For a typical **insurance** company, this is a
risk with these characteristics: it is one of a large homogeneous group of similar risks; the loss produced by the risk
is definable and quantifiable; the occurrence of loss in
individual cases is accidental or fortuitous; the potential
loss is large enough to cause hardship; the cost of insuring
is economically feasible; the chance of loss is calculable;

and it is sufficiently unlikely that loss will occur in many individual cases at the same time.

Insurance   1. A contract in which one person (or company or agency) pays money and the other person (or company or agency) promises to reimburse the first person for specified types of **losses** if they occur. The person agreeing to compensate for losses is usually called the *insurer* or *underwriter*; the person who pays for this protection is the *insured*; the payment to the insurer is a *premium*; the written contract is a *policy*; the thing or person being protected is the **insurable interest;** and the types of harm protected against are **risks** or *perils*. A few of the more common types of insurance (and the situations they cover) are as follows: *credit life* (to pay off a car or other major purchase in case of death while **installments** are still owed); *group* (insurance provided at lower rates through an employer or other defined group or people); *self* (putting aside money into an account that will be used to pay **claims** if they come up or merely being prepared to pay for possible losses or claims); *unemployment* (a government program); and **workers' compensation.** *Marine insurance* compensates the owners of goods transported overseas in the event of loss that cannot be legally recovered from the carrier.   2. A company's *insurance administrator* or *planner* predicts as far as possible the likelihood of any given catastrophe occurring to any particular **asset,** the extent of loss or disruption that would be incurred if the catastrophe actually happened, the advisability of protecting the asset with insurance, and if advisable whether to turn to outside insurance companies or to *self-insure*. See **actuary.** *Insurance management* is that aspect of **risk management** concerned with **self-insurance** or the transferral of risk by purchasing insurance. An *insurance pool* is an organization of insurers through which particular types of risks are shared or pooled. The risk of high loss by any particular insurance company is transferred to the group as a whole with **premiums,** losses, and expenses shared in agreed amounts. The advantage of a pool is that the size of expected losses can be predicted for the pool with much more certainty than for any individual party to it. Pooling arrangements are often used for catastrophic coverage or for certain high risks. An *insured loan* in the context of federal credit programs is a loan in which a private lender is assured of repayment by the federal government on part or all of the principal or interest due on a loan.

Intangibles Property that is really a right, rather than a physical object; for example, bank accounts, **stocks, copyrights, goodwill** of a business, etc. *Intangible rewards* are those satisfactions of no monetary value that an individual gains from a job.

Integrated agreement An agreement is *integrated* when the persons making it agree on a document or documents as the final and complete expression and explanation of the agreement. This complete and written document is called an *integration*.

Integration 1. See **integrated agreement.** 2. The combination of different businesses. *Horizontal integration* combines firms in the same kinds of business; for example an auto company buying another auto company. *Vertical integration* combines businesses in successive stages of production and marketing; for example an auto company buying a steel plant. A *circular combination* consists of a group of businesses that are to some extent both horizontally and vertically integrated.

Intelligence 1. An individual's ability to cope with his or her environment and deal with mental abstractions. An *intelligence test* is any of a variety of standardized tests that seek to measure a range of mental abilities and social skills. The most commonly tested factor is *intelligence quotient (IQ)*, a measure of an individual's general intellectual capability. 2. The military, as well as some other organizations, use the word *intelligence* in its original Latin sense—as *information. Competitive intelligence* is legally spying on the competition.

Intelligent terminal A typewriter, **VDT**, etc. containing a computer for stand-alone operation. The opposite of **dumb terminal.**

Intended use doctrine In **product liability** cases, a manufacturer is responsible for harm done by a product if its advertising and marketing indicates that the product can be used a certain way and if the harm done is a foreseeable result of such use.

Interest 1. A broad term for any right in property. For example, both an owner who **mortgages** land and the person who lends the owner money on the mortgage have an *interest* in the land. 2. The extra money a person receives back for lending money to another person; money paid for the use of money. See **compound interest** and **simple interest.** 3. For the various types of interest, such as **compound, future, public,** or **security,** see those words. For the *abstinence theory of interest,* see **agio.** 4. An *interest arbitration* is an **arbitration** of a dispute arising during the course of contract negotiations where the arbitrator must decide what will or will not be contained in the agreement. For *interest cap,* see cap. The *interest elasticity of the demand for money* is the degree to which loan demand varies with interest rates. An *interest equalization tax* is a U.S. tax on long-term investment interest earned by U.S. citizens on foreign stocks, bonds, etc. An *interest inventory* is a questionnaire designed to measure the intensity of interest that an individual has in various objects and activities. It is widely used in vocational guidance. For *interest paying agent,* see **transfer agent.** The *interest rate risk* refers to fluctuations in the price of securities resulting from the rise or fall of market interest rates. An *interest-rate swap* occurs when floating or variable rate payments are traded for fixed-rate payments or vice versa. 5. A benefit or advantage that one seeks to gain through the political process. 6. A group of persons who share a common cause, which puts them into political competition with other groups or interests. Thus the oil interests want better tax breaks for the oil industry; and the consumer interests want new laws protecting consumer rights vis-a-vis the business interests, who want fewer laws protecting consumer rights. 7. *Interested officers* are officers of corporations (or of other organizations) who have personal interests or financial stakes in matters in which the corporation has an interest or financial stake; usually officers whose interests in a particular matter, transaction, or piece of property are **adverse** to the interests of their corporation in the same thing.

Interface 1. The boundary between two areas of concern. 2. Communication or interaction with someone not in one's immediate organizational unit. 3. The way that parts of a computer system link together, the way systems link together, or the way the operator links into the system. This includes both **hardware** and **software.** See **serial interface, parallel interface** and **port.**

Interference 1. The state of affairs when two different persons claim a **patent** on what may be the same discovery or invention. 2. An **unfair labor practice.** The **National Labor Relations Act** makes it unlawful for an employer "to interfere with, restrain, or coerce employees" who are exercising their right to organize and **bargain** collectively.

Interim Temporary; meanwhile. An *interim agreement* is a **collective bargaining** agreement designed to avoid a strike or to maintain the current conditions of employment while the settlement of a dispute or the signing of a final comprehensive contract is pending. *Interim certificates* are certificates issued by a corporation which certify that the corporation will deliver to the certificate bearers, upon surrender of the certificates, certain specified bonds or shares of stock of the corporation. They are issued as temporary proof of ownership to purchasers of new issues of bonds or stocks while definitive or permanent bonds or stock certificates are being prepared. In some cases interim certificates have been held to be **negotiable,** and in others non-negotiable. An *interim dividend* is one of the annual series of **dividends** other than the *final dividend* for that year or **fiscal** period. Interim dividends may be **declared** and paid before the year's final or **net** income figure is known. *Interim financing* is a short-term construction loan, with final financing provided later by a **mortgage.** An *interim report* is a report to **stockholders** to keep them informed concerning the activities and business of the company during intervals between **annual reports.**

Interlocking directorate Several of the same persons serving on the **boards** of directors of more than one company. Federal and state laws limit the extent of interlocking in certain industries and between certain types of businesses. Also, courts look more closely at deals between companies with common directors than at other deals.

Intermediate customers Any buyer other than a producer of raw materials or a final consumer; the people who buy things for business.

Intermediation Investing through a bank or other financial institution.

Internal Inside. *Internal alignment* is the relationship among **positions** in an organization in terms of rank and pay. In theory, the most desirable internal alignment calls for similar treatment of like positions, with the differences in treatment in direct proportion to differences in the difficulty, responsibilities, and qualifications needed for a position. *Internal auditing* is a control technique used by top management to protect itself, the owners it represents, and the organization as a whole through ascertaining: that established plans, policies, and procedures are being carried out efficiently and effectively; that financial **statements,** statistical and other reports and records are accurate; that all controls, managerial as well as **accounting,** are adequate and effectively maintained; that company **assets** are properly safeguarded and used; and that management is informed promptly of significant facts. This is often accomplished by following a written *internal audit program. Internal check* is the methods and procedures set up by management to prevent or detect errors and **fraud.** Internal check is a part of the broader effort of *internal control.* As such, it focuses on designing effective controls over transactions by: subdividing or allocating work so that no one person has complete control over an entire transaction, asset, or other record established to account for a transaction; establishing the flow of work so that one employee automatically verifies the work of another; and providing physical and mechanical facilities to aid in verifying the work of employees. *Internal control* is the sum of many diverse procedures instituted by management to insure effective administration of the company: to develop and maintain a functional line of authority among the various departments within the company; to clearly define duties and responsibilities of the various units and activities of the company so that there are no overlapping areas; to develop a system of **accounting** that provides prompt, complete, and accurate information about the company and its various departments; to set up a system of reporting to **line** and administrative management based upon accounting and other records; and to set up *internal checks* for protection against fraud within the company. Management's tools in realizing the broad objectives of *internal control* include such things as administrative regulations, employee procedure manuals, special directives, *internal auditing*, and employee training and participation programs. For *internal equity,* see **external**

equity. *Internal financing* is raising money for projects by keeping earnings, by getting back money from taxes due to **depreciation**, and other methods that do not involve selling stock or borrowing. The *internal rate of return* is a calculation which equates the full cost of an investment with future cash flows that can be expected from the investment **discounted** back to current values. *Internal reports* are reports intended primarily for use within the corporation only. Principal internal reports are financial, operating, sales, production, purchasing, statistical and special. The *Internal Revenue Code* is the United States tax laws.

International Worldwide. The *International Bank for Reconstruction and Development (World Bank)* was created in 1944 to help finance the reconstruction of Europe after World War II; today the World Bank mainly lends funds and provides technical assistance to **developing countries.** The *International Development Association* is the *World Bank's* **soft-loan** window. It lends money to the poorer *developing countries* on highly concessional terms (no interest, long term of repayment, and grace periods of up to 10 years). The *International Finance Corporation* is the part of the *World Bank* that promotes the private sectors of *developing countries*. The *International Labor Organization* is a United Nations agency that tries to improve labor conditions, raise living standards, and promote economic and social stability by advancing an international labor **code** concerning employment, freedom of association, hours of work, migration for employment, protection of women and young workers, prevention of industrial accidents, **workers' compensation,** conditions of sailors and **social security.** The *International Monetary Fund* was created to maintain international monetary stability. The *IMF* lends funds to member countries to finance temporary **balance-of-payments** problems, facilitates the expansion and balanced growth of international trade, and promotes international monetary cooperation. It also creates **special drawing rights** as an additional source of member countries' reserves. *International reserves* are acceptable international means of payment, mainly gold, certain currencies (such as the dollar), *special drawing rights* and a country's reserve position at the *International Monetary Fund*. The *International Shoe Doctrine* is the principle that a corporation must have at least minimal contacts with a state (carry on at least some activity there) for it to be sued in that state. The *International Trade Commission* furnishes studies, reports, and recommendations involving international trade and tariffs to the President, the Congress, and other government agencies. It is involved in anti-dumping decisions. An *international* (or *national*) *union* is a parent union composed of affiliated unions known as locals. Many international unions in the United States are international solely because of their affiliates in Canada.

Internship Any of a variety of formal training programs for new employees or students that allows them to learn on-the-job by working closely with professionals in their field.

Interstate and Intrastate Commerce 1. The Constitution gives the federal government power to regulate "commerce among the several states" (Article I, Section 8). But it does not define either *commerce* or *interstate commerce*. Today, *interstate commerce* includes transportation, transmission of power, and communication—radio, television and telecommunications services. Many operations, even though local, are part of the general flow of interstate commerce. Federal regulatory laws are not consistent in their definition of what is interstate commerce, although the tendency is toward uniformity. Thus, a business cannot take for granted that because it is in *intrastate* commerce under one law and exempt from federal regulation, it has a similar exemption under other laws. A company is engaged in *intrastate commerce* if the bulk of its business takes place entirely within a state, and is not part of an interchange or movement of tangible or intangible commodities (such as stock). As a general rule, a state cannot prohibit foreign corporations (corporations chartered in other states) from doing interstate business within its borders; however, it can prohibit them from doing intrastate business unless they meet certain qualifying conditions. Usually, the conditions include registration and filing of certain documents with state officials; designation of an **agent** to accept service of process; and payment of certain fees and taxes. A company that is engaged only in interstate commerce cannot be considered as **doing business** in a given state even if it actually gets business in the state. But courts have differed greatly as to exactly what is "doing business." The *Interstate Commerce Act* is a federal law that regulates the surface transportation of goods and persons between states; regulates rates for railroads, pipelines, etc. all through the *Interstate Commerce Commission*. 2. The **intrastate offering exemption** of the Securities Act, Section 3(a)(11), exempts from **registration** any **security** that is a part of an issue offered and sold only to persons who are residents of a single state or territory, where the issuer of such security is a person who is both a resident and **doing business** within the state or territory. This exemption is intended to facilitate the local financing of local business operations. To qualify for the exemption, the company must: be incorporated in the state in which it is making the **offering;** carry out a significant amount of its business in such state; and make offers and sales only to residents of the state.

Intervention 1. One of the most basic techniques of **organization development** which calls for a **change agent** to interact with an ongoing system of organizational relationships to improve behaviors. 2. Government action to directly lower interest rates, change the **money supply,** settle strikes, or change any other basic economic condition. 3. In foreign trade, this is the purchase or sale of **foreign exchange** by the central bank of a country to influence the foreign exchange rate of that country's currency.

Intrapreneurship The use of entrepreneurial skills within an already established large organization.

Inventory 1. The total items in a group of material or their value, usually based on cost; also, the process of counting, listing, and pricing such items, or the actual listing in which they are itemized. There are four principal types of inventory; *finished goods* (products that are ready for sale to the purchaser), *work in process* (the product, in semifinished form, which needs more material and further labor before it becomes finished goods), *raw materials* (inventory items on which neither labor nor further cost has yet been expended) and *indirect materials* (see **indirect**). Inventory is an essential part of total **capital** investment in any business not concerned with the sale of services alone. For *inventory analysis,* see *inventory control* and *inventory turnover*. An *inventory buffer* (or *cushion* or *reserve*) is a safety inventory. An *inventory certificate* is a preprinted form which a public accountant asks a company official with responsibility and knowledge of inventory matters to fill out and to sign as part of an audit. It contains statements as to quantities and dollar amounts of inventory classes, questions about title to goods, representations about the methods and procedures used in inventory valuation, and questions about purchase commitments, the condition of goods in the inventory, and the like. *Inventory control* is maintaining supplies of *inventory* at appropriate levels to meet production and sales requirements. Inventory control attempts to maintain the smallest possible inventories consistent with good service to customers and efficient use of capital. It involves both the control of inventory investment (a financial function) and physical control (an operations function). When effective, it prevents such costly mistakes as over-investment in inventories, which leaves a firm shy of working capital, raises storage costs, crowds available space, and hikes losses due to deterioration and obsolescence; underinvestment in inventories, which frequently means stockouts in critical items, slowing of production and loss of customers; and unbalanced inventories, which contains the worst features of both. *Inventory financing* is the process of obtaining needed capital for a business by borrowing money with inventory used as collateral, or a method used for financing the purchase of inventories such as a bill of lading, trade acceptance, banker's acceptance, warehouse receipt, trust receipt, factor's lien, conditional sale, or chattel mortgage. For *inventory investment*, see changes in business inventories. *Inventory profits* are profits from inventory sales when costs have increased since acquisition; they are considered *ghost profits* because the cost to replace the inventory has increased proportionately. *Inventory taking* is making an actual count of inventory to determine the goods on hand, if no inventory records are available; or to determine if inventory records are correct. For tax and for general accounting purposes, an inventory count should be made at least once a year. *Inventory turnover* is an activity ratio: net sales divided by average inventory. This is equal to the number of times inventory is replaced during a time pe-

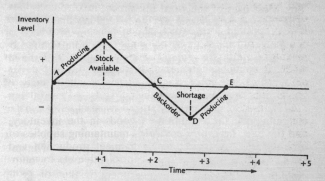

A typical inventory cycle

riod. *Inventory valuation* is determining which costs are properly attributed to inventory and then to which items. *Inventory valuation adjustment* is an adjustment to book profits—profits before taxes—in order to exclude the gains or losses due to differences between the replacement cost of goods taken out of inventory and their recorded acquisition cost.   2. Any general list of items; for example, a questionnaire designed to obtain non-intellectual information about a subject. Inventories are often used to gain information on an individual's personality traits, interests, attitudes, etc.

Inverse seniority   A concept that allows workers with the greatest **seniority** to elect temporary **layoff** so the most recently hired (who would normally be subject to layoff) can continue working. The key to making the concept practical is the provision that senior workers who are laid off receive supplementary compensation in excess of state **unemployment compensation** and have the right to return to their previous jobs.

Investing institutions   Institutions that invest other people's money. These include banks, trust companies, investment companies, etc. **Security** purchases by investing institutions are subject to special rules and restrictions. See **prudent person rule** and **institutional investors**.

Investment   Using money to make money by, for example, lending it for interest, buying property for gain in value, leasing property, buying an ownership share in a business, etc. Most uses of the word *investment* involve **securities**. The *Investment Advisors Act* is a federal law that **regulates** all persons who give professional investment advice or who manage investments for a fee. It is administered by the **Securities and Exchange Commission**. *Investment banking* is a field of business that raises money for companies and governments by buying and selling **issues** of their **securities.** This may be done in several ways: outright purchase and sale by either *private negotiation* (an investment banker called an *underwriting house* negotiates a price with a company for the right to buy a new securities issue); *competitive bidding* (a group of investment bankers bids for the issue against other groups); *standby underwriting* (the investment banker or group agrees to buy all unsold securities from an issue); and *best efforts selling* (the investment banker acts as the selling agent for the issuing company, but does not buy the securities or guarantee a sales price or volume). Typically, but not exclusively, private negotiation is used for small issues, competitive bidding for large or government issues, standby underwriting for **rights issues,** and best effort for highly speculative issues. In a typical deal, an *originating underwriter* negotiates a price with a company for its new stock issue, then shepherds the issue through **SEC registration.** Other investment bankers are then invited to form a *buying group*. Next, a *selling group*, which may overlap the buying group, is formed and selling prices and terms are set. The securities are then sold to institutions and the public with the price often stabilized by inside purchases and sales. Finally, the purchase group buys the unsold portion. Investment bankers also perform other services such as giving investment advice, managing securities holdings, etc. Many investment banking houses are completely integrated, providing a full range of wholesaling, retailing, agenting, advising, and managing functions. An *investment club* is a formal or informal group of persons who meet to learn more about investing, pool their money to invest, or both. A *qualified investment club* is one which qualifies as an individual investor under certain **SEC** rules for *securities* purchases. An *investment company* is a financial institution that invests the funds of a large number of individuals in many different types of *securities* of a variety of corporations and in other investments, such as real estate. (It is different from a **holding company,** which also tries to control the companies in which it invests.) It usually raises money by selling its own stock. Some stress income, some **capital gains.** They include such things as **trust companies, mutual funds,** and closed-end investment companies. The *Investment Company Act* is a federal law that **regulates** persons and companies that trade in securities and **commodity options** (or claim to trade in them); that invest in large blocks of securities; that invest in other companies, etc. An *investment contract* under federal law is any deal that involves an investment of money pooled with others' money to gain profits solely from the efforts of others. For *investment counselor,* see *Investment Advisors Act. Investment credit* refers to either **credit** given to a business for the purchase of **fixed assets** or to a tax break on fixed assets bought for business purposes. This **investment tax credit** is more than a **deduction.** It is a direct subtraction from income of a percentage of the purchase price of major machines, buildings, etc. *Investment grade* refers to securities that fall into the top four categories, AAA to BBB or Aaa to Baa, for **Standard & Poor's** and **Moody's** ratings respectively. Some institutions are required by law to buy only investment grade issues. *Investment tests* are ways of deciding whether or not an investment in **securities** should be made. Traditional tests include: safety of **principal** and **income;** rate of **return;** tax satus of income; protection against **inflation** or deflation; extent of attention required in reappraising security or **market;** nature and terms of the security **instrument;** nature of the enterprise and the industry; reputation of the **issue** and company management; marketability of the security; trend of **interest** rates in the market; **balance sheet** tests; tests of earning power; and **dividend** payments tests. For *investment trust,* see **investment company**.

Invoice   A commercial *invoice* is a document containing a record of the transaction between buyer and seller (a bill for merchandise) prepared by the seller. It contains a complete description of the merchandise, quantity, weights and measurements, prices, type and number of packages, marks and numbers, and terms of sale. It usually enumerates all charges and commissions to be paid by the buyer as may have been agreed upon and lists the name and address of the seller and of the purchaser.

Involuntary conversion   Loss of property by theft, casualty, or public condemnation. Any financial gain (from insurance on the lost property, payment for the condemnation, etc.) can be treated as *unrecognized* for tax purposes (and no tax paid at the time) if property similar to what was lost is bought soon after.

Issue   1. A group of **stocks** or **bonds** that are offered or sold at the same time. A stock is *issued* even if not yet bought.   2. The first transfer of a **negotiable instrument** such as a check.

Item   1. A separate **entry** in an **account** or list.   2. The smallest unit of an employment test; a test question. *Item analysis* is the statistical description of how a particular question functioned when used in a particular test. And *item validity* is the extent to which a test item measures what it is supposed to measure.   3. A *line item* is the most basic element of a budget. See **line item budget.**

J

J In newspaper **stock** transaction tables, an indication, low-ercase (j), that a **dividend** was paid earlier than usual.

Jason clause A provision in a **bill of lading** that requires a cargo owner to contribute to the **general average loss** even if the loss was caused by **negligence,** as long as the shipowner was careful in outfitting and crewing the ship.

Jeopardy assessment The right of the **IRS** to assess and collect a tax immediately if tax **evasion** is probable. (For example, if the taxpayer plans to leave the country.)

Job 1. *Job* has three common meanings: a **position** or **occupation;** a group of identical positions; or a discrete unit of work. 2. A *job action* is a strike or work slow-down, usually by public employees. *Job analysis* is the determination of a position's specific tasks and of the knowledge, skill and ability that an incumbent should possess. This information can then be used in making recruitment and selection decisions, creating selection de-vices, developing compensation systems, approving train-ing needs, etc. See also **functional job analysis.** For *job audit,* see **desk audit.** A *job bank* is a computer fed each day with information on new job openings and on jobs just filled. Its daily printout provides up-to-the-minute information for all job-seekers, greater exposure of employers' needs, and a faster referral of job applicants. A *job ceiling* is the maximum number of employees au-thorized at a given time. *Job coding* is a numbering sys-tem used to categorize jobs according to their *job families* or other areas of similarity. For example, all positions in a clerical series might be given numbers from 200 to 299 with higher numbers usually indicating higher skill levels within a series. A *job cycle* is the amount of time required for an employee to perform a discrete unit of work. *Job depth* is a measure of the relative freedom that the incum-

277

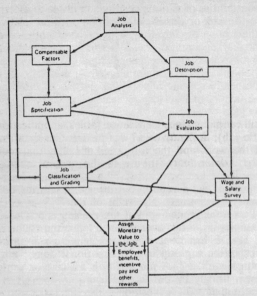

JOB ANALYSIS INFORMATION FLOW

bent of a **position** has in the performance of assigned duties. A *job description* (or *definition*) is a formal statement of the duties, qualifications, and responsibilities of a particular job. Its purpose is to give both employer and employee a clear understanding of what the employee should do, how it should be done, and why it should be done that way. *Job design* (or *redesign*) is a general term for increasing job satisfaction or **productivity** by making jobs more interesting and efficient. *Job dilution* is dividing a relatively sophisticated job into parts that can be performed by less skilled labor. *Job enlargement* is adding additional, similar duties to a job. *Job enrichment* is building into lower-level jobs the factors that make work at higher levels of an organization more satisfying and more responsible. Two such factors would be personal responsibility for discrete units of work and the ability to set one's own pace within an overall schedule. See **job loading.** *Job evaluation* is a formal comparison of the duties and responsibilities of various positions in order to ascertain the worth, rank or **classification** of one position relative to all others in an organization. This involves both job content and market conditions. *Job factors* are main elements of a factor evaluation system that group the various aspects of a job into specific categories. While there are an infinite number of specific factors that pertain to differing jobs, the factors themselves can usually be categorized within the following groupings: *job requirements* (the knowledge, skill, and ability needed to perform the duties of a specific job); *difficulty of work* (the complexity or intricacy of the work and the associated mental demands of the job); *responsibility* (the freedom of action required by a job and the impact of the work performed upon the organizational mission); *personal relationships* (the importance of interpersonal relationships to the success of mission accomplishment); and *other factors* such as physical demands, working conditions, accountability, or number of workers directed). A *job family* is a group or series of jobs in the same general occupational area, such as accounting or engineering. A *job freeze* is a temporary, formal halt to an organization's discretionary hiring and promoting. *Job grading* is the process of **position ranking.** *Job loading* is assigning a job more, different duties: "horizontal" for more of the same level, and "vertical" for increased responsibility and recognition. A *job lot* is a quantity of goods that is available in an amount less than the market unit of sale for that product; or a quantity of mixed goods, often leftovers and incomplete batches, bought at one time for one low price. See **odd lot.** A *job number* is assigned to each job or batch to readily identify it during the manufacturing process. A *job order* is a document authorizing the production (or delivery) of goods or services. A *job order cost system* is a way of collecting costs in which each job is treated as a separate unit. It is used by manufacturers who produce on order separate lots of clearly distinguishable goods. *Job range* is a measure of the number of different tasks that a job has. *Job ranking,* the most rudimentary method of *job evaluation,* simply ranks jobs in order of their importance to an organization. *Job restructuring* occurs when an employer finds it necessary to rearrange or adjust the contents (tasks performed) of jobs within a system because of economic conditions, technological changes, and the inability to fill vacant positions among other reasons. *Job rotation* is the transfer of a worker from one assignment to another in order to minimize boredom or enhance skills. For *job sampling,* see **work sampling.** *Job satisfaction* is the totality of an employee's feelings about the various aspects of his or her work; an emotional appraisal of whether one's job lives up to one's values. *Job scope* is the relative complexity of a task. This is usually reflected by the *cycle time*—the time it takes to complete the task. *Job security* is the presence of safeguards that protect an employee from capricious assignments, demotion, or discharge. *Job sharing* has two persons—each working part-time—sharing one whole job. A *job shop* is a manufacturer with custom-order capability; a functional organization for production which has a product travel from one work center (drilling, soldering, etc.) to another; or an employment agency. For *job specification,* see **specification.** For *job spoiler,* see **ratebuster.** A *job ticket* is a report of how much time was spent on a task; also known as a *time ticket.* *The Job Training Partnership Act* provides for job-training programs to be planned and implemented under the joint control of local elected officials and private industry councils in service delivery areas designated by the governor of each state. A *job-vacancy rate* is the ratio of the number of job vacancies to the sum of actual employment plus vacancies. See also **work.**

Jobber 1. A person who buys and sells for other persons. 2. A **wholesaler.**

Joint Together; as a group; united; undivided. A *joint adventure* (or *enterprise* or *venture*) is a "one-shot" grouping together of two or more persons in a business. If they have a continuing relationship, it may be a **partnership.** *Joint and several* means both together and individually. For example, a **liability** or debt is *joint and several* if the creditor may sue the debtors either as a group (with the result that the debtors would have to split the loss) or individually (with the result that one debtor might have to pay the whole thing). A *joint bank account* is a bank account held in the names of two or more persons, each of whom has full authority to put money in or take it out, and all of whom share equally in the money. *Joint bargaining* occurs when two or more unions unite to

negotiate with a single employer. *Joint costs* are costs
incurred for two or more products prior to the point that
they separate and become *joint products*. *Joint costs* occur
when two or more products are the result of one production process and there is no logical way of apportioning
costs between them. A *joint council* is a labor-management
committee established to resolve disputes arising during
the life of a **contract**. *Joint debtors acts* are either state
laws that allow a judge to grant a **judgment** for or against
some defendants who owe money and allow the trial to go
on against the others, or state laws that allow a plaintiff to
go ahead with a lawsuit and get a judgment against every
defendant when only some of the defendants who owe
money have been served with **process** (formally told to
show up in court). *Joint demand* occurs when goods (or
services) are usually sold together; an increase in the
demand for one would cause a corresponding increase in
demand for the other. Examples include gasoline and
tires, baseballs and baseball gloves, computers and software, etc. *Joint products* are two or more products made
from the same materials. Joint products are of approximately equal value. If not, the products of lesser value
are known as **by-products**. A *joint purchasing agreement*
is a formal agreement among two or more organizations
to purchase professional services, equipment or supplies.
The agreements simplify purchasing and result in **economies of scale** which lower costs. A *joint return* is a single
income tax report filed by both husband and wife. A *joint
stock company* is a company that is more than a **partnership**, but less than a **corporation**. It is similar to a corporation in most ways, but all owners are **liable** for company
debts. For *joint tenant,* see **tenant**. A *joint through rate*
is the charge for shipping something from a point on one
transportation line to a point on another.

Joker   A clause or phrase inserted in a contract, legislative
bill, or other document that is superficially harmless, but
actually destroys the document's effectiveness.

Journal   A book that is written in regularly, such as an
account book in which all expenses and all money taken
in are written down as they happen.

Journey worker (or journeyman)   1. A person who has
completed **apprenticeship** training in a trade or craft or
who has a certain number of years of proven experience.

See **guild.** *Journey worker's pay* (or *union scale*) is the minimum wage paid to an experienced worker in a particular job in a geographic area. 2. A day worker or hired hand.

Judgment The official decision of a court about the rights and claims of each side in a lawsuit. *Judgment* usually refers to a final decision that is based on the facts of the case and made at the end of a trial. It is called a *judgment on the merits*. For other types of *judgments,* such as **cognovit note, confession of, default, deficiency,** etc., see those words. A *judgment creditor* is a person who has proven a debt in court and is entitled to use court processes to collect it. The person owing the money is a *judgment debtor*. A *judgment note* is the paper a debtor gives to a creditor to allow **confession of judgment.** *Judgment-proof* refers to persons against whom a money *judgment* will have no effect (persons without money, persons protected by wage-protection laws, etc.). A *judgment sample* is a **sample** which is selected on the basis of personal opinion rather than on the theory of probability. Contrast **random sample.**

Judicial sale A sale held under a court **judgment** or **order** or held under court supervision. See also **execution.** It is usually against the owner's wishes to satisfy a debt.

Junior An interest or a right that collects after, or is subordinate to, another interest or right.

Junior board of directors 1. An advisory board under a formal system of **multiple management. 2. A management development** process used to introduce junior executives to top management decisionmaking by allowing them to mirror the activities of, and make advisory recommendations to, the senior **board of directors.**

Junk Not good; not safe. A *junk bond* pays higher interest than other **bonds** because it is a riskier investment. A *junk CD* is a **certificate of deposit** that is a bank's own debt instrument; it is not insured by the federal government. A *junk IOU* is **commercial paper** not backed by **collateral.**

Junket A trip for reporters, critics, buyers, etc., paid for by the company whose products they will review.

Jurisdiction 1. The geographical area within which a court, public official, union, etc. has the right and power to operate. 2. The persons about whom and the subject matters about which a court, public official, union, etc. has the right and power to make decisions that are legally binding.   3. A *jurisdictional dispute* is a conflict between unions, either as to which union should represent certain workers or as to which union's members should do a certain type of work. Strikes based on these disputes have been made illegal because the employer is caught in the middle.

Jury   A group of persons selected by law and sworn in to look at certain facts and determine the truth. *Jury duty pay* is the practice of giving employees leave with pay if they are called to *jury duty*. Many organizations reduce such pay by the amount the employee is paid by the court for jury service.   2. The *jury of executive opinion* is a forecasting technique for making decisions in the face of uncertainty by allowing the collective wisdom of top management to bear upon a problem.

Just   1. Legal or lawful.   2. Morally right; fair. Words like *just cause* and *just compensation* include both meanings (no. 1 and no. 2) of *just*.

Just in time   A **production** and **inventory control** system that calls for parts and materials to be delivered from suppliers to work stations just as they are needed; this avoids the expense of and need for warehousing.

K

K 1. One thousand. In computerese, either 1,000 or 1,024. 2. In newspaper stock transaction tables, an indication, lowercase (k), that **preferred stock** dividends) are in arrears.

KD Knocked down. A shipping term indicating that machinery or equipment will be received by the purchaser in a disassembled condition.

Keep To carry on or manage (a hotel); to tend or shelter (a dog); to maintain continuously (a record book); to store (a box); to continue without change (a ship's course); or to protect (a child).

Kentucky rule The principle that all **dividends** (except for some **stock** dividends) are **income** to a **trust,** not an addition to **principal.**

Keogh Plan (HR10 Plan) A tax-deferred retirement account for persons with self-employment income that is similar to an **individual retirement account.** It is a voluntary **pension** plan. [pronounce: *key*-oh].

Key class Occupations or positions for which data are gathered from other employers (via a **salary survey**) in order to serve as a basis for establishing wage rates.

Key industry Any industry of such size and importance that its health is considered a **barometer** of the nation's economy.

Key-person insurance see **business life insurance.**

Key punch A machine which perforates tabulating cards for data processing systems. Blank cards, containing rows of numbers, must be punched with the desired information before processing of the data can begin. The *key punch operator* inserts the card and uses a *keyboard* to transfer information to the card. The punch perforates the blank card in a pattern which corresponds to this information. The punched cards then serve as *input* for the data-processing system.

Keying Measuring the effectiveness of an advertising medium by having customers respond to differing box or department numbers. For example, the same ad in each of several magazines might have responses sent to different post office boxes.

Kick upstairs A slang term for the removal of an individual from a position where his or her performance is not thought satisfactory by promotion to a higher position in the organization.

Kickback Employers or third parties who extort money from employees or **contractors** by threatening to sever or have severed the employment relationship are soliciting *kickbacks*. Most kickbacks are obviously unethical if not illegal. The Copeland Act prohibits kickbacks by federal contractors and subcontractors. More generally, it is also a *kickback* to give a company or government employee something for doing a favor for another company.

Kicker 1. Loan charges in addition to the **interest.** 2. Any extra charge or penalty.

KISS principle Keep It Simple, Stupid.

Kiting Writing checks on an **account** before money is deposited to cover them.

Knocked down 1. Unassembled when packaged. 2. Auctioned off.

L

L   In newspaper **stock** transaction tables, an indication that the stock has reached a new 52-week low.

LCL   Less than carload; a factor in railroad freight rates.

LIBOR   London Interbank Offered Rate. The rate at which banks in London are prepared to lend to high-quality banks. The interest rate on **Eurocurrency** loans is often expressed as a markup, or spread, over *LIBOR*.

LIFO   "Last in, first out." A method of calculating the worth of a merchant's **inventory.** Under this method if a merchant buys a blivit for a dollar, then buys another for two dollars, then sells either blivit, the remaining blivit is worth one dollar. See **FIFO** and **NIFO.**

LTL   Less than truckload; a factor in freight rates.

Label   1. Any writing added onto a larger document.   2. A tag (either temporary or permanent) on a product. A *private label* bears the **brand** of the store which sells it and not the name of the manufacturer.

Labor   A collective term for an organization's workforce exclusive of management or for all workers. For types of *labor,* see those words. A *labor agreement* is the formal result achieved by **collective bargaining.** *Labor costs* are the total expenses an employer must meet to retain the services of employees. The *unit labor cost* is the expense for labor divided by the number of units of output produced. A *labor costs audit* is made to determine whether the services received for the salaries paid are adequate and that salary expenditures are applied correctly in determining the costs of manufactured goods. The *Labor Department* is the U.S. cabinet department that regulates working conditions, labor-management relations, minimum wages, discrimination, unemployment insurance, workers' compensation, pension rights, etc. However, the **National Labor Relations Board** (NLRB) is an independent agency.

A *labor dispute* is a controversy between an employer and employees or an employer and a union involving wages, hours, working conditions, or the question of who has the right to speak for the employees. The *labor efficiency variance* is the difference between standard and actual direct labor hours expended in manufacturing under a **standard cost system.** A *labor grade* is one of a series of steps in a wage-rate structure established by a process of **job evaluation** or **collective bargaining.** *Labor intensive* refers to any production process requiring a large proportion of human effort relative to **capital** investment. For the *Labor-Management Relations Act,* see **Taft-Hartley Act.** For the *Labor-Management Reporting and Disclosure Act,* see the **Landrum-Griffin Act.** The *labor movement* is an inclusive term for the history of U.S. unionism. A *labor organization* is any group, whether or not a labor **union** and whether or not formally organized, that deals with pay, hours, or any other working conditions or **grievances.** For *labor organizer,* see **organizer.** The *labor pool* is the group of trained workers from which prospective employees are recruited. *Labor racketeer* is a broad term that applies to a union leader who uses his or her office as a base for unethical and illegal activities. The *labor rate variance* is the difference between direct labor paid at the standard rate and at the actual rate in a **standard cost system.** The *labor theory of value* is the theory that the value of a product is dependent on or determined by the amount (or value) of the labor needed to produce it. A *labor time ticket* is a form or a computer record used to distribute the total hours worked to specific job orders or to types of production operations. In plants where workers are paid on a straight piece rate basis or salary plus production bonus, labor time tickets also include information on quantities produced for payroll purposes. For *labor union,* see **union.**

Laboratory training   A general term for training exercises that are designed to increase an individual's sensitivity to the motives and behaviors of self and others and to analyse those elements of interpersonal interactions that either help or hurt a group's **effectiveness.** *Sensitivity training* is the most common form of laboratory training. This is the popular name given to almost all *experience-based learning* exercises—artificial experiences which seek to simulate real life. The basic vehicle for sensitivity training is the *T-Group* (T for Training). *Laboratory method* or *laboratory education* are terms used interchangeably for all the formal means of learning about human behavior through experiencing group activities that have been specially created for such a purpose.

Laborer's lien See **mechanic's lien.**

Laden in bulk Carrying loose cargo such as grain rather than carrying containers of grain or individual items such as chairs.

Lading See **bill of lading.**

Lagging indicator An **economic time series** which measures such factors as **inventories,** unemployment beyond 15 weeks, expenditures for new plant and equipment, etc. These indicators serve mainly to complete the history of a **business cycle** by experiencing its highs and lows several months after a general change in overall economic activity. See **leading indicator.**

Laissez faire (French) The theory of a free economy in which the government does not meddle with private economic decisions. The word also refers to a "hands off" style of leadership that emphasizes loose supervision. [pronounce: *lay*-say fair]

Lame duck 1. An elected official who is serving out the end of a term after someone else has been elected to take his or her place. Since the official will soon be leaving, the official's authority is considered impaired or *lame.* The term is used in an organizational sense to refer to anyone whose leaving has been announced, whether for retirement, promotion, transfer, etc. 2. An investor in stock who has overbought and cannot meet financial commitments.

Land In the law, *land* is not just the surface. It includes everything underneath plus the airspace above, and means the same thing as **real estate** or property. The *land bank* refers to either a federal program in which land is taken out of agricultural production and used for conservation or trees (also called *soil bank*) or to a federally created bank that makes low-interest farm loans. A *land sales contract* is a **contract** for the sale of real estate, not recorded in the land records, in which the seller keeps **title** to the property until an agreed future time. This is often done to keep a low interest rate on an existing **mortgage.**

Also called a *contract for deed* and *installment contract.* One common type, a **land contract mortage,** permits a seller to hold onto his or her original below-market rate mortgage while "selling" the home on an **installment** basis. The installment payments are for a short term and may be for **interest** only. At the end of the contract the unpaid balance, frequently the full purchase price, must still be paid. The seller continues to hold title to the property until all payments are made. Thus the buyer acquires no **equity** until the contract ends. These loans are popular because they offer lower payments than market rate loans. Land contracts are also being used to avoid the **due on sale clause.** The buyer and seller may assert to the lender who provided the original mortage, that the due on sale clause does not apply because the property will not be sold until the end of the contract. Therefore, the low interest rate continues. However, the lender may assert that the contract in fact represents a sale of the property. Consequently, the lender may have the right to call it due or raise the interest rate to current market levels.

Landrum-Griffin Act   A federal law to curb union corruption, especially in financial dealings and election procedures. It also gave several new rights to individual union members (such as the requirement that unions must have a fair constitution). It is formally called the *Labor-Management Reporting and Disclosure Act of 1959.*

Lapping   Stealing or "borrowing" from an employer by taking money paid by a customer, not recording the payment, then covering the theft by putting the next customer's payment into the first's account, and so on.

Last dollar coverage   Insurance coverage without upper limits or maximums no matter how great the benefits payable. See **first dollar coverage.**

Last in, first out   See **LIFO.**

Last offer arbitration   See **final offer arbitration.**

Latent   Hidden. For example, a *latent defect* is something wrong (with an article sold or with the validity of a legal document) that cannot be discovered by ordinary observation or care. In this sense, its opposite is **patent.** Compare to **hidden agenda.**

Lateral entry   Appointment of an individual from outside of the organization to a position above the bottom level of a generally recognized **career ladder.**

Launder To "wash" illegally obtained money by placing it in a legitimate business.

Law 1. That which must be obeyed. 2. A **statute;** an act of a legislature. 3. The whole body of principles, standards, and rules put out by a government. 4. The principles, standards, and rules that apply to a particular type of situation; for example, **contract law.** 5. Any theory or principle. 6. A *law day* (or *date*) is a court-set day after which a **mortgagee** can no longer pay off a debt on real estate and get the land back from **foreclosure.** The *law merchant* is the generally accepted customs of merchants. These customs have standardized over the years and become a part of the formal law. The *law of demand* is that, in general, **demand** for an item falls as its price rises. There are many exceptions to the "law." The *first law of demand* holds that the rate of individual demand will not increase with a rise in prices. The *second law of demand* holds that the *substitution effect* (the purchase of less expensive products) is greater the longer that prices remain higher than they were before. The *law of diminishing returns* is that, in general, there comes a point where one more unit of energy (or other input) expended will produce less of a result than the last one did. In a production process there is a point at which the **return** upon invested **capital** and labor are at a maximum; beyond this point, the application of further capital and labor will not cause a proportionate increase in the rate of return. The *law of downward sloping demand* is a version of the *law of demand:* more of a product will sell at lower, rather than higher prices. The *law of supply and demand* is that prices and values tend to vary directly with demand and inversely with supply.

Layaway Putting down a deposit to hold a purchase for later pickup. This is *not* necessarily an **installment** sale involving credit.

Layoff A temporary or indefinite loss of a job due to a reduction in work to be done. **Seniority** rights are usually kept.

Lead time 1. The time expected between the completion of planning and the start of operations. In manufacturing, this is a preliminary **production** scheduling phase to coordinate the flow of raw materials and work-in-progress among machines, work centers, or plants. 2. In **inventory**

control, the elapsed time between placing an inventory order and its arrival. The shorter the procurement lead time, the smaller the order need be.

Leader prices Bargain prices designed to get the customer into the store in the expectation that other full price items will be bought as well. See **loss leader.**

Leadership The exercise of **authority,** whether formal or informal, in directing and coordinating the work of others. See **charismatic leadership, contingency management-effectiveness, functional leadership,** and **management** and **manager.**

Leading indicator An **economic time series** which measures such factors as new building permits, new business formations, average workweeks, stock market prices, new unemployment insurance applicants, etc. It seeks to anticipate movements in the **business cycle** from 1 to 12 months ahead of the actual activity. Each month the **Bureau of Economic Analysis** of the Department of Commerce publishes data on hundreds of economic indicators in its *Business Conditions Digest.* Several dozen of these are classified as "leading." The Bureau's composite index of 12 leading indicators is a popular means of assessing the general state of the economy. For contrasting terms, see **coincident indicator** and **lagging indicator.**

Learning curve In industry, the learning curve concept holds that when workers repeatedly perform a task, the amount of labor required per unit of output decreases according to a constant pattern. Generally speaking, with traditional, mass-production processes, each time output doubles, the new average of effort per unit should decline by a certain percentage, and so on for each successive doubling of output. Of course, as production processes become more dependent upon machines, the learning curve becomes less and less significant. The *learning curve* as a concept in *training* describes a learning process in which increases in performance are large at the beginning but become smaller with continued practice. Learning of any new thing eventually levels off as mastery is attained, at which point the curve becomes horizontal. This is called a *learning plateau.*

Lease A **contract** for the use of land or buildings, but not for their ownership. The **lessor** is called the **landlord** and the **lessee** is the **tenant.** 2. A contract for the use of something, but not for its ownership. 3. A long-term loan of something in exchange for money. Also, a *sublease* is a lease made to another person by a person to whom something is leased. 4. For special types of *leases* such as a **mineral lease** and **percentage lease,** see those words.

Leaseback   A sale of property with a **lease** of the same property from the buyer back to the seller. This is often done with land or industrial equipment for tax purposes.

Leasehold   Land or buildings held by lease.

Least and latest rule   Pay the least amount of taxes legally possible as late as legally possible.

Least developed countries   Those **developing countries** without significant economic growth, with very low per capita incomes, and with low literacy rates.

Ledger   A business **account** book, usually recording the day-to-day transactions, and usually showing **debits** and **credits** separately.

Legacy   1. A gift of money by will. 2. A gift of personal property (anything but real estate) by will. 3. A gift of anything by will.

Legal   1. Required or permitted by law. 2. Not forbidden by law. 3. Concerning or about the law. 4. *Legal capital* is variously defined as the **par** or stated value of a company's stock; the amount of money a company must keep to protect its creditors; or property with enough value to balance a company's stock **liability.** A *legal description* is the identification of a piece of land that is precise enough to locate it without ambiguity and to show any **easements** or reservations. This may be done by government survey, recordation of precise measurements, lot numbers on a recorded **plat,** or similar formal means. A *legal entity* is a living person, a **corporation,** or any organization that can sue and be sued or otherwise function legally as an individual. A *legal holiday* is a day on which normal legal business may not be transacted. This varies widely from state to state, but the businesses may include **service of process,** court proceedings, banking, etc. For *legal investments* or *legal list,* see **prudent person rule.** A *legal reserve* is the percentage of total funds that an insurance company or a bank must set aside to meet possible claims. For *legal value,* see **par value, book value,** and **face value.**

Lessee   A person who **leases** or rents something *from* someone. A *lessee* of land is a **tenant.**

Lessor A person who **leases** or rents something *to* someone. A *lessor* of land is a *landlord*.

Let To **award** a **contract** (such as a building job) to one of several bidders. 2. To **lease**.

Letter A written document. A *letter of advice* is a **drawer's** (for example, a person who makes out a check) notice to a **drawee** (for example, a bank) that a **draft** (a check for a certain amount to a certain person) has been *drawn* (made out). A *letter of attornment* goes from a landlord to a tenant saying that the property has been sold and telling who now should get the rent payments. A *letter of comment* is a letter from the SEC to persons registering a proposed sale of **securities** (stocks, etc.) that the **registration** statement does not comply with law and must be changed. A *letter of credit* is a statement by a bank or other financer that it will back up or pay the financial obligations of a merchant involved in a particular sale. It may be a **negotiable instrument** to pay a certain sum, a letter that the person's **credit** is good to a certain amount, or something in between. *Import, export* and *travelers' letters* authorize a foreign bank to cash checks or make other payments in local currency to be reimbursed by the bank that writes the letter. A *stand-by letter of credit or guarantee letter of credit* is a way of financing multinational corporations. Such a corporation asks its U.S. bank to issue a letter of credit in favor of the foreign bank from which its overseas **subsidiary** or **affiliate** seeks to borrow. If the foreign operation does not repay its loan, the foreign bank then draws upon the stand-by letter of credit. Otherwise, the letter of credit is not used. A *letter of intent* is a preliminary understanding that forms the basis of an intended contract; for example, a letter (often from a government agency) to a **contractor** stating that a contract **award** will be made. This gives the contractor some, but not all, of the rights of a signed contract. A *letter ruling* is a written answer to the **IRS** to a taxpayer about how the tax laws apply to a specific set of facts (often a proposed transaction). Sometimes this is called a *private letter ruling* because it is advice for one specific situation and one specific person only. *Letter stock* is **stock** that does not need to be **registered** with the **SEC** because buyers give the seller a letter saying that the stock will be held for investment and not resold for a long time.

Level annual premium funding A method of setting up a **pension** so that after the pension costs for a new employee are **actuarially** determined, pension contributions or premiums are paid into a **fund** (or to an insurance company) in equal installments during the employee's remaining working life so that upon retirement the pension benefit is fully funded.

Leverage 1. Any borrowing (especially for investment purposes). 2. Putting down a small investment (usually as a down payment) to control a large amount of **stock** (and usually borrowing the rest). This makes the eventual profit or loss quite large when compared to the money actually put up if the price of the stock changes. A *leveraged buy-out* allows a small group to take over a target company by using company assets as **collateral** to finance much of the debt incurred in the takeover. 3. The proportion of a company's **bonds** and **preferred stock** compared to its **common stock.** The common stock is called *highly leveraged* if there is proportionately little common stock, because small changes in the company's income can result in big changes in the stock's value, since payments that must be made on bonds and preferred stock are large, but unchanging. 4. *Leverage ratios* are measures of the degree to which the owners or the creditors have financed a firm. The leverage ratio, also known as the *debt ratio,* is total debt divided by the total assets. See **debt-equity ratio** and **fixed-charge coverage.** 5. A *leveraged lease* is a deal in which leased items are financed by a third person. This is often done to shift tax benefits from users of the property to the owners who gain more. See **equity investor.**

Liability A broad word for legal obligation, responsibility, or debt. If you have a liability, you are *liable* for it. In a business context, *liabilities* are *current* if due within the current **fiscal** year, *long-term* if not, and *contingent* if dependent on an uncertain event. A *liability reserve* anticipates a future claim against cash, the exact amount of which may be unknown but can be estimated with a reasonable degree of accuracy; for example, taxes, insurance, and interest.

License Formal permission to do something specific; for example, the *license* given by one company to another to manufacture a **patented** product. A *governmental license* is a permission granted to an individual or organization by competent authority to engage in a practice, occupation or activity otherwise unlawful. A *license tax* is a tax exacted (either for revenue raising or for regulation) as a condition to the exercise of a business or non-business privilege, at a flat rate or measured by such bases as **capital** stock, capital surplus, number of business units, or capacity. It excludes taxes measured directly by transactions, gross or net income, or value of property except those to which only nominal rates apply.

Licensee 1. A person who holds a **license.** 2. A person who is on property with permission, but without any enticement by the owner and with no financial advantage to the owner; often called a *mere licensee* as opposed to an invitee in negligence law. In some situations, an invited personal guest is a *licensee, not an invitee.*

Lien A claim, charge, or **liability** against property that is allowed by law, rather than one that is part of a **contract** or agreement. For example, a *mechanic's lien* is the right of a worker to hold property worked on until paid for the services; and a *tax lien* is the government's placing of a financial obligation on a piece of property that must be paid because taxes have not been paid. Other types of *liens* include **judgment,** landlord's, maritime, etc. [procounce: leen]) For *lien creditor,* see **secured creditor.** A *lien theory state* (or *jurisdiction*) is a state in which a **mortgage** is considered a *lien* on property, and the **title** does not transfer to the lender.

Life cycle From beginning to end. For *life cycle of product,* see **product life cycle.** *Life cycle costs* are the costs of buying (or leasing, renting, etc.), operating, servicing and disposing of a product. *Life cycle estimates* are all anticipated costs directly and indirectly associated with an alternative during all stages: preoperational, operational, and terminal.

Like-kind exchange A trade of certain types of business property that will not be taxed. There are detailed **IRS** rules.

Limit order See **order.**

Limited 1. Partial or restricted. For example, *limited liability* is the legal rule that the owners (shareholders) of a **corporation** cannot usually be sued for **corporate** actions and, thus, the most they can usually lose is the value of

their investment. But see **piercing the corporation veil.**
2. *Limited* is the British and Canadian word for **corporation.**
It is abbreviated "Ltd." 3. A *limited partnership* is a
special form of unincorporated business ownership, available under most state laws, that allows the business to be
run by *general partners* and financed partly by *limited
partners,* who may take no part in running the business
and have no **liability** for business losses, lawsuits, etc.,
beyond the money they put in.

Lincoln incentive plan A combination **profit sharing** and
piecework incentive system which incorporates many aspects of **industrial democracy** and is famous for the fact
that employees have received bonuses of up to 150 percent of their base pay.

Line A place where production occurs; a row or a column.
Line balancing is a production method which provides for
an even flow of product from one work station to another
in order to avoid idle time at any one station. See *line of
balance technique.* A *line item budget* is the classification
of budgetary **accounts** according to narrow, detailed objects of expenditure (such as motor vehicles, clerical workers, or reams of paper) used within each organization unit
generally without reference to the ultimate purpose or
objective served by the expenditure. For *line of authority,*
see **scalar chain.** A *line of balance technique* is a method
of follow-up and control used to forecast production progress or trouble. It uses a three-part chart and reports of
work accomplished at certain key points along the production line. The *line of command* is the route through
which orders pass from top to bottom in an organization.
A *line of credit* is the promise of **credit** up to a certain
maximum that a merchant or bank will give to a customer, usually for an ongoing series of loans and pay-
backs. A *line organization* is the simplest form of
organizational structure in which there is a direct line of
responsibility and control from the very top to the very
bottom. *Line personnel* are those who directly carry
out the essential tasks of an organization. Production,
sales, and finance departments are usually considered line
or operating units. For contrast, see **staff.** A *line printer* is
a high-speed computer printer that prints a line at a time
rather than a character at a time.

Linear responsibility chart A graphic presentation of organizational structure and functional operations (the vertical portion) combined with a distribution of responsibilities across department lines (the horizontal portion).

Link financing One person depositing a **compensating balance** in a bank for another person's loan.

Liquid 1. Having enough money to carry on normal business. A "live" business is *liquid*, but a "dead" business is *liquidated* (made *liquid* in the totally different sense of being turned entirely into cash).   2. Easily turned into cash. *Liquid assets* consists of money in bank accounts plus **stocks, bonds** and anything else that could be readily sold.

Liquidate 1. Pay off or settle a debt.   2. Adjust or settle the amount of a debt.   3. Settle up affairs and distribute money, such as the money left by a company that goes out of business.

Liquidated 1. Paid or settled up.   2. Determined, settled, or fixed. For example, a *liquidated claim* is a claim or debt with a definite amount fixed either by agreement or by a court's action.

Liquidation 1. See **liquidate.**   2. Winding up business and ending a company. A proportionate distribution of **assets** among a business's stockholders or creditors may be called a *liquidation dividend*.

Liquidity 1. See **liquid.**   2. The ability to turn **assets** easily into cash.   3. In foreign trade, a country's international purchasing power.   4. *Liquidity preference* is an individual (or aggregate) desire to hold currency or **demand** deposits rather than equivalent amounts of **securities.** *Liquidity ratios* are measures of how adequately a firm can, if it has to, meet all short-term obligations. See **current ratio, quick (acid test) ratio,** and **cash ratio.** A *liquidity trap* occurs when any further increases in a nation's money supply would be hoarded in liquid form rather than invested.

Lis pendens 1. A pending lawsuit.   2. A warning notice that **title** to property is in litigation and that anyone who buys the property gets it with legal strings attached.

List 1. See **listing.**   2. See **docket.**   3. *List price* is the price of goods set by the manufacturer. It may be reduced for many reasons.

Listed security A **stock** or other **security** that has met the requirements of an **exchange** (financial reports, supervision, etc.) and is traded on that exchange. Stock can

Listing 298 **Loan**

sometimes be traded without being listed and listed without being traded.

Listing 1. A **real estate agent's** right to sell land. An *open* or *general listing* is the right to sell that may be given to more than one agent at a time. An *exclusive agency listing* is the right of one agent to be the only one other than the owner who may sell the property during a period of time. An *exclusive authorization to sell listing* is a written **contract** that gives one agent the sole right to sell the property during a time period. This means that even if the owner finds the buyer, the agent will get a **commission.** *Multiple listing* occurs when an agent with an exclusive listing shares information about the property sale with many members of a real estate association and shares the sale commission with an agent who finds the buyer. A *net listing* is an arrangement in which the seller sets a minimum price he or she will take for the property, and the agent's commission is the amount the property sells for over that minimum selling price. 2. See **listed security.**

Living trust A **trust** that will take effect while the person setting it up is still alive, as opposed to one set up under a will. It is also called an *inter vivos trust.*

Lloyd's of London The world's largest association of insurance underwriters (persons and companies that insure things).

Load 1. That part of **insurance, mutual fund,** or other business charges that represents **commissions** and selling costs. 2. Put data or instructions into a computer; in particular, transfer it from external storage (such as a **disk**) to internal computer storage. 3. *Loading* compares the total work to be done against the individual work center capabilities and then assigns work to the specific areas and facilities that can handle it. *Scheduling* is an extension of loading; it is the time-phasing of loading. While loading assigns work, scheduling determines when the work will be started and finished.

Loan A lending or advance of money or property which the borrowing person or organization promises to repay. To be a loan, there must be a sum of money, or certain property; delivery or placing of it in the account of the borrower; an agreement that it will be returned; and *usually* an agreement that **interest** will be paid at an agreed rate. Loans may be *straight,* or *flat,* meaning that they are for a definite term of days or years, and that the borrower pays only interest on the **principal.** Loans also may be **amortized,** meaning that the borrower pays back part of the principal at periodic intervals, instead of returning the lump sum at the end of the term of the loan. A *loan commitment* is a promise by a bank, mortgage company, etc., that it will lend a buyer a certain amount of money at a certain rate for a certain length of time on a particular piece of property and hold the loan open for a certain length of time for the buyer to complete the real estate purchase. A *loan discount* (often called "points"), is a one-time charge used to adjust the **yield** on the loan to what the market conditions demand. It is used to offset constraints placed on the yield by state or federal regulations. Each "point" is equal to one percent of the mortgage amount. A *loan guarantee* is an agreement by which a government pledges to pay part or all of the loan principal and interest to a lender or holder of a security in the event of default by a third-party borrower. The purpose of a *guaranteed loan* is to reduce the risk borne by a private lender by shifting all or part of the risk to the government. A *loan ratio* is a comparison of the amount of a loan to the value of the property on which the loan is made. The closer together the two numbers are, the higher the interest a bank is likely to charge for the loan. A *loan shark* is a person who lends money at an interest rate higher than the legal maximum or who uses extortion to get repaid. A *loan value* is the highest amount a lender will lend (or can safely lend) on a piece of property, on a life insurance policy, etc.

Loaned servant doctrine The legal principle that in most cases when an employer lends a person to another employer, that person becomes an employee of the second employer for many purposes, such as **liability** to others.

Local Nearby. A *local agent* is a person who takes care of a company's business in a particular area. Many states require a company doing business in the state to **register** a *local agent* for the **service** of **process** for lawsuits against the company. A *local assessment* (or *local improvement assessment*) is a tax on only those properties benefiting from an improvement such as a sidewalk or sewer. A *local union* is affiliated with a national or international union, while a *local independent* is not.

Locative calls The description of land in a **deed** or other document by using landmarks, physical objects, and other things by which the land can be precisely located and identified.

Lockbox system First, a company's customers send payments to a local post office box, then a local bank collects the payments and sends them on to the company's main bank, sometimes sending lists of the checks ahead. This is a common form of *concentration banking,* in which local payments feed into local banks for transfer.

Locked in 1. A person is *locked in* who has profits on **stocks** or other **securities,** but who will have to pay a high tax on them if he or she sells them now. 2. A person may also be *locked in* who owns an **option** to purchase something at a certain price even if the price goes up.

Lockout An employer's refusal to allow employees to work. This is not an individual matter between an employer and a single employee, but a tactic in employer-union disputes. The closing of a business in order to pressure the employees and the union to accept the employer's offered terms of employment is the employer's version of a strike.

Lock up An agreement (typically a contractual offer of **assets** or **stock**) between two parties in a **merger** or acquisition which makes it difficult for a third party to interfere.

Lodge An organizational unit of some labor unions, equivalent to a local union.

Logistics See **business logistics.**

Logo A symbol used by a company as its emblem.

Lombard Street London's Wall Street.

Long (or long position) A person who has large amounts of **stock** or who has contracted to buy large amounts of stock for future delivery in expectation of a price rise is called *long* and has a *long position.*

Long-arm statute A state law that allows the courts of that state to claim **jurisdiction** over (decide cases directly involving) persons or property outside the state. Even with a *long-arm statute,* a person cannot be sued unless he or she has certain *minimal contacts* with the state.

Long run 1. A time so far in the future that **fixed costs** can no longer be predicted. 2. Any period of time beyond the *current* or next **fiscal** period.

Long-term debt Debt payable more than one year later or in the next fiscal year. *Long-term debt offsets* are **reserves** and **sinking funds.**

Longevity pay Salary additions based on length of service.

Loophole Someone else's way of legally avoiding taxes. See **deduction, credit, exclusion,** etc. for *your* way.

Loose-leaf service A set of books in loose-leaf binders that gives up-to-the-minute reports on one area of business or law, such as federal taxes. As the techniques or law change, new pages replace old ones. Three big publishers of these are Prentice-Hall, Commerce Clearing House, and Bureau of National Affairs.

Loss A broad word that can mean anything from *total loss* (dropping a coin accidentally in the ocean) through *partial loss* (a drop in the value of a **stock**) to *technical loss* ("loss" of an eye might mean the loss of the use of the eye for practical purposes). In general, the financial and legal uses of the word are close to its ordinary use. For various types of *loss,* such as **capital, casuality, general average, hobby,** etc., see those words. *Loss* is most frequently used in a **balance sheet,** tax, or **insurance** context. A *loss leader* is merchandise sold below cost to attract customers who may buy other items. When this is done with no intention of selling the promised items, it is called **bait and switch.** A *loss payable clause* is a provision in an insurance policy that lists the order of payments if the insurance is not enough to pay everyone involved. A *loss ratio* is the proportion between insurance premiums collected and loss claims paid.

Lot 1. An individual piece of land. 2. A thing or group of things that is part of one separate sale or delivery. 3. The number of **shares** of a **stock** or other **security** that is the normal minimum trading size. See **odd lot** and **round lot.**

Low-balling Getting a **contract** by agreeing to a price that is unrealistically low in anticipation that extras associated with the job (subsequent contracts or contract adjustments) will make the contract profitable in an overall sense.

Lower of cost or market A method for **inventory** valuation in which the cost of goods is compared to current replacement price (the market price) as of a **balance sheet** date; the lower of the two values is then reported.

Lump-sum settlement   1. Payment of an entire amount of money owed at one time, rather than in payments.   2. Payment at one time of less than an entire amount owed or in dispute.   3. Payment of a fixed amount of money to take care of an obligation that might otherwise have gone on indefinitely.

M

M In newspaper financial transaction tables, an indication, lowercase (m), that a **bond** has matured and is not earning **interest** anymore.

MBA Master of Business Administration.

MBO **Management by objectives.**

MIS **Management information system.**

MIT A **market-if-touched** order.

MM Master of Management.

MPA Master of Public Administration.

MPPM Master of Public and Private Management.

MSBA Master of Science in Business Administration.

MSIA Master of Science in Administration.

MSIM Master of Science in Management.

MTN **Multilateral trade negotiations.**

Machine hour A method of allocating expenses based upon the number of hours a machine is used in the manufacturing process, usually where machines are the predominant factor in the production operation. Time-meter records also show when individual machines are due for periodic servicing and help allocate **overhead** expenses such as electric power, **depreciation,** etc.

Machine language A set of instructions which can be directly understood and obeyed by a computer.

Mag card Magnetized card for (usually typewriter) data storage.

Mailbox rule The rule that an **acceptance** of an **offer** is made (and forms a valid **contract**) when it is mailed, so neither the person making the offer nor the person accepting it can take it back after the acceptance is in the mail. This rule applies only in situations where mailing is a reasonable practice. The general principle (that sending, not receipt, makes an acceptance) applies to other ways of communicating also.

Main purpose doctrine   The principle that if the *main purpose* of a person's promise to pay another's debt is the person's own benefit, that promise need not be in writing to be enforceable. This is an exception to the general rule that the promise to pay another's debts must be in writing because it comes under the **statute of frauds.**

Mainframe   A large computer.

Maintenance-of-membership shop   A union security provision found in some **collective bargaining agreements.** It holds that employees who are members of the union at the time the agreement is negotiated, or who voluntarily join the union subsequently, must maintain their membership for the duration of the agreement as a condition of employment.

Major dispute   A *major dispute* in transportation labor law concerns the creation or change of a labor contract, while a *minor dispute* concerns the meaning of an existing contract as it applies to specific situations.

Major medical   Insurance designed to offset the heavy medical expenses resulting from catastrophic or prolonged illness or injuries. Generally, such policies do not provide **first dollar coverage,** but do provide benefit payments of 75 to 80 percent of all types of medical expenses above a certain base amount paid by the insured. Most major medical policies sold as private insurance contain maximums on the total amount that will be paid; thus, they do not provide **last dollar coverage** or complete protection against catastrophic costs. See **third party payment.**

Make-up pay   Allowances paid to piece workers to make up the difference between actual piece-work earnings and guaranteed rates (or statutory minimum wages).

Make whole   Put a person who has suffered legal **damages** back into the financial position he or she was in before the wrong was done.

Maker   1. A person who initially signs a **negotiable instrument** such as a **note,** and by doing so promises to pay on it.   2. A person who signs, creates, or performs something.

Managed trade   A reference to protectionist devices other than **tariffs** which governments, particularly those of the industrialized West, have adopted since the late 1970s, usually to restrict the volume of imports from Japan and the new industrializing countries of the **Third World** (or else to regulate trade between the United States and the

Europen Community). *Managed trade* includes voluntary **quotas,** special levies, **orderly marketing agreements,** and government subsidies to domestic producers. Such measures have chiefly affected the steel, textile, auto, shipbuilding, and electronics industries, and agriculture.

Management Both the people responsible for running an organization and the running process itself; use of numerous resources to accomplish an organizational goal. See **contingency, generic, first-line, principles of, project, reaction, scientific,** and **systems management.** Also see **administration.** *Management accounting* is those aspects of **accounting** such as budgets, cost records, performance reports, etc., which are primarily designed for internal management use, as opposed to **financial accounting,** which is for both internal and external consumption. A *management audit* is any comprehensive examination of the **administrative** operations and organizational arrangements of a company or government agency which uses generally accepted standards of practice for the purpose of evaluation. *Management by exception* is a management **control** process that has a subordinate report to an organizational superior only exceptional or unusual events that might call for decisionmaking on the part of the superior. In this way, a manager may avoid unnecessary detail that only confirms that all is going according to plan. *Management by objectives* is an approach to managing whose hallmark is a mutual—by both organizational subordinate and superior—setting of measurable goals to be accomplished by an individual or team over a set period of time. For *management clause,* see **management rights clause.** A *management committee* is made up of various corporate officers, certain **directors,** and general managers representing important divisions of the company. Its function varies with the particular company, but essentially it serves as coordinator of the company's policies and practices. For *management control,* see **control.** *Management development* is any conscious effort on the part of an organization to provide a manager with skills that he or she might need for future duties (such as rotational assignments or formal educational experiences). A *management information system* is an automated or computer-based system which produces the necessary information in proper form and at appropriate intervals for the *management* of a program

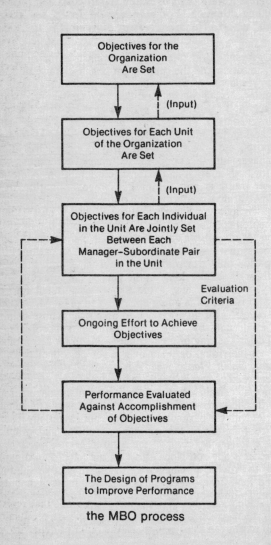

the MBO process

or other activity. The system should measure program progress toward objectives and report costs and problems needing attention. For *management letter,* see **accountants' report.** The *management movement* is the totality of events, starting in the last century, that led to the recognition of *management* as a professional discipline. A *management rights clause* is that portion of a **collective bargaining agreement** that defines the scope of management rights, functions, and responsibilities—essentially all those activities which management can undertake without the consent of the union. *Management science* has three overlapping meanings, depending on who is using the term. First, it means an outgrowth of the **scientific management** movement in which time and efficiency studies were paramount. Second, the phrase refers to the use of sophisticated scientific and mathematical techniques, in particular mathematical modeling, to solve problems in management. In this sense, it overlaps with **operations research.** Finally, *management science* is used to mean the whole field of technical management studies, whether quantitative or qualitative, theoretical or applied. *Management trainee* is the administrative job title loosely assigned to a wide variety of entry-level positions that are often reserved for new college graduates. *Collegiate management* is consensus management by colleagues, as in a **partnership.** See **managerial.**

Manager Generally, any organization member whose job includes supervising others. A *top manager* is one of those who makes policy for, and is responsible for, the overall success of the organziation. A *middle manager* is responsible for the execution and interpretation of top management policies and for the operation of the various departments. A *supervisory manager* is responsible for the final implementation of policies by **rank and file** employees. A *managerialist* believes that organizations should be run by those who are specially trained to do so.

Managerial See **management.** The *managerial grid* is a graphic gridiron which has an X axis locating various degrees of orientation toward production and a Y axis locating various degrees of orientation toward people. Individuals can place themselves at positions that register their relative orientations toward people or production. Grid scores can then be used as the point of departure for a discussion of individual and organizational growth needs. A *managerial philosophy* guides all organizations. It need not be formally expressed; many managers would deny that they have one, but it's always there, stated or unstated, conscious or unconscious, intentional or unintentional.

Mandatory bargaining items Those **collective bargaining** items that each party must bargain over if introduced by the other party.

Manifest A written document that lists goods being shipped or stored, giving descriptions, values, shipping information, etc.

Manipulation A series of **stock** (or other **securities**) transactions intended to raise or lower the price of the stock or to convince others to buy or sell. This is usually done by creating a false impression of active trading or by trying to trigger a major trading trend.

Manning table A **personnel inventory.**

Manpower See **human resources.**

Manufacturer's liability See **strict liability.**

Manufacturers' representative An independent sales representative for two or more manufacturers in a sales territory defined either geographically or by customer classification. The representative, who can be one individual or a group, generally works for a **commission** and carries related product lines so that the sale of one product often leads to the sale of another.

Manufacturing management That aspect of **management** most concerned with **production;** it is responsible for producing particular products at appropriate costs within specified times.

Manufacturing overhead standard The predetermined cost of factory **overhead** that is chargeable to a product.

Manufacturing resource planning A term which combines with **production planning** the *higher* concerns of overall business planning and the *lower* concerns of *master scheduling.*

Margin 1. A boundary or boundary line. 2. The percentage of the cost of a **stock** (or other **security**) that must be paid in cash by the buyer. A **broker** who offers such a *margin* transaction then makes a loan for the balance of the cost, keeping the stock as **collateral** in the *margin account.* 3. For **margin of profit,** see **profit margin.**

Margin call 1. A **stock broker's** demand for more cash or more **collateral;** for example, when a stock bought on **margin** has gone down in value. This is also called *remargining* and is done by others, such as **commodity** dealers. 2. A stock broker's notice to a buyer that a certain stock has been bought and that the purchase price must now be paid.

Marginal Toward the end. *Marginal analysis* is any technique that seeks to determine the point at which the cost of something (for example, an additional employee or machine) will be worthwhile or will pay for itself. *Marginal cost* is the cost of adding one more identical item to a bulk purchase, of manufacturing one more item in a production run, of borrowing one more dollar in a loan, etc. *Marginal efficiency of capital* is either the marginal or declining rate of **return** from increased **capital** investment, or the cost of capital (for an economy as a whole) increasing directly with its greater use; also known as the *marginal efficiency of investment. Marginal employees* are those members of an organization who contribute least to the organization's mission because of their personal nature or the inherent nature of their duties. *Marginal income* is the amount of each sales dollar left after **variable costs** are subtracted. It is then used to pay **fixed costs** and possibly contribute to profits. The *marginal income ratio* (also called the *profit/volume ratio*) is the percentage of sales (in dollars) that is marginal income. *Marginal income analysis* is an approach to **profit planning** which seeks to break down costs according to how they behave in order to quickly determine **break-even points,** gain a measure of a product's profitability, and obtain a basis for sound pricing. *Marginal product* is the increase in total product resulting from the addition of one more unit of input. Also known as *marginal physical productivity and incremental product. Marginal propensity* is the ratio of a change in economic activity to an underlying change in income. The *marginal propensity to consume* is the rate of change in consumption which follows an increase in income. The *marginal propensity to save* is the rate of change in saving with respect to a change in income. For *marginal (tax) rate,* see **tax rate.** *Marginal rate of substitution* is the rate at which one item can replace another while maintaining a constant level of satisfaction.

Marginal revenue is the rate at which **revenue** varies with increases in sales volume; the difference in revenue between selling or not selling one more unit. Also known as *incremental revenue*. *Marginal utility* is the usefulness to a consumer of an additional unit of a commodity as determined by the amount of the existing supply.

Mark A **trademark, service mark, collective mark** or **certification mark** that can be **registered** under federal law because it is "used in commerce" by being displayed on or with a product or service sold or advertised in more than one state or country.

Markdown See **markup.**

Market 1. The geographical region in which a product can be sold, the economic and social characteristics of potential buyers, the **demand** for something, or the price it will sell for if sold. 2. An abbreviation for **stock** market, **commodities** market, or the range of **bid and asked** prices for **over-the-counter** stocks. 3. *Market access* refers to the availability of a national market to exporting countries, i.e., reflecting a government's willingness to permit imports to compete relatively unimpeded with similar domestically produced goods. *Market analysis* is the process of determining the characteristics of the buying market and the measurement of its capacity to buy a commodity. It investigates the potential market for an industry. See **marketing research.** *Market development* is an attempt to increase sales by offering current products to new markets. The *market leader* is the firm with the greatest sales of a given product. A *market letter* is either a brokerage firm's in-house publication (often a newsletter) offering investment advice or a similar publication put out by an investment advisory service. *Market making* is establishing a sales price for **over-the-counter** stocks and other **securities** by placing **bid and asked** quotations. For *market manipulation* see **manipulation.** *Market maturity* is the time in the life of a product when sales level off. For *market order,* see **order.** *Market oriented* means being responsive to the needs of those who buy your product. A *market niche* is a place in the market (such as the high end) where there is little or no competition for a product that fits the niche. For *market penetration,* see **penetration.** *Market price* is either the price at which something has just sold in a particular market or it is **market value.**

For *market research,* see **marketing research.** *Market risk* is the possibility that securities will not sell for a price near the last quoted price. *Market saturation* occurs when few additional widget sales are possible because practically everyone already has a widget. *Market segmentation* calls for the identification of subsets of a market and then the development of the most appropriate **marketing mix** for them. *Market share* is the percentage of sales of a particular item that one company controls in a particular market. *Market value* is the price to which a willing seller and a willing buyer would agree for an item in the ordinary course of trade. It is also called *actual market value, actual value, cash market value, clear market value, current market value, fair cash value, fair market value, fair value, just compensation,* etc. A *market-directed economic system* allows the individual producers and consumers to make their own economic decisions as to what to make, buy, or sell. A *market-if-touched* (MIT) order is an instruction to a securities broker to buy or sell a security if a particular price is touched, meaning reached.

Marketable 1. Easily sold for cash. For example, a *marketable security* is a **stock, bond,** etc., that can be sold in the proper **exchange** or through normal business channels. *Marketable securities* also refers to a company's temporary investments of extra cash in such short-term, low-risk things as **treasury bills** and **commercial paper.** 2. Commercially valid. For example, a *marketable title* to land is ownership that can be freely sold because it is clear of any reasonable doubts as to its validity. *Marketable title acts* are state laws that make it possible to determine whether or not a **title** to land is good by searching the public records for a limited time only (for example, back to forty years ago).

Marketing An extremely broad term which encompasses all those efforts a business makes to sell its products and services. A *marketing channel* is the distribution route that products travel from manufacturer to consumer. The *marketing concept* or *marketing orientation* is a view that the marketing process begins not when a product is manufactured and ready for sale, but before the product is even conceived; conception then becomes a function of perceived market demand. For *marketing contract,* see that term. *Marketing cost analysis* is the examination of

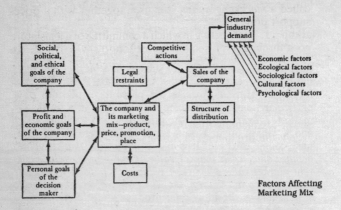

Factors Affecting
Marketing Mix

all those expenses incurred from the time a product is manufactured to the time final payment is received for its sale. *Marketing mix* is a concept that calls for marketing managers to mix the controllable **variables** of product characteristics, price, distribution, service, and promotion in a way that will obtain the most profitable result. For *marketing order*, see that term. *Marketing research* is the systematic gathering and analyzing of information on who is likely to buy what in order to help marketing managers make better decisions on advertising tactics, product design, sales methods, etc. A *marketing target* is a specific group of potential customers. For *marketing utilities,* see **form, place, possession,** and **time utility.** *Pull marketing* seeks to motivate purchasers with the image and quality of a product. *Push marketing* seeks to motivate purchasers with price-off promotions and coupon discounts.

Marketing contract   1. Any agreement between an **agent,** a **broker,** or a merchant and a producer in which goods, **securities,** etc., are sold.   2. An agreement between a producers' **co-operative** and its members in which the members promise to sell through the co-op and the co-op promises to get the best possible price.   3. An **output contract** or a **requirements contract.**

Marketing order   A federally approved limit on the amount of a particular vegetable or other argicultural commodity that can be sold by farmers in a particular area. Also called a *marketing quota,* it is used together with a price-support program.

Markup   1. The meeting in which a committee of a legislature goes through a bill section-by-section to revise it.   2. An amount of money added to the cost of an item to give the merchant selling costs plus a profit. If a merchant buys a shirt for ten dollars and sells it for fifteen, it has a "50 percent markup" or a "five dollar markup."   3. Additions that raise the selling price above the original retail price. Deductions that do not decrease the selling price below the original retail are called *markup cancellations.* A *markdown* reduces the selling price.

Marshaling   1. Arranging, ranking, or disposing of things in order. For example, *marshaling assets and claims* is collecting them up and arranging the debts into the proper order of priority and then dividing up the assets to pay them off. This is done by a **trustee** when someone goes **bankrupt** and by an **executor** or **administrator** during the **probate** of a dead person's estate.   2. The *rule of marshaling* is that if one **creditor** could collect from either of two pots of a **debtor's** money and a second creditor can collect from only one of them, the first creditor will be required to take from the singly claimed pot first.

Mass marketing   Producing and marketing a product aimed at a large proportion of a nation's population.

Mass merchandiser   A big self-service retail or "discount" store. The *mass merchandising concept* holds that low prices and fast turnover will yield a great volume of sales, which will increase profits for retailers.

Mass picketing   When a union wants to indicate broad support for a **strike** it sometimes assembles a "mass" of strikers to picket a place of business in order to discourage nonstrikers from entering the premises.

Mass production   Generally, a high volume of output; but more specifically, *mass production* also assumes product simplification, standardization of parts, continuous production lines, and the maximum use of automatic equipment.

Massachusetts trust   A **business trust.**

Master   1. An employer who has the right to control the actions of an employee.   2. A *special master* is a person appointed by a court to carry out the court's orders in certain types of lawsuits. A *special master* might, for example, supervise the sale of property under a decree that it be sold.   3. A skilled worker in a trade who is qualified to train apprentices.   4. Overall or controlling; for example, a *master agreement* is an agreement between a large union and the leaders of one industry (this becomes a model for labor contracts with each individual company); a *master budget* is the combined budgets of a company's departments; a *master contract* is a basic agreement to buy or lease equipment as needed, each time under the same general terms; a *master policy* is a *group insurance* plan; a *master schedule* is a production planning and control device for coordinating all the major aspects of a manufacturing process, establishing deadline requirements for each major assembly that supports the end item so that the products are ready at the appropriate time and in the appropriate quantity, and translating sales forecasts into production requirements to help insure that production capabilities match anticipated sales.

Matched sale-purchase agreements   When the **Federal Reserve** makes a *matched sale-purchase agreement,* it sells a *security* outright for immediate delivery to a dealer or foreign **central bank,** with an agreement to buy the security back on a specific date (usually within 7 days) at the same price. The reverse of **repurchase agreements,** *matched sale-purchase agreements* allow the Federal Reserve to withdraw **reserves** on a temporary basis.

Matching   An **accounting** concept which holds that expenses should be **recognized** in the same **accounting period** that is used to recognize the revenues they produced.

Matching orders   Giving one **broker** an order to sell a **security** and another broker an order to buy the same security, for the purpose of creating the appearance of activity in the issue. The practice is forbidden by federal law.

Material fact   1. A basic reason for a **contract,** without which it would not have been entered into.   2. A fact that is central to winning or deciding a case.   3. A fact which, if told to an insurer, would influence the insurer to refuse insurance, cancel insurance, or raise its cost.

Materials control   See **inventory control.**

Materials handling   The movement of materials. Movement within a plant has accounted for as much as 25 percent of manufacturing costs.

Materialman   A person who supplies building materials for a construction or repair project. A more general word is *supplier*.

Maternity leave   A formally approved absence from work for childbirth and after. The U.S. Supreme Court has held that **arbitrary** mandatory *maternity leaves* are unconstitutional, and that women forced to take maternity leave cannot be denied their previously accumulated **seniority** rights when they return to work. See **birth leave** and **Pregnancy Discrimination Act.**

Matrix organization   Any organization using a multiple command system in which an employee might be accountable to one superior for overall performance as well as to one or more leaders of particular projects. *Matrix* is a generic term that is used to refer to various organizational structures. See **project management** and **task force.** A *matrix diamond* is a basic structural form of matrix organizations; this is in contrast to the pyramid—the basic structural form of traditional organizations. A *matrix manager* is any manager who shares formal **authority** over a subordinate with another manager.

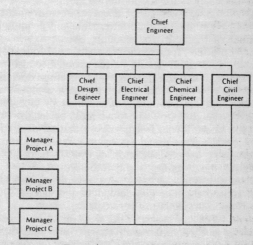

Typical matrix organization

Matrix printer See **dot matrix.**

Matured 1. See **liquidated.** 2. See **maturity.**

Maturity The time when a debt or other obligation becomes due or a right becomes enforceable. It is usually the date when the borrower on a loan, note or bond must pay the full amount of the debt. The *maturity value* is the **face value** plus any unpaid **interest.**

Maturity curve A technique for determining the salaries of professional and technical employees that relates the employee's education and experience to on-the-job performance. For example, after it is determined what the average compensation for a professional employee is for each of various categories of experience, the individual employee is assigned a salary based upon whether he or she is considered average, below average, or above average in performance.

Maximax A decisionmaking principle from **game theory** which calls for choosing the alternative that would maximize chances for the maximum gain at any cost. Only true gamblers use this tactic.

Maximin A decisionmaking principle from **game theory** which calls for choosing the alternative that would maximize the chances for the minimum gain.

Mean A simple average of a set of measurements, obtained by summing the measurements and dividing by the number of them. If, for example, six persons score "10 right" on a test, four score "15 right" and four score "20 right," "14.3 right" would be the *mean.* See also **median** and **mode.** For *mean deviation,* see **average deviation.**

Means test 1. The requirement that if a company makes choices that are potentially *discriminatory* (see **discrimination**), the company's purpose must be legally justified and the *means* it uses to accomplish that purpose (or end) must be the least drastic possible. 2. Any formula for determining the eligibility for, or cost of, receiving something that takes **ability to pay** into account.

Measured day work (or rate) An **incentive** wage plan that is premised upon a guaranteed base wage rate that is based upon previous job performance.

Mechanic's lien A worker's legal claim to hold property (such as a car) until repair charges are paid or to file formal papers securing a right to property (such as a car or a house) until charges for work done are paid.

Mechanization See **automation.**

Median The middle score in a population or distribution;
the 50th percentile; the point that divides the group into
two equal parts. Half of a group of scores fall below the
median and half above it. If the population has an even
number of items, the median is obtained by determining
the **mean** of the two middle values. If, for example, six
persons score "10 right" on a test, four score "15 right,"
and four score "20 right," "15 right" would be the median.
Also, see **mean** and **mode.**

Mediation Outside help in settling a dispute. The person
who does this is called a *mediator*. This is different from
arbitration in that a *mediator* can only persuade, not
force, people into a settlement. The **Federal Mediation
and Conciliation Service (FMCS)** helps to settle **labor
disputes.** *Mediation* and *conciliation* may be used interchangeably for the entrance of an impartial third party
into a labor dispute, but there is a technical distinction.
Conciliation refers to efforts to bring the parties together
so that they may resolve their problems themselves.
Mediation, in contrast, implies that an active effort will be
made to help the parties reach agreement by clarifying
issues, asking questions, and making specific proposals.

Meeting of creditors In the *first* meeting of **creditors,** under **bankruptcy** law, the bankrupt person is questioned,
and claims are made (and allowed or disallowed by the
trustee). *Interim* meetings may do more of the same. A
final meeting closes the bankrupt's affairs prior to a final
court hearing.

Meeting of minds Agreement by each person entering into
a deal on the basic meaning and legal effect of the **contract.**

Melioration Improvements, rather than repairs, to property.

Member 1. One of the persons in a family, corporation,
legislature, union, etc. 2. A bank that is **affiliated** with
one of the **Federal Reserve** banks, or a **brokerage** firm
that is affiliated with a stock or other **securities exchange.**

Membership corporation A nonprofit, nonstock corporation created for social, charitable, political, etc., purposes.

Memorandum 1. An informal note or summary of a meeting, a proposed agreement, etc. 2. A note from one
member of an organization to another. 3. A written
document that proves a **contract** exists. 4. A brief of law
submitted to a judge in a case.

Memory The place in a computer where data and **programs** are stored. See also **RAM** and **ROM.**

Mentor Wise counselor. The word comes from Homer's *Odyssey.* The role of mentors in furthering organizational careers is considered an important aspect of **management development.**

Menu A list of **programs,** computer operations, data files, questions, or other choices for a computer operator. The choices are usually displayed on a screen.

Mercantile Commercial; having to do with buying and selling, etc. For *mercantile agency,* see **credit agency.**

Merchandising The process of adjusting to customer demand the merchandise that is produced or offered for sale. It involves selecting and securing the appropriate products, ascertaining the proper quantities and quality to have in stock at the proper times, and setting the appropriate prices for them.

Merchant banking 1. As practiced abroad, the conduct of a commercial and investment banking business, involving lending, borrowing, **underwriting** or dealing in **securities,** and providing financial advice. Domestic merchant banking was prohibited for U.S. banks by the **Glass-Steagall Act,** although U.S. banks can engage in it abroad with regulatory approval. 2. A loose term for the lending and underwriting activities of **brokerage** firms.

Merchantable 1. Fit to be sold; of the general type and quality described and fit for the general purpose for which it was bought. 2. A *merchantable title* is a **marketable title.**

Merger 1. The union of two or more things, usually with the smaller or less important thing ceasing to exist once it is a part of the other. Companies, rights, contracts, etc., can *merge.* The following definitions divide these mergers by type. 2. When **corporations** *merge,* it is a *horizontal merger* if business competitors selling the same product in the same area join; a *vertical merger* occurs when a company joins with its customers or suppliers; and a *conglomerate merger* occurs when unrelated companies join. These *conglomerate mergers* are of three types: when two totally unrelated companies join, it is a *pure merger;* when companies selling similar products in different **markets** join, it is a *geographical extension merger;* and when two companies selling related but different products join, it is a *product extension merger*. When a **subsidiary** merges with its **parent** company, many states allow a quick, cheap *short-form merger*. 3. In **contract** law, if the persons who make a contract intend it, one contract may end and become a part of another through *merger*. Also, all prior oral agreements may be ended by establishing a written contract as the entire agreement by including a *merger clause*.

Merrick differential (or multiple) piece rate An incentive wage plan that establishes three different piece rates on the basis of performance—one for beginners, one for average workers, and one for superior workers.

Methods engineering Procedures that relate the work of individuals to the processes and tools used in manufacturing the product. **Efficiency** in work performance, including the application of **time and motion studies,** is among its goals.

Mezzanine financing A **venture capital** term for the private placement of medium-risk capital.

Micro marketing Perceiving the needs of customers and directing a flow of goods or services that will both satisfy those needs and further the ends of the producing organizations.

Middle management A vague term for organizational **authority** and **leadership** that lies below top management and above first-level supervisors.

Middleman 1. A person who brings others together and helps them make deals. A more general term is *intermediary*. 2. A person who buys from one person and sells to another. 3. An **agent** or **broker.**

Migratory corporation A **corporation** organized in a state other than that in which the persons interested in it reside, for the purpose of **doing business** primarily outside of the state in which the corporation is incorporated.

Mill One-tenth of a cent. Some property taxes are expressed in *mills*. A mill rate of "one" would be a dollar for each thousand dollars of assessed property.

Milline rate The cost of reaching one million readers with one **agate line** of advertising.

Mineral As defined in land laws, *mineral* may mean any nonanimal, nonvegetable substance found on or in the ground, any commercially valuable mineral, or one specific type of mineral. A *mineral lease* is an agreement giving a right to explore for *minerals* and then to remove those minerals found upon payment of rent for use of the land or **royalties** based on what is taken. A *mineral right* is a right to either take minerals out of the ground or to receive payment for minerals taken out.

Mini-shift A tour of duty for a permanent part-time employee.

Minimal (or **minimum**) **contacts doctrine** The rule that a person must carry on a certain minimum amount of activity within a state, or have formal ties to the state, before that person can be sued in the state.

Minimax A decisionmaking principle from **game theory** which calls for choosing the alternative that would minimize chances for the maximum loss.

Minimum inventory A **safety inventory.**

Minimum wage The lowest hourly rate that may be paid to a worker. While many *minimum wages* are established by union contracts and organizational pay policies, *the* minimum wage usually refers to the federal minimum wage law—the **Fair Labor Standards Act** (FLSA). The minimum wage at any given time is established by Congress via FLSA amendments. The Secretary of Labor regulates some exceptions to the minimum wage.

Minor dispute See **major dispute.**

Minority stockholder A person who holds too few **shares** of **stock** to control the way the corporation is managed (or to elect any **directors**). The *minority interest* is the **equity** in a **subsidiary** company belonging to those who are not part of the controlling interest.

Minutes The official record of the proceedings of a meeting of an organized body, such as the **stockholders** or **directors** of a corporation. *Minutes* are often required by law or charter. It is not always essential to the validity of acts done by an organized body that minutes be kept, but accurate minutes avoid future misunderstandings and lawsuits based on these misunderstandings. The general form of minutes is fairly well standardized: time and place; proof that the meeting was properly called and that notice was given or waived; the names of the chair and secretary of the meeting; proof of **quorum;** and a statement that the minutes of the previous meeting were read. Next should come a clear, accurate, and complete report of all business transacted.

Misbranding Any intentionally false information on a product label.

Misery index The total of the rates of inflation and unemployment.

Misrepresentation A false statement that is not known to be false is an *innocent misrepresentation*. A false statement made when you should have known better is a *negligent misrepresentation*. A false statement known to be false and meant to be misleading is a *fraudulent misrepresentation.*

Missionary sales representative An **agent** of a producer who seeks to create a demand for a new product among wholesalers and their customers.

Mitigation of damages 1. Facts showing that the size of a claim for **damages** is unjustified. 2. The rule that a person suing for damages must have done everything reasonable to minimize those damages, or the amount of money awarded will be lowered.

Mixed car Different commodities shipped in the same vehicle.

Mixed costs **Fixed** and **variable costs** combined.

Mixed economy If at one end of a continuum were **laissez-faire capitalism** and at the other end were **socialism,** then an economic system that lies somewhere in the middle would be a *mixed economy*. All of the industrialized countries of the **First World** have mixed economies.

Mode The value that occurs most frequently in a distribution. If, for example, six persons score "10 right" on a test, four score "15 right" and four score "20 right," "10 right" would be the *mode*. Also see **mean** and **median.**

Modem Modulator/demodulator. It converts a computer's *digital* signal to an **analog** signal and back for transmission (such as overphone lines) between computer systems. This may also require an **acoustic coupler.**

Modified union shop A variation of the **union shop** that exempts certain classes of employees from joining the union. Such exemptions might include employees who were employed before a certain date, seasonal workers, work study students, etc.

Mom and pop operation A business enterprise so small that its workforce consists solely of immediate family members.

Mommy track   An alternative career track for women who would work fewer hours, make less money and have fewer opportunities for advancement because it is presumed that they are not committed to the organization for the long term.

Monetary   Having to do with money. A *monetary economy* uses money as opposed to barter as a means of exchange; a *monetary equilibrium* is a state of balance where the aggregate **demand** for money equals the supply; a *monetary indemnity* has insurance pay a specific amount for a loss rather than reimbursing actual expenses; a *monetary indicator* is a variable that shows the direction of **monetary policy;** for example, the **federal funds rate;** *monetary reserves* are those things held as **security** for currency (gold, silver, etc.); a *monetary standard* is the basis upon which money is issued (gold, silver etc.); the *monetary theory of the business cycle* attributes variances in economic activity to changes in interest rates and the money supply; and a *monetary unit* is a nation's basic currency (the *dollar* for the U.S., the *pound* for the United Kingdom, etc.). For **monetary policy,** see next entry below.

Monetary policy   A government's formal efforts to manage the money in its economy in order to realize specific economic goals such as economic growth, full employment, price stability, and international financial balance. Three basic kinds of *monetary policy* decisions can be made: decisions about the amount of money in circulation; decisions about the level of interest rates; and decisions about the functioning of credit markets and the banking system. Controlling money is, of course, the key variable. In 1913, the United States passed into law the **Federal Reserve Act,** which created a strong central bank for the country, similarly titled—the Federal Reserve. Like most central banks, the Federal Reserve is empowered to control the amount of money in circulation by either creating or cancelling dollars. Implementation of money control is achieved through the process of putting up for sale or buying government **securities.** This is usually termed **open market operations**—which means that the Federal Reserve competes with other bidders in the purchasing or selling of securities. The difference is that when the Federal Reserve buys securities, it pays in the form of new currency in circulation. If it sells some of its securities, it decreases money available since it, in effect, absorbs currency held by others. This does not mean, however, that the **money stock** fluctuates greatly. It steadily increases. It is in the margin of the increase that money supply has its impact. The other major tools involve **interest** rates and the amount of **credit** being made available by banks. By varying interest rates and controlling bank **reserve** requirements, the Federal Reserve can attempt to affect investments and loans. It does this in two ways: first, by changing its discount rate—that is, the interest rate it charges other banks for loans of money which these banks can use to make loans; and second, by changing the reserve requirements—which is the ratio of the amount of money a bank must have on hand in comparison to the amount of money it has out on loan.

Money Strictly defined, *money* is only currency and coin. More loosely, money includes anything, such as **demand deposits** in banks, that performs all the functions of *currency*. Money is a *standard of value*. It measures the relative value of different goods. Money is a *medium of exchange*. It is a method of payment. And money is a *store of value*. It saves purchasing power for a future date. The *money market* is the sum of the institutions and intangible mechanisms that deal with short-term loans and near-term transfers of funds. It includes the **commercial paper** market, **acceptance** market, **collateral** loan market, government **securities** market, **foreign exchange** market, etc. A *money broker* is an individual (or firm) who helps those in need of significant funds find those who might be willing to lend. *Money management* is financial planning, whether for an individual or an organization. A *money market certificate* is a savings certificate, sold by banks and other savings institutions, that is usually held for at least six months and is based on the interest rate paid by U.S. **treasury bills.** A *money market fund* is a **mutual fund** that invests in safe short-term securities such as treasury bills. A *money order* is a type of **draft** sold by banks, post offices, and other companies to persons who want to make payments in check form, but who do not use their own checks. A *money-purchase plan* is a **pension plan** in which an employer contributes a fixed amount each year. The ultimate value of the **benefits** paid will vary, depending on how much the invested sums earn.

Money rates are **interest** rates. The *money stock* is the totality of currency and coin outside of the U.S. Treasury and the **Federal Reserve** banks. Also called *money in circulation*. The *money supply* is the amount of money in circulation as defined by the Federal Reserve. *Dirty money* consists of profits from illegal operations; it is sometimes "cleaned" by "laundering" it through legitimate businesses.

Monopoly The ability of one or a few companies to control the manufacture, sale, distribution, or price of something. A *monopoly* may be prohibited if, for example, a company deliberately built its power to fix prices, exclude competition, etc. The term *monopoly* suggests gigantic national or international business firms, but smaller firms can illegally *monopolize* a local or regional market. *Monopoly power* has been assumed to exist by courts when a single firm is responsible for the sales of 70 percent or more of a specific product within a specific geographic market. *Monopolistic competition* exists when the few producers who dominate a market try to get a larger share by emphasizing **product differentiation** in advertising (which also allows them to influence pricing).

Monopsony A market with only one buyer.

Monotony curve See **fatigue curve.**

Moody's Investors Service A major publisher of financial data well known for its **bond** ratings that range from Aaa (highest grade) to C (lowest speculative grade).

Moral obligation bonds State or local government **bonds** backed only by the jurisdiction's promise to repay; they are specifically not backed by a jurisdiction's **full faith and credit.** They often carry a higher interest rate than other municipal bonds, because full faith and credit bonds will always be paid first.

Morale The collective attitude of the workforce toward their work environment and a crude measure of the organizational climate.

More favorable terms clause A labor contract provision in which a union promises not to give more favorable terms (as to wages, benefits, hours, working conditions, etc.) to competitors of the company.

More or less A **contract** term meant to keep the delivery of small variations in quantity from being a **breach.** What is *more or less* the right amount varies with what is customary in the trade and between the persons.

Mortgage 1. One person putting up land or buildings (or, in the case of a **chattel mortgage,** personal property) in exchange for a loan. A mortage usually takes one of three forms. In one form, the ownership of the property actually transfers in whole or in part to the lender. In another form, the ownership does not change at all, and the mortgage has the same effect as a **lien.** In a third form, the property is put into a **trust** with an independent person until the debt is paid off. 2. For various types of *mortgages* such as **amortized, blanket, closed-end, conventional, FHA, first, junior, purchase-money, second, wraparound,** etc., see those words. 3. *Mortgage-backed securities* are **bonds** backed by a grouping of mortgages. A *mortgage banker* makes (usually short-term) mortgage loans using his own or others' money. A *mortgage certificate* is a document showing a share owned in a mortgage. A *mortgage commitment* is a letter agreeing to a specific loan on specific terms. A *mortgage company* makes mortgage loans, then sells them to others. A *mortgage contingency clause* makes a sale depend on finding mortgage money. A *mortgagee* is a lender who takes a mortgage. *Mortgaging out* is 100 percent financing, or buying property without using any of your own money. A *mortgagor* is someone who borrows on a mortgage.

Most-favored-nation provision 1. A promise in a treaty or agreement to extend to the contracting nation the best trade privileges or **tariff** rates granted to any other nation. The United States has an "unconditional" most-favored-nation provision in its trade agreements, meaning that the extension of privileges or the reduction of tariffs negotiated with one nation automatically apply to all trading partners unless specifically excluded by law. All contracting nations to **GATT** have agreed to grant equal treatment to each other. When a country agrees to cut tariffs on a particular product imported from one country, the tariff reduction automatically applies to imports of this product from any other country eligible for most-favored-nation treatment. Tightly controlled exceptions have been made for **customs unions,** free trade areas, and **developing countries.** 2. For a *most-favored-nation clause* in a **labor contract,** see **more favorable terms clause.**

Most suitable use See **highest and best use.**

Motion study See **time and motion study.**

Mouse A device that can be hand-rolled along a flat surface to move symbols across a computer screen.

Multicompany A conglomerate.

Multilateral agreement An agreement among several persons, companies, or governments.

Multilateral development banks International financial institutions organized on a multilateral basis to provide financial and technical resources for social and economic development of less developed countries.

Multilevel distributorship A pyramid sales scheme.

Multinational Either a company with major centers of operation or **subsidiaries** in several countries, or a company that merely does business in several countries. They create wealth and jobs, pay taxes, help to generate and transfer technology, provide management skills and generally contribute to the development of foreign economies. However, they have the potential power to manipulate prices and profits and the uses of new technology; intracompany transactions constitute a large part of world trade; they tend to be centrally controlled by parent companies whose foreign activities are beyond the control of their home governments; and they have been accused of illegally interfering in the internal politics of both home and host governments.

Multiple management 1. A formal system of advisory boards of employees that serve to generate new ideas, further communications, and develop managerial potential. Typically, multiple management systems operate with a factory board, a sales board, and a **junior board of directors.** 2. A loose term to describe any of a variety of programs in which workers are able to participate in the development and execution of policy.

Multiple party account A bank **account** such as a **joint** account or a **trust** account, but not an account for an organization.

Multiple-step A financial **statement** offering a variety of subtotals (such as "earnings before taxes") before computing **net** earnings. For a contrast, see **single step.**

Multiple time plan A wage **incentive** plan that provides higher base rates as progressively higher levels of production are reached.

Muni A municipal bond.

Municipal Having to do with a local government. For example a *municipal ordinance* is a local law or regulation.

Municipal bonds are put out not only by local governments, but also by states, territories or possessions of the United States, or any municipality, political subdivision (including cities, countries, school districts and special districts for fire prevention, water, sewer, irrigation and other purposes) or public agency or instrumentality (such as an authority or commission). While the interest on municipal bonds is exempt from federal taxes, state and local exemptions may vary. *Municipal revenue bonds* are municipal bonds whose interest and principal are paid from the revenues of rents, tolls, or other user charges flowing from specific projects financed by the bonds.

Must buy An advertising medium that a retailer *must buy* exposure from to reach a particular audience; for example, the local newspaper, when there is only one to choose from.

Mutual Done together; reciprocal. A *mutual benefit association* is a social organization or corporation for the relief of members of the organization from specified perils or costs such as the costs of illness. Such associations pay losses with assessments on their members for specific losses rather than by fixed premiums payable in advance. A *mutual company* is a company in which the customers are the owners who get the profits. A *mutual fund* is an **investment company** that pools investors' money and buys shares of stock in many companies. It does this by selling its own shares to the public. A *mutual insurance company* is an insurance company with no **capital** stock, owned by the policyholders. **Trustees** of the company are chosen by the policyholders. Earnings over and above payment of losses, operating expenses, and **reserves** are the property of the policyholders and returned to them in some way such as dividends or reduced premiums. See also **stock insurance company.** A *mutual investment trust* is a *mutual fund.* A *mutual savings bank* is historically a state-chartered and depositor-owned organization that accepts deposits from individuals, in order to invest primarily in residential mortgages. Found in only 17 states, these banks may often invest in commercial **mortgages,** corporate bonds, and corporate stock. Because of recent changes in federal laws, they may receive federal charters and may now enter into broader banking relationships with commercial customers (if federally chartered) and consumers. On the federal level, the **Federal Home Loan Bank Board** is the primary regulator of federally-chartered mutual savings banks, and the **Federal Deposit Insurance Corporation** is the primary regulator of federally insured state-chartered mutual savings banks. *Mutual rating* is the same as peer rating. A *mutual will* has a husband and wife leave all assets to each other. A *split mutual fund* is a **split investment company.**

Muzak   The trade name for the soothing background music played in workplaces and retail outlets.

N

N 1. A mathematical symbol commonly used to represent the number of cases in a distribution, study, etc. The symbol of the number of cases in a subgroup of *N* is *n*. 2. In newspaper stock transaction tables, an indication, lowercase (n), that a **stock** is new and has been listed for less than a year. 3. An indication that the stock is traded on the **New York Stock Exchange.**

NAM **National Association of Manufacturers.**

NAR National Association of Realtors

NASD National Association of Securities Dealers. An association of dealers in **over-the-counter stocks** and other **securities.**

NIFO Next in, first out. Valuing current **inventory** by its replacement cost. Under this accounting method, if a merchant buys a blivit for a dollar, but knows that once it is sold a replacement blivit will cost two dollars, the owned blivit is worth two dollars. See **FIFO** and **LIFO.**

NIOSH National Institute for Occupational Safety and Health

NLRA **National Labor Relations Act.**

NLRB **National Labor Relations Board.**

NOW **Negotiable order of withdrawal.**

NSF 1. National Science Foundation. 2. Not sufficient funds.

NTB **Nontariff barrier.**

NTIS **National Technical Information Service.**

NYSE **New York Stock Exchange.**

National For the nation; common to the whole nation. The *National Association of Manufacturers* is the largest non-trade **employer's association** in the United States. A *national bank* is a bank incorporated under the laws of the U.S., rather than state laws, even though it does business primarily in one state only. It is usually a member of the **Federal Reserve** system, and the **FDIC.** For *national brand,* see **brand.** The *National Credit Union Administration* charters, supervises, and provides deposit insurance for federal **credit unions.** The *national debt* is the debt of the U.S. federal government or the debt of any central government. The *National Environmental Policy Act* is the federal law requiring **environmental impact statements** on major projects and setting out the major environmental goals of the U.S. *National income* is the total earnings of labor and property from the production of goods and services; the income earned, but not necessarily received, by all people and companies in a given country during a stated period. The *National Labor Relations Act* is the federal law that set up the National Labor Relations Board and established rules for most types of employer-employee contact affecting **interstate commerce,** union **recognition,** strikes, secret ballots for selection of a union, union elections, **collective bargaining, unfair labor practices,** etc. It is a combination of the **Wagner, Taft-Hartley,** and **Landrum-Griffin Acts.** The *National Labor Relations Board* has two principal functions: preventing and remedying unfair labor practices by employers and labor organizations or their agents, and conducting secret ballot elections among employees in appropriate collective bargaining units to determine whether or not they desire to be represented by a labor organization. The NLRB also conducts secret union ballots for other purposes and decides **jurisdictional disputes** between unions. The NLRB can act only when it is formally requested to do so. Individuals, employers, or unions may initiate cases by filing charges of unfair labor practices or petitioning for employee representation elections. The *National Mediation Board* is a federal agency that provides the railroad and airline industries with specific mechanisms for the adjustment of labor-management disputes through collective bargaining, investigation of questions of representation, and the **arbitration** and establishment of procedures for national emergency disputes. The *National Railroad Adjustment Board* is a federal agency that decides disputes growing out of **grievances** or out of interpretation or application of agreements concerning rates of pay, rules, or working conditions in the railroad industry. The *National Technical Information Service* is the central point for the public sale of government-funded research and development reports and other analyses prepared by federal agencies, their contractors, or grantees. A *national union* is composed of a variety of widely dispersed affiliated local unions.

Nationalization A country taking over a private industry, owning and running it, with or without payment to the ex-owners.

Natural business year An **accounting** or **fiscal period** that ends with the close of the month in which the activities of a business are at or near their lowest point.

Natural monopoly A **monopoly** that is due to the nature of the business; for example, a **public utility** is a natural monopoly. Most natural monopolies are owned or regulated by governments.

Near-money Quick assets.

Necessaries doctrine The rule that a seller may collect from a spouse or parent the price of goods sold to the other spouse or to a child for the basic support of that spouse or child.

Needs analysis 1. **Marketing research** to determine who might be interested in a new product. 2. A comparison of an organization's skills and skill deficiencies to determine what needs should be met by training present employees or new hires.

Negative amortization When **mortgage** payments are not adequate to cover the interest due, the shortfall is added to the **principal;** such *negative* **amortization** will necessarily require an adjustment in the schedule of payments.

Negative covenant 1. An agreement that prohibits an employee or the seller of a business from competing in the same area with a similar product. 2. Any agreement in a contract to refrain from doing something.

Negative income tax A welfare program in which citizens with incomes below a specified level receive cash payments.

Negative pledge clause A restriction (usually in a bond **issue** or **debenture**) that prohibits the corporation from allowing any subsequent debt to gain **priority** over the restricted debt. Negative pledge clauses often have exceptions for later purchases in which the purchases themselves are secured by a stronger **lien.**

Negative strike See **positive strike.**

Negotiable Something transferable by **endorsement** from one owner to another is *negotiable.*

Negotiable instrument A signed document that contains an unconditional promise to pay an exact sum of money, either when demanded or at an exact future time. Further, it must be marked **payable** "to the **order** of" a specific person or payable "to **bearer**" (the person who happens to have it). *Negotiable instruments* include **checks, notes,** and bills of **exchange.** There is a whole branch of law concerning negotiable instruments and a special vocabulary of ordinary sounding words (such as **holder**) that have specialized meanings in this area. However, if you look at a *check* and think about the bank's rules for cashing it, you have a basic idea of what *negotiable instruments* are about.

Negotiable Order of Withdrawal (NOW) Accounts An interest-earning check-like account, on which individuals and nonprofit organizations can write orders of withdrawal that are treated as if they were checks. It is technically not a checking account, since the offering institution can impose a hold before honoring the orders. NOW accounts are offered nationwide by banks and **thrift institutions.**

Negotiate 1. Discuss, arrange, or bargain about a business deal or discuss a compromise to a situation. 2. Transfer a **negotiable instrument** from one person to another.

Neocolonialism Economic control of the **Third** and **Fourth Worlds** by former colonial powers.

Net The amount remaining after subtractions. For example, *net assets* (or *net worth*) are what is left after subtracting what you owe from what you have; *net weight* is the weight of a product not counting the container; and the *net cost* of a car might be what you pay the dealer minus what you get back from the automaker as a **rebate.** *Net book value* (or *net asset value*) is the amount of a company's property backing each share of **stock** or **bond** it puts out. Calculating this amount is complex. A *net contract* (or *listing*) is a sale in which a **broker's commission** is equal to the amount by which the sale price exceeds a particular amount. *Net exports of goods and services* is the balance of goods and services, excluding transfers under military grants, as reported in the **balance of payments** statistics. *Net income* is revenue and gains minus expenses and losses. The *net income/net worth ratio* divides this figure by net worth for one indication of a company's earning efficiency. *Net income on sales* is a

profitability ratio: net income divided by net sales. *Net interest* is a measure of the excess of **interest** payments made by the domestic business sector over its interest receipts, plus net interest received from abroad. Interest paid by one business firm to another is a transaction within the business sector and has no effect on the net interest payments or receipts of the sector. The same is true of interest payments within other sectors as from one individual to another, or one government to another. A *net lease* is a **lease** in which the tenant pays rent plus all the costs of ownership, such as taxes and maintenance. Sometimes a distinction is made between a *net lease* (rent and some costs such as heat) and a *"net net" lease* (rent and all expenses such as taxes). *Net pay* is take-home pay. A *net position* is the difference between **long** and **short** **contracts** held in one thing by a **commodities** or **securities** trader; more simply, the amount that a person will gain or lose by a change in a commodity's or a stock's value. *Net present value* is the **present value** of cash inflows less the present value of cash outflows. For *net profit margin,* see **profit margin.** *Net realizable value* is the net cash or equivalent that can be expected from the sale of an asset. *Net sales* represents gross dollar sales minus merchandise returns and allowances. Some accountants also deduct cash discounts granted to customers on the theory that these are actually a reduction of the net selling price; others credit the discounts to "other" expenses. Trade and quantity discounts are, of course, concessions off price, and should be deducted from the gross sales. The *net sales/inventory ratio* is a **turnover** ratio used as a test of **inventory.** It indictates how often **raw materials** and finished goods have been converted into cash during the year. The test reveals overstocking or overvaluation of inventory. The *net sales/receivables ratio* is a test of the **liquidity** of customers' **accounts receivable** and is known as the receivables **turnover.** It indicates the number of times receivables have turned over during the year; the more rapid the rate, the larger the volume of receivables which a given amount of **working capital** is supporting. This information matters in formulating both sales and credit policy. The *net worth method* is a way the IRS proves that a person has understated taxable income by showing that the person has acquired more **assets** than could be bought by the stated income. The *net worth/ total debt ratio* is the relation of the investment of stockholders to the investment of creditors (**equity capital** to borrowed capital). For *net yield to maturity*, see **yield.**

New-product development   An integrated effort of the marketing, research and development, and production departments to generate and evaluate ideas for new items that can be mass produced and profitably sold. Companies rely on new-product development to increase growth, to replace obsolete products, and to productively use surplus physical plant and managerial energy.

New York Curb Exchange   Former name of the **American Stock Exchange.**

New York Stock Exchange   The largest **security exchange** in the world, formed in 1927 and located on Wall Street. The *New York Stock Exchange Index* covers the price movements of all **common stocks** listed with the exchange.

Nibbling   Any practice of cutting the **piece rates** paid to employees upon an increase in their output.

Ninety day letter   A notice that the **IRS** claims you owe taxes. During the 90 days after receiving the notice, you must either pay the taxes (and claim a refund) or challenge the IRS's decision in tax court.

No   Negative. A *no action clause* is a provision in many **liability insurance** policies that the insurance company need not pay anything until a lawsuit against the insured person results in a **judgment** or agreement about the amount owed. A *no action letter* is a letter from a government **agency** lawyer that, if the facts are as represented in a request by a person for an agency decision, the lawyer will recommend that the agency take no action against the person. For *no-commission account,* see **house account.** *No fault* is a type of automobile insurance required by some states in which each person's own insurance company pays for injury or damage up to a certain limit no matter whose fault it is; or the popular name for a type of divorce in which a marriage can be ended simply because it has broken down. A *no limit order* is instructions from a client to a **broker** to buy or sell a certain amount of stock or other **securities** without any limits on price. A *no load fund* is a **mutual fund** that charges no initial sales **commissions.** *No par stock* is stock with no nominal or face value, only the price at which it sells.

Nominal 1. In name only. For example, a *nominal interest rate* is the interest stated on a stock or other **security**, rather than the actual **interest** earned as computed by the cost of the stock and other factors. 2. Not real or substantial. Slight; token. 3. Estimated. For example, a *nominal price quote* is one estimated when there has been no recent sale, or the best available estimated average of two or more prices being quoted currently by traders whose price views differ.

Nominee 1. A person chosen as another person's representative (deputy, **agent, trustee**, etc.). 2. A *nominee trust* is an arrangement in which one person agrees in writing to hold land, stock, etc., for the benefit of another (undisclosed) person. See **street name.**

Nonacquiescence The **IRS's** announced disagreement with a decision of the U.S. **tax court.**

Nonconforming Not standard. *Nonconforming goods* are goods that fail to meet contract specifications. A *nonconforming lot* is a piece of land with a size, shape, or location that is not permitted by current **zoning** laws. A *nonconforming use* is the use of a piece of land that is permitted, even though that type of use is not usually permitted in that area by the zoning laws. This can come about either because the use (building size, use, etc.) existed before the zoning law or because a **variance** has been granted.

Noncontestable clause A provision in an insurance policy that prohibits the insurance company from refusing to pay a claim if the refusal is based on **fraud** or mistake in the original application after a certain amount of time.

Noncontributory pension plan A pension program that has the employer paying the entire cost.

Noncumulative preferred stock See **cumulative preferred stock.**

Nonmarket economy An economic system in which economic activity is regulated by central planning as opposed to market forces such as supply and demand.

Nonmember depository institution A **depository institution** that is not a member of the **Federal Reserve System.** Those that offer **transaction accounts** or nonpersonal **time deposits** are subject to **reserve** requirements set by the Federal Reserve, and they also have access to the Federal Reserve **discount window** and Federal Reserve services on the same terms as member banks.

Nonparticipating preferred stock   A class of **stock** that entitles its owners only to a fixed or stated rate of **dividends** and to nothing more. See **participating preferred stock.**

Nonproduction bonus   A payment to workers that is in effect a gratuity, upon which employees cannot regularly depend; for example, a year-end bonus.

Nonprofit corporation   A corporation that has no "owners" and gives none of its income to its members, **directors,** or **officers** can apply for special tax-exempt status for contributors when it can demonstrate that it is set up for religious, charitable, educational, or similar purposes.

Nonpublic enterprise   A company that does not trade its debt or equity **securities** on a stock **exchange** or **over-the-counter** market; and consequently, is not required to file financial **statements** with the **Securities and Exchange Commission.**

Nonrecourse loan   A loan in which the lender cannot take more than the property borrowed on as repayment for the loan. This type of loan is used in surplus crop price support programs in which the crop is the only **security** for the loan. Some **mortgages** are also of this type, but most are not.

Nonsuability clause   That portion of a labor contract where a company agrees that it will not sue a labor union because of a **wildcat** strike, provided that the union lives up to its obligation to stop the strike.

Nontariff barriers   Practices other than the imposition of **tariffs** that tend to restrain international trade. They may be financial (internal taxes, anti-**dumping** or countervailing duties, customs fees) or nonfinancial (domestic regulations concerning sanitation or labeling of a product, quantitative restrictions, excessive documentation requirements). As tariff barriers to trade have decreased as a result of **GATT,** nontariff barriers have taken on increased importance in multilateral trade negotiations.

Nontax payments   Payments required by law that are not ordinarily considered taxes, such as fines, user fees, special assessments, etc.

Norms   1. Average or standard behavior for members of a group. The *norm* is what is "normal."   2. Socially enforced requirements and expectations about basic responsibilities, behavior and thought patterns of members in their organizational roles.   3. In psychological testing, *norms* are tables of scores from a large number of people who have taken a particular test. And a *norm-referenced test* is any test that describes a candidate's performance in terms of its relation to the performance of other candidates.

Notary public A semipublic official who can administer oaths, certify the validity of documents, and perform other witnessing-type duties needed by the business and legal worlds.

Note 1. A document that says the person who signs it promises to pay a certain sum of money at a certain time or on **demand.** If payable "to the order of" a particular person or "to bearer" and if certain other formalities are followed, it is a **negotiable instrument.** A *note register* is a book with information on a company's notes **receivable** and notes **payable.** This information is summarized periodically in reports, with a separate section on those that have been **discounted.** 2. A financial **statement** may or may not have accompanying *notes.* If there are notes, they should be considered an integral part of the statement because important **contingent liabilities** or contractual obligations are often described in such notes. Unless the notes are read and interpreted, any analysis of a financial statement will be incomplete.

Nothing job 1. A job that gives nothing (no satisfaction, no prestige, etc.) to an incumbent except wages. 2. An easy task, quickly done.

Notice 1. Knowledge of certain facts. Also, *constructive notice* means a person *should have known* certain facts and will be treated as if he or she knew them. 2. Formal receipt of the knowledge of certain facts. For example, *notice* of a lawsuit usually means that formal papers have been delivered to a person (*personal notice*) or to a person's **agent** (*imputed notice*). 3. For various types of real estate transaction *notice* laws (such as a *race notice statute or act),* see **recording acts.** 4. A *notice of dishonor* is notice that payment on or **acceptance** of a **negotiable instrument** has been refused. A *notice to creditors* is the *notice* in a **bankruptcy** proceeding that a **meeting of creditors** will be held, that claims must be **filed,** or that **relief** has been granted. A *notice to quit* is the written notice from a **landlord** to a **tenant** that the tenant will have to move.

Novation The substitution by agreement of a new **contract** for an old one, with all the rights under the old one ended. Usually, the substitution of a new person who is responsible for the contract and the removal of an old one.

NOW Account A **negotiable order of withdrawal account.**

Number cruncher 1. A person who is generally engaged in the mathematical tasks related to computers, accounting, and statistical research. 2. A huge computer.

Numeraire A measure of value (such as gold or currency) used to express the value of goods and services.

O

O In newspaper stock transaction tables, an indication of an **over-the-counter stock.**

OASDI Old age, survivors, and disability insurance.

OD Organization development.

OFCCP Office of Federal Contract Compliance Programs.

OECD Organization for Economic Cooperation and Development.

OMA Orderly marketing agreement.

OMB Office of Management and Budget.

OPEC Organization of Petroleum Exporting Countries.

OPIC Overseas Private Investment Corporation.

OPM 1. Other people's money. 2. **Office of Personnel Management.**

OSHA Occupational Safety and Health Administration.

OTC Over-the-counter.

Object classification A uniform classification identifying transactions by the nature of the goods or services purchased (such as personnel compensation, supplies and materials, equipment) without regard to the organizational unit involved or the purpose of the programs for which they are used.

Obsolescence The loss in value of an **asset** due to new inventions, change in styles, legislation, and other causes apart from the wear and tear of ordinary use. *Planned obsolescence* is the intentional design of a product so that it will wear out or be out of style sooner than might be expected.

Occupation A relatively continuous pattern of activity that provides a livelihood for an individual and serves to define an individual's general social status. *Occupational certification* permits practitioners in a particular occupation to claim minimum levels of competence. It usually prevents uncertified people from supplying the same services. An *occupational disease* (or *illness*) is a disease, but not an injury, that is widespread among workers in a particular job, such as "black lung" disease among miners. **Workers' compensation** and some federal programs may pay workers who contract these diseases if the disease is peculiar to the industry or if the job puts workers at a much higher risk than other workers of contracting the disease. An *occupational grouping* consists of **classes** within the same broad occupational category, such as engineering, nursing, accounting, etc. *Occupational health* is the physical, mental and social well-being of workers in relation to their work and working environment. The concern is thus wider than the safety of the workplace, and includes **job satisfaction.** *Occupational obsolescence* is a concept usually associated with professional employees who lack currency in their discipline. For example, an engineer who has served as an administrator for a significant number of years may be unable to function in his or her engineering specialty because the "state of the art" has moved too far. The obsolescence could have occurred even if the engineer in this example had continued functioning as an engineer because so much of what technical specialists need to know is new information that they could not have learned about in school. For *occupational parity,* see **parity.** For *occupational psychology,* see **industrial psychology.** For *occupational rehabilitation,* see **occupational therapy.** The *Occupational Safety and Health Administration* is the federal agency that puts out occupational safety and health standards and regulations, conducts investigations and inspections, and issues citations and proposes penalties for noncompliance. The *Occupational Safety and Health Review Commission* handles appeals from OSHA rulings. *Occupational socialization* is the process by which an individual absorbs and adopts the values, norms, and behavior of the occupational role models with whom he or she interacts. An *occupational survey* is an organization's study of all positions in a given **class,** series of classes, or occupational group in whatever departments or divisions they may be located. *Occupational therapy* seeks to restore health to the ill and to retrain the disabled, while *occupational rehabilitation* is more specifically concerned with the restoration of earning capacity.

Odd lot   A number of shares of **stock** less than the number usually traded as a unit. This is often fewer than one hundred shares.

Off A declining **market** (as in "the market is off").

Off-board A **stock** or other **securities** transaction that does not take place through a national securities **exchange.** *Off-board* exchanges are either between private individuals or **over-the-counter.**

Off-book financing Financing which exists, but which is not presented on a **balance sheet.** This may occur when a corporation **guarantees** the debt of another. While the debt appears on the balance sheet of the latter company, the former does not necessarily record the guarantee on its balance sheet.

Off-the-books Wages or other payments (usually in cash) for which no records are kept.

Off-line A computer system whose operations are not under the control of a central processing unit, or a computer system that does not process information as it is received, but stores and processes it at a later time.

Offer In **contract** law, a proposal to make a deal. It must be communicated from the person making it to the person to whom it is made, and it must be definite and reasonably certain in its terms.

Offering A sale of **stock** (or other **securities**). A *primary offering,* also called a "new issue," is the sale of a new stock by a company. A *secondary offering* is a sale by persons who hold already-issued stock. A *private offering* is made to a small group of persons who know something about the company. It is not as strictly regulated by the **SEC** as a *public offering* (a sale of stock to the general public). Private stock sales require an *offering circular* (a document similar to a **prospectus**). An *offering price* is a price per share, usually of a **mutual fund.**

Office of Federal Contract Compliance Programs An agency within the Department of Labor that combats employment **discrimination** by government contractors.

Office of Management and Budget The central budget and planning office of the United States government.

Office of Personnel Management The central personnel agency of the federal government.

Office title A job title that differs from the **classified** title assigned to a job and that is used to describe a particular **position** for other than payroll, budget, or official purposes.

Officers The persons who actually run an organization at the top (president, secretary, etc.).

Offset 1. Any claim or demand made to lessen or cancel another claim. 2. An *offset account* is a **bookkeeping** device to balance one set of figures against another to make the books come out even at the end. 3. *Offset requirements* in foreign trade include requiring an exporter to purchase a specified amount of locally-produced goods or services from the importing country, to establish manufacturing facilities in the importing country, or to buy a specified percentage of the components used in manufacturing the product from established local manufacturers. 4. A legal **kickback** connected with a contract; a sweetener that seals a deal.

Offshore banking center A country in which nonresident banks locate foreign branches primarily or exclusively to borrow from depositors elsewhere and to lend to nonresidents of the country.

Offshore funds 1. **Mutual funds** outside the U.S. 2. Investments made outside the U.S. to avoid taxes, **SEC** regulations, etc.

Old age, survivors, and disability insurance Commonly known as "social security," this is the federal program funded by employer and employee payments that pays for monthly retirement, disability, dependent, and widow/widower benefits.

Old money Substantial wealth that was gained by earlier generations.

Oligopoly A situation in which a few sellers dominate the market for a particular product. Prices tend to be higher than in a more competitive market.

Oligopsony A situation in which a few buyers dominate the market for a particular product.

Ombudsman An official who investigates complaints concerning public services. An *organization ombudsman* is a high-level staff officer who receives complaints and **grievances** about the organization directly from employees.

Omnibus account A **broker's account** in which the transactions of several persons are combined.

On or about Approximately. A phrase used to avoid being bound to a time more exact than a business deal or the law requires; for example, "*on or about* July 15."

On account As a part payment for something bought or owed.

On demand (or on call) Payable immediately when requested.

On-the-job training   Any training that takes place during regular working hours and for which normal wages are paid.

On-line   A computer system whose operations are under the control of a central processing unit or a computer system in which information is processed as received.

One-line consolidation   See **equity method.**

Open   Not closed. An *open account* (or *open end credit*) is a "charge account" in which purchases (or loans) can be made without going through separate **credit** arrangements each time. This is often done on credit cards and "revolving charges" where you can pay a part of what you owe each month on several different purchases. See **open end mortgage.** An *open bid* is an offer to do work or supply materials (usually in the construction business) that reserves the right to lower the bid to meet the competition. An *open end agreement* is a **collective bargaining** agreement providing for a **contract** that will remain in effect until one of the parties wants to reopen negotiations. An *open end company* is a **mutual fund.** An *open end contract* is a **requirements contract.** For *open end credit,* see **consumer credit.** An *open end lease* is a **lease** that may involve a **balloon payment** based upon the value of the item leased when it is returned to the lessor. An *open end mortgage* is a **mortgage** agreement in which amounts of money may be borrowed from time to time on the same agreement. See **open account, open mortgage,** and **closed-end mortgage.** An *open end settlement* is **workers' compensation** payments that continue until a person can work again. An *open interest* is either the total desire at any given time for the buying or selling of a product on the **commodities** market, or those **futures** contracts still unsettled at the end of the day. An *open listing* is a **real estate** contract by which any **agent** who produces a sale gets a **commission.** An *open market* is any freely competitive market in which buyers and sellers of **commodities, securities,** and **commercial paper** trade. It is distinguished from organized markets, such as the **New York Stock Exchange,** in that trading is not limited to members and there is no particular location set aside for trading. Prices and money rates are determined by competition. Buyers and sellers include the **Federal Reserve** banks, commercial banks, **brokers, acceptance** and discount houses, and commercial credit houses. *Open market credit* is the short-term financing of **commercial paper.** The *open market operations* of the **Federal Reserve** are purchases and sales of government **securities** by the New York Federal Reserve Bank as directed by the Federal Open Market Committee to influence the volume of money and credit in the economy. Purchases inject **reserves** into depository institutions and stimulate growth of money and credit. Sales have the opposite effect. An *open mortgage* is a **mortgage** that can be paid off without a penalty at any time before **maturity** (the time it ends). See **open end mortgage** and **closed-end mortgage.** An *open office* or *open plan* is an approach to office space planning that eliminates traditional private offices and conventional walls in favor of freestanding dividers and modular work stations. An *open price term* is an unspecified price in a contract. For example, it is possible to have a valid **contract** without setting an exact price for something if this *open price term* depends on some standard market indicator or if the persons intend the contract to read that way and don't agree on price. In this case a reasonable price at time of delivery will be set. An *open shop* is any work organization that is not unionized. The term also applies to organizations that have unions but do not have union membership as a condition of employment. Historically, an "open shop" was one that discriminated against unions. An *open system* is any organism or organization that interacts with its environment. An *open union* is a union willing to admit any qualified person.

Opening (or closing) range The price fluctuations that occur at the beginning (or end) of a trading session, at the time of the opening (or closing) of the day's market.

Operating 1. The running of a business. *Operating expenses* are expenses incurred in conducting the ordinary major activities of an enterprise, including manufacturing expenses, selling expenses, administrative expenses and the costs of maintenance and repair. *Operating profit* is sales minus the cost of the goods sold and operating expenses. *Net operating assets* are **assets** used in the ordinary course of business (after **depreciation** and **bad debts** are subtracted). These assets do not include things like **stocks** and **bonds.** *Net operating income* (or *loss*) is income (or loss) after subtracting for depreciation of operating assets, but not yet accounting for any interest gained or income taxes paid. *Operating margin* is *net operating income* divided by sales, and the *operating ratio* is *operating expenses* divided by sales. For *operating efficiency ratios, see* **activity ratios.** 2. An *operating budget* is a short-term plan for managing the resources necessary to carry out a program. "Short-term" can mean anything from a few weeks to a few years. Usually an operating budget is developed for each **fiscal year** with changes made as necessary. A company's *operating cycle* is the time requried for a complete business cycle; for example, from the purchase of raw materials to the receipt of cash for the finished product. An *operating lease* is a short-term **lease** that can be canceled. An *operating report* contains various **statements** for management's use; for example, those on income, sales, and personnel. 3. An *operating system* is a computer's internal **programs** that allow it to respond to the user's commands.

Operation of law The way in which rights or liabilities sometimes come to or fall upon a person automatically, without his or her cooperation.

Operations management Because **production** management has grown to encompass so much more than the traditional concerns of manufacturing, it is slowly being replaced by the more general terms *operations management* or *production/operations management.*

Operations research 1. Mathematical methods for the efficient allocation of scarce resources such as capital, labor and materials. 2. An interdisciplinary effort to apply scientific principles to management problems. Specialists from many different areas (such as economics or physics) work with managers to solve a broad range of problems in marketing, manufacturing, finance, etc.

Opportunity cost The value that resources, used in a particular way, would have if used in the best possible or another specified alternative way. When opportunity costs exceed the value the resources have in the way they are being used, they represent lost opportunities to get value from the resources. *Opportunity cost* is sometimes more narrowly defined as the rate of profit you could get by investing your money, rather than putting it into a particular project. See **hurdle rate.** *Opportunity costs* are the appropriate *cost* concepts to consider when making resource allocation decisions. **Actual costs** often, but not always, can be assumed to represent (be proportional to) opportunity costs. See **marginal cost.**

Option A **contract** in which one person pays money for the right to buy something from, or sell something to, another person at a certain price and within a certain time period. For example, a *commodity option* gives a person the right to buy (a **call**) or the right to sell (a **put**) a certain **commodity** (such as a ton of rice) at a certain price (the striking price) by a certain time. The option holder pays a fee (a *remium*) for this right and may use (exercise) it or not depending on **market** conditions. A combined right to either buy or sell is called a *straddle.* And an option sold by a person who owns no stocks or commodities to back it up is called a *naked option.* Options are known as *derivative* investment instruments because their value derives from the security on which they are based—the underlying security.

Optional bond A callable bond.

Optional dividend A **dividend** payable in either cash or stock, as the stockholder prefers. The stockholder is usually given a certain number of days to choose.

Oral board A committee formed to interview candidates for employment, promotion, or evaluation.

Oral contract A **contract** that is not entirely in writing or not in writing at all.

Order 1. A written command or direction given by a judge. For example, a *restraining order* is a judicial command to a person to temporarily stop a certain action or course of conduct. 2. A command given by a public official. 3. *To the order of* is a direction to pay something. These words (or "pay to the **bearer**") are necessary to make a document a **negotiable instrument.** A document with these words on it is called *order paper.* 4. Instructions to buy or sell something. In **stock** sales, for example, a *day order* is an instruction from a customer to a **broker** to buy or sell a stock on one particular day only; a *limit order* is an instruction to buy only under a certain price or sell only over it; a *market order* is an instruction to buy or sell right away at the current **market** price; a *scale order* is an instruction to buy or sell a certain amount of stock at each of several price levels; and a *split order* is an instruction to buy or sell some stock when it reaches one price and some when it reaches another. For **stop order,** see that word. 5. *Order cost* is the increased per-item cost of buying a relatively smaller amount of an item.

Orderly marketing agreement A formal trade agreement between the U.S. and a foreign country in which the latter voluntarily agrees to limit for a specified period of time its exports to the U.S. of a particular commodity. This form of import relief is an alternative to the imposition of quotas or higher **tariffs** as a method of protecting domestic industry.

Ordinary income Income from business profits, wages, interest, dividends, etc., as opposed to **capital** gains.

Organization Almost any group of persons with legal or formal ties may be an *organization.* So may almost any business. *Organization* is any structure or process of allocating jobs to achieve common objectives. An *organization chart* displays individuals or jobs connected to one another by lines, showing the prescribed **hierarchy** and lines of **authority.** See also **Q-chart.** *Organization climate* is either why things are as good or as bad as they are in a particular organization or an organization's overall ambience. *Organization development* is an applied behavioral science process for increasing an organization's effectiveness. The *organization expenses* of a corporation include incorporating taxes, attorney's fees, promotion expenses, printing of stock certificates, minute books, costs of registration of **securities,** etc. The *Organization for Economic Cooperation and Development* is an international organization of industrialized countries to promote economic growth and further world trade. An *organization man* or *woman* is any individual within an organization who accepts the values of the organization and finds harmony in conforming to its policies. *Organization theory* seeks to explain how groups and individuals behave in varying organizational structures and circumstances. The *organizational iceberg* concept holds that the greater part of the organization—the feelings, attitudes, and values of its members—remain covert or hidden from obvious view. In short, the formal organization is visible, while the informal is hidden and waiting to sink any ship that ignores it. *Organizational picketing* is picketing an employer in order to encourage union membership. The **Landrum-Griffin Act** severely limited such picketing. *Organized labor* consists of workers represented by labor unions. An *organized market* is any **market** created by traders to buy and sell their products which operates at a regular place under recognized rules. An *organized market* is often called an **exchange.** An *organizer* is an individual, employed by a union, who acts to encourage employees of a particular plant or organization to join a union.

Original issuance **Stock** issued at the time a **corporation** is organized is the only truly "original" *issuance* of stock. However the term *original issue* also is used for any issue of stock which is not the result of a transfer or exchange, and which does not involve the surrender of outstanding certificates. In addition, a corporation may make additional issue of stock already authorized, or it may make an increase in the amount of its authorized stock. These latter issuances of stock are not truly *original issuances*.

Origination fee A charge for finding, placing, or starting financing; for example, for a **mortgage** on a house. This fee covers the lender's administrative costs in processing the loan. Often expressed as a percentage of the loan, the fee will vary among lenders and from locality to locality. Generally the buyer pays the fee unless another arrangement has been made with the seller and written into the sales contract.

Out-of-pocket 1. A small cash payment. 2. A loss measured by the difference between the price paid for an item and the (true, lower) value of that item.

Outage 1. Unaccounted-for money. 2. An electrical failure.

Outplacement Counseling and career-planning services offered to terminated employees to reduce the impact of "being fired," improve job search skills, and ultimately place the "displaced" person in a new job in another organization.

Output contract An agreement in which a manufacturing company agrees to sell everything it makes to one buyer, and the buyer agrees to take it all. This is a valid contract even though the amounts are indefinite.

Output curve A work curve.

Outs Conditions or promises which, if not complied with by a customer, allow a banker to get out of a deal.

Outside broker 1. A **broker** who is not a member of an **exchange,** but who operates through others who are.

2. A broker who deals in **securities** not listed on an exchange. Such a broker is sometimes referred to as a *street broker* or an **over-the-counter** broker.

Outside director See **director.**

Outside salesperson A person whose full-time job is making sales away from the employer's business and who may **deduct** all work expenses from taxes.

Outstanding 1. Still unpaid; not yet collected. 2. Remaining in existence; not brought in, gathered up, or bought back.

Over-the-counter **Securities,** such as **stocks** and **bonds,** sold directly from **broker** to broker or broker to customer rather than through an **exchange.** Much *OTC* business is done by telephone.

Overbought A **security** or **market** whose price(s) has risen to an unreasonable high.

Overcapitalization A condition that occurs when a corporation's earnings are not large enough to yield a fair **return** on the amount of **stocks** and **bonds** that have been issued, or when the amount of **securities** outstanding exceeds the current value of the **assets.** Overcapitalization may result from promotional optimism, from having overestimated earnings, from having chosen too low a capitalization rate for earnings in terms of the risks involved, or from the issuing of **watered stock.** In each case the **market value** of the stock will fall below the original purchase price of the stock. When overcapitalization results in financial difficulties, **recapitalization** and readjustment of capital structure are necessary. This can be done by putting earnings back in the business, reducing the amount of stock, or reducing the stock's **par value.**

Overdraft (or **overdraw**) Taking out more money by check from a bank account than you have in the account. An *overdraft checking account* is a **line of credit** that allows a person to write checks for more than the actual balance in the account, with a finance charge on the overdraft.

Overhead The general and administrative expenses of a business that cannot be directly allocated to a particular product or department. These include such things as power, water, supervision, maintenance, rent, real estate tax, etc. An *overhead agency* is an **auxiliary agency.** An *overhead rate* is the ratio which *overhead* bears to some chosen base, usually **labor** or material. In a non-manufacturing business, an overhead rate is sometimes used to allocate administrative expenses to the various departments. In manufacturing companies, overhead rates may be established for a company as a whole (blanket rate) or for each department.

Overissue Putting out more shares of a company's **stock** than are permitted by the company's incorporation papers or by the law.

Overqualified Having qualifications considerably beyond those required for a job. Paradoxically, this can lose the job for an applicant.

Overrate Same as **flagged rate.**

Overreaching Taking unfair commercial advantage by **fraud** or **unconscionability.**

Override 1. A **commission** paid to a supervisor when an employee makes a sale. 2. A commission paid to a **real estate agent** when a landowner sells directly to a purchaser who was found by the agent before the **listing** was ended.

Overseas Private Investment Corporation A U.S. government-owned corporation that encourages U.S. private investment in **developing countries** by insuring U.S. investors against the political risks of expropriation, revolution, or inconvertibility of local currencies, and by guaranteeing payment of principal and interest on loans to eligible private enterprises.

Oversold A **security** or **market** whose price(s) has fallen to an unreasonable low.

Overstay Remaining in a market too long so that **paper profits** are lost.

Oversubscription A situation in which more orders for shares of **stock** exist than there are shares of stock to fill the orders.

Overtime Work performed in excess of the basic workday or workweek as defined by law, collective bargaining, or company policy. An *overtime premium* is a **work premium** calling for compensation in excess of the normal. For employees covered by the **Fair Labor Standards Act,** overtime must be paid at a rate of at least 1½ times the employee's regular pay rate for each hour worked in a workweek in excess of the regular hours in a given type of employment.

Owners' equity statement See **statement.**

P

P In newspaper stock transaction tables, an indication that the **stock** is traded on the Philadelphia Stock Exchange.

Pa In newspaper stock transaction tables, an indication that the **stock** is traded on the Pacific Stock Exchange.

PA Professional association.

PAIR Personnel and Industrial relations.

PBGC Pension Benefit Guarantee Corporation. Most private **pension plans** must pay into this federal agency (through an insurancelike plan) to protect against insufficient pension funds.

PC 1. Professional **corporation.** A special type of corporation set up by doctors, lawyers, or other professionals. 2. Personal computer.

P/E ratio Price-earnings ratio.

PEFCO Private Export Funding Corporation

PERT Program Evaluation and Review Technique. A planning and control process that requires identifying the activities of programs and the time and resources needed to go from one activity to the next. A *PERT diagram* would show the sequence and interrelationships of activities from

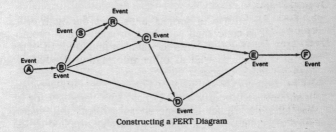

Constructing a PERT Diagram

351

the beginning of a project to the end. *PERT* uses probability theory to help decide how long it is likely that each
program activity in a project will take, and can sometimes
also show what optimistic versus pessimistic time estimates will mean, as well as determine probable costs for
normal versus "crash" schedules. See **CPA.**

PHC   Personal **holding** company.

PITI   Principal, interest, taxes and insurance.

POD   Payable on death. A bank or other account payable
to a person (or a group of persons) and, on that person's
death, payable to someone else.

POP   Point of purchase.

PPI   Producer Price Index.

PR   Public Relations.

PUC   Public Utilities Commission. A state agency that
regulates power companies, railroads, etc.

PUD   Planned unit development.

PTI   Previously taxed income.

P/V analysis   Profit/volume analysis.

P-system   Reordering **inventory** at set times with the quantity varying according to need. Contrast **Q-system.**

Pac-man strategy   Make a **tender offer** for a company that
is trying to gobble up yours.

Package mortgage   A **mortgage** that includes things like
stoves and refrigerators in addition to the building.

Package settlement   The total money value (usually quoted
as dollars and cents per hour) of an increase in wages and
benefits achieved through **collective bargaining.**

Packager   1. A **broker.**   2. An **underwriter.**   3. A person
who puts together deals, such as group travel, a television
series, etc.

Packing   All efforts to protect a product during transit.
Packaging is concerned with both protection and promotion. A *packing list* shows the number and kinds of items
being shipped, as well as other information needed for
transportation purposes.

Paid-in   Supplied by the owners. For example, *paid-in capital*
is money or property actually paid to a company for its
capital stock, rather than merely **subscribed;** and *paid-in
surplus* is that part of a company's **surplus** supplied by the
stockholders, such as donations and assessments, rather
than generated from profits. It sometimes also includes a
company's profits from dealing in its own stock and con-

tributions from outsiders such as a local development agency.

Paid-up capital The total value of **stock** for which full payment has been received by the corporation.

Palletization The system of shipping goods on comparatively lightweight, double-decked wooden platforms called *pallets*.

Palm off Sell goods made by one manufacturer as if they were made by another (better or more famous) manufacturer.

Paper 1. *Paper* may be short for **commercial paper** or for a **negotiable instrument.** 2. *Paper* may mean "only paper." A *paper title* is a **document of title** to something that may or may not be valid. A *paper profit* is an increase in value (of a **stock, bond,** etc.) that might be lost again if the value goes down before sale. A *paper local* is a local union created as a vehicle for unethical or illegal actions.

Par 1. The **face** value of a **stock** or **bond.** For example, if a hundred-dollar bond sells in the bond market for one hundred dollars, it sells *at par*. 2. *Par items* are things a bank will process and send on without charge to another bank. 3. In an international context, the official value of a unit of a country's currency stated in terms of a **numeraire** (customarily gold or another currency); meaningful only in the context of a fixed exchange rate system.

Parallel interface (or **port**) A printer or other **peripheral** hooked up to a computer in a way that transmits all the **bits** of a **byte** of information at once. One standard parallel interface is called *Centronics*. Contrast **serial interface.**

Parallel ladder A **dual ladder.**

Paramount title 1. A **holder in due course** has the best right to a document (and to all the money or property it stands for) in all but a few circumstances. For example, if the property were originally stolen, the real owner has *paramount title*. 2. In **real estate** law, *paramount title* originally meant original title but has come to mean simply "better" or "superior."

Paraprofessional Any individual with less than standard professional credentials who assists a professional. For example, paralegals assist lawyers and paramedics assist medical doctors.

Parent corporation A company that fully controls another company.

Parity 1. Equality; equivalence; even-exchangeability.
2. *Employment parity* exists when the proportion of **EEO**-
protected groups in the external labor market is equivalent to their proportion in an organization's total workforce
without regard to job **classifications.** *Occupational parity*
exists when the proportion of an organization's protected
group employees in all job classifications is equivalent to
their respective availability in the external labor market.
Wage parity requires that the salary level of one occupational classification be the same as for another. The most
common example of wage parity is the linkage between
the salaries of police and firefighters. 3. *Farm parity*
began in the 1930s when the federal government started
using price supports (accompanied by production controls) to stabilize the prices of agricultural commodities.
A *price support* is a guarantee to buy or make loans
against farm products at set prices. It is in this setting that
price parity comes in; it is the price designed to allow a
farmer to maintain a purchasing power equal to a previous base period. In theory, the *parity price* that the government is willing to pay gives a farmer a fair return on
investment when contrasted with costs. 4. *Parity of
authority* is the management principle that a manager
should have the amount of authority that is appropriate
for his or her responsibilities.

Parking 1. The placement of uncommitted funds in short-
term investments while awaiting favorable long-term investment opportunities. 2. Illegal practices whereby
securities are sold to an associate not in **good faith** but as
a means of avoiding legal requirements.

Parliamentary procedure Formal rules of conduct governing the holding of meetings.

Partial incapacity An injury that disables a worker from
doing part of his or her job or that lowers the value of
that person's labor. The term does *not* mean the loss of
part of an arm, part of the use of an arm, part of the
ability to lift things, etc. This is usually called *partial loss*.

Participating preferred stock A class of **preferred stock**
that gives the stockholder a right to **dividends** beyond the
fixed preference rate. The preferred stock might, for example, share with the **common stock** in additional dividends after the common has received a certain amount of
dividends.

Participation 1. An **insurance** policy in which the person insured pays a certain percentage of any loss. 2. A loan arrangement in which several banks combine to make a large loan. 3. A **mortgage** agreement in which the lender gets a share of the profits of the venture in addition to interest on the loan.

Participative management See **industrial democracy.**

Particular average loss A loss of property at sea that is the result of negligence or accident and that must be borne by the owner of the property.

Particular lien A right to hold specific property because of a **claim** against that property; for example, a garage's right to hold a car until the repair bill is paid.

Particulars 1. The details of a legal **claim** or of separate items on an **account.** 2. A detailed description of property to be sold.

Partner A member of a **partnership.** A *full* or *general partner* participates fully in running the company and sharing the profits and losses. A *dormant, silent,* or *sleeping partner* is a person who is in a partnership, but is not known as a partner by the public, does not take an active hand in the business, and, if also a *special* or *limited partner,* puts in a fixed amount of money, gets a fixed amount of profit, and is usually not liable for anything beyond the investment itself. Finally, a *nominal* or *ostensible partner* is *not* a partner, but only someone who *looks like* a partner to the public.

Partnership A **contract** between two or more persons to carry on a business together and to share money and labor put in and profits or losses taken out. It is not a **corporation.** For *limited partnership* and other types, see **partner.** Partnerships are usually formed because they allow several persons to combine talents and resources, because they allow the businss to retain the personal character of the individual partners, and because they are easier to form than corporations. Partnerships do, however, have several disadvantages. Most important, partners (except for *limited* partners) remain fully liable for business debts. If, for example, the business goes **bankrupt,** each partner could lose nearly all his or her personal **assets.** Also, partnerships are legally dissolved on the death of one of the partners. This makes long-term financing difficult to obtain. Because of these problems, partnerships should be avoided unless those involved share a strong personal understanding and have a well-constructed *partnership agreement*. This agreement must include, at a minimum, a definition of the partners' rights and obligations, the way that profits and losses should be divided, information on salaries, expenses, and other financial matters, and provisions for ending the partnership. These provisions can bind the partners, but not creditors or other outsiders. Finally, *partnership accounting* is similar to corporate accounting except, of course, that profits and losses are divided among the partners, whether or not taken out of the business, and that the partners are individually taxed on profits. See **corporation** and **sole proprietorship** for the other major ways of owning a business.

Party   A person taking part in any matter, especially a legal proceeding. A *third party* is a person who is not directly involved in a matter, such as a contract, but who is or might be affected by it. See **third party payment.**

Pass-through   1. Payment through another person.   2. An interest in certain **trusts** and **partnerships** that qualifies for a prorated income tax **deduction.**   3. **Ginnie Mae's mortgage**-backed **securities** program which **guarantees** principal and **interest** payments on securities issued by private mortgage lenders if those securities are backed by pools of government-guaranteed mortgages.   4. A process by which a state government receives federal grants and passes the money through to local governments.

Passalong   A price increase caused by an increase in costs.

Passbook account   An **account** at a commercial bank or a **thrift institution** whose ownership is evidenced by entries in a nonnegotiable book that must be presented with each deposit or withdrawal. In general, a savings account, although **time deposits** may be in passbook form.

Passing a dividend   Omitting the **declaration** of a regular or expected **dividend.**

Past practice   The manner in which a similar issue was resolved before the occasion of a present **grievance.**

Pat. Pend.   Patent pending. A **patent** has been applied for and, if granted, will be valid as of the date of the original application.

Patent   1. Open, evident, plainly visible.   2. A grant of land by the government to an individual.   3. A right (given by the federal government to a person) to control the manufacture and sale of something that person has discovered or invented. The *patent and copyright clause* is the U.S. constitutional provision protecting the rights of authors and inventors to exclusive use of their products for a limited time (Article I, Section 8, Clause 8). The *Patent and Trademark Office* is a federal agency in the **Commerce** Department that decides on and keep tracks of *patent* and **trademark** applications, keeps a complete public reference file, publishes related information, etc. *Patent pooling* is an agreement among companies (usually manufacturers) to share *patent* information and rights.

Paternalism In U.S. labor relations, the word is a derogatory reference to an organization's "fatherly" efforts to better the lot of its employees. Historically, the **labor movement** has considered *paternalistic* efforts to be a false and demeaning charity which inhibited the growth of union membership. In other societies where there are well-established paternalistic traditions, the derogatory connotations of the word may be absent.

Paternity leave See **birth leave.**

Patronage 1. All the customers of a business; giving a company business. (A *patronage dividend* is the refund given to a member of a **cooperative** based on purchases made from the cooperative.) 2. The right of some public officials to give out some jobs, contracts, or honors on their own **discretion,** without going through a merit selection process.

Pattern bargaining **Collective bargaining** in which key contract terms agreed to by one **bargaining unit** are copied by other companies in the same industry during subsequent negotiations.

Pay Salary (or wages) plus, sometimes, fringe benefits. For various *types* of *pay* (such as **call-in, longevity, well,** etc.) see those words. *Pay for performance* is the concept of paying an employee on the basis of job performance—all bonuses, raises, promotions, etc., would be directly related to the measurable results of the employee's efforts. A *pay grade* or *pay level* is the range of pay, or a standard rate of pay, for a specific job. The totality of the pay grades make up the *pay structure*. A *pay plan* is a listing of rates of pay for each job category in an organization. A *pay range,* also known as *salary* or *wage range,* indicates the minimum through maximum rates of pay for a job. The various increments that make up the pay range are known as the *pay steps*. A *pay-as-you-go plan* is a **pension plan** that has employers paying pension benefits to retired employees out of current income.

Payable   1. Owing, and to be paid in the future.   2. Owing, and due for payment now.   3. For *payable to bearer* and *payable to order,* see **bearer** and **order.**

Payables   Accounts payable.

Payback   In its simplest form, the length of time it will take an investment to return what was put in. For example, if a $10,000 investment in a new machine will save $5,000 per year, the *payback period* is $10,000 divided by $5,000, or two years. It is also referred to as the *payoff* or *cash recovery period.* The calculation of the payback period, the payback method, is an important aspect of **capital budgeting.** The *payback reciprocal* is an approximation of the **internal rate of return** when the life of a project will be more than twice the payback period and cash income from the project will remain the same over time.

Payee   The person to whom a **negotiable instrument** (such as a check) is made out; for example, "pay to the **order** of John Doe."

Payment cap   A ceiling on the amount by which monthly **adjustable rate mortgage** payments (**interest** and **principal**) are allowed to rise in any one period.

Payoff period test   A method for comparing the amount of an investment in equipment with the annual cost savings. It is a type of **payback** calculation.

Payola   Bribes or unethical gifts.

Payout ratio   The **dividend** a company pays on each share of **common stock** divided by its **earnings per share.** This percentage shows how much money a company pays its investors compared to what it can plow back into the business.

Payroll tax   See **employment tax.**

Peak-period pricing   User pricing that charges higher rates during higher periods of demand for a service (e.g., a utility), and lower rates during lower periods of demand.

Pegging   Officially, arbitrarily, or artificially fixing or setting the value of something. For example, a country can *peg* the relative value of its money or allow it to **float** relative to other countries'. Also, an **underwriter** selling a

new stock **issue** can *peg* the price by placing repeated
buying orders at a certain price in the stock market. See
crawling peg.

Penalty clause A **contract** provision that requires payment
of an exact sum of money if something is done to vary the
contract's requirements; for example, if you pay off a
mortgage before it is due to avoid further **interest** payments.

Pendency A *notice of pendency* is a formal warning, placed
on property records, that a lawsuit or claim has been
placed against a property and that anyone who buys it
may have to pay off a **lien,** a **judgment,** etc.

Penetration rate 1. A company's sales of a product relative
to the total market for the product. *Penetration pricing* is
an especially low (usually introductory) price for a product in order to quickly penetrate as much of the market as
possible. 2. In the context of **equal employment opportunity,** the *penetration rate* for an organization is the proportion of its workforce belonging to a particular minority
group. The *penetration ratio* is the ratio of an organization's penetration rate to the penetration rate for its geographic region (usually the **standard metropolitan statistical
area,** or SMSA).

Penny stock Speculative **stock** selling at less than a dollar
a share.

Pension Periodic payments to an individual who retires
from employment (or simply from a particular organization) because of age, disability, or the completion of a
specific period of service. Such payments usually continue
for the rest of the recipient's life and sometimes extend to
legal survivors. The *Pension Benefit Guaranty Corporation*
is a federal agency that sets up an employer-contributing
mandatory fund to pay pension **benefits** to persons whose
defined-benefit pension plans go broke. A *pension plan* is
a plan set up by an employer to pay employees after
retirement. A pension plan may be either a fund of money
(called "funded" if it is fully paid-in to meet the promised
pension needs) set up by the employer or payments by
the employer to or for the employee. A *qualified plan* is
one that meets **IRS** requirements for the payments to be
deducted by the employer and initially tax-free to the
employee. A *defined-benefit plan* is one with employer
payments varying to pay for fixed, specifically promised
benefits (or a fixed benefit formula). A *money-purchase*

plan (or *defined-contribution plan*) is one with benefits varying depending on the ultimate value of fixed, specifically promised regular payments (or a fixed payment formula) by the employer. See also **IRA, Keogh Plan, Employee Retirement Income Security Act, vested,** and **annuity.**

Per capita tax   An equal tax on each head (person). A *per capita* "anything" (such as **GNP,** income, etc.) is that thing divided by total population.

Per diem   (Latin) By the day; day by day; or each day. A fixed amount of money paid to a person each day for either a salary or expenses of employment such as food and lodging. [pronounce: per *dee*-em].

Per se   (Latin) In and of itself; taken alone; inherently. For example, some types of business arrangements are called *per se violations* of **antitrust** laws because, even without specific proof that **monopoly** power has hurt competition, the arrangements are in and of themselves bad. [pronounce: per *say*]

Percentage of completion method   An **accounting** process used when a period of production goes beyond an accounting period; then revenues and expenses are recorded in proportion to the costs incurred in relation to the total expected costs of the job or contract.

Percentage depletion   **Depletion allowance.**

Percentage lease   A **lease** of a building with the rent based on the dollar value of sales by the tenant in the building.

Percentage order   Instructions from a customer to a **broker** to buy or sell a certain number of shares of **stock** after a specific number of shares have been traded on the **market.**

Perfect   1. Complete; enforceable; without defect. Also called *perfected.*   2. To tie down or *make perfect.* For example, to *perfect a title* is to **register** it in the proper place so that your ownership is protected against all persons, not just against the person who sold it to you. This is called *perfection.*   3. *Perfect competition* is a theoretical situation existing when there is no **discrimination,** perfect mobility of resources, and all buyers and sellers know all relevant facts in a competitive market; thus no one would buy or sell above or below the **market price.** See **pure competition.** *Perfect elasticity of demand* means that a small price change (lower) would result in an unlimited increase in demand. *Perfect elasticity of supply* means that a small price change (higher) would result in an unlimited increase in supply. *Perfect inelasticity of demand* means that a small price change (lower) would result in no change in demand. *Perfect inelasticity of supply* means that a small price change (higher) would result in no change in supply.

Perfect tender rule The rarely applied rule that exact **performance** of the details of a commercial **contract** is required to make the contract enforceable.

Performance 1. Carrying out a **contract,** promise, or other obligation according to its terms, so that the obligation ends. *Specific performance* is being required to do exactly (or as close to exactly as is fair) what was required. A court may require *specific performance* if one person fails to perform one side of a deal and money **damages** will not properly pay back the other side for harm done. *Part performance* is doing something in *reliance* upon a contract. If the contract is oral, it may not be enforceable unless *part performance* has been made. 2. *Performance analysis* is the review of data on sales, costs, profits, etc., to make comparisons, appraise performance and recommend improvements. A *performance appraisal, evaluation, rating* or *report* is a method by which an organization documents the work performance of its employees. A *performance* (or *completion) bond* is a **bond** that guarantees that a **contractor** will do a job correctly and finish it on time. A *performance report* compares budgeted expenditures to actual expenditures.

Period cost A **fixed cost.**

Periodic inventory Any **inventory** system whose **accounting** is done at various times; only at those times is there a physical count of actual inventory. For a contrast, see **perpetual inventory.**

Periodic tenancy A **lease** that continues from month-to-month or year-to-year unless ended (usually by someone giving a notice that it will be ended).

Peripheral Computer input, output or auxiliary equipment such as a printer.

Perks **Perquisites.** A *perker* (or *perkman*) is a person whose real income is substantially enhanced because of job *perquisites*.

Permanent *Permanent* can mean anything from "for an indefinite time" (as in *permanent employment*), to "definitely right now" (as in *permanent residence*), to "definitely for a definite time" (as in a *permanent* **arbitrator,** whose work lasts for the life of a labor contract or other term) to "definitely for a long time" (as in *permanent disability*), to "forever." *Permanent income* refers to income that can be anticipated into the foreseeable future; the amount that can be consumed each year without reducing overall wealth.

Permit 1. An official document that allows a person to do something (usually something legal that is not allowable without the permit). 2. A *permit card* is a document given by a union to a non-member allowing that person to work on a job for which there are not enough union members.

Perpetual inventory Any **inventory** system whose **accounting** is kept current; each physical addition or subtraction to inventory is recorded immediately. For a contrast, see **periodic inventory.**

Perpetual succession The continuous existence of a **corporation** as the same "being," even though its owners, **directors,** and managers may change.

Perpetuity An investment that gives equal future payments essentially forever.

Perquisites Also called "perks," these are the special **benefits,** frequently tax exempt, usually made available only to the top executives of an organization. There are two basic kinds of executive perquisites: those with "take-home" value (such as company cars, club memberships, etc.) and those that have no "take-home" value, but serve mainly to confer status (such as the proverbial executive washroom, office size and decor, etc.).

Person A human being (a "natural" person); a **corporation** (an "artificial" person, treated as a person in many legal situations); or another "being" entitled to sue as a legal entity (a government, an association, a group of **trustees,** etc.).

Personal income An aggregate measure of economic activity consisting of **national income** minus any kind of income not received by individuals. *Disposable personal income* is the income remaining to individuals after personal tax and nontax payments (fines and fees) that can be used for discretionary spending and savings.

Personal outlays An aggregate measure of spending which consists of personal consumption expenditures, interest paid by consumers, and personal transfer payments to foreigners. It represents the disbursements made by individuals of that portion of **personal income** available after payment of personal taxes. The residue is **personal saving.**

Personal saving The excess of **personal income** over the sum of **personal outlays** and personal tax and **nontax payments.**

Personal space The area that individuals actively maintain around themselves, into which others cannot intrude without arousing discomfort.

Personal time That time an employee uses to tend to personal needs. This time is usually separate from lunch and rest breaks and is sometimes written into union contracts.

Personnel A collective term for all of the employees of an organization. See also **human resources.** A *personnel action* is a process necessary to appoint, separate, reinstate, or make other changes affecting an employee, such as change in position assignment, tenure, etc. *Personnel administration* (or *managment*) is that aspect of management concerned with the recruitment, selection, development, use and compensation of the members of an organization. *Personnel examiner* is a job title for a professional staff member of that unit of a personnel department concerned with selection. A *personnel inventory* is a listing of all employees in an organization by job and personal characteristics which serves as a basic reference for planning and other purposes. A *personnel jacket* is a file folder containing all personnel data on, and personnel actions pertaining to, an employee. A *personnel manual* is a written record of an organization's personnel policies and procedures. *Personnel officer* is a job title for the individual who runs the personnel program of an organizational unit. *Personnel planning* is the process of forecasting **human resources** supply and demand and developing plans to meet organizational needs. The *personnel ratio* is the number of full-time employees of a personnel department (usually exclusive of clerical support) per 100 employees of the total organization. A *personnel runaround* is what is given to job applicants who apply for positions for which individuals have been preselected. *Personnel technician* is a job title for an individual who is a professional staff member of a specialized unit (recruitment, classification and pay, examinations, etc.) of a personnel department. *Personnelist* is jargon for personnel specialist or manager.

Peter Principle In a **hierarchy** every employee tends to rise to his level of incompetence.

Petition in bankruptcy A paper filed in **bankruptcy** court by a debtor requesting **relief** from debts. It can also be filed by creditors asking that a person be put into bankruptcy involuntarily.

Petrodollars Oil earnings of petroleum-exporting countries in excess of their domestic needs and deposited in dollars in Western banks.

Phantom freight See **basing-point system.**

Phantom stock plan An incentive plan that grants an executive a number of theoretical shares of **stock**—*phantom stock*. Since the executive is told that he or she will be paid a cash bonus at some later date that is equal to the then value of the theoretical or phantom shares, there should exist within the executive a great desire to see the value of the company's stock appreciate.

Physical distribution All movement of materials from supplier to manufacturer to consumer. It may also include market planning and customer service functions if integrated by a company in an overall *physical distribution plan*. The job of the *physical distribution engineer* includes not only transportation and traffic management, but areas such as **materials handling, warehousing, inventory control,** order processing, etc., that border on **production** and sales as well.

Picketing Persons gathering outside a place of business to disturb its activities or to inform persons outside of grievances, opinions, etc., about the place. This usually takes place when a **labor union** tries to publicize a **labor dispute** with a company, influence customers to withhold business, influence workers to withhold services, etc. For **chain, common situs, cross,** and other types of *picketing,* see those words.

Pictogram A bar chart using figures instead of bars to show the comparative size of various quantities.

Piece of the action Participation in a business venture.

Piece (work) rate An incentive wage program in which a predetermined amount is paid to an employee for each unit of output. See **differential piece rate** and **nibbling.**

Piercing the corporate veil A judge's holding individual owners, **directors, officers,** etc., liable for a **corporation's** debts or wrongdoing. This is done in unusual circumstances such as to punish fraud or when the corporation's **stock** is not fully paid for.

Piggy-back service The transporting of loaded truck trailers on rail cars.

Pink-collar jobs Those jobs in which noncollege women form the bulk of the labor force, in which the pay is usually low in comparison to men of the same or lower educational levels, in which unionization is nil or weak, and where "equal-pay-for-equal-work" provisions are of little effect because women tend to compete only with other women. *Pink-collar workers* include nurses, elementary school teachers, typists, telephone operators, secretaries, hairdressers, waiters and waitresses, private household workers, etc.

Pink sheets The National Daily Quotation Service directory of information on **over-the-counter** stocks, published on pink paper.

Pioneer patent A **patent** for an invention or device that is entirely new, rather than a small improvement; or a patent that may open up a whole new area of experimentation or development.

Pit A **commodity exchange's** trading area.

Place (and **placement**) Arrange a sale or other financial transaction. *Placement* could be arranging the sale of a new **issue** of stock, arranging a loan or **mortgage** by matching up borrower and lender, or finding a job for a person. *Private placement* is the sale of new **securities** directly to **institutional investors** such as insurance companies.

Place utility Having a product available where a customer wants it. See also **form, time** and **possession utility.**

Planned unit development An area of land to be developed as one unit of various housing groups plus commercial or industrial development, government-required parkland, etc.

Planning The formal process of making decisions for the future of individuals and organizations. There are two basic kinds of business planning: *strategic* and *operational.* *Strategic planning,* also known as long-range, comprehensive, corporate, integrated, overall, and managerial plan-

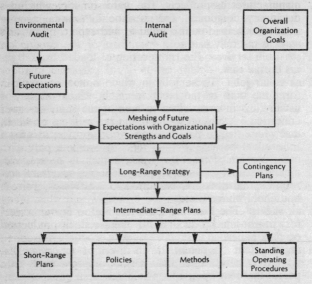

The planning process

ning, has three dimensions: the identification and examination of future opportunities, threats and consequences;
the process of analyzing an organization's environment
and developing compatible objectives along with the appropriate strategies and policies capable of achieving those
objectives; and the integration of the various elements of
corporate planning into an overall structure of plans so
that each unit of the organization knows in advance what
must be done, when and by whom. *Operational planning,*
also known as divisional planning, is concerned with the
implementation of the larger goals and strategies that
have been determined by strategic planning; improving
current operations; and the allocation of resources through
the **operating budget.** See **situation audit.**

Planning horizon The time limit of organizational planning
beyond which the future is considered too uncertain or
unimportant to waste time on.

Plant Any building or group of buildings where a company manufactures its products. The word sometimes includes machinery, equipment, and even tools. *Plant engineering* is another term for maintenance and repair. *Plant and part integration* is the coordination of the production schedules of several integrated plants.

Plant layout The determination of the particular relationship between equipment and operations that will result in the greatest degree of economy and **effectiveness.** For locating machinery, the two general types of layouts used are based on the process used and the product made. In the *process type of layout,* all machines or operations for a specific function are grouped together in one department, and the product travels from department to department. This arrangement maintains a high degree of production flexibility. It is used when a product is not standardized, when the volume of each job lot is low and when many types of products are being made. *Product layout* is used for straight-line production. All the pieces of production equipment needed to produce a single product are grouped together, and the material flows directly from one operation to another. This arrangement requires large-scale production of a standardized product.

Plat (or **plot**) A map showing how a piece of land will be subdivided (divided up) and built upon. A *platmap* gives the legal description of pieces of property by lot, street, and block numbers.

Play An investment. A **direct play** is the purchase of the **stock** of a firm that concentrates in one industry as opposed to one that has more diversified operations. **In play** means a corporation is in the process of being taken over.

Pledge Handing over physical possession of a piece of personal property (such as a radio) or of a document (such as shares of stock) to another person, who holds it until you pay off a debt to that person. *Pledging receivables* is using existing **accounts receivable** as this **collateral** for a loan.

Plottage The extra value two pieces of land may have because they are side-by-side and can be sold as a unit.

Plow back Reinvest profits into a business rather than pay them out to owners.

Plural executive A concept that has a committee assuming the normal responsibilities of an executive.

Point 1. One percent. A term used by **mortgage** companies to describe an initial charge made for lending money. See **loan discount.** 2. One unit of measure. For example, if a stock goes up in price one dollar, it has gone up "one point," since stocks are usually expressed in dollar amounts. 3. A *point estimate* is an estimate which is expressed in terms of a single numerical value rather than a range of values. *Point of purchase* is the very end of the retail chain, where money is exchanged for a product.

Point-of-sale terminal systems A variety of systems using electronic terminals which are located in places convenient to consumers, such as shopping centers, and which provide access to accounts maintained with depository institutions such as banks. Depending on the complexity of the *POS system,* various services associated with a purchase transaction may be possible, such as transferring of funds between accounts, authorization of credit, or verification of checks. A complete POS system would allow transfer of funds from a customer's to a merchant's account, even if such accounts were maintained at different depository institutions. See also **electronic fund transfer systems.**

Point system (or **method**) The most widely used method of **job evaluation,** in which the relative worth of the jobs being evaluated is determined by totalling the number of points assigned to the various factors applicable to each of the jobs.

Poison pill An issue of new **stock** by a target corporation to thwart a hostile *takeover* attempt. Such an issue might be initially worthless *preferred stock* that could be turned in for cash if the takeover succeeds.

Poison-put bond A **bond** which gives the owner the right to cash it in at **par** in the event of a hostile **takeover.**

Policy 1. A general rule indicating a course of action that should be taken under established circumstances. *Corporate policy statements* are sometimes issued separately, but more frequently they are included in other company publications such as the employee handbook. *Procedures* implement policies by stating how they will be carried out. *Public policy* is either the general purpose of a **statute** or the general good of the state and its people. A contract is "against public policy" if carrying it out will be harmful to the public. For various types of *insurance policies,* see insurance and the individual words. 2. *Policy analysis* is the application of systematic research techniques to create a more rational administrative system. For *policy formulation*, see **corporate strategy**.

Polyopsony The fewness of buyers of a particular item or commodity.

Polypoly The fewness of sellers of a particular item or commodity.

Pool 1. A joining together of resources (by individuals or companies) in a common commercial venture. 2. An agreement between companies to not compete and to share profits. These types of arrangements are usually illegal under **antitrust** laws.

Pooling of interest Directly combining the **balance sheets** of two companies when they **merge.** This **accounting** method disregards **goodwill** as a measure of the difference in company values. See **purchase method.**

Port A plug that connects parts of a computer system. A type of **interface.**

Port authority Various federal, state, or interstate agencies that **regulate** boat traffic, promote port business, and maintain other services such as airports, tollroads, etc.

Port of entry 1. A place where immigrants and imported goods may enter the country by sea, air or land and where **customs** offices exist. 2. A point of entry for some U.S. states where vehicles may be inspected for weight, cargo, etc.

Portability The characteristic of a **pension plan** that allows participating employees to have the monetary value of **accrued** pension **benefits** transferred to a succeeding pension plan should they leave their present organization.

Portal-to-portal pay Wages paid while traveling from a plant, factory, or mine's entrance to the employee's specific work station and vice versa.

Portfolio All the investments (usually **stock** and other **securities**) held by one person or organization. The *portfolio effect* is the offsetting of one investment risk by another investment so that the combined risk is lessened. The *portfolio risk* is the inherent risk in any group of investments. *Portfolio theory* deals with the relationship between risk and **return** to portfolios.

POSDCORB A mnemonic device to call attention to the various functional elements of the work of an executive.

It stands for *Planning* (working out in broad outline the things that need to be done and the methods for doing them to accomplish the purpose set for the enterprise); *Organizing* (the establishment of the formal structure of authority through which work subdivisions are arranged, defined and co-ordinated for the defined objective); *Staffing* (the whole personnel function of bringing in and training the staff and maintaining favorable conditions of work); *Directing* (the continuous task of making decisions and embodying them in specific and general orders and instructions and serving as the leader of the enterprise); *Coordinating* (the all important duty of interrelating the various parts of the work); *Reporting* (keeping those to whom the executive is responsible informed as to what is going on, which thus includes keeping self and subordinates informed through records, research and inspection); *Budgeting* (with all that goes with budgeting in the form of fiscal planning, accounting and control).

Position 1. A defined group of duties and responsibilities requiring the full or part-time employment of one individual. A position may, at any given time, be occupied or vacant. *Position classification* is the process of using formal *job* (or *position*) descriptions to organize all jobs in a given organization into **classes** on the basis of duties and responsibilities for the purpose of delineating authority, establishing chains of command, and providing equitable salary scales. 2. A *position paper* is a formal statement of opinion, a report or analysis. 3. One's stake in a **securities** or **commodities** market. 4. An **accounting** summary. 5. *Positioning* is the use of comparative advertising (or selling to a well-defined submarket or target market) to gain sales for a product at the direct expense of similar products.

Positive recruitment Aggressive action designed to encourage qualified individuals to apply for positions, as opposed to just waiting for the right person to "knock on the door."

Positive strike A **strike** to gain new benefits. A *negative strike* is to prevent the loss of present benefits.

Possession utility Being able to transfer legal possession of a product to a customer. See also **form, time** and **place utility.**

Post audit An **audit** made after transactions have been recorded and approved by appropriate authority.

Postdate To put a date on a document that is *later* than the date the document is signed.

Posting 1. Writing down an *entry* (such as money spent for a lamp) into an **account** book. 2. The same as no. 1, but by transferring the information from an original record or notation to an account in a ledger.

Postponement Subordination of a **lien, mortgage,** or **judgment** when it would normally have priority over the lien, mortgage, or judgment now given priority.

Potentially dilutive Any **security** which may be converted into **common stock.**

Power The ability or the right (or both) to do something. *Power of appointment* is a part of a will, deed, or separate document that gives someone the power to decide who gets money or property or how it will be used. *Power of attorney* is a document authorizing a person to act formally for the person signing the document. A *power base* is the organizational or interpersonal support one has to advance one's self or policies. A *power broker* is a trader in influence. The *power elite* consists of the leaderships of major segments of society—business, government, military, etc. *Power of sale* is the right of a **mortgage** holder or mortgage **trustee** to sell the property if payments are not made. The *power structure* is the group making basic decisions for an organization or community. A *power test* is a test intended to measure level of performance unaffected by speed of response—there is either no time limit or a very generous one.

Practice 1. Custom, habit, or regular repetition. *Practices* are operating *procedures* that have not been put into written form. 2. Formal court procedure; the way a lawsuit is taken to and through court as opposed to what it is about. 3. Engaging in a profession, such as law, medicine or accounting, or doing things that are only permitted to be done by a member of a profession. 4. The *practice effect* is the influence of previous experience with a test on a later administration of the same test or a similar test—usually an increase in score.

Pre-emption The first right to buy or do something. For example, *pre-emptive rights* are the rights of some stockholders to have first chance at buying any new stock the company issues.

Precautionary demand   Money or **liquid assets** held for emergencies. The *precautionary balance* is the cash held in an **account** for unexpected needs.

Precedent   A court decision on a *question of law* that gives direction on how to decide a similar question in a later case with similar facts. The American court system is based on judges making decisions supported by *past precedent*, rather than by the unsupported logic of the judge alone.

Precontract   A **contract** that keeps you from entering into a similar contract with someone else.

Predatory intent   Lowering prices solely to put a competitor out of business.

Preference   1. A **creditor's** right to be paid before other creditors.   2. The act of an **insolvent** (broke) **debtor** in paying off a creditor more than a fair share of what is left. For example, if John has ten dollars and owes both Mary and Don ten dollars each, his decision to pay Mary ten dollars is a *preference*. If a debtor gives a creditor preference shortly before going into **bankruptcy,** the bankruptcy court may be able to get that money back in to be divided fairly.   3. A country's granting of more generous **tariff** or non-tariff treatment to particular trading partners.

Preferential shop   A place of business where union members will be hired first and laid off last.

Preferred creditor   A **creditor** whose claim, by law, must take preference over those of others.

Preferred stock   A type of **stock** entitled to a fixed rate of income before the company's **common** stock is paid **dividends,** and often entitled to a share of the company's **assets** before common stock can take a share. This usually makes it less speculative than common stock but more speculative than **bonds.**

Pregnancy Discrimination Act   A 1978 amendment to Title VII of the **Civil Rights Act** which holds that discrimination on the basis of pregnancy, childbirth or related medical conditions constitutes unlawful sex **discrimination.**

Premium   1. The money paid for **insurance coverage.** 2. An extra amount of money paid to buy something or as a bonus.   3. The amount by which a **stock or other security** sells above its **par (face** or **nominal)** value.   4. *Premium pricing* means charging more for a product because the high price enhances its attractiveness. Also called **prestige pricing.** For *premium pay,* see **work premium.**

Prepay Paid before. A *prepaid expense* is any expense or debt paid before it is due. This may have special tax consequences. A *prepaid health plan* is a contract between an insurer and an employer, a subscriber, or group of subscribers in which the plan provides a specified set of health benefits in return for a periodic **premium.** *Prepaid income* is money received but not yet earned or due to you. This may have special tax consequences. *Prepaid legal services* works the same way as a *prepaid health plan.* A *prepayment penalty* is extra money that must be paid if you pay off a loan early. This compensates the lender for lost **interest** or extra paperwork.

Present worth (or value) Future payments, earnings, or debts **discounted** to their value today (as if a sum of money were invested today to make the future payments). *Present value benefit* is a calculation of each year's expected monetary benefit multiplied by its discount factor and then summed over all years of the planning period. *Present value cost* is a calculation of each year's expected cost multiplied by its discount factor and then summed over all years of the planning period. For *present worth method,* see **profitability index.**

Presentment (or presentation) Showing a **negotiable instrument,** such as a check, and asking for payment on it.

Presort Arranging mail in zip-code order to take advantage of lower postage rates.

Press kit Packages of materials (press releases, pictures, etc.) for distribution to individual media representatives.

Prestige prices Sufficiently high prices to allow customers to feel that they are getting a "quality" product.

Prevailing wage Average pay for a specific job in a given geographical region.

Preventive discipline Actions to heighten employees' awareness of organizational rules and policies.

Preventive mediation To avoid last-minute **crisis bargaining,** the negotiating parties sometimes seek the use of a **mediator** before an **impasse** has been reached.

Previously taxed income Earnings that have been taxed but not yet distributed. (This usually happens when a **Subchapter S corporation** holds onto earnings.) This income will not be taxed a second time when given out to the company's owners.

Price Costs; the money for which items are bought or sold. Also see **leader prices** and **prestige prices**. For *price discrimination,* see **predatory intent**. The *price/earnings ratio* is the cost of a **share** of **stock** divided by the yearly **dividend** paid by that stock. For example, a $20 stock that paid $2 has a ten-to-one ratio. This figure is used in comparing stocks' investment potential. The *price elasticity of demand* is a measure of the probable percentage change in **demand** for a given product in response to a one-percent change in its price. See **elasticity**. *Price fixing* occurs primarily two ways. *Horizontal price fixing* is different companies (or associations of companies) agreeing to charge similar prices for similar things. *Vertical price fixing* is controlling the resale price of something (by requiring a retailer to sell at no lower than a certain price, etc.) All of these arrangements are violations of **antitrust** laws. Firms need not actually sign an agreement to be found liable for price fixing. In fact, rarely does a written agreement exist among *price fixers*. Proof of conspiracy can be found from "circumstantial" evidence such as a pattern of unexplained identical contract terms. There is no defense for price fixing. Defendants may not justify their behavior by arguing, for example, that the prices were reasonable to consumers or were necessary to avoid cutthroat competition or that the price fixing actually stimulated competition. For *price guides,* see **deceptive pricing guides.** A *price index* shows the relative changes in a price over time or the relative change in an average of prices over time; examples include the **Consumer Price Index** and the **Producer Price Index.** See **index**. *Price leadership* is a situation in which one large company regularly sets selling prices for something, and the rest of the industry then sets the same price. This is not a violation of antitrust laws unless the companies worked together on the pricing or tried to drive other companies out of the market. A *price limit* is the maximum fluctuation in the price of a **commodities futures contract** allowed during any one trading session. *Price lining* calls for a seller to set a few price levels for a class of products and then assign each product in the class to one of these levels. A *price loco* is the price for goods at the location of purchase. A *price out of the market* is a price so high that there are few, if any, buyers. *Price sovereignty* is the theory that goods or services should go to those who can pay the most. *Price supports* are government loan, subsidy, and buying programs designed to keep prices (usually farm prices) above a certain level. See **parity** for more on how they work. *Pricing* is setting or adjusting the price of goods for sale. Some of the operating and marketing considerations for pricing are replacement costs, the **profit/volume ratio,** profit maximization, flexibility (for example, in setting credit terms), market share, etc.

Primary activity A **strike, boycott,** or **picketing** against an employer with which a **union** has a dispute. In contrast, a boycott directed against, for example, a store that handles the employer's products is a **secondary boycott.** While the mere withholding of patronage is not unlawful, contracts, combinations, and conspiracies to do so may be.

Primary earnings per share See **fully diluted earnings per share.**

Primary market 1. The place in which, or the method by which, the first sale of a **stock** or other **securities issue** is made. 2. A **market** established for trading in a **commodity** in its natural form. The *primary iron market,* for instance, is the market for newly mined iron ore rather than the market for products of the iron ore. 3. The principal trading market for a particular commodity. 4. Large cities that serve as the basic markets for certain goods.

Prime 1. Original. 2. Most important. 3. For *prime contractor,* see **contractor. 4.** *Prime costs* of manufacture include labor and material but not **overhead.** 5. The *prime rate* is the lowest **interest** a bank will charge its best low-risk customers for short-term, **unsecured** loans. This is an indicator of what the bank's other interest rates will be. The *prime rates* of **national banks** are one major economic indicator.

Principal 1. Chief; most important; primary. For example, a company's *principal office* is its legal home for purposes of incorporation, whether or not that is its real headquarters. (This is more important to the incorporating state than to the company.) 2. A sum of money, as opposed to the profits (**interest**) made on that money. 3. An employer or anyone else who has another person (an **agent**) do things for him or her.

Principles of management   Fundamental truths or working hypotheses that serve as guidelines to management thinking and action.

Printers ink statute   A state law that makes it illegal to advertise anything that is false or deceptive.

Prior   Earlier in time or importance. A *prior act* is a device or process similar enough to one in a **patent** application to justify rejecting the patent. *Prior deposits* are government requirements that an importer must deposit, in domestic or foreign currency, a sum corresponding to a certain percentage of the value of the product to be imported, usually a **licensing** requirement. They are held without **interest,** sometimes for many months from the time an order is placed until after an import operation has been completed. Since the purpose of prior deposits is usually to discourage imports, they are considered **nontariff** measures that impede trade. A *prior lien mortage* is a **mortgage** made after other mortgages on the same property, but with a prior claim on the property. Sometimes when a company is already heavily mortgaged and still in need of funds, it will seek the consent of its **mortgagees** for a *prior lien mortgage*. Sometimes the mortgagees will recognize that new money is necessary to keep the business going and, for the protection of all, will agree to **subordination** of their claims. However, in practice, prior lien mortgages are rare since mortgagees are reluctant to give up their **senior** claims. *Prior preference stock* is **preferred stock** issued after one or more preferred stock issues have been made, and having preferential or priority rights ahead of the prior issue or issues. It may be issued only with the consent of all stockholders.

Private   1. Concerning individuals, not the general public and not the government.   2. For **private letter ruling, offering, placement,** etc., see those words.

Private Export Funding Corporation   A private corporation, owned by American commercial banks and industrial corporations, that makes fixed-rate medium- and long-term loans to foreign buyers. Its loans are unconditionally guaranteed by the **Export-Import Bank** and generally issued together with Eximbank and commercial bank loans.

Private remittances   Unilateral transfers of goods, services, cash, etc., between U.S. residents and residents or governments of foreign countries.

Private sector All of those industries or activities considered to be within the domain of free enterprise. See **public sector** and **third sector.**

Privity 1. Private or "inside" knowledge. 2. A close, direct financial relationship. *Privity of contract* exists among those persons who actually took part in making a deal and have rights and duties because of it. For example, a manufacturer and a seller may be "in privity," but not the manufacturer and the buyer. *Privity* may determine who may be sued and other rights.

Privilege 1. An advantage; a right to preferential treatment. 2. An exemption from a duty others like you must perform. 3. The right to speak or write defamatory (personally damaging) words because the law allows them in certain circumstances. For example, most words are privileged if spoken completely "in the line of public duty." 4. A basic right. For example, the privileges and immunities guaranteed to all by Article IV and the Fourteenth Amendment of the U.S. Constitution. 5. A special advantage, as opposed to a right; an advantage that can be taken away again. 6. The right, and the duty, to withhold information because of some special status or relationship of confidentiality. These privileges include: husband-wife, doctor-patient, clergy, journalist-source, executive, etc. 7. An **option** on a **security** or **commodity.** A *privilege dealer* sells options. A *privileged issue* is a security that has an additional right such as a **stock** or **bond** that can be converted into **common** stock under specified conditions.

Pro bono publico A Latin phrase meaning "for the public good." Often abbreviated to *pro bono,* it usually stands for work done by lawyers without pay for some charitable or public purpose.

Pro forma (Latin) 1. As a matter of form; a mere formality. 2. Projected. A *pro forma* financial **statement** is one that is projected on the basis of certain assumptions. A *pro forma* **balance sheet,** for example, is prepared in connection with new financing, **mergers, recapitalizations, reorganizations,** and the like. They are sometimes called "giving-effect" balance sheets.

Pro rata (Latin) Proportionately; by percentage; by a fixed rate; by share. For example, if Tom, Dick, and Harry are owed two, four, and six dollars respectively by John, but

John has only six dollars to give out, a *pro rata* sharing would be one, two, and three dollars respectively. A *pro rata clause* in an **insurance policy** says that the company will not pay a higher percentage of a loss than the percentage that company covers of the total insurance coverage from all companies. And a *pro rata distribution clause* in an insurance policy says that the amount of insurance on each piece of property is in proportion to the value of that property compared to the total value of all property covered. Thus, if property in several locations is underinsured, then under this clause it is equally underinsured in every location. To *prorate* is to allocate *pro rata*.

Proactive 1. An administrative style which encourages risk taking on behalf of one's clients or one's moral values. 2. A management orientation which exhibits a tendency to act in response to ideas, goals, and opportunities as opposed to a *reactive orientation,* which is a tendency to avoid any initiatives that are not in response to some outside stimulus.

Probate 1. The process of proving that a *will* is genuine and giving out the property in it. 2. The name in some states for a court that handles the distribution (giving out) of decedents' estates (dead persons' property) and other matters.

Proceeds Money or property gained from a sale.

Process 1. A court's ordering a defendant to show up in court or risk losing a lawsuit without being represented; a summons. 2. Any court order that "takes jurisdiction over" (brings formally under the court's power) a person or property. 3. A series of actions designed to achieve something. *Process analysis* is an examination of the method for producing a part or product to discover the most cost effective and efficient means of production. A *process chart* is often used to graphically represent a production process under study. A *process cost system* is **batch costing.** *Process engineering* means making engineering preparations for a sequence of manufacturing processes. It is a part of **industrial engineering.** A *process patent* is a **patent** for a new way of making something or of bringing about a result that has commercial value. A *process server* is a person with legal authority to formally deliver court papers such as writs and summonses to defendants.

Procuration Doing something as someone's **agent,** buyer, or representative.

Procurement Purchasing.

Procuring cause A **broker** who has started in motion a chain of events leading to the sale of real estate and who is entitled to a **commission** for this service.

Producer Price Index The **Bureau of Labor Statistics'** most comprehensive monthly measure of wholesale prices.

Producer's risk The risk that a lot of goods will be rejected by a **sampling** plan even though it is a good lot.

Product 1. The result of mathematical multiplication. 2. Something to be sold. *Product design* is the drawing, modeling, patterning, or delineating of a new product. *Product differentiation* is a marketing tactic which promotes the differences between products whether they are real or imagined; for example, a new toothpaste with sex appeal or a breath mint that has a bold new flavor. *Product engineering* follows up on product design, in contrast with **process engineering,** which plans the manufacturing process. *Product liability* is the responsibility of manufacturers (and sometimes sellers) of goods to pay for harm to purchasers (and sometimes other users or even bystanders) caused by a defective product. A *product life cycle* is the changing sales volume of a product from introduction to death. Each stage of the cycle (through "growth," "maturity," and "decline") has typical sales patterns and typical customers depending on the type of product, type of marketing, introduction of competing products, etc. A *product line* is a group of related products. A *product* (or *brand*) *manager* is responsible for promoting a specific product or line of products. The *product mix* is how much of each product a company makes and sells. *Product planning* is determining which products are profitable and which products should be dropped from production. These decisions use information on **marketing, cost accounting, budgeting,** etc. *Product positioning* is a **marketing research** concept for how a present or potential customer views a product in relation to its competition. See **positioning.** *Product reliability* is the extent to which a product will continue to perform as designed. *Reliability engineering* consists of the managerial and technical aspects of production that have the goal of assuring a product's performance to specified standards.

A *product review* is a critical analysis of a product's features and usefulness written by an independent journalistic source.

Production The manufacturing process. A *production bonus* is a regularly scheduled additional payment to workers for exceeding production quotas. A *production budget* is an estimate of the number of units of each item that must be produced during a stated period, based on the sales budget and **inventory** requirements. Its primary purpose is to determine the production facilities and the finances necessary to manufacture quantities determined salable by the **marketing** division. *Production control* is a comprehensive program of planning a **master schedule** and controlling all production activities, from **purchasing** of **raw materials** to **shipping** the finished **product**. Production control creates stability, which makes for long manufacturing runs, with a minimum of set-ups, delays, and interruptions. It sees that production stays on schedule and that goods are finished on time. *Production cost control* is a system for allocating all expenses to their actual sources. It explains how much it costs to make and sell each item. This information serves as a basis for the *production budget*, and it gives a realistic basis for cost-cutting. The *production fit* is a measure of the compatibility of a proposed product with present production capabilities. A *production function* is a measure of the sensitivity of production output to variations of production inputs such as labor, equipment and materials. For *production management*, see **operations management**. A *production payment* is an advance payment for a purchase that is really a loan to allow its production. *Production planning* is basically the scheduling aspects of *production control* The *production possibility boundary* is a curve on a graph showing the various products that can be produced if all available resources are used. *Production preplanning* (or *prior planning*) is the part of *production control* that establishes feasible goals, prescribes the availability of the means of production, and outlines the limitations within which further planning can proceed. It begins with a **budget** or sales forecast, an estimate of the number of units of each product that the sales division can sell during a specified period, usually a year. This is translated into a **master schedule,** then into separate plans for different products and different production departments. This breakdown shows the movements of parts and materials into production and indicates the timing necessary for subassembly and assembly stations to receive, fabricate, and release items. These schedules remain flexible until shortly before actual production begins. The *production schedule* is usually a chart which shows in detail the manufacturing operations to be carried out over a period of time. *Production workers* are those employees directly concerned with the manufacturing or operational processes of an organization, as opposed to supervisory and clerical employees.

Productivity A measured relationship between the quantity (and quality) of results produced and the quantity of resources required for production. Productivity is, in essence, a measure of the work **efficiency** of an individual, a work unit, or a whole organization.

Productivity bargaining **Collective bargaining** that seeks increases in **productivity** in exchange for increases in wages and benefits.

Profession An occupation requiring specialized knowledge that can only be gained after intensive preparation. A *professional association* is any group of professionals organized for social, educational, or other purposes; for example, a bar association. *Professionalism* is conducting one's self in a manner that characterizes a particular occupation. *Professionalization* is the process by which occupations acquire professional status.

Profit All gains, including both money and increases in the value of property. Economists define it as "**return** on **capital** investment," and, in the context of sales, it is "sales minus costs and expenses (and taxes)." For *profit and loss statement,* see **statement** of income. A *profit center* is either a unit of a company that is considered a separate entity for profit **accounting** purposes (as large as a department store or as small as its smallest counter) or any major source of a company's profit (whether an organization division or product line). A *profit margin* is sales minus the cost of sales and **operating** expenses; that figure then divided by sales. A company's *gross profit margin* (also called *operating margin*) is its operating profit divided by its money made on sales. Its *net profit margin* (also called *net ratio*) is its net profit divided by its sales.

These percentage figures can be used to compare the
company with others and to compare **efficiency** and profitability with prior years. *Profit planning* is either an
aspect of **planning** by which factors that affect profit (prices,
volume, costs, etc.) are coordinated in order to achieve
the balance among them that will result in the highest
profits; or the disposition of profits after they have been
made. *Profit sharing* is a plan set up by an employer to
distribute part of the firm's profits to some or all of its
employees in current or deferred sums based not only
upon individual or group performances, but on the business as a whole. A *qualified* profit sharing plan (one that
meets requirements for tax benefits) must have specific
criteria and formulas for who gets what, how, and when.
A *profit squeeze* occurs when costs rise faster than selling
prices. The *profit/volume (or marginal income) ratio* is a
measurement of the rate at which a dollar of sales contributes to **fixed costs** and profits. This ratio is:

$$ P/V = \frac{\text{fixed costs} + \text{profits}}{\text{total sales}} $$

A *profit-volume chart* is a graphical method of reviewing
cost-volume-profit relationships in order to project earnings (or losses) at various activity levels. The vertical axis
shows earnings and losses; the horizontal shows sales.
The **breakeven point** then occurs when **net** earnings cross
the horizontal axis. The *profitability index* (also known as
the *discounted cash flow method* and *present worth method*)
evaluates proposed investments by comparing the value
of future income (such as annual cost savings from an
investment in equipment) with the expenditure needed to
finance the investment. The profitability index method
shows the rate of **interest** at which the amount of **capital**
required to make the investment would have to be invested to equal the **return** on the investment. To use this
method for equipment purchase it is necessary to know
five things: total investment expenditure and its time schedule; annual cost savings; the equipment's useful life; probable **depreciation** allowance; and expected income tax
rates on profits (or cost savings). See **discounting**. *Profitability ratios* are measures of the relative value of profits

compared to a **base.** See **dividend yield, earnings per share, net income on sales, price-earnings ratio,** *profit margin,* **return on assets, return on investment,** and **return on net worth.** *Profiteering* is making unreasonable profits by taking advantage of unusual circumstances; for example, by selling scarce goods at high prices during a war.

Program 1. In computer terminology, a set of instructions telling the computer what to do. A *programmer* is a person who writes a computer program. As the programmer does his or her job, he or she can be said to be *programming* the computer. 2. A major organizational effort defined by the principal actions required to achieve a significant end **objective.** In this sense, *programming* is the process of deciding on specific courses of action to be followed in carrying out **planning** decisions on objectives. It also involves decisions in terms of total costs to be incurred over a period of years as to personnel, material, and financial resources to be applied in carrying out programs. *Program budgeting* is a long-range approach that relates future expenditures to organizational goals that go beyond a single **budget cycle.** This allows a manager to see the estimated cost of a program over several years as opposed to only seeing that portion of the cost covered in the current budget. *Program evaluation* is a systematic examination of any activity or group of activities by an organization to know their impact or effects, both short and long range. For *Program Evaluation and Review Technique,* see **PERT.** For *program management,* see **project management.** *Programmed costs* are **fixed charges,** such as long-term research, that do not directly produce or sell goods and services; the opposite of **capacity costs.** 3. *Programmed learning* is an instructional technique that has learning materials presented in a predetermined order, with provisions that permit the learner to proceed at his or her own pace and gain immediate feedback on his or her answers.

Program trading 1. Decisions to buy or sell *securities* generated by computers that have been previously programed to process buy or sell orders when a certain price or date is reached. 2. Index **arbitrage,** the simultaneous computer-generated trading of a stock index *futures* contract and the *equities* that make up the index. The goal is to find a profit in discrepancies between stock prices and futures prices.

Progress payments   Periodic payments made as work on a **contract** progresses; used extensively in defense and construction contracts.

Progressive discipline   An approach to employee discipline that invokes increasing severe penalties as infractions continue to occur.

Progressive tax   A tax that charges the rich a larger proportion of their income or wealth than it charges the poor. For example, federal *income tax* is *progressive*, at least in theory. The opposite of a *progressive tax* is a *regressive tax*. This hits the poor harder. An example is a sales tax. Even though everyone pays the same tax, it takes a larger part of a poor person's money to pay it.

Project management   A project is an organizational unit created to achieve a specific goal. While a project may last from a few months to a few years, it has no further future. Indeed, a primary measure of its success is its dissolution. The project staff necessarily consists of a mix of skills from the larger organization. The success of project management is most dependent upon the unambiguous nature of the project's goal and the larger organization's willingness to delegate sufficient authority and resources to the **project manager.** *Project* or *program management* is an integral part of **matrix** organizations.

Project manager   A manager whose task is to achieve a temporary organizational goal using as his or her primary tool the talents of diverse specialists from the larger organization.

Promise   In legal language a *promise* is an oral or written statement from one person to another, given for something of value in return. It binds the person making the promise to do something and gives the other person the legal right to demand that it be done.

Promissory estoppel   The principle that if Person A makes a promise and expects Person B to do something in reliance upon that promise, then Person B does act in reliance upon that promise, the law will usually help Person B enforce the promise.

Promissory note   A written promise, with no strings attached; to pay a certain sum of money by a certain time. A **negotiable** *promissory note* is a signed written promise, with no strings attached, to pay an exact sum of money immediately, when asked for, or by a certain date to either "the **order** of" a specific person or to **bearer** (the person who physically has it).

Promoter A person who forms a **corporation.** The **SEC** defines *promoter* as anyone who receives a certain percentage of a corporation's stock (or proceeds from the sale of that stock) in exchange for services or property. *Promoters' stock* is issued to the *promoters* of a corporation as payment, in full or in part, for their services in organizing the corporation, or other services.

Proof 1. A body of evidence supporting a contention. Those facts from which a conclusion can be drawn. In this sense, proof can be convincing or unconvincing. (But see no. 2.) 2. The result of convincing evidence. The conclusion drawn that the evidence is enough to show that something is true or that an argument about facts is correct. There are various standards of proof, including beyond a reasonable doubt (how convincing evidence must be in a criminal trial); by clear and convincing evidence; and by a preponderance (greater weight) of the evidence. In this sense, proof is always convincing. (But see no. 1.) 3. *Proof of claim* is a sworn statement in a **bankruptcy** or **probate** proceeding of how much a **creditor** is owed. *Proof of loss* is a sworn statement made to an insurance company of a loss suffered under an insurance policy. *Proof of notice* is a copy of the notice of a **stockholders'** meeting with the date of mailing and mailing list in **affidavit** form and, if the notice has been published in the newspapers, a clipping.

Property Anything that is owned or can be owned, such as land, automobiles, money, stocks, patents, the right to use a famous actor's name or picture, etc. Property is usually divided into *real* (land and things attached to or growing on it) and *personal* (everything else). Some things fall in between or are both (a partly built-in bookcase, a *title* document to a piece of land, etc.). A *property dividend* is a **dividend** paid in the form of *stocks* or *bonds* of other corporations held as investments, property of other corporations received in payment of claims against them; stock of **subsidiaries;** or merchandise owned by the corporation. Any **asset,** if physically divisible, may be paid out as dividends if there is a **surplus.** *Property management* is performing all a landlord's functions (such as upkeep, rent collection, finding tenants, etc.) for another person's building. A *property tax* is a state or local tax based on the value of certain property (homes, cars, etc.) owned.

Proposal 1. An **offer** that can be accepted to make a **contract.** 2. A preliminary or exploratory idea for discussion that is *not* an offer as in no. 1.

Proprietary Having to do with ownership, especially with ownership to make a profit. *Proprietary rights* or interests are the rights or interests a person has because of, or attached to, property ownership. For example, if one person has the sole right to make and sell a medicine, it is a *proprietary drug*. And the right to vote a **share** of **stock** is a *proprietary interest* of owning it. The *proprietary functions* of a city (as opposed to its public functions) may include such things as sidewalk repair and trash pickup.

Proprietorship 1. The running of a business. 2. **Sole proprietorship.**

Prorate To divide or share proportionately or by shares; see **pro rata.**

Prorogation An agreement in a **contract** to allow the courts of one particular state or country to decide all disputes involving the contract.

Prospectus 1. A document put out to describe a **corporation** and to interest persons in buying its **stock.** When new stock is sold to the public, the **SEC** requires a *prospectus* that contains such things as a **statement** of income, a **balance sheet,** an **auditor's report,** etc. 2. Any offer (written, by radio or television, etc.) to interest persons in buying any **securities,** such as stock. 3. A document put out to interest persons in any financial deal (such as the offer to sell a building).

Prosumer A consumer of one's own products.

Protected classes (or **groups**) See **affirmative action groups.**

Protected preferred stock Preferred stock issued with a provision that a special **surplus** account will be maintained by the corporation for the regular saving of funds to be kept available for the **declaration** of **dividends** for this **class** of stock. This assures the availability of funds for dividends even in lean years.

Protectionism The setting of trade barriers (such as quotas and *tariffs*) high enough to discourage foreign imports or to raise their prices sufficiently to enable relatively inefficient domestic producers to compete successfully with foreigners.

Protective committee A group of stockholders appointed to protect the interests of all holders of that type of stock during the **reorganization** or **liquidation** of a corporation.

Protective inventory A **safety inventory.**

Protest 1. A written statement that you do not agree to the legality, justice, or correctness of a payment, but you are paying it while reserving your right to get it back later. 2. A formal certificate of the **dishonor** of a **negotiable instrument** you have presented for payment. It is signed by a **notary** and gives **notice** to all persons **liable** on the negotiable instrument that they may have to pay up on it.

Protocol The conventions about **software**, content, format, speed, etc. that allow different parts of a computer system and different computerized systems to communicate.

Provision 1. Money or property held by or sent to the **drawee** of a **bill** of exchange in order to pay it upon **presentment.** 2. See **reserve.**

Proxy A person who acts for another person (usually to vote in place of the other person in a meeting the other cannot attend) or a piece of paper giving that right. A *proxy statement* is the document sent or given to stockholders when their voting *proxies* are requested for a **corporate** decision. The **SEC** has rules for when the statements must be given out and what must be in them. *Proxy solicitation agents* are individuals or companies who solicit proxies, usually by mail and newspaper campaign, for a fee, as agents for individual stockholders, directors, or officers of corporations, for groups of interested persons, or for management.

Prudent person rule A **trustee** may invest **trust** funds only in traditionally safe investments or risk being personally responsible for losses. These safe investments may be restricted to a state-selected group of **securities** called *legal investments* or the *legal list*.

Public 1. Having to do with a state, nation, or the community as a whole; for example, a tax or a government function that will benefit the community as a whole, and not merely individual members, has a public purpose. 2. Open to all persons. 3. *Public administration* can mean three things: the implementation of public policy; administrative policy making and implementation in support of legislative intent; or the study of governmental decision-making and **management**. *Public affairs* is that aspect of *public relations* which deals with political and social issues and, most important, relations with governments; or a more genteel sounding name for a *public relations* department. The *public domain* is either land owned by the government or something that is free for anyone to use (no longer protected by **patent** or **copyright**). A *public enterprise* is a company that trades its debt or equity **securities** in a stock **exchange** or **over-the-counter** market and is required to file financial statements with the **Securities and Exchange Commission**. For a contrast, see **nonpublic enterprise**. *Public enterprise (revolving) funds* are federally owned funds that are credited with receipts generated by and earmarked to finance a continuing cycle of business-type operations (e.g., the **Federal Deposit Insurance Corporation**). *Public finance* is an imprecise term for the gaining and spending of funds by governments and of the management of government debt. *Public goods* are **commodities** typically provided by government that cannot, or would not, be separately parceled out to individuals since no one can be excluded from their benefits. Public goods such as national defense, clean air, or public safety are neither divisible nor exclusive. *Public lands* are either land owned by the government or land owned by the government and not set aside for a particular purpose, so subject to possible sale. *Public relations* is a management function (or department) which involves building and maintaining good relationships with other groups or "*publics*," such as employees, stockholders, customers, government, and the general public. *Corporate public relations* are efforts designed to enhance the image of the corporation as a good place to work, as being socially responsible, etc. *Financial public relations* are those efforts on the part of a corporation which seek to generate interest in its stock among current and prospective stockholders. *Marketing public relations* are efforts to improve the image of a company's products for distributors and sales representatives as well as for the general public. A *public sector organization* is any agency or institution funded, directly or indirectly, by public taxation. See **private sector** and **third sector**. A *public services com-*

mission (or *public utilities commission*) is a state agency that **regulates** private businesses that have a public **charter,** perform a necessary public function, and need special government help (such as the power of **eminent domain**). These private businesses (such as railroads or power companies) are called *public utilities;* they are often **monopolies,** and must provide service to all persons without **discrimination.** A *publicly held corporation* is a **corporation** with stock sold to a large number of persons.

Publication Making public. For example, in **copyright** law, *publication* is offering a book, a movie, etc., to the public by sale or distribution; and *publication of notice* of a forthcoming stockholders' meeting is often required to be in a newspaper.

Publicist One who practices **public relations** in the entertainment industry.

Puffing 1. Salesmanship by a seller that is mere general bragging about what is sold, rather than definite promises about it or intentionally misleading information. 2. Secret bidding for the seller at an auction to raise the price.

Pull (or **pulling**) **strategy** A **marketing** plan that concentrates on creating consumer demand for a product. Contrast **push strategy.**

Pump priming Government spending designed to increase overall employment and purchasing power to generate economic activity during an economic slowdown.

Punitive damages Money awarded by a court to a person who has been harmed in a particularly malicious or willful way by another person. This money is not necessarily related to the actual cost of the injury or harm suffered. Its purpose is to keep that sort of act from happening again by serving as a warning. It is also called *exemplary damages*.

Purchase Buy. However, according to the **Uniform Commercial Code,** *purchase* includes "any voluntary transaction creating an interest in property, including a gift." A *purchase forecast* is an estimate of material needs for a given period. To make the forecast, the **sales budget** must be studied in conjunction with the **production schedule,** and the material needs determined on the basis of both production plans and delivery dates, keeping in mind: revisions in production schedules; failure of suppliers to deliver material; price changes in major items; or extra buying because of strikes, unexpected shortages, etc. A *purchase fund* is a provision in an **issue** of **preferred stock** that the company must set aside a certain amount of money each year with which to purchase the stock if it can do so at or below the price at which the stock was offered. If stock is not available at that price, the money is kept in the fund. The purpose is to support the market for the stock. The *purchase method* is an **accounting** procedure for **business combinations** which essentially adds the actual amounts paid for the acquired company's **assets** to the assets of the acquiring company. For a contrast, see **pooling of interest method**. A *purchase money mortgage* has a buyer financing part of a purchase by giving a **mortgage** on the property to the seller as **security** for the loan. A *purchase money resulting trust* occurs when one person puts up money to buy something to be held in another person's name. **Title** to that property is held by a *purchase money resulting trust* in favor of the person putting up the money. A *purchase order* is a document that authorizes a person or a company to deliver goods or perform services. It promises to pay for them. A *purchasing department* buys an organization's materials for production, office use, transportation, resale, etc.

Pure competition 1. A **market** in which no individual participant is significant enough to influence prices. 2. A market situation in which buyers and sellers don't care who they deal with so long as they get the best price, and the amounts offered by any given seller are small in proportion to the whole market. See **perfect competition**.

Push (or **pushing**) **strategy** A **marketing** plan that concentrates on convincing wholesalers and retailers to stock and sell a product. Contrast **pull strategy**.

Put An **option** to sell a particular **stock** or **commodity** at a certain price for a certain time. The person who buys a *put option* expects prices to fall. If they don't, he or she loses the purchase price of the *put*, but does not have to **exercise** (use) it.

Pyramid 1. A colloquial term for an organization's **hierarchy**. When top **management** offices are located on the highest parts of a building, the organizational pyramid becomes a literal as well as a figurative notion. 2. A *pyramid sales scheme* is a type of sales pitch that promises that once you buy an item, you get paid for each additional buyer you find for the company. It is also known as a *referral sales plan,* a *chain referral plan,* and a *multilevel distributorship.* It is illegal in many forms.   3. **Pyramiding** is the use of a small amount of money or of **paper profits** to finance buying large amounts of *stock,* to control companies, etc. This is **leverage** plus the additional idea of adding on as you go along.

Q

Q In newspaper stock transaction tables, an indication, lowercase (q), that an **over-the-counter** firm is in **bankrupcy** proceedings.

Q-chart Any **organization chart** that assigns numerical values to its various boxes. Sometimes these "quantitative" values are indicated by using boxes proportionate in size to the represented values.

Q-rating A measure of the popularity of a person or product, usually expressed in a dual score: first, whether the person or product is recognized; second, whether he, she or it is liked.

Q-ratio The ratio of a company's physical *assets* to their current replacement costs.

Q-system Reordering **inventory** in set quantities with the reorder periods varying according to need. Contrast **P-system.**

Qualification (or **qualifying a prospect**) Making sure that a person is a genuine prospect for a business deal. This may involve testing the person's sincerity, checking the person's financial resources, etc.

Qualified 1. Meeting certain requirements. For example, a *qualified corporation* is a **corporation** that has met the requirements of a state for **doing business** within the state. This usually includes maintaining a **statutory agent** for **service of process.** Corporations usually keep a state-by-state *qualification file* of necessary papers and information which may also contain documents showing how the corporation's **securities** *qualify* for sale under various state and federal laws. For *qualified pension*, see **pension plan.** 2. Limited. For example, a *qualified acceptance* is not an **acceptance** at all, but a **counteroffer** because an acceptance of a deal must be unqualified and unrestricted. *Qualifed circulation* is controlled circulation. A *qualified* *endorsement* is signing a **negotiable instrument** "without recourse" and limiting your **liability** for payment. A *qualified report* is an opinion of an **auditor** which cannot be given full credence because the auditor was unable to examine, or has some doubts about, some relevant matters.

Quality Level of excellence. *Quality assurance* is the systematic **auditing** of *quality control* operations. A *quality B school,* in corporate recruiting notices, usually refers to an MBA program in one of a specific list of *top* business schools. Other management programs have, however, been known to deliver a quality business education. *Quality circles* are small voluntary groups of employees who meet regularly to identify and solve work problems. *Quality control* is both an independent staff function and a responsibility of **production** supervisors. It is responsible for establishing product quality specifications (performance capability, appearance, ease of operation, durability, etc.); insuring that the product design incorporates all quality requirements; determining that processes and processing equipment are capable of meeting quality production requirements; establishing quality specifications for materials and inspecting incoming materials; determining standards for inprocess inspection and providing measuring devices and other inspection tools; testing finished products; establishing packaging and shipping specifications; and establishing installation and service instructions. *Quality management* is a new phrase for *quality control* in its most expanded sense of a total concern for quality in **production management.** A *quality market* is those customers who are more concerned with quality than price. *Quality of working life* is an ill-defined area of concern that generally deals with the problem of creating more humane work environments through greater **industrial democracy.** The *quality system* consists of all those activities, including *quality control* and *quality management,* that are designed to ensure that a product, process, or service meets appropriate **standards.** Used interchangeably with *quality plan* and *quality program.*

Quantitative controls The **Federal Reserve System's** instruments of monetary policy such as changes in **reserve** requirements or **discount rates.**

Quantity discount A reduction in **net** price that is systematically related to purchased amounts.

Quasi (Latin) "Sort of"; analogous to "as if." A *quasi* (or *constructive*) *contract* is an obligation "sort of like" a **contract** that is created, not by an agreement, but by law. The principle of *quasi contract* is used to bring about a fair result when a person's actions or the relationship between persons makes it clear that one person has an obligation to the other that is similar to a contract. A *quasi corporation* is a **joint stock company**. A *quasi-public corporation* is a private corporation, such as a **public utility,** that is **regulated** by government and must make available goods or services for the general public. A *quasi-reorganization* is a **reorganization** designed to eliminate a **deficit** (by absorption) from a past operation. This results in a new basis of accountability which should make it easier for a company to borrow money for its profitable operations.

Queue A line. Customers waiting for service and receiving service, products waiting for processing and receiving processing, etc. *Queuing theory* is a set of mathematical techniques which attempt to explain or influence queues to avoid or lessen bottlenecks in production lines, checkout counters, etc.

Quick assets A company's cash, plus its **assets** that are easily turned into cash for immediate use or to meet emergencies. *Quick assets* are **current** assets minus **inventory.** *Net quick assets* are quick assets minus **current liabilities** (what the company owes that comes due soon). The *quick asset ratio* (or *quick ratio* or *acid test*) is quick assets divided by current liabilities. These are measures of whether a company can meet unexpected obligations, can take advantage of unexpected opportunities, and has good short-term prospects or even survivability.

Quickie strike A spontaneous or unannounced **strike** of short duration.

Quid pro quo (Latin) "Something for something." The giving of one valuable thing for another. **Consideration** that makes a **contract** valid.

Quiet Free from interference or disturbance. For example, an *action to quiet title* is a way of establishing clear ownership of land, and a *covenant for quiet enjoyment* is, among other things, that part of a **deed** that promises that the seller will protect the buyer against **claims** or lawsuits based on ownership rights.

Quitclaim deed A **deed** that passes on to the buyer all those rights or as much of a **title** as a seller actually has. A *quitclaim deed* does not **warrant** (promise) that the seller actually has full title to the land to pass on.

Quorum The number of persons who must be present to make the votes and other actions of a group (such as a **board**) valid. This number is often a majority (over half) of the whole group, but is sometimes much less or much more.

Quota 1. An assigned **goal,** such as a certain minimum amount of sales a salesperson must make. 2. A limit, such as the maximum number of cars that may be imported from a particular country. 3. A proportional share of a **liability.**

Quotation (or **quote**) The selling or asking price of a **stock,** other **security,** or **commodity. Brokers** exchange *quotes*. Also, **purchasing** departments usually request written prior *quotations* (or bids) from several suppiers when deciding on a purchase or when gathering information for possible future purchases.

R

R 1. **Registered,** as in registered **trademark.** The symbol is®. 2. In newspaper financial transaction tables, an indication, lowercase (r), that an **option** was not traded; that a **mutual fund** has a redemption charge when shares are sold; or that a **bond** is registered; or that a cash as well as a stock dividend was paid in the preceding year.

R & D Research and development.

RAM 1. **Reverse annuity mortgage.** 2. Random access memory. A computer memory storage device, such as a **chip** or **disk,** that can give or take information quickly because it need not be transferred in any set order. The information, however, can usually be erased. Contrast **ROM.**

REIT. **Real estate investment trust.**

REMIC A real estate **mortgage** investment conduit; a package of mortgages sold as **bonds.**

RESPA Real Estate Settlement Procedures Act. A federal law concerning **disclosure** of **settlement (closing)** costs in real estate sales financed by federally insured lenders.

RFP Request for proposals. A government notice soliciting applicants to perform a **contract.**

ROG Receipt of goods.

ROI Return on investment. The profit that might be earned with a given investment within a given time expressed as a percentage.

ROM Read only memory. A computer chip or other information-storage device that stores data or instructions permanently; gives it back as many times as needed or requested; and cannot be changed. Contrast **RAM.**

RRM **Renegotiable rate mortgage.**

Rackjobber A wholesaler who supplies and stocks display racks for retailers and who takes back unsold items.

Raid One company's attempt to take over another company by buying its **stock** to gain control of its **board of directors.** This is often accomplished by a **tender** offer. A **takeover** is more often called a *raid* when the raiders want something the company has (such as **retained earnings** or a salable **asset**) rather than wanting the company's ongoing business. A **raider** is an individual who uses his own and or the money of others to buy large blocks of stock in a corporation in a hostile takeover attempt. He may truly wish to take over the company or merely want to be bought off with **greenmail.** *Raiding* refers to efforts by one organization to gain, for their own, members of a competing organization.

Railway Labor Act A federal law that protects the **collective bargaining** rights of railroad and airline employees and established the *National Railroad Adjustment Board* to **arbitrate grievances** that arise from labor-management contracts. There is also a *Railroad Unemployment Insurance Act* that covers unemployment and sickness benefits and a *Railroad Retirement Act* for retirement with a Railroad Retirement Board that handles all these benefits.

Rake-off An illegal bribe, payoff, or **skimming** of the profits of a business.

Ramp Direction. **Ramp up** means profits are up. **Ramp down** means declining profits.

RAMPS A Resource Allocation and Multi-Project Planning technique for large projects—an offshoot of **CPA.** It is useful for planning multiple projects simultaneously, and especially for resolving conflicts among competing priorities.

Random access A way to get data from a computer that does not depend on the last data taken out. This is much faster and easier than data retrieval in only a set order. For *random access memory,* see **RAM.**

Random sample A **sample** chosen so that each unit of the larger group sampled has a known chance (usually equal) of being selected for the sample. This selection requires a scientific plan to assure *randomness* because human *random* selection often has an unplanned pattern.

Rank and file 1. Those members of the organization who are not part of **management.** 2. Those members of a union having no status as officers or **shop stewards.**

Rank performance rating A method of **performance appraisal** that requires superiors to rank order employees according to their merit.

Rapid payoff mortgage See **growing equity mortgage.**

Ratable 1. Proportional; adjusted by some formula or percentage. 2. A proportional but unequal division. 3. Capable of being evaluated. 4. Taxable.

Rate 1. An amount fixed by mathematical formulas or adjusted according to some standard (such as an **interest** rate); or a charge that is the same to all persons for the same service (such as a shipping rate). A *rate base* is the property value (or investment amount) upon which a **public utility**'s profit is calculated. *Rate buster* is a slang term for any employee whose production level far exceeds the norms established by the majority of the workforce. Rate busters usually face considerable peer pressure to conform to average production levels, and sometimes this pressure can be physical. *Rate fixing* is the power of some **administrative agencies** (such as state power commissions) to set the charges a company may get for its services. This is *not* the same as **price fixing.** *Rate of return* is profit as a percentage of money or property value invested. 2. A classification by quality; for example, a "first-rate" **insurance risk.** The process of determining insurance costs by evaluating risks is called *rating*. 3. For **discount** rate, **prime** rate, etc., see those words.

Ratification Formal confirmation of a previous act done by you or by someone else; for example, formal confirmation by the union membership of a contract that has been signed on their behalf by union representatives.

Ratio One number divided by another for a comparison between the two.

Ratio analysis Analysis of the relationship of items in financial **statements.** The relationships are expressed either as ratios or percentages, with the second item in the ratio usually divided into the first. When correctly chosen and properly interpreted, the ratios serve as guides in determining the solvency, adequacy of earning power, and the relative **efficiency** of the management operations of a given firm. Ratios also provide a common denominator for comparing the operations of one firm to another, or the performance of one firm to that of its industry as a whole. Commonly used ratios include **acid test, activity,**

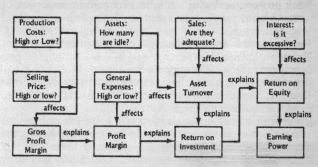

Factors Affecting Profit and the Interrelation of Profitability Ratios

average collection period, bad debt, balance sheet, capital turnover, cash turnover, collection, contribution margin, current, delinquency, debt, debt-equity, dividend yield, earnings per share, fixed asset turnover, fixed charge coverage, gross profit margin, inventory turnover, leverage, liquidity, margin, marginal income, net income on sales, net income/net worth, net profit, net sales/inventory, net sales/receivables, net worth/total debt, operating, operating efficiency, pay-out, price-earnings, profitability, profit/volume, quick, receivables turnover, return on assets, return on net worth, and total assets turnover.

Ratio delay A work sampling technique that uses a large number of observations taken at random intervals to determine the parts of the work day (expressed in minutes or hours) during which an employee is working productively or is engaged in activities other than productive work.

Rationalization 1. A psychological process of explaining behavior by making excuses either to one's self or to others. 2. Administrative actions which seek to increase productivity. 3. The merging of industrial plants in given industries to achieve greater efficiency and lower costs. This presupposes a large degree of government **regulation** of production (as well as consumption) which has not been possible in the United States since World War II.

Raw materials Commodities on which productive labor will be expended to change their form during the manufacturing process, and which will be an integral component of the finished product. In many cases, the finished product of one manufacturer is the raw material of another. A *raw materials inventory* is a list of these materials not yet changed or used.

Reacquired stock   Treasury stock.

Reaction management   A **management** posture that is limited to responding to immediate problems and pressures.

Read only memory   See **ROM.**

Readjustment   A **reorganization** of a company in financial trouble that is done voluntarily by the owners without court or other intervention.

Reaffirmation   Agreeing to pay a prior, possibly now uncollectable, debt. Under **bankruptcy** and **contract** law, if you *reaffirm* a debt (under court approval in the case of bankruptcy), you are again **liable** for it.

Real estate   Land, buildings, and things permanently attached to land and buildings. Also called *realty* and *real property*. A *real estate investment trust* is an arrangement in which investors buy shares in a **trust** that invests in real estate. To qualify for special **income tax** benefits, a *REIT* must meet certain requirements, such as being unincorporated, having fewer than a certain number of investors, and gaining most of its income from real estate and related financial ventures. For the *Real Estate Settlement Procedures Act,* see **RESPA.**

Real rate of interest   The nominal rate of **interest** corrected for **inflation.** For example: if inflation is 5 percent and the nominal rate of inflation is 12 percent, then the *real rate of interest* is 7 percent.

Real time processing   Immediate computations or changes made when information is put into a computer. This is most important when the computer is used to control an ongoing process. See also **batch processing.**

Real wages   **Wages** after they have been adjusted for changes in the level of prices. The buying power of wages, the *real wages,* is computed by dividing the dollar amount by an index measuring changes in prices (such as the **Consumer Price Index**).

Realized   Actual; cashed in. For example, a *realized investment* is one made, not merely planned; a *realized profit* is a cash-in-hand gain as opposed to a *paper profit,* which is the increase in value of property (such as stock) that might be lost again if the value goes down; and a *realized gain or loss* is the difference between the **net** sale price of something and its net cost (or, in tax terms, its **adjusted basis**). Income or loss is *realized* when a "taxable event" takes place; typically, a sale or exchange of property. *Realization* means "now is the time to see whether income or loss will have tax consequences." **Recognition** means "the income or loss *does* have tax consequences now." In most cases, *realization* and *recognition* mean the same.

Realtor   A *real estate agent* (see **real estate** and **agent**) who belongs to the *National Association of Realtors*.

Realty   **Real estate.**

Reasonable   A broad, flexible word used when a decision must be based on specific facts rather than general principles. For example, *reasonable accommodation* is the idea that once a handicapped employee is hired, an employer is required to take *reasonable* steps to accommodate the individual's disability unless such steps would cause the employer undue hardship. This might be providing adequate workspace for an employee confined to a wheelchair.

Reassessment   A government's reestimating of the value of property and changing the official value it gives to that property for tax purposes.

Rebate   A discount, deduction, or refund.

Recall   1. Notify car (or other product) owners of a safety defect and offer to fix it.   2. Rehire employees from a **layoff.** Union contracts usually require that the union be given both notice of the recall and the names of the employees to be recalled. This enables the union to determine if employees were being called back in the order required by the agreement.   3. A *recall item* is a test question that requires the examinee to supply the correct answer from memory, in contrast to a *recognition item*, in which the examinee need only identify the correct answer.

Recapitalization   Readjusting the types, amount, values and priorities of a **corporation's stocks** and **bonds.**

Recapture   1. The **IRS** requirement that a person pay taxes on profits created by some prior **deduction** or **credit,** such as the *investment tax credit*. For example, when **accelerated depreciation** is taken on some types of property that is later sold at no loss, the IRS *recaptures* this depreciation by then treating it as **taxable income.**   2. A **contract**

provision that limits profits or provides for the recovery of goods in special situations. 3. A **lease** provision giving the landlord a percentage of profits and allowing the landlord to end the lease if profits are not high enough.

Receipt Written acknowledgment that something has been received or put into your hands; or the act of getting or receiving.

Receipts Money that comes into a business (usually through sales).

Receivables **Accounts receivable.** The *receivables turnover* is an **activity ratio**: sales divided by accounts receivable.

Receivership A court putting money or property into the management of a *receiver* (an independent, court-appointed person) to perserve it for the persons ultimately entitled to it. This is often done when the **creditors** of a business suspect **fraud** or **gross** mismanagement and ask the court to step in and watch over the business to protect them.

Recession A decline in overall business activity that is pervasive, substantial and of at least several months' duration. Historically, a decline in **gross national product** for at least two consecutive quarters has been considered a recession.

Reciprocal 1. Mutual; bilateral (two-sided or two-way). For example, *reciprocal sales* involve buying from customers on terms better than others get (or favoring customers by buying goods from the customer), in possible violation of **antitrust** laws; and *reciprocal trade agreements* are agreements between countries to lower import taxes or to reduce other trade restraints on goods traded between the countries. The term *relative reciprocity* refers to **developed countries** accepting less than full reciprocity from **developing countries.** 2. One of two numbers which, when multiplied together, equal 1; for example, 3 and ⅓.

Recision To **rescind.**

Reclassification of stock A change in the **capital structure** of a corporation. It may be done by the issuance of one or more additional classes of stock. For example, a corporation that has only **common stock** may change its capital structure by issuing a smaller amount of common stock and a new issue of **preferred stock.** Reclassification may also be done by a change in the number of shares, the **par** value, designations, relative preferences, participation rights or other special rights of existing shares. However, not all changes in the structure of a corporation are a reclassification of stock. This depends on state law and the corporate **charter.**

Recognition 1. In most cases, when a taxpayer has received some financial gain, it is *recognized.* This means that it must be reported on tax forms, and tax must be paid on it. Some gains, however, are *nonrecognized.* This means that paying taxes on them may be put off to a later year. See **realized** for a more complete understanding of *recognition.* 2. Acknowledgment that something done by another person in your name was authorized by you. 3. An employer's acceptance of a union as the **bargaining agent** for all of the employees in a particular **bargaining unit.** *Recognition picketing* is **picketing** to encourage an employer to recognize a particular union as the bargaining agent for his or her employees. Recognition picketing is usually an **unfair labor practice.** The same is true of some *recognition strikes.*

Reconciliation Bringing two differing **accounts** into agreement; for example, adjusting the **balance** in a checking account book to agree with the bank's monthly statement.

Reconsignment A change made in the **consignee** or destination of goods while they are still in transit.

Record 1. A **corporation's** *records* include its **charter, bylaws,** and **minutes** of meetings. The *record date* for payment of a company's **stock dividends** or for voting is the date on which stockholders must be **registered** as the *record owners* on the company's books to vote or to receive dividends. This is usually set by the company's **board of directors** when a dividend is **declared** or a vote is set. 2. A formal, written account of a legal case, containing the complete formal history of all actions taken, papers filed, rulings made, opinions written, etc. 3. A *public record* is a document filed with, or put out by, a government agency and open to the public for inspection. For example, a *title of record* to land is an ownership interest that has been properly filed in the public land records. The official who keeps these records is usually called the *recorder of deeds,* and the filing process is called *recordation.* 4. A set of related facts; usually a set of related computer data **fields** treated as a unit (such as a customer account). 5. A *record copy* is a document that is considered the most important or the key official copy.

Recording acts State laws establishing rules for **priority** among persons who claim the same **interests** in **real estate** (and sometimes other property). These laws have many different forms and time limits in different states, but the three basic types are *race statutes* (a person who first **records** a claim has the legal right to that claim); *notice statutes* (the person with a *later* valid claim—whether or not recorded—has priority over an earlier unrecorded claim unless the later person *knew* about the earlier claim); and *race-notice statutes* (the first person to record without knowledge of a prior unrecorded claim wins).

Records management The total process of creating, maintaining, and finally disposing of an organziation's stored information. While *records management* and *information management* tend to be used interchangeably, some prefer the latter because it better connotes both paper and nonpaper records. The *records cycle* consists of the creation of a record, its use, its storage for easy retrieval, its transfer to inactive status, and its destruction.

Recourse The right of a person who holds a **negotiable instrument** to receive payment on it from anyone who endorsed (signed) it when the person who originally endorsed the negotiable instrument fails to pay up—unless the endorser signs the negotiable instrument "no recourse" or "without recourse."

Red A *red-circle rate* is a rate of pay that is higher than the established rate for a particular job. A *red herring* is an advance copy of a **prospectus** that must be filed with the **SEC** before a company sells **stocks** or **bonds.** It is "for information only" and marked in red for identification. *Red lining* is a bank or mortgage company's refusal to make loans in a particular neighborhood solely because of deteriorating conditions. This practice violates federal laws and is often a "cover" for racial discrimination. *Red tape* is a term for excessive formal requirements, paperwork and attention to routine that has its origins in the red ribbon with which clerks bound up official documents in the last century.

Redeem Buy back; gather up and pay off; reclaim from mortgage or **pledge;** turn in for cash; etc. A *redeemable bond* is either a **callable** bond (one that can be called in by the company and paid off at any time before **maturity**), or a bond that has a maturity date (as opposed to a consol). Sometimes only part of a bond **issue** is redeemed each time. The process is called *redemption*. A *redemption period* is also the time during which a **mortgage** or similar debt that has gone into **default** can be paid off without losing the property. Some states have mandatory redemption periods for home mortgages.

Rediscount rate The rate at which a **Federal Reserve Bank** can make loans to **member banks** on **commercial paper (bills, notes,** etc.) already *discounted* (resold) by those banks. See **discount rate.**

Redraft A second **note** or **bill** offered for payment after the first has been refused payment. It includes the costs of delayed payment and collection in addition to the original amount.

Reduction Turning something abstract into something concrete. For example, *reduction to possession* is turning a right to something (such as a debt) into the thing itself (getting payment), and *reduction to practice* is turning an idea for a device or process into a useful device or process or filing a **patent** application on it. This often includes a demonstration of workability by a working model. See **conception.**

Redundancies Excess employees; those declared to be *redundant* are laid off.

Reefer A refrigerated vehicle for transporting perishable goods.

Re-employed annuitant An employee who, having retired with a **pension** from an organization, is again employed by the same organization. This may affect either salary or pension benefits.

Re-employment list A list required by most union contracts. In the event of **layoffs,** employees will be ranked on a *re-employment list* in order of their **seniority.** Usually, re-employment lists must be exhausted before new hires can be considered.

Reexchange The expenses caused by the refusal to pay a bill of **exchange** in a foreign country are *reexchange* expenses.

Referee in bankruptcy An old word for a federal judge who runs **bankruptcy** hearings.

Reference 1. An agreement in a **contract** to submit certain disputes to an **arbitrator** for decision. This may be an *arbitration clause.* 2. The act of sending a case to a *referee* for a decision. 3. A person who will provide information for you about your character, credit, etc. 4. A *reference group* is a social group with which an individual identifies to the extent that his or her personal values are derived from the group's norms and attitudes. 5. A *reference price* is a **trigger price.**

Referral plan (or **referral sales scheme**) See **pyramid sales scheme.**

Refinance Pay off a debt with money from a new debt.

Reformation A procedure in which a court will rewrite, correct, or *reform* a written agreement to conform with the original intent of the persons making the deal. The court will do this only if there was **fraud** or a mutual mistake in writing up the original document.

Refunding Refinancing a debt; usually refinancing a long-term debt by taking on a new long-term debt.

Reg. 1. **Regulation.** 2. **Registered.**

Register 1. A book of public facts (such as a *land register*); the person responsible for these public records (such as a *register of deeds*); or the process of placing information into these records. The book is also called a *registry,* and the person a *recorder* or *registrar.* See also **record.** 2. Any official record or chronological list. *Registered* means listed on an official record. For example, a *registered stock* can only be cashed in by the person who is listed as the owner, and each time ownership changes that fact must be registered. A *registered bond* might have the **bond** or only the **interest** payments registered this way. (See also **transfer agent.**) A *registered check* is a check sold by a bank but not **certified.** And a *registered representative* is a person approved by the government to sell **securities.** 3. *Registration* is recording a fact. A *registration statement* is a financial and ownership **statement,** including a **prospectus** and other documents, required by the **SEC** of most companies that want to sell stock or other **securities** and of all companies that want their securities traded in **markets** such as the New York Stock Exchange. Some stocks may be sold to a small number of persons without full registration.

Regressive tax The opposite of a **progressive tax.**

Regs. Abbreviation for **regulations.**

Regular 1. Steady; uniform; with no unusual variations. 2. Lawful; legal; in conformity with usual practice.

3. *Regular course of business* means books and records kept, or sales made, normally and in **good faith.**

Regulate To control. For example, a government *regulates* businesses that have a big effect on the general public (such as power companies) by writing laws on the subject and setting up government organizations called *regulatory agencies* (or **administrative agencies**) to write rules and **regulations** that explain what such companies can and cannot do and how they may operate. The agencies also administer and enforce the rules by giving **orders,** holding **hearings,** etc.

Regulation 1. A "mini-law." A rule that is put out by a low-level branch of government, such as an **administrative agency,** to *regulate* conduct. For example, **IRS** *regulations* are rules about how the tax **code** applies to specific situations; and local governments put out parking *regulations.* 2. What a government does when it **regulates** conduct. *Regulation of business* includes such things as pure food and drug laws, **antitrust** laws, **labor** laws, utility rate laws, consumer protection laws, etc. See **deregulation.**

Rehabilitation See **Chapter Thirteen.**

Reindustrialization A loose term for public and private efforts to make American industry more competitive by rejuvenating its physical plant.

Reinforcement An inducement to perform in a particular manner. *Positive reinforcement* occurs when an individual receives a desired reward that is contingent upon some prescribed behavior. *Negative reinforcement* occurs when an individual works to avoid an undesirable reward.

Reinstatement The restoration of an employee to his or her previous position without any loss of **seniority** or other benefits.

Reinsurance The practice of one insurance company buying **insurance** from a second company for the purpose of protecting itself against part or all of the losses it might **incur** in the process of honoring the claims of its policyholders. The original company is called the *ceding* company; the second is the *assuming* company or *reinsurer.*

Reinvestment The use of **dividends, interest** or proceeds from the sale of **securities** to buy more securities. Arrangements can sometimes be made to automatically reinvest dividends in additional shares of **common stock** or shares of a **mutual fund.**

Release The giving up or relinquishing of a **claim** or a right by the person who has it to the person against whom it might have been enforced. For example, most persons demand a *written release* in exchange for paying money to settle an accident claim.

Relevant market The geographic area in which a particular type, price, and quality of product is sold.

Remainder An interest or estate in land or **trust** property that takes effect only when another interest in the land or trust property ends. See **reversion.**

Remargining See **margin call.**

Remittance Money (or a check, etc.) sent by one person to another, often as payment for a debt owed.

Remote service unit An electronic terminal operated by a **savings and loan association,** often located in shopping areas which allows customers easy access to their accounts. See also **electronic fund transfer systems.**

Renegotiable rate mortgage A fully **amortized** long-term **mortgage** whose **interest** rates (and thus total monthly payments) are renegotiated (or "rolled over") once every 3 to 5 years. Within each of these intervals, the monthly payments stay level. As authorized in 1980 for federal savings and loan associations, changes in *RRM* rates are tied to nationwide mortgage rates. *RRM* rates may rise 0.5 percentage point per year, up to 5 percentage points in all, or may decrease by these amounts.

Rent control Local laws that regulate the amount by which landlords can raise rents on residential rental properties. A rent strike is an organized refusal by tenants to pay their rent in an effort to force their landlord to do something such as make repairs.

Reopener clause A provision in a **collective bargaining** agreement stating the circumstances under which portions of the agreement, usually concerning wages, can be renegotiated before the agreement's normal expiration date. Typically such clauses provide for renegotiation at the end of a specified time period (such as one year) or when the **Consumer Price Index** increases by an established amount.

Reorganization 1. See **Chapter Eleven** for a *reorganization* in bankruptcy. 2. Any restructuring of a large organization. This may be by **recapitalization** of ownership only, by a shakeup of management and organizational structure, or both. A financial reorganization is usually done under an agreement involving various classes of owners and **creditors,** and usually done to reduce debt, raise **working capital,** make a company more efficient and competitive, or protect a vital public interest.

Repair   1. Fix a defect. *Repairs* and **improvements** are treated differently for tax purposes. A *business repair* can be taken as an immediate **deduction;** while a *home repair* has no tax benefits unless made soon before the sale of the home (when it can be added to the tax **basis** of the house). Both business and home *improvements* can be added to the property's basis.   2. *Repair* and *reconstruction* (making something new) of *patented* objects are treated differently under **patent** laws. Reconstruction may be an **infringement.**

Replacement cost   The cost of buying something that does the job of something lost; for example, to build a house comparable to one that burns down. Compare this with **reproduction cost.** In **inventory** valuation, *replacement costs* are more significant than *purchase costs* when negotiating selling prices or when a current valuation of **assets** is desired (especially in periods of rapidly increasing costs).

Repo.   1. **Repurchase agreement.**   2. **Repossession.**

Repossession   Taking back something sold because payments have not been made.

Representation   1. In the law of **contracts,** a *representation* is any statement (or any attempt to give an impression about a state of facts) that was done to convince the other person to make a contract.   2. A *representation election* is an **authorization election.**

Representative action   1. A lawsuit brought by one stockholder in a **corporation** to claim rights or to fix wrongs done to many or all stockholders in the company; it is also called a **derivative action.**   2. Any **class action.**

Reprimand   A formal censure for some job-related behavior. A repimand is less severe than an **adverse action** but more forceful than an admonition.

Reprivatization   The assignment of functions to the private sector that were previously performed by government (i.e., trash collection, fire protection, etc.).

Reproduction cost   The cost of replacing a lost or destroyed item with an *exact* duplicate. See **replacement cost.**

Repudiation   Rejection or refusal. For example, *repudiation* of a **contract** is the refusal to go through with it (usually with a legal right to do so).

Repurchase agreement   Two simultaneous transactions. One is the purchase of **securities**—used as **collateral**—by an investor from a **dealer** (which can be a bank). The other is an agreement by the dealer to repurchase the securities at a specified date and price and structured so that the investor receives a known return. A *repo* is thus a short-term loan from the investor to the dealer. The **Federal Reserve** often engages in repurchase agreements—and the mirror-image transactions known as *reverse repurchase agreements*—when it wishes to affect **reserves** on a short-term basis. A *repo* by the Federal Reserve supplies reserves; a *reverse repo* by it drains reserves.

Requirements contract   A **contract** for the supply of goods in which the exact amount of goods to be bought is not set but will be what the buyer needs for the life of the contract (so long as the needs are real, reasonable, and the buyer's total needs for that type of goods).

Requisition   A routine written request for supplies or services, made from one department of an organization to another.

Resale price maintenance   See **fair trade** laws.

Resale rights   The right of a seller to resell (usually perishable) goods if the buyer does not pay for or does not claim them in time.

Rescind   To take back, "unmake," or **annul.** To cancel a **contract** and wipe it out "from the beginning" as if it had never been.

Research and development   Research is a systematic and intensive study for the fuller knowledge of the subject studied; *development* is directing that knowledge toward the production of useful materials, systems, methods, or processes. In other words, corporate research uncovers facts and principles in order to benefit development. *Pure* or *basic* research attempts to uncover new scientific knowledge and understanding with little regard to when, or specifically how, the new facts will be used; and *applied* research is conducted with a special purpose in mind. It is usually directed toward a specific problem, or toward a series of problems that stand in the way of progress in a particular area.

Reserve   1. Hold back a thing or a right. For example, a **deed** to land can *reserve* the right to cross the land for the person selling it; and to *reserve* **title** is to keep an ownership right as **security** that the thing will be fully paid for. And *with reserve,* in an auction, means that the thing will not be sold if the highest **bid** is not high enough; while *without reserve* means that the thing will be sold at whatever is the highest price bid. For the phrase *reserved rights* in a *labor* context, see **management rights.**   2. A *reserve bank* is a member of the **Federal Reserve System** and the *Reserve Board* is the Federal Reserve *Board of Governors. Reserve requirements* are the percentages of deposit **liabilities** that U.S. reserve banks and all other depository institutions are required to hold as *reserves* at their Federal Reserve bank, as cash in their vaults, or as directed by state banking authorities. The reserve requirement is one of the tools of **monetary policy.** Federal Reserve officials can control the lending capacity of the banks (thus influencing the **money supply**) by varying the ratio of reserves to deposits that banks are required to maintain. The *primary reserve ratio* is a comparison between the cash a bank has in its vault plus what it has with the *Federal Reserve Banks* and the amount of its **demand** deposits (money that could be withdrawn by depositors at any time). The *secondary ratio* is a comparison between government *securities* held by a bank and its demand deposits.   3. An **accounting** device that designates funds for specific future purposes. This restricts cash available for current spending and for **dividends.** Technically, a *reserve* does not set aside any actual cash; this is a **fund.** For example, a company might have a *reserve for replacement* of **fixed assets** as a disposition of **paper · profits** and a parallel *replacement fund* of cash set aside for the purpose. There are three general types of *reserves: Valuation reserves* provide for losses in **asset** value; for example, a **bad debt** *reserve* might offset projected losses in **accounts receivables.** *Liability reserves* provide for known or easily estimated future claims; for example, **tax** or **pension** reserves. And *surplus reserves* are either earmarked for future projects or are *contingency reserves* to allow for possible future losses such as lost lawsuits.

Resident agent   See **statutory agent** under **statute.**

Residual value The difference between the cost of an **asset** (original value) and that portion of it which has been **amortized** or treated as an expense or loss.

Respondeat superior (Latin) "Let the master answer." A legal rule that an employer is responsible for certain (often negligent) actions of an employee done in the course of employment. This is a type of **vicarious liability**.

Responsible bidder A company competing for public work must be financially sound, honest and competent to do the job bid on. The government may reject a low **bid** if the bidder is not *responsible*.

Responsibility accounting (or **reporting**) A type of budgetary control in which costs are accumulated and charged on a departmental rather than a product basis. In this system, supervisors receive **budget allowances** only for those items that are used exclusively by their departments and over which they exercise direct control. This method fixes responsibility and helps evaluate individual administrative ability.

Resting order An order which waits for the **market** in the **commodity** concerned to change. If the order is, for example, to purchase, it is a *resting order* when the market price is above that set in the purchase order.

Restitution Giving something back; making good on something. There are various rules for how much "giving back" is full *restitution*. For example, in **contract** law, restitution is usually the amount that puts the plaintiff back in the financial position he or she was in before the contract.

Restocking costs The expenses incurred each time an **inventory** count is replenished. This includes the costs of gathering information needed to write the order, the expense of actually writing the order, and the expense of receiving and inspecting the shipment when it arrives.

Restraint of trade An illegal agreement or **combination** that eliminates competiton, sets up a **monopoly,** or artificially raises prices. See **antitrust acts.**

Restricted securities **Stocks** or **bonds** which were issued in a private sale or other transaction not registered with the **Securities and Exchange Commission.**

Restriction of output Reduced **productivity** on the part of a worker or workforce because of informal group norms, personal grievances, or sloth.

Restrictive Limiting. A *restrictive covenant* is a clause in a group of **deeds** that forbids all the landowners (and all later owners) from doing certain things with their land; for example, a prohibition on buildings over a certain height. More generally, it is any provision in an agreement limiting or restricting the action of one of the parties to the agreement. For example, a seller of a business may agree not to engage in the same business within a certain number of years. A *restrictive indorsement* is signing a **negotiable instrument** in a way that ends its negotiability; for example, "Pay to Robert Smith only."

Retail credit See **consumer credit.**

Retained earnings A company's yearly **net profit** minus the **dividends** it paid out that year. Retained earnings are a part of **stockholders' equity** and are added to **capital stock** when figuring a business's **net worth.** *Accumulated retained earnings* is that year's retained earnings plus profits left over from prior years. It is a measure of what a company can use for future improvements and expansions as well as to ride out possible bad years. The *retained earnings statement* is a required part of most **corporate annual reports.** See **statement.** Most payments to shareholders made by a company with *retained earnings and profits* will be taxed as dividends, no matter what they are called.

Retention schedule A timetable showing how long any business record is to be kept. The period of retention for each record is affected by requirements of tax laws, other regulatory legistation, and the usefulness of the record.

Retirement 1. Making the final payment owed on a **bond, note,** or other **security** and ending its existence and all obligations under it. 2. The removal of **fixed assets** from service accompanied by adjustments of the **accounts** containing their costs and accumulated **depreciation.** It is immaterial whether the retired assets are sold for use, for junk, or just abandoned. 3. The voluntary or involuntary termination of employment because of age, disability, illness or personal choice. *Retirement counseling* is a systematic effort by an organization to help its employees who are retiring to adjust to their new situation. For various *retirement plans,* such as **fixed-benefit,** see those words.

Retroactive pay Wages for work performed during an earlier time at a lower rate or a payment that makes up the difference between an old and new rate of pay.

Retroactive seniority Seniority status that is *retroactively* awarded back to the date that a woman or minority group member was proven to have been discriminatorily refused employment.

Return 1. Yield or profit. 2. See **tax return.** 3. *Return on assets* is a **profitability ratio:** net profit after taxes divided by total tangible **assets.** *Return on equity* is either the profit a company makes compared to its value—especially the annual profit made compared to the total cost of its **common stock**—(see **statement** and **equity**); or the profit an investor makes on shares of stock or other investments, such as rental housing. *Return on net worth* is a **profitability ratio:** net income divided by net worth.

Revaluation Raising the value of a country's money relative to other countries' money.

Revenue 1. Income. 2. **Return** on an investment. 3. Money raising or taxing by the government. 4. *Revenue anticipation notes* are forms of short-term borrowing used by a jurisdiction to resolve a cash flow problem occasioned by a shortage of necessary revenues or taxes to cover planned, or unplanned, expenditures. *Revenue bills* raise tax money legislatively. *Revenue bonds* are sold by governments and backed by money-making projects. They are **municipal bonds** whose repayment and **dividends** are guaranteed by revenues derived from the facility constructed from the proceeds of the sale of the bonds (i.e., stadium bonds, toll road bonds, etc.) rather than guaranteed by general tax revenues. A *revenue enhancer* is a euphemism for a tax increase. A *revenue gainer* is another euphemism for a tax increase. *Revenue procedures* are **IRS** opinions on procedural tax matters and *revenue rulings* are IRS interpretations of tax laws as it applies to specific cases. They have slightly less legal "weight" than tax **regulations** and slightly more than private **letter rulings.**

Reverse 1. Set aside. For example, when a higher court *reverses* a lower court on **appeal,** it sets aside the **judgment** of the lower court and either substitutes its own judgment for it or sends the case back to the lower court with instructions on what to do with it. 2. The *reverse annuity mortgage (RAM)* was created to allow recovery of the

equity of elderly homeowners in their residence without forcing them to sell the property; the RAM combines a **mortgage** and an **annuity.** With specific terms varying widely from case to case, the RAM typically provides an annuity to the borrower, while the lender recovers the mortgage amount after the death of the borrower through **probate.** There are still legal uncertainties surrounding the RAM. *Reverse collective bargaining* occurs when economic conditions force **collective bargaining agreements** to be renegotiated so that employees end up with a less favorable wage package. *Reverse discrimination* is preferential treatment of women and minorities, as opposed to white males. A *reverse stock split* is a calling in of all **stock,** reducing the number of shares, and increasing the value of each share, without changing the total value of all the stock.

Reversion Any **future interest** kept by a person who transfers away property. For example, John rents out his land for ten years. His ownership rights during those years, his right to take back the property after ten years, and his heirs' right to take back the property after ten years (if he dies) are *reversionary interests.* See **remainder.**

Revised statutes 1. A **code.** 2. A book of **statutes** in the order they were originally passed, with temporary and repealed statutes removed.

Revive Restore to original force or legal effect. For example, if a **contract** has expired, it can be *revived* by acknowledging it and making a new promise to perform it.

Revocation 1. The taking back of some **power** or **authority.** For example, taking back an **offer** before it is accepted ends the other person's power to accept. 2. Wiping out the legal effect of something by canceling, rescinding, etc. If something can be revoked, but has not yet been revoked, it is *revocable.*

Revolving charge **Credit,** often provided through credit cards or department stores, by which purchases may be charged and partially paid off month-by-month. New purchases may be made, charged, and paid off during the same period.

Revolving fund A **fund** established to finance a cycle of operations through amounts received by, and paid back into, the fund.

Rigging the market Artificially driving up the price of a stock by making a series of **bids** that make it look like demand for the stock has soared.

Right 1. Morally, ethically, or legally just. 2. One person's legal ability to control certain actions of another person or of all other persons. Every right has a corresponding **duty**. For example, if a person has a right to cross a street on a green light, most drivers have a duty to avoid hitting the person with their cars. (When lawyers speak of "a right," they mean a legal, not moral, right.) A *right of first refusal* is the right to have the first chance to buy property when it goes on sale, or the right to meet any other offer. This also refers to the right of **stockholders** in some **close corporations** to first buy stock offered for sale. For *right of way,* see **easement**. *Right-to-work laws* are state laws that make it illegal for **collective bargaining** agreements to contain **maintenance of membership,** preferential hiring, **union shop,** or any other clauses calling for compulsory union membership. Twenty states have these laws. *Rightful place* is the legal rule that a person who has been discriminated against should be restored to the job as if there had been no **discrimination,** and given appropriate **seniority,** merit increases, and promotions. For *rights arbitration,* see **grievance arbitration.** A *rights issue (or offer)* is stock (or other **securities**) that is sold only to current stockholders.

Ringed rate A red circle rate.

Ringi The Japanese decisionmaking process of seeking a consensus from all levels of management before implementation begins.

Ringing up Brokers exchanging sales **contracts** to cancel them out, with leftover differences paid.

Risk 1. A **hazard** (fire); the danger of hazard or loss (one chance in ten thousand per year); the specific possible hazard or loss mentioned in an **insurance** policy (John's house burning down); or the item insured itself (the house). *Risk charge* is the fraction of a **premium** which goes to generate or replenish surpluses which an insurer must develop to protect against the possibility of excessive losses under its policies. 2. *Risk capital* is money or property invested in a business (usually as **stock** or a share of the business) as opposed to loans or **bonds.** (Even "risky" bonds are not *risk capital.*) 3. The *risk premium* is the amount an investment with a variable return earns over a safer investment with a certain return.   4. *Risk management* includes all of an organization's efforts to protect its assets, its earning power, and its human resources against accidental loss. Accordingly, the major elements of risk management are safety and insurance management. A *risk manager* is generally an insurance specialist who has the technical ability to diagnose risk and advise appropriate insurance coverage.

Robber barons   The label applied to the big-business titans of the U.S. toward the end of the 19th century. Now it is an invidious term for corporate leadership in general.

Roberts Rules   *Roberts Rules of Order* are a set of rules by which many legislatures and other meetings are conducted.

Robinson-Patman Act   A federal law that prohibits **price discrimination** and other anticompetitive practices in business. It forbids a seller from furnishing services or an allowance to some of its customers unless they are made available to all competing customers on proportionally equal terms. In addition, if sellers pay **commissions** or brokerage fees to buyers, the buyers must actually perform some services to earn them. The Act also has criminal sanctions for certain practices and for sales at unreasonably low prices if the purpose is to destroy competition.

Roll   A record of official proceedings or a list of taxable persons or property.

Rolling over   1. Extending a short-term loan for another short period. *Rollover paper* is a short-term **note** that can be extended.   2. Refinancing a debt. A *rollover mortgage* is either a **renegotiable rate mortgage** or a loan which must be financed or *rolled over* after a period of years with no guarantee that the current lender will refinance.

Round   Cycles of multilateral trade negotiations under **GATT,** culminating in simultaneous agreements among participating countries to reduce **tariff** and **non-tariff** trade barriers.

Round lot   A normal unit of trading in **stocks** or **bonds.** Fewer shares are an **odd lot.**

Route 128   A high-technology area; this highway, near Boston, is an East Coast **Silicon Valley.**

Routine   A set of instructions telling a computer to perform a particular task. It is usually one part of a **program.**

Rowan Plan   An incentive wage plan that gives a worker a standard rate for completing a job within an established time, plus a **premium** determined on the basis of the percentage of time saved.

Royalty   A payment made to an author, an inventor, an owner of oil or other mineral lands, etc., for the use of the **property.**

Rucker plan   An employee incentive plan which uses **participative management** to reduce costs and improve profits. Its hallmark is the precise measurement of increases in productivity in monetary, as opposed to physical unit, terms.

Rule   1. Settle an issue as a judge, chairperson, etc.   2. A **regulation,** often one to govern an agency's internal workings, or a court's procedure.   3. *Rule making authority* is the power exercised by administrative agencies that have the force of law. Agencies begin with some form of legislative mandate and translate their interpretation of that mandate into policy decisions, specifications of regulations, and statements of penalties and enforcement provisions.

Run   One complete cycle of a task such as a computer completing a **program,** a researcher completing one test group in an experiment, or a manufacturer turning out one batch of a product.

Running account   An open and as yet unsettled account; a charge account.

Runaway shop   A business that closes and moves away to avoid unionization or the effects of union wages.

S

S In newspaper financial transaction tables, an indication, lowercase (s), that a **stock** has **split** or that a stock dividend was at least 25 percent higher than earlier in the year.

SA Abbreviation of **corporation** in French and Spanish.

SAR **Stock appreciation rights.**

SBA Small Business Administration. A U.S. agency that provides loans and advice for small businesses and ensures that small business concerns receive a fair proportion of government purchases, contracts, and subcontracts.

SBIC Small Business Investment Company.

SBU **Strategic business unit.**

SEC **Securities and Exchange Commission.**

SIC **Standard Industrial Classification.**

SM **Service mark.**

SMSA **Standard Metropolitan Statistical Area.**

SOP Standard operating procedure.

S & P **Standard and Poor's.**

Safe harbor 1. An approved way of complying with a **statute** when the statute is phrased in general terms. For example, **SEC regulations** list ways that are sure to keep you out of trouble when making certain types of stock **offerings** (even though other ways might be legal also). 2. *Safe harbor leasing* is a way for companies to sell tax breaks to each other.

Safe investment rule 1. **Prudent person rule.** 2. One way to calculate **future earnings,** by estimating what sum of money, safely invested, would equal the earnings.

Safety inventory (or **safety stock**) The quantity of goods carried as a hedge against stockouts. It ensures having a certain amount of reserve on hand at all times in each **inventory** account.

Sag A minor drop in the price of a **security** or commodity.

Salary A rate of pay (usually based on a yearly amount) that does not depend primarily on hours worked. It is usually earned by managers and professionals who get paid as long as they do their jobs. See **wages.** For types of *salary*, such as **straight,** see those words. For *salary curve,* see **maturity curve.** For *salary range,* see **pay range.** A *salary review* is a formal examination of an employee's rate of pay in terms of his or her recent performance, changes in the cost of living, and other factors. For *salary survey,* see **wage survey.**

Sale Either a **contract** in which property is exchanged for money or the actual exchange of property for money. For **approval, bootstrap, bulk, consignment, foreclosure, judicial, short,** and other types of *sale,* see those words. A *sale against the box* is a **short sale** in which the seller actually owns that stock. For *sale and leaseback,* see **leaseback.** A *sale and return* is a sale in which the buyer may return any unused items. A *sale note* is a summary of a sale, given by a **broker** to the seller and buyer. A *sale on approval* does not have **title** to goods passed to the buyer until the goods are approved or until a preset time period has passed without disapproval. *Sale value* is the price an **asset** will bring if it must be sold, less any selling costs. *Sales* is a field of law, now covered primarily by the **Uniform Commerical Code,** that deals with the sale of goods and that partly replaces general **contract** law for those sales. A *sales allowance* is a reduction in price given to a buyer because the goods received were not exactly as ordered. A *sales analysis* is an examination of a detailed breakdown of sales records to discover patterns of sales or non-sales that will allow managers to allocate their sales resources more effectively. A *sales budget* is a forecast of projected sales in dollars for a given time period. For *sales commission,* see **commission** earnings. A *sales curve* is a graphic representation of **demand.** A *sales finance company* is either a company that buys **account receivable** at a discount and then tries to collect the debts, or a finance company that specializes in **consumer** sales. A *sales journal* is a book of original entry for records of sales. For *sales load,* see **load.** *Sales management* is that aspect of **marketing** concerned with the planning of sales strategies along with the hiring and training of a sales force capable of carrying out those strategies. A *sales mix* is the combination of individual product types and sales volume that make up total sales. *Sales price variance* is the difference between the standard selling price and the actual price for which products are sold. *Sales promotion* is short-term **marketing** activity directed toward sales workers, distributors, or consumers that seeks to directly or indirectly generate future sales. Examples include convention displays, shows for distributors, and other non-recurrent selling efforts. A *sales tax* is a state (or local) tax on sales, paid by the buyer to the merchant, then sent on to the state. Some states tax items (such as cars) at different rates, and some states do not tax some items (such as food) at all.

Sallie Mae   Student Loan Marketing Association; a quasi-governmental business.

Salvage   1. Property recovered after an accident or other damage or destruction.   2. Business property that is disposed of simply because it has been replaced or is of no further use to the company, whether it is still valuable or only scrap.   3. Money paid to someone who rescues property from destruction at sea.   4. *Equitable salvage* is a lien in favor of the last person to make a payment that prevents the loss of property through lapse, foreclosure, etc.   5. In tax law, a value given to property for **depreciation** calculations. *Salvage value* is the amount that is expected to be realized from the disposal of an **asset** at the end of its useful life. The cost of an asset subject to depreciation is reduced by estimated salvage value in most methods of depreciation.

Sample   1. Any deliberately chosen portion of a large population that is representative of that population as a whole. See **random sample**. *Sample size* is the number of items selected for study from the population. Sample size is affected by the **standard deviation** of the population and the required degree of precision and reliability in the study. For many statistical applications, such as **acceptance sampling,** tables are available that give the necessary sample sizes for specific risk factors. A *sample statistic* is the value of the chosen criterion for decision in a sample. The choice of a particular measurement such as *sample* mean or *proportion defective* is governed by the nature of the problem. *Sampling error* is the relative precision of the sample estimate compared to the value that could be obtained by a complete count of the population. 2. A *sale by sample* usually means that the items bought must "conform to" the sample. In commercial law, this may mean "substantially identical" and may mean "similar and accepted in the trade as of equal quality."

Sandwich lease A **lease** in which the person who leases property then sublets it for more money; for example, leasing a shopping center and renting out the stores in it.

Satisfaction 1. Taking care of a debt or **obligation** by paying it. See **accord and satisfaction.** 2. A *satisfaction contract* is one in which one person promises to do work or supply goods that will satisfy another. *Satisfactory* in this sense does not mean "to every personal whim" but "to any reasonable need" or "according to the judgment of an impartial expert." 3. A *satisfaction* of **judgment, lien,** or **mortgage** is a written document signed by the person paid, stating that an obligation has been paid.

Saturation The point at which further **penetration** of a **market** is improbable or excessively costly.

Saving clause A provision in a law or **contract** that makes its parts **severable.**

Savings Reserved money. A *savings account* is an **interest**-bearing account on which advance notice of intent to withdraw funds may be required. Savings accounts may be passbook accounts or **statement** savings accounts, which involve periodic issuance of summaries of deposits and withdrawals. Savings accounts do not have **maturity** dates. A *savings account loan* is **secured** by funds on deposit. A *savings and loan association* is one of several different types of institutions that primarily make loans to home buyers. Some are **cooperatives;** some banks; some state chartered; some federally chartered under the **Federal Home Loan Bank Board.** The difference between most of these associations and ordinary banks is not as great as it used to be. A *savings bank* was once distinguishable from a commercial bank by its inability to offer checking accounts. Now that this distinction no longer applies (because of **NOW accounts**), a *savings bank* is generally any bank accepting savings accounts other than a full-service commercial bank. For *savings bank trust,* see **Totten trust.** The *savings rate* is the ratio of income saved to income earned. *Savings ratios* compare the comings and goings of deposits in savings institutions. The *savings turnover ratio* is savings received divided by total savings for a given period. The *savings withdrawal ratio* is savings received divided by savings withdrawn in a given period.

Scab   Slang for a person who works for lower than union wages, works under nonunion conditions, takes the place of a striking worker, passes through a picket line, etc.

Scalar chain   The chain of superiors ranging from the ultimate authority to the lowest ranks. The *line of authority* is the route followed—via every link in the chain—by all communications.

Scale-down   1. A composition.   2. To make smaller; to reduce the size of a corporation.

Scale order   See **order.**

Scalper   1. A small-scale speculator in **stocks, bonds,** tickets, etc. See **speculate.**   2. An investment advisor who buys **securities,** such as stocks, and then recommends them without disclosing the fact that a price rise will be to his or her benefit.

Scanlon Plan   An employee incentive plan which seeks to enchance **productivity** and organizational harmony through bonus and suggestion systems.

Schedule   1. Any list.   2. A list attached to a document that explains in detail things mentioned generally in the document. For example, *scheduled property* is items on a list attached to an insurance policy, with the value of each piece and what the company will pay if it is lost or hurt. The supporting pages of calculations attached to the main sheet of a **tax return** are called *schedules*, as are the charts for computing the tax rates of high-income persons. 3. A *scheduled payment* is a payment due at a specified time, such as **installment** payments in a credit agreement.

Scheme   1. Any general plan or system, especially one to produce a business profit.   2. A plan to trick or defraud someone.   3. See **common scheme.**

Schlock   Merchandise of poor quality.

Schmoozing   A collective term for all employee social interactions that are seemingly unrelated to organization productivity.

Scientific management   A systematic approach to managing that seeks the "one best way" of accomplishing any given task by discovering the fastest, most efficient, and least fatiguing production methods.

Scope of bargaining Those issues over which management and labor negotiate during the **collective bargaining** process.

Scope of employment An action of the general sort a person was employed to do, even if not exactly what the employee wants.

Scorched earth policy The selling off of **crown jewels** before a company that wants to take you over to get them can do so; to deliberately incur debt for the same purpose.

Scrambled merchandising A retailer's practice of stocking any products that will sell.

Scrip A piece of paper that is a temporary indication of a right to something valuable. *Scrip* includes paper money issued for temporary use; partial **shares** of **stock** after a stock **split; certificates** of a deferred stock **dividend** that can be cashed in later; etc. *Scrip* was originally token money commonly used to pay workers in lieu of cash. As the scrip could only be redeemed at a company store with inflated prices, some states passed laws making it illegal to pay employees with anything but legal tender.

Scut work Unpleasant or menial tasks.

Seal A wax identification mark or a paper impression. Originally, for a document to be valid, it had to have a wax seal on it to show that it was done seriously, correctly, and formally. Now there is no need for the seal at all, except for making sure that the right person actually signed it (for example, in front of a **notary public,** who has a seal), or to formalize certain corporate documents with a **corporate seal.**

Sealed bidding A way of taking offers to do work or supply materials. Each **bid** is submitted in a sealed envelope, all are opened at the same time, and the best bid is chosen.

Seasonal discount A price reduction to encourage buyers to stock up sooner than they really need to.

Second mortgage A **mortgage** that is considered **subordinate** to another (usually the initial or "first") mortgage on a property, and usually bears a higher rate to reflect the higher risk. Sometimes referred to as a second **trust,** such a mortgage is usually for a shorter term than the first mortgage and is generally provided by the seller of the property or through mortgage bankers, rather than depository institutions.

Second World The countries of Eastern Europe plus the USSR. Contrast to **First World.**

Secondary Lower ranking; happening or coming later or farther away. A *secondary boycott* is a concerted effort by a union engaged in a dispute with an employer to have another union **boycott** a fourth party (usually their employers) who, in response to such pressure, might put like pressure on the original offending employer. Secondary boycotts are forbidden by the **Taft-Hartley Act.** *Secondary cash resources* are any **marketable securities** such as stocks, bonds or notes. A *secondary distribution or offering* is the sale of a large block of stock that is not a new **issue,** but one that has been held by the company or an investment firm. A *secondary liability* is a duty that does not come due unless someone else fails to perform his or her duty. A *secondary market* is a stock exchange or other organized, regular method for buying already issued **securities.** A *secondary mortgage market* is a nationwide market (place, organization or method) for the purchase and sale of existing **mortgages.** A *secondary strike* is a **strike** against an employer because it is doing business with another employer whose workers are on strike.

Secrete Hide something away, especially to keep it from **creditors,** by putting **title** in someone else's name.

Secured Protected by a **mortgage, lien, pledge,** or other **security** interest. The person whose money is protected is called a *secured* **creditor** or *secured* **party** and the money protected is a *secured loan.*

Securities Stocks, bonds, notes, or other documents that show a share in a company or a debt owed by a company. *Securities acts* are federal and state laws **regulating** the sale of securities (stocks, bonds, etc.). These include the *Securities Act of 1933* (which requires the **registration** of securities to be sold to the public and the disclosure of complete information to potential buyers); the *Securities and Exchange Act of 1934* (which regulates stock **exchanges** and **over-the-counter** stock sales); the *Uniform Securities Act* (a model for the states that includes **blue sky laws** and **broker-dealer** requirements); and several others involving investments (the Public Utility Holding Company Act, the Investment Adviser's Act, etc.). Federal securities acts are administered by the *Securities and Exchange*

Commission, which seeks the fullest possible disclosure to the investing public and seeks to protect the interests of the public and investors against malpractices in the securities and financial markets. The *Securities Investor Protection Corporation* is a private agency set up by the U.S. government to help protect investments with stockbrokers and others in financial trouble. *Securities ratings* are evaluations of the degree of risk involved with a security. See **bond rating** and **security.**

Securitization Packaging traditional loans into **securities** that can then be bought and sold as **bonds.**

Security 1. Property that has been pledged, mortgaged, etc., as financial backing for a loan or other obligation. A *security interest* is any right in property that is held to make sure money is paid or that something is done. Most property **secured** this way may be sold by the **creditor** if the debt it backs is not paid. 2. A share of **stock,** a **bond,** a **note,** or one of the many different kinds of documents showing a share in a company or a debt owed by a company or a government. There are different technical definitions of *security* in the various **securities acts—** the **Uniform Commercial Code,** the *Federal* **Bankruptcy** *Act,* the *federal tax code,* etc. Some of these definitions overlap and some conflict. See **securities.** 3. For **assessable, equity, hybrid, listed,** etc., *security,* see those words. A *security deposit* is money put up in advance by a tenant to pay for possible damage to property or for leaving before the end of the lease. *Security management* is that aspect of **management** most concerned with the protection of a company's people, property and cash; marketing and industrial secrets; and computer-stored data.

Seed money The initial financing of a business which is premised on further financing at a later date.

Segmentation The division of a market for a product into sub-markets based on the characteristics of similar types of persons. The products may then be sold in only some sub-markets, sold differently in each, etc.

Seigniorage A government's profit (or costs) from coinage.

Selection ratio The number of job applicants selected compared to the number of job applicants who were available.

Selective demand A customer's demand for a specific brand rather than just for a particular product; for example, a desire for Levi's as opposed to a desire for jeans.

Selective distribution   Selling products only to those wholesalers and retailers who will give what is felt to be appropriate attention to your product's promotion or who have good credit.

Self   Personal. For *Self-Employed Individuals Tax Retirement Act,* see **Keogh Plan.** The *self-employment tax* is the means by which persons who work for themselves are provided **social security** coverage. Each self-employed person must pay a self-employment tax on part or all of his or her income, to help finance social security benefits, which are payable to self-employed persons as well as wage earners. A *self-help eviction* is a landlord's removing the tenant's property from an apartment and locking the door against the tenant. In some situations this is legal, in others, not. *Self-insurance* is setting aside a fund of money to pay for future losses (or not providing for such losses at all) rather than purchasing an insurance policy to cover possible losses. A *self-liquidating loan* is a loan to buy or produce **assets** which will be sold by the borrower to obtain cash with which to repay the debt. These **secured** loans are usually, but not always, short term.

Seller's   Belonging to one offering something for sale. A *seller's lien* is a legal remedy used by an unpaid seller in possession of goods sold. The **lien** imposes a charge on the goods by which they become **security.** Although **title** may have passed to the buyer, the seller is sometimes entitled to retain possession under a lien until payment of the purchase price. Many seller's liens have been replaced by specific portions of the **Uniform Commercial Code.** A *seller's market* is a situation in which goods are scarce so that buyers compete among themselves to obtain supplies. This market usually exists in a period of rising prices. A *seller's option* is the right of a seller of **commodities** to select, within the terms of the contract, the quality of the commodity to be delivered as well as the time and place of delivery. The word *option* should not be used to describe the contract itself. A *seller's surplus* is the difference between the price received and the lowest price that would have been accepted.

Selling   Offering something for sale. *Selling against the box* is a variation of the **short sale.** The difference is that in a short sale, the seller is not the owner of the shares sold short; in *selling against the box,* while the seller borrows the stock to sell short, the seller at the same time owns an equal number of shares. This is a **hedging** procedure to safeguard an investment position. *Selling expenses* include such expenses as sales solicitation costs, transportation costs, advertising, packing and shipping costs, showroom rent, **depreciation,** etc. For *selling flat,* see **flat bonds.** A *selling formula approach* has a sales representative give a potential customer a "canned" pitch about a product. A *selling group* is a group of **securities dealers** organized by an **investment banker** to participate in selling an **issue** of **securities.** See **underwriter.** *Selling off* refers to a market whose prices are declining because there are more sellers than buyers. For *selling short,* see **short sale.**

Semivariable costs   Costs that do not fluctuate in direct proportion to changes in volume. Semivariable costs are also referred to as *semifixed, partially fixed,* and *partially variable.* Electricity, for example, has both fixed and variable elements. The fixed element is the minimum charge for maintaining service; the variable element is all the costs above the minimum that are due to the demand.

Senior interest   An **interest** or right that takes effect or that collects ahead of others; for example, a *senior mortgage* has preference or priority over all others.

Seniority   Preference or priority; often, but not always, because the person or thing came first in time. In employment, *seniority* may be a formal or informal mechanism that gives priority to the individuals who have the longest service in an organization. Seniority is often used to determine which employees will be promoted, subjected to **layoff,** or given other employment advantages. For types of *seniority,* such as **benefit, dovetail, super,** etc., see those words.

Separability clause   A **saving clause.**

Separation pay   Same as **severance pay.**

Sequential marketing   Introducing a product or service in one subset at a time of a total market.

Serial bonds   Bonds of the same **issue,** put out at the same time, that have varying dates of **maturity,** so that the entire debt does not fall due at once. Usually the group carrying the longest term of years pays a higher rate of **interest** than those with a shorter term. *Serial bonds* should not be confused with **series bonds.** Serial bonds are frequently used in **equipment trust** financing because they are a means of financing recurring demands. Serial bonds are often used by firms that have a relatively stable income from year to year.

Serial interface (or **port**) A printer or other **peripheral** hooked up to a computer to transmit the **bits** of a **byte** of information one after another. Contrast **parallel interface.**

Serial note A **promissory note** that is paid back in **installments.**

Series bonds Groups of **bonds** put out at different times with different cash-in times, but all part of the same deal; often a complex **mortgage.** Each bond in a series has identical **maturity, interest,** terms and conditions; but each *series* may vary from the others. When issued as part of an equipment **lien** deal, no new series may usually be put out to **mature** prior to earlier bonds with earlier maturities. In the case of **equipment trust** certificates, different series represent, not open-ended debt, but obligations **secured** by different lots of equipment. Railroads and public utilities often employ series bonds because of their large borrowing for large, continuing equipment. Do not confuse these with **serial bonds,** which are similar and have similar uses.

Series of classes All classes of **positions** involving the same kind of work, but which may vary as to the level of difficulty and responsibility and have differing grade and salary ranges. The classes in a series either have differing titles (e.g., assistant accountant, associate accountant, senior accountant) or numerical designations (e.g., Accountant I, Accountant II, Accountant III). Be wary of numerical designations, however: Accountant I could be either the most junior or most senior level.

Service 1. An intangible commodity; useful work. 2. An expense that supports production. 3. The delivery (or its legal equivalent, such as publication in a newspaper in some cases) of a legal paper (such as a writ) by an officially authorized person, in a way that meets all formal requirements. It is a way to notify a person of a lawsuit. 4. Regular payments on a debt. This is called *servicing the debt* or *debt service.* 5. A *service charge* for *consumer credit* includes any cost that has anything to do with the credit, no matter what it is for or called. These include **time-price** differentials, credit investigations, **carrying charges,** creditor insurance, etc. *Service credit* is a credit arrangement allowing bills to be paid at the end of a month for services provided during that month. Utility companies and the medical professions often extend this kind of credit. A *service establishment* is any place that sells *services* to the public (barber shops, laundries, auto repair shops, etc.). A *service fee* is either money (usually the equivalent of union dues) that nonunion members of an *agency shop bargaining unit* pay the union for negotiating and administering the **collective bargaining** agreement; or a *service charge*. The *service life* of property is how long it should be useful. This is not necessarily the same as its **depreciable** life. A *service mark* is a mark used in the sale or advertising of services, usually to identify a company by a distinctive design, title, character, etc. See **trademark.** *Service of debt* is regular payments on a debt. This is also called *servicing the debt* or *debt service. Service of process* is the delivery (or its legal equivalent, such as publication in a newspaper in some cases) of a legal paper by an officially authorized person in a way that meets all the formal requirements. A *service unit* is a unit of measurement for a business activity when activities are divided up by functional areas or departments to allocate costs. *Service value* is the difference between the current value of an item and its **salvage** value.

Servicing Service of debt.

Servitude A **charge** or burden on land in favor of another. For example, the owner of a piece of land may be required by the **deed** to allow the owner of adjoining land to walk across a part of the land. This type of *servitude* is called an **easement.** The land so restricted is the *servient estate* and the land benefiting from the restriction is the *dominant estate*.

Set asides Government purchasing and contracting provisions that *set aside* or allocate a certain percentage of business for minority-owned companies.

Set of exchange An original and copies of a foreign **bill** of exchange.

Set-up time The time during the normal work day when a worker's machine is being set up (usually by the machine's operator) prior to commencing production. Union contracts frequently provide time **standards** for set-up operations.

Setback   A distance from a street, property line, building, etc., within which building is prohibited by **zoning** laws, **building codes,** etc.

Settle   1. Come to an agreement about a debt, payment of a debt, or disposition of a lawsuit.   2. Transfer property in a way that ties it up for a succession of owners, such as in a **trust.**   3. One of several words for end-of-day closing price, especially in the **futures** market.

Settlement   1. See **settle.**   2. The meeting in which the ownership of **real property** actually transfers from seller to buyer. All payments and debts are usually adjusted and taken care of at this time. These financial matters are written on a *settlement sheet,* which is also known as a **closing** statement.   3. A *settlement price* is a price set by **commodities brokers** in settling outstanding transactions when they **clear** their **balances** with each other. For *settlement day* in **securities** and **commodities,** see **account day.**

Sever   To separate. *Severable* means capable of carrying on an independent existence. A *severable* **contract** or **statute** is one that can be divided up without harm to the part remaining. Most statutes and some contracts have a *severability* or **saving clause.** *Severally* means distinctly; separately; each on its own. *Severalty ownership* is sole ownership; ownership by one person. *Severance pay* is a lump-sum payment by an employer to an employee who has been permanently separated from the organization because of a workforce reduction, the introduction of labor-saving machinery, or for any reason other than **cause.** A *severance tax* is a tax on the volume or value of a natural resource (oil, coal, etc.) taken from the land.

Sex   Gender. *Sex discrimination* is any disparate or unfavorable treatment of an individual in an employment situation because of his or her sex. The **Civil Rights Act** makes sex discrimination illegal except where a **bona fide occupational qualification** is involved. *Sexual harassment* exists whenever an individual in a position to control or influence another's job, career, or grade, uses such power to gain sexual favors or to punish one for the refusal of such favors. Sexual harassment on the job varies from inappropriate sexual innuendo to coerced sexual relations. An employer has a responsibility to provide a place of work that is free from sexual harassment or intimidation.

Shape-up A method of hiring which had men line up at the beginning of each day so that they could be selected (or rejected) for work.

Share 1. One piece of **stock** in a corporation. A *share certificate* (or **warrant**) is a document certifying that a person is entitled to own (or buy) a certain number of shares of stock. 2. A *share account* is one of an assortment of accounts offered by a **credit union** which closely parallel the time and savings accounts offered by commercial banks and **thrift institutions.** A *share draft* is similar to a **NOW account** but is offered by credit unions. 3. With a *shared appreciation mortgage,* monthly payments are at a relatively low **interest** rate; but the lender shares a sizable percent (usually 30 to 50) of the appreciation in the home's value when it is sold or after a specified number of years. *Shared equity* is a real-estate purchase arrangement in which an investor puts up part of the purchase price and pays part of the **mortgage** in exchange for tax benefits and a share of the eventual profits of a sale. 4. The percentage of homes watching a given TV show out of all TV sets in use at the time. 5. The percentage of sales that a given **brand** represents of the total sales of a product.

Shark repellent Anything a company can do to inhibit a **takeover** by a *shark,* a would-be acquirer. Typically, **bylaws** would be altered so that 75 percent of the stockholders have to approve a takeover.

Sharp A **mortgage** or other **security** document is *sharp* if it allows the creditor to take quick summary action to collect if the debtor fails to pay.

Shave A slang expression for buying **notes** or other **securities** at a discount; for discounting a promissory note or similar instrument at a rate higher than market or higher than legal; for paying an extra charge to get a time extension for the delibery of a security; for cutting prices secretly to a few persons; for using extortion to get something; etc.

Shelf life 1. The length of time a product remains for sale in a retail outlet. 2. The length of time a product (such as food or drugs) has before it naturally deteriorates and should be discarded.

Shell branch   A foreign branch that acts as a booking office
for financial transactions negotiated beyond U.S. borders
with the ledgers of the shell branch usually maintained at
the head office of the U.S. bank. Often located in offshore banking centers, particularly the Bahamas and Cay-
man Islands, shell branches provide low-cost access to
Eurocurrency markets for U.S. banks.

Shelter   1. A way of investing money to minimize your
total tax burden.   2. The principle that a buyer has as
good a **title** to property as the seller had. For example,
under the **UCC** *shelter doctrine*, the **holder** of a **negotiable instrument** has **holder in due course** rights if the
person who sold the instrument was a holder in due
course.   3. A *sheltered workshop* is a place of employment that offers a controlled, noncompetitive environment for persons unable to compete in the regular world
of work because of physical or mental disabilities.

Sherman Act   The first **antitrust** or antimonopoly law, passed
by the federal government to break up "combinations in
restraint of trade."

Shift work   A formal tour of duty that is mostly outside of
"normal" daytime business hours.

Ship's manifest   A document signed by the captain of a
ship that lists the individual shipments constituting the
ship's cargo.

Shipping   1. Transporting goods for a charge. *Shipping
documents* include **bills of lading, letters of credit,** etc. A
company's **shipping department** packs, loads, and ships
the product. The shipping department is often headed by
a traffic manager who is responsible for selecting methods
of shipment.   2. Having to do with ships or moving goods
by sea. *Shipping articles* are a written agreement between
a sailor and the ship's master concerning the voyage, the
pay, etc.

Shop   Workplace. A *shop committee* is a group of union
members in the same organizational unit who have been
selected to speak for the union membership on any of a
variety of issues. The *shop right rule* is the legal rule that
when an employee gets a **patent** on an invention worked
on during work hours and using employer's materials, the
employer has a right to use the invention free, but not to
take the patent away from the inventor. For *shop steward,*
see **steward.**

Shopping goods   Retail products that customers are likely to take the time to compare for price and quality. See **heterogeneous** and **homogeneous shopping goods.**

Short   1. A *short position* is the trading position of a person who has sold **securities** or **commodities** that he or she does not own, in the hope of being able to buy them later at a lower price. *Short covering* is usually the purchase of **stock** to return stock previously borrowed to make delivery on a *short sale;* or the repurchase of previously sold contracts to even up or balance off sales made in a commodity. A *short interest* is the total amount of securities or of a commodity that has been sold and remains uncovered by actual ownership on an exchange. This is also called a *total short position.* A *short sale* is a **contract** for the sale of something, such as a stock, commodity, or **futures** contract, that the seller does not own. It is a method of profiting from the expected fall in price of a stock, but risky because if the stock goes up, the person will have to buy at whatever price it reaches to *cover* the short sale. A *short tax year* is a tax year of less than 12 months because the taxpayer had not existed as yet for a full year, or the taxpayer is changing tax years.   2. *Short term* is defined for various tax and other financial purposes as less than a week, a month, six months, nine months, and a year. The *short term,* in economic theory, is the time during which some costs are **fixed** (such as the costs of a just built factory). *Short swing profits* are profits made by a company **insider** on the *short-term* sale of company stock.

Show cause   A court **order** to a person to show up in court and explain why the court should not take a proposed action.

Showing of interest   The requirement that a union must show that it has adequate support from employees in a proposed **bargaining unit** before a **representation election** can be held. A *showing of interest* is usually demonstrated by signed **authorization cards.**

Shrinkage   1. The loss of goods or raw materials due to a naturally occurring physical depletion.   2. The loss of goods or raw materials due to employee theft or incompetence.

Shut-in royalty   Money paid to keep a mineral **lease** active when nothing is being produced.

Sick-leave bank An arrangement that allows employees to pool some of their paid sick-leave days in a common fund so that they may draw upon that fund if extensive illness uses up their remaining paid time off. Sick-leave banks have tended to discourage **absenteeism;** because, with everyone jointly owning days in the bank, there is some psychological pressure on workers not to use their sick-leave unless they are really sick.

Sick-out A mass absence from work by a group of aggrieved employees.

Sight *At sight* means **payable** when shown and requested. A **bill** or **draft** payable when shown is a *sight bill* or *sight draft*. *Sight drafts* can be sent by a seller of goods to a new, faraway buyer's bank. When the buyer tells the bank to pay the draft, the ownership documents for the goods are given to the buyer.

Silent partner See **partner.**

Silicon Valley That part of the San Francisco Bay Area where there is a concentration of manufacturers who produce semiconductors, microelectronic chips out of silicon, and computers. The phrase is gradually coming to mean any concentration of computer-related industries.

Simple capital structure A corporation's **capital structure** is *simple* when it has issued only **capital stock** and no **potentially dilutive common stock equivalents** that would dilute **earnings per share** by more than an aggregate 3 percent. See **complex capital structure.**

Simple interest **Interest** on original **principal** only. It is a method of calculating interest on an outstanding balance that produces a declining finance charge with each payment of an installment loan. Contrast **compound interest.**

Simulate Take on the appearance; imitate; fake. For example, a *simulated sale* is a fake sale to make it look to creditors as if the property is out of their reach. This is also called a **fraudulent conveyance.**

Single One. For *single column tariff,* see **tariff.** *Single lump sum credit* is a **closed-end credit** arrangement in which the total outstanding **balance** is due on a specified date. *Single name paper* is a **negotiable instrument** that has only one **maker** (original signer) or, if more than one original signer, persons signing for exactly the same purpose (for example, as **partners**). This is opposed to **accommodation paper** (where one person signs as a favor to another) or a **surety**ship (where, usually for a fee, one person cosigns to back up another person's debt). A *single rate* is a **flat rate**. *Single step* is a financial statement where expenses are deducted from revenues to compute **net** earnings. For a contrast, see **multiple step.**

Sinking fund Money or other **assets** put aside for a special purpose, such as to pay off **bonds** and other long-term debts as they come due or to replace worn-out or outdated machinery or buildings.

Sister corporation Two companies with the same or mostly the same owners.

Sit-down strike Any work stoppage during which the strikers remain at their work stations and refuse to leave the employer's premises in order to forestall the employment of strikebreakers.

Site license An agreement whereby a company is sold the right to use specific computer software in any manner so long as the use remains in the company.

Situation audit A **strategic planning** technique for assessing an organization's performance in absolute terms or in comparison to a competing or parallel organization. Major aspects include a **capability profile** and a **WOTS-UP** analysis.

Situational leadership An approach to the study of leadership based on the idea that situational factors (such as organization structure, interpersonal relations, etc.) bear heavily on leader effectiveness.

Situational management Same as **contingency management.**

Sixty-day notice The federal requirement that both employers and unions must give a notice sixty days before reopening and ending a labor contract. During this time **strikes** and **lockouts** are prohibited.

Skeleton bill A **bill** of exchange written or signed **in blank.**

Skilled labor Workers who, having trained for a relatively long time, have mastered jobs of considerable skill requiring the exercise of substantial independent judgment.

Skimming 1. To take the best parts of a group of something. A *skimming pricing policy* seeks the "cream" of a market (those consumers who are the least price sensitive) before pricing the product for other, more price-conscious consumers. 2. In **insurance,** *skimming* refers to the intentional selection of favorable **risks.** 3. A slang term for illegally concealing business income from **partners** or tax authorities.

Skiptracing A detective **service** that finds missing **debtors** and other missing persons.

Skunkworks A slang term for a **research and development** unit.

Slide-rule discipline An approach to discipline that eliminates supervisory discretion and sets very specific quantitative standards as the consequences of specific violations. For example, a discipline policy based on this concept might hold that any employee who is late for work more than four times in a 30-day period would be "automatically" suspended for three days. With the demise of the *slide rule,* "automatic" discipline is a more common phrase.

Sliding scale A rate that varies according to another **(fixed)** rate.

Slowdown A deliberate reduction of output by employees. Such efforts are usually meant to bring economic pressure upon an employer without incurring the costs of a **strike.**

Slush funds 1. Discretionary funds. 2. Funds used for bribery. 3. Secret funds. All *slush funds,* because of their lack of formal accountability, have an unsavory connotation—even when they are perfectly legal.

Small Little. A company may be a **small business** if it has few employees, a low sales volume, few stockholders, etc. The definition differs, depending on who (**SBA, workers' compensation, IRS,** state law, etc.) defines it. A *small denomination savings certificate* (and a *small saver certificate*) are specially regulated **certificates of deposit** that are **time deposits** in small amounts. A *small group* is a number of individuals who interact with each other in a restricted social setting. Groups are usually called *small* when each member can recognize and interact with all other members. A *small loan act* is a state law setting maximum interest rates on **consumer** loans or on all small short-term loans.

Smart money 1. Profitable investing generally, but more often profitable investing because of inside information. See **insider.** 2. Punitive damages.

Smorgasbord plan A **cafeteria plan.**

Social Relating to society. A *social audit* is a systematic assessment of a company's actions that have social impact. It is a major way of measuring how *socially responsible* a company is, often as defined by the auditor. *Social insurance* is any **benefit** program that a state makes available to its citizens in time of need and as a matter of right. Coverage is often compulsory, and benefits are not usually directly related to individual contribution amounts. The *social responsibility of business* implies that a business has an obligation to its society other than seeking a profit in a legal manner. The *Social Security Administration* is a federal agency, set up by the *Social Security Act* and the *Federal Insurance Contribution Act (FICA),* that administers a national old age, survivors, and disability insurance program and other insurance, medical, and welfare programs.

Societé (French) A **partnership.** A *societé anonyme* is a **corporation.**

Socio-technical systems The concept that work groups are neither technical nor social systems, but interdependent.

Soft Easy. For *soft funding,* see **hard funding.** For *soft goods,* see **goods.** A *soft landing* is an economy that is going from a situation of rapid unsustainable growth to one of stable growth without a **recession.** A *soft-loan window* is a special lending facility extending loans on significantly easier terms than those applicable to conventional loans. In international finance, these loans are made by organizations such as the **International Development Association** to the poorer **developing countries.** A *soft market* is a declining market or one in which sales are slow. *Soft money* may mean paper currency as opposed to coins; easy borrowing because of low interest rates; a nation's currency that is not desired by foreigners; or temporary funding. A *soft spot* is a rapid decline in one kind of **securities** while the **market** as a whole remains firm. *Software* means computer **programs.**

Sole actor doctrine The rule that a **principal** (such as an employer) will be held legally responsible for knowing what his or her **agent** (such as an employee) knows and for what that agent does.

Sole proprietorship A business owned by one person. There are several advantages to this form of ownership. Most important, the *sole proprietor* has full managerial power over the business. This is important both from the point of view of control and the psychological advantage of owning and controlling. The owner also has the right to all profits of the venture and the benefit of single taxation of these profits, as opposed to the double taxation of corporate profits. Balanced against these advantages are the disadvantages: limited size due to greater difficulties in raising **capital** and in generating enough time and energy to expand; the limited (personal) lifetime of the company; and the unlimited personal liability for company debts and losses. See **partnership** and **corporation** for other major ways of owning a business.

Solvency (or **solvent**) Either the ability to pay debts as they come due, or having more **assets** than **liabilities.** These are *different* tests of financial strength.

Sophisticated investor A person who has the background and knowledge to understand what he or she is getting into by buying shares in a business venture. Some **stock** sales can avoid **SEC registration** requirements by selling to only *sophisticated investors* who can afford the investment.

Span of control The extent of a manager's responsibility. The *span of control* has usually been expressed as a number of subordinates that a manager should supervise.

Special Unique. A *special assessment* is a real estate tax that singles out certain landowners to pay for improvements (such as a sidewalk) that will benefit all those owners. *Special bank credit plans* are **lines of credit** extended to borrowers by banks, based upon a prearranged limit which borrowers may use all, or part of, by writing a check. **Interst** charges are based on the amount of credit used during the month and the total amount outstanding. *Special drawing rights* are a type of international money, created by the **International Monetary Fund** and allocated to its member nations. Although *SDRs* are only accounting entries (not actual coin or paper money and not backed by precious metal), they are an international **reserve asset.** The *special facts rule* is the legal rule that **corporate insiders** must reveal certain types of financial and ownership information to stockholders. *Special interests* are groups that have common interests such as consumers, banks, milk producers, etc. Each *special interest* tries to lobby the government to influence the passage of laws and their enforcement. A *special master* is a person appointed by a court to conduct an investigation or to carry out a court order; for example, a special master might supervise the sale of property that the court has ordered to be sold. A *special use permit* (or *permit of exception*) is government permission to use property in a way that is allowed by **zoning** rules, but only with a permit. (This is *not* a **variance**.) A *special use valuation* is the option of a person handling a dead person's land to call its tax value the value of its current use—not what it would be worth if used most profitably. Users of this option must conform to several provisions of the tax code. A *special warranty deed* is a transfer of land that includes the formal, written promise to protect the buyer against all claims of ownership of the property that are based on relationships with, or transfers from, the seller. In some states, it is the same as a **quitclaim deed.**

Specialist A stockbroker who handles other brokers' orders in a specialized type of stock.

Specialization of labor See **division of labor.**

Specialty goods (or **products**) Items that a consumer would be willing to make a special effort to find and buy. They are often to be found in a *specialty shop*—a store aimed at a small **market** segment.

Specie 1. Coins, especially gold and silver coins. 2. *In specie performance* of a **contract** means according to the exact terms; and return of an item *in specie* means return of the same—not "an identical" item.

Specific duty or tariff An import tax set at a fixed amount per unit, or per unit of measure, regardless of the value of the item imported. See **duty** and **tariff.**

Specific performance See **performance.**

Specification 1. A detailed listing of all particulars, such as the "how to build it" part of a **patent** application. 2. A written description of the duties and responsibilities of a **class** of **positions.**

Speculate Hope to profit from rapid changes in a stock's (or other item's) price, or to profit from a huge price increase in a very risky (*speculative*) investment. A person taking such risks is a *speculator*.

Speculative demand (or **speculative motive for money**) A general withdrawal of money from markets in the belief that prices will fall or **interest** rates will rise.

Speculative grade **Bonds** below **investment grade;** those rated **BB** (double B) or lower.

Speed rating A performance rating that compares the speed with which an employee performs specific tasks against an observer's **standard** or norm. See also **power test.**

Speed-up An effort by employers to obtain an increase in **productivity** without a corresponding increase in wages.

Spike A rapid up-and-down movement in the price of a **stock** or in any trend on a graph.

Spillover effect Benefits or costs to persons other than the buyer of goods or services. A new airport, for example, not only benefits its users but *spills over* onto the population at large in both positive and negative ways.

Spin-off 1. A **corporation** sets up and funds a new corporation and gives the **shares** of this new corporation to the old corporation's stockholders. This new corporation is a *spin-off* and the process is a *spin-off*. See also **split-off** and **split-up**. 2. A production **by-product.**

Split 1. The division of a corporation's outstanding **shares** into a larger number. While each stockholder gets a pro-rated number of additional shares, overall **equity** remains the same. This often occurs when the price of a stock gets so high that it discourages new buyers; a split then lowers the price in the expectation that this will increase demand and thus ultimately raise the price. A *splitback* or *splitdown* is the reverse of this process; shares are recalled and fewer shares issued in their place. 2. A *split-off* occurs when a corporation sets up and funds a new corporation and gives the **shares** of this new corporation to the old corporation's stockholders in exchange for some of their shares in the old company. This new company is a *split-off* and the process is a *split-off*. See **spin-off** and *split-up*. A *split-up* occurs when a corporation divides into two or more separate new corporations, gives its shareholders the shares of these new corporations, and goes out of business. This process is a *split-up*. 3. A *split commission* awards partial credit and compensation to each of several salespersons when each was directly involved in completing a sale. *Split-dollar insurance* is one person helping another to pay insurance premiums. This may have tax advantages. In *split dollar* (or *supplemental*) *life insurance,* where an employer helps employees pay, when the employee dies the employer totally recovers the paid **premiums** from the benefit sum with the remainder distributed to the employee's **beneficiaries.** *Split funding* combines the purchase of **mutual fund** shares with life insurance. A *split investment company* is a **closed end investment company** that has two kinds of stock: one receives income and the other receives **capital gains.** A *split offering* is a **bond** issue of both serial and long-term bonds with the same **maturity** date. The *split-off point* in **accounting** occurs when the **joint costs** associated with two or more products end so that costs can then be attributed to the individual products. A *split opening* occurs on an **exchange** when there are different opening prices for the same thing because two groups of traders have started simultaneously. For *split order,* see **order.** A *split shift* is the same as **broken time.**

Spot 1. Immediate. For example, a *spot exchange rate* is the conversion rate for money exchanged at the time the rate is quoted. The *spot price* is the price of things sold for immediate delivery with immediate payment. This is called *spot trading.* 2. *Spot zoning* is changing the **zoning** of a piece of land without regard for the zoning plan for the area. 3. A short advertising message. A commercial that is not part of those run on a sponsored program. *Spot advertising* is picking selective markets (and stations) in which to advertise a product.

Spread The difference between two prices, amounts, or numbers; for example, between **bid and asked** prices in **commodity** trading.

Sprinkling trust A **trust** that gives income to many persons at different times.

Squatter's rights The "right" to ownership of land merely because you have occupied it for a long time. This is different from **adverse possession** and is not recognized as a *right* in most places.

Squeeze out A **merger** or other change in a corporation's structure that is done by majority owners to get rid of (or further reduce the power of claims of) **minority stockholders.** See **freeze-out.**

Stabilization 1. Any action by government to stabilize prizes, employment levels, exchange rates, etc. A *stabilization policy* is a government's efforts to reduce cyclical fluctuations in the **business cycle.** 2. The buying and selling of a **security** to hold its price steady.

Stabilized bond A **bond** that has its **principal** or **interest** adjusted to reflect changes in **inflation** or **deflation** as indicated by an **index.**

Staff 1. Specialists who assist line managers in carrying out their duties. Generally staff units do not have the power

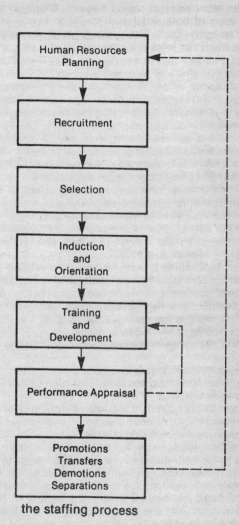

the staffing process

of decision, command, or control of operations. Rather, they make recommendations to (which may or may not be adopted by) the **line personnel.** Legal, **personnel,** and **purchasing** departments are examples of *staff, service* or *auxiliary units.* 2. All employees. 3. To *staff out* is a process that involves soliciting a variety of views or recommendations on an issue so that a decisionmaker will be aware of all reasonable options. The *staff principle* is a principle of administration stating that the executive should be assisted by officers who are not in the line of operation, but are essentially extensions of the personality of the executive, and whose duties consist primarily of assisting the executive in controlling and coordinating the organization, and of offering advice. *Staffing* is the process of hiring people to perform work for the organization. *Staffing* structures a work system by establishing who will perform what function and have what authority. Staffing must also make the employment, advancement, and compensation processes satisfy the criteria of **equity** and **due process.** *Staffing dynamics* is a phrase used by those who are not content with calling **turnover** turnover. A *staffing plan* is a planning document that minimally lists an organization's projected **personnel** needs by occupation and grade level and identifies how these needs will be met. *Staffing program planning* is the process of developing this plan and the specific steps needed to implement it.

Stagflation High **unemployment** and high **inflation** at the same time.

Stale check A check that has been made uncashable because it has been held too long. This time period is often set by state law.

Stamp tax A tax on certain legal documents, such as **deeds,** that requires that revenue stamps be bought and put on the documents to make them **valid.**

Standard A model, example, or measurement unit established by authority, custom, or general consent. In industry, it is usually an element of a cost, time, or quality determination system. See **industrial standardization.** A *standard allowance* is an established amount of time by which the normal time for employees to complete their tasks is increased to compensate for the expected amount of personal or unavoidable delays. *Standard & Poor's Corporation* is a major publisher of financial data that is perhaps best known for its ratings of **securities**. A *standard cost system* uses predetermined **standards**, computed before production, for all phases of **cost accounting**. The costs collected on the basis of these standards are compared with the actual costs, and **variances** between them are computed. These variances spotlight costs that are out of line. *Standard absorption costing* calls for calculating the cost of a finished product as the total of labor, material, and **overhead** that went into it—each taken as a standard rather than actual cost. *Standard direct costing* is the same except that the overhead costs are actual rather than standard. *Standard deviation* is a measure of the variability of a distribution about its **mean** or average. A *standard hour* is the normally expected amount of work to be done in an hour. It is a unit of measurement for use in nearly all **production** activities. Standard hours do not correspond to clock times; the standard hour notation on an incoming job order may indicate that the job will require 40 standard hours, but this does not mean that the job can be completed by one person in a regular 40-hour work week. The available clock time of a facility does not take into account, for example, personal time, absenteeism, stoppages, and reduced efficiency. The only way to correlate standard hours and maximum gross hours is to reduce the maximum gross hours available by total lost time. A *standard-hour plan* is an incentive plan that rewards an employee by a percent premium that equals the percent by which performance beats the *standard time*—a unit of measure that specifies the time it takes an average worker to perform a given task. The *Standard Industrial Classification System* is the federal government's numbering system for the classification of industries and enterprises which develops comparable statistics on the composition and structure of the economy. This system is an important resource for **marketing** research because census reports based upon this data allow companies to easily determine the location and size of potential customer groups. *Standard of living* is a measure of the material affluence enjoyed by a nation or by an individual. The *standard mileage rate* is what the **IRS** allows taxpayers to deduct for business use of their vehicles. A *Standard Metropolitan Statistical Area* is a Census Bureau device to more accurately portray urban populations; an *SMSA* includes the population in all counties contiguous to an urban county (that is, one with a city over 50,000 in a common total) if the population of these counties is involved in the urban county work force. SMSAs are used in **marketing research.** A *standard price report* is an analysis of sales volume by product groups that indicates any sales price variance and its effect on planned profits; it contains a comparison of sales volume at actual and at standard selling prices. The standard selling price is the price at which management would like to sell goods to ensure a certain profit margin. It is not necessarily the only price at which they will sell, but it is the target figure. Exceptions to the stardard price may be made for a variety of reasons, such as competition or the desire to penetrate new sales territories. The standard price report enables management to see, on an individual product basis, how close they are to achieving a desired return on sales. A *standard rate* is a **flat rate.** A *standardized test* is any objective test given under constant conditions, or any test for which a set of **norms** is available. *Standards of conduct* are an organization's formal guidelines for ethical behavior. *Standards of performance* are statements that tell an employee how well he or she must perform a task to be considered a satisfactory employee.

Standby letter of credit   See **letter.**

Standing   1. A person's right to bring or join a lawsuit because he or she is directly affected by the issues raised. This is called *standing to sue.*   2. Reputation.   3. A *standing committee* of a house of a legislature is a regular committee, with full power to act within a subject area.

Standing (or **continuing**) **plans**   Documents to guide organizations in policies, standard methods, or procedures when dealing with recurring objectives or problems.

Standstill agreement   An agreement between a target company and a **raider** (or company) seeking to take it over whereby the potential acquirer agrees not to buy any more of the target's **stock** for a specified period.

Staples   Routinely bought goods; what customers consider to be necessities.

State   1. Say, set down, or declare.   2. The major political subdivision of the U.S. (*State action* is action by a state, such as New York).   3. A nation. (An *act of state* is by a country, such as France.)   4. Condition; situation.

5. Department of State; the U.S. cabinet department that handles relations with foreign countries. 6. A **state bank** is a commercial bank chartered by a state and subject to **regulation** by the state and also in many instances by the federal financial regulatory agencies. See **dual banking system.** *State of the art* is the level of development in a given scientific or technological field at a given time, usually the present. *State trading nations* are countries such as the Soviet Union and the People's Republic of China that rely heavily on government entities, instead of corporations, to conduct their trade with other countries.

Stated 1. Regular. For example, a *stated meeting* of a **board of directors** is one held at regular intervals according to law or **charter.** 2. Settled or agreed upon. For example, a *stated account* is an agreed amount owing.

Statement 1. A document laying out facts. For example, a *statement of account* or *bank statement* lists all the transactions made by a customer for that month; a *statement of affairs* is the summary financial form filled out when filing for **bankruptcy;** and a *statement of identity* is a questionnaire used by real estate **title** companies to more accurately identify a person. 2. There are several technical **accounting** *statements* that supplement a **corporation's** basic **balance sheet** in its reports. These include statements of **income** (profits and losses); **earnings per share;** money in and out for such things as wages, supplies, **interest,** taxes, etc., all compared with prior years; *changes in financial position* or *sources and application of funds* (**cash balances, working capital,** etc.); *changes in accounting* (the way **inventory** is valued, the way **assets** are **depreciated,** etc.); *owners' equity* (basically, assets minus **liabilities,** but for a corporation, it is measured by **paid-in** capital plus **retained earnings**); and *retained earnings* (basically, profit kept by a corporation after paying out profits as **dividends,** etc.). See **combined, comparative,** and **consolidated** statements. *Statement analysis* is the process of applying financial **ratios** and other evaluative techniques to financial statements. A *statement of condition* or a *statement of financial position* is a **balance sheet.**

Statistical Dealing with numerical data. A *statistical inference* is the use of information observed in a **sample** to make predictions about a larger population. *Statistical quality control* is a statistical technique for maintaining product quality at the desired level without 100 percent inspection. Statistical quality control uses **acceptance sampling** to determine whether a large lot of finished products meets pre-set quality levels. Using statistical techniques, a **random sample** is taken from a lot of **goods** and the sample is inspected. From this analysis an inference as to the quality level of the entire lot is made. This technique is often used in conjunction with periodic inspection along the production line that permits corrective action to be taken before final assembly of the product. *Statistical sampling* consists of sampling techniques which are based on the mathematical laws of probability.

Status quo objective A conservative **marketing** management goal that minimizes the risk of loss in an already established market.

Status symbols Visible signs of an individual's social status or importance in an organization. Under varying circumstances almost anything can be a status symbol: a key to the executive washroom, an assigned parking space, wood, as opposed to metal, office furniture, etc.

Statute A law passed by a legislature. *Statutes of frauds* are various state laws, modeled after an old English law, that require many types of **contracts** (especially those that are large, longterm, or involve land sales) to be signed and in writing to be enforceable in court. *Statutes at large* is a collection of all *statutes* passed by a particular legislature (such as the U.S. Congress), printed in full and in the order of their passage. *Statutes of limitations* are laws that set a maximum amount of time after something happens beyond which time it may no longer be taken to court; for example, a "three-year statute" for lawsuits based on a contract, or a "six-year statute" for a criminal prosecution. *Statutory* means having to do with a *statute;* created, defined, or required by a statute. A *statutory agent* is a corporation's legal representative in a state. Most state statutes require a company doing business within the state to maintain a statutory agent for, among other things, **service of process** in a lawsuit against the company. Many companies pay a commercial service or an individual to do this. A *statutory fee* may refer to the administrative costs of making a loan.

Stay To stop or hold off. For example, when a judge *stays a judgment*, the judge stops or delays its enforcement. And *stay laws* are **statutes** that hold off legal actions, usually to protect **debtors** in times of national financial crisis.

Steamship conference   A group of steamship operators that operate under mutually agreed-upon freight rates.

Step bonus   A feature of wage **incentive** plans that calls for a substantial increase in incentive payments when the quantity or quality of output reaches a specified level.

Step increase   See **increment.**

Step up (or down) basis   1. An increase (reduction) in the **basis** of a property for income tax purposes. This usually occurs when heirs take a dead person's property and their basis becomes the **market value.**   2. The *step down method* in **accounting** allocates service-department costs to appropriate production departments.

Stepped cost   A cost that increases by increments, or steps, with increased volume.

Steward   A local union's most immediate representative in a plant or department. Usually elected by fellow employees (but sometimes appointed by the union leadership), the *shop steward* handles **grievances,** collects **dues,** solicits new members, etc. A shop steward usually continues to work at his or her regular job and handles union matters on a part-time basis, frequently on the employer's time. A *steward chief* is a union representative who supervises the activities of a group of shop stewards.

Stint-plan wage system   A system that assigns a definite output to an employee's day's work; if the work is completed in less than normal time, the employee is credited with a full day's work and allowed to go home.

Stipulation   1. An agreement between lawyers on opposite sides of a lawsuit.   2. A demand.   3. One point in a written aggreement.

Stock   1. The goods held for sale by a merchant. *Stock control* is keeping **inventory** records. *Stock in trade* is either an inventory of goods or the nature of the services offered by a business. A *stockout* is a lack of inventory that should have been available. The *stock turnover* (or *stockturn*) *rate* is a measure of how often a given amount of inventory is sold per year.   2. Shares of ownership in a corporation. Some of the many types of stock are *assessable* (the owner may have to pay more than the stock's cost to meet the company's needs); *blue-chip* (excellent investment ratings); *callable* or *redeemable* (can be bought back by the company at a prestated price); *control* (that amount of stock, often less than a majority, that can control the company); *cumulative* (unpaid **dividends** must be paid before any **common stock** gets paid); *donated* (given back to the company for resale); *floating* (on the open market for sale); *growth* (bought for an increase in value, not dividends); *guaranteed* (dividends guaranteed by another company); *letter* (a letter is required stating that the buyer will not resell before a certain time); *listed* (traded on an **exchange**); *participation* (gets a share of profits); *penny* (cheap and speculative); **preferred** (getting a fixed rate of income before other stocks); and *registered* (**registered with the Securities and Exchange Commission**). Some stocks are *restricted* or *unregistered*—so designated because they were originally issued in a private sale or other transaction where they were not registered with the **SEC**. These stocks may be subject to certain limitations and conditions when resold. Other types of stock with more complex definitions (such as **capital, common, convertible,** etc.) are defined under their own words. So are some *stock-* words (such as **broker, exchange, market,** etc.). Others follow here: For *stock acquisition plan,* see **executive stock acquisition plan.** *Stock appreciation rights* are executive compensation programs similar to **phantom stock** that pay the cash equivalent of the increase in value of a stock during a predetermined period. A *stock association* is a **joint stock company.** The *Stock Clearing Corporation* is the New York Stock Exchange's central agency for clearing stock transfers and settling financial balances. A *stock dividend* is the profits of stock ownership paid out by a corporation in more stock rather than in money. This additional stock reflects the increased worth of the company. A *stock insurance company* is an insurance company owned and controlled by stockholders and operated for the purpose of making a *profit*. Contrast with a **mutual** insurance company, in which profits go to the insured. A *stock-option plan* is any of a variety of plans that allow employees to purchase shares of the company's stock at a future date at a price that is significantly lower than the stock's market value. If the price of the stock rises, the employee would find it profitable to exercise the option and buy the stock at a discount unavailable on the open market. A *stock power* is a power of attorney which allows a person other than the owner of a stock to legally transfer ownership of the stock. A *stock purchase plan* allows employees to buy stock in their company, often by payroll deduction and often with the employer paying a portion of the costs, or offering terms below market costs. *Stock rights* are documents (usually **warrants**) that give existing stockholders (or those to whom the documents are later sold) rights to buy new stock later. See *pre-emptive rights* under **pre-emption.**

Stockholder's derivative suit A lawsuit in which a shareholder of a corporation sues in the name of the corporation because a wrong has been done to the company and the company itself will not sue.

Stockholder's equity A corporation's *net worth* (**assets** minus **liabilities**) expressed, not in terms of the assets themselves (buildings, **inventory,** etc.), but in terms of the way the assets are owned by the stockholders. It consists of **capital stock, capital surplus,** and **retained earnings.**

Stop order 1. A customer's notice to his or her bank that tells the bank to refuse payment on a check the customer has written to another person. 2. Instructions from a customer to a **stockbroker** to buy a particular **stock** at a price above the current **market** price or sell it at a price below the current price. A *stop-limit order* gives a price above which it can't be bought and below which it can't be sold. A *stop-loss order* is to buy or sell at a particular price to limit loss on an existing purchase. 3. An **order** from a judge, from an **administrative agency,** etc., to stop doing something, such as building a house without a **permit.** See **cease and desist order.**

Stoppage in transit The right of a seller to stop the delivery of goods even after they have been given to a **carrier** (railroad, etc.) is, for example, the seller finds out that the buyer is **insolvent** and will not be able to pay for the goods.

Straddle A combination of **put** and **call options** in which a person buys the right to buy or sell a **stock** at a certain price within a certain time.

Straight 1. Direct. 2. In proper order. 3. *Straight commission* is a method of compensating sales employees by solely paying them a percentage of the value of the goods they sell. A *straight rebuy* is a routine repurchase. *Straight* *salary* is a method of compensating sales employees by solely paying them a fixed salary without regard to the dollar value of the sales that they generate within a specified time period. *Staight-line depreciation* is dividing the cost of a thing used in a business by the number of years in its **useful life** and deducting that fraction of the cost each year from **taxable income.** See also *accelerated depreciation* under **depreciation.** *Straight-time hourly earnings* are wages earned per hour exclusive of **premium** payments and **shift differentials.**

Strategic business unit   A section of a larger company which concentrates on a particular product or market and is considered a distinct **profit center.**

Strategic control point   A control **standard** for measuring the quality of a good or service at key times or places; for example, the number of formal **grievances** filed in a particular unit, the quality of a product midway through its assembly, etc. The whole purpose of *strategic control points* is to catch errors or problems before they become serious and expensive.

Strategic management   Any managerial decisionmaking style which consistently attends to both internal and external organizational concerns. Its most basic instrument is strategic **planning,** which develops the specific tasks needed to implement a given strategy.

Strategic planning   See **planning.**

Straw (or straw man)   A "front"; a person who is put up in name only to take part in a deal. See **street name.** *Straw boss* is a colloquial term for a supervisor who has no real authority, power or status with which to back up orders.

Stream of commerce   Goods held within a state for a short while, but which come from another state and will go to another state, are in the *stream of commerce* and cannot be taxed by the state.

Street certificate   A **share** of **stock** signed **in blank,** so anyone can transfer it.

Street name   1. **Stock** or other **securities** held in the stockbroker's own name instead of the customer's (for convenience, to hide the owner's name, because the stock was bought on **margin,** etc.) are held in a *street name.*   2. The made-up name used by investment companies, banks, etc., to hide the real owners of stock, of a business, etc. Also called *straw, front name,* and *nominee.*

Strict foreclosure A **creditor's** right, in some circumstances, to take back property and cancel the debt. In these situations, the property acts as an exact cancellation of the debt, and neither the **creditor** nor the **debtor** can sue the other for any additional money.

Strict liability The legal responsibility for damage or injury, even if you are not at fault or negligent. For example, a manufacturer may be liable for injuries caused by a defective product even if the person hurt cannot prove how the manufacturer was careless.

Strike 1. Employees stopping, slowing down, or disrupting work to win demands from an employer. An *economic strike* is to make changes (in wages, hours, conditions, etc.) as opposed to one caused by an employer's **unfair labor practices**; a *general strike* is throughout an industry or country; a *jurisdictional strike* protests assignment of work to members of another union; a *secondary strike* is by one union against an employer who does business with another employer whose employees are on strike; a *sit-down strike* includes a refusal to leave the workplace; a *sympathy strike* is where one union helps another against the same employer; and a *wildcat strike* is unauthorized by union officials. A *strike authorization* is a formal vote by union members that (if passed) gives the union leadership the right to call a strike without additional consultation with the union membership. *Strike benefits* are payments by a union to its striking members or to non-members who are out on strike in support of the union. *Strike-bound* means struck by employees or attempting to function in spite of the strike. A *strikebreaker* is a person who accepts a position vacated by a worker on strike or is a worker who continues to work while others are on strike. The **Taft-Hartley Act** guarantees a strikebreaker's right to work and makes it illegal for unions to attempt to prohibit strikebreakers from crossing picket lines. A *strike counselor* is a **union counselor**. *Strike duty* consists of tasks assigned to union members by the union leadership during the course of a strike. A *strike fund* is money reserved by a union for use during a strike to cover costs such as strike benefits or legal fees. Strike funds are not necessarily separate from a union's general fund. 2. A *strike suit* is a stockholder's **derivative suit** brought purely for the gain of the stockholder or to win large lawyer's fees. 3. A *striking price* is the price at which a person can *exercise* an **option** to buy or sell a **stock** or **commodity.** 4. Take out, remove, or delete.

Strong-arm provision A part of the federal **bankruptcy** law. It says that a bankruptcy **trustee** has all the powers of the most powerful **secured creditor,** whether or not one actually exists, so he or she has the *strong-arm power* to gather in all the bankrupt's property.

Struck work Products produced by **strikebreakers.**

Structural unemployment Unemployment resulting from changes in technology, consumption patterns or government policies—a mismatch between available labor and demand for skills. The "cure" for structural unemployment is worker retraining.

Subchapter S corporation A legal status, sometimes chosen by *small* (defined by number of owners) *business* **corporations,** that allows them to be taxed primarily as **partnerships,** thus avoiding the **corporate** income tax and passing on *tax losses* to the owners.

Subcontractor A person who contracts to do a piece of a job for another person (a *prime* contractor) who has a contract for a larger piece or for the whole job. Many subcontractors are small businesses; but many large government defense and construction projects are so large that even the subcontractors are huge. Many government contracts require that a certain proportion of subcontractor business go to small businesses, that a certain percentage of the work satisfy equal opportunity requirements, etc. A *subcontractor's audit* is a survey of subcontractor records by the prime contractor to provide a basis for future time-and-material rates charged. It covers workers, supplies, accounting practices, etc.

Subdelegation Same as **delegation** of **authority.**

Subdivision Land divided into many lots by a developer and sold to different persons under a common plan.

Subletting A **tenant** renting property to another person.

Suboptimization Accepting alternatives that are less than ideal, but that accommodate the conflicting objectives of the various organizational interests.

Subordinate rating The evaluation of an organizational superior by someone of lesser rank.

Subordination A ranking of rights; for example, signing a document that admits that your **claim** or **interest** (for example, a **lien**) is weaker than another one and can collect only after the other one collects.

Subpoena A court's **order** to a person that he or she appear in court to testify (give evidence) in a case. Some **administrative agencies** may now **issue** subpoenas. A *subpoena duces tecum* commands a person to bring certain documents to court or to an administrative agency. [pronounce: sub-*pee*-na due-ces *tay*-kum]

Subrogation The substitution of one person for another in claiming a lawful right or debt. For example, when an insurance company pays its policy holder for damage to his or her car, the company may become *subrogated to* (gets the right to sue on or collect) any claim for the same damage that the policy holder has against the person who hit the car. This right is contained in a policy's *subrogation clause*.

Subscribe 1. Sign at the end of a document (as the person who wrote it, as a witness, etc.). 2. Agree to purchase some initial **stock** in a **corporation.** The act is *subscription*.

Subsidiary Under another's control; lesser. *Subsidiary* is often short for *subsidiary corporation*, or one that is controlled by another company, which is called the **parent corporation.** *Subsidiary accounts* are a group of related **accounts** maintained in a subsidiary **ledger** and controlled by an account in the general ledger; for example, individual customer **accounts receivable.**

Subsistence allowance Payments for an employee's reasonable expenses (meals, lodging, transportation, etc.) while traveling.

Succession A passing on of rights; a following. *Intestate succession* is the transfer of property by law to heirs if the person does not leave a will. *Perpetual succession* is the continuation of a **corporation** even though its owners, **directors,** and managers change. A *successor company* is a company that has taken over another company with all its rights and burdens by **reorganization** or by other legal process.

Suggested retail prices Until recently, many states permitted manufacturers to fix retail prices under so-called "fair trade laws," but those laws were forbidden in 1975 by the Consumer Goods Pricing Act. Yet, many manufacturers continue to "suggest" retail prices. But now that the fair trade laws are off the books, there are very few circumstances under which a seller can lawfully influence prices charged by its customers. A manufacturer may not request its distributors to agree to suggested retail prices; may not require wholesalers to report retailers' "violations" of suggested prices; and may not use its own field representatives, distributors, or even independent contractors to police a suggested retail price scheme.

Suitability rule The rule that a stockbroker should recommend only those stocks suitable for a customer's particular financial situation.

Sum certain An exact amount of money, usually of money owed. The amount is exact even if it includes **interest,** costs, etc., so long as these added amounts are exactly computable. A *sum certain* is a legal requirement for such things as the *negotiability* of a **negotiable instrument.**

Sumptuary laws Laws controlling the sale or use of socially undesirable, wasteful, and harmful products.

Sunk costs Past spending that no longer directly affects current decisions. For example, except for taxes, the original cost of a car is not as important as its current sale value. In an organizational context, *sunk costs* are resources committed to the achievement of an objective that cannot be regained if the objective is abandoned.

Sunshine bargaining **Collective bargaining** sessions open to the press and public. This process is more likely to be used in *public sector* negotiations.

Superannuation A **pension.**

Supernumerary Someone who is extra and not immediately needed.

Supernumerary income That portion of a worker's income which is not needed for the essentials of everyday life and consequently available for luxuries and other optional spending.

Superseniority **Seniority** that supersedes ordinary seniority, which is dependent on an individual's length of service. Because a union may be detrimentally affected if its key union officials are subject to **layoffs,** union **contracts** often grant them *superseniority*.

Supplemental Extra. For *supplemental compensation,* see **bonus** and **executive supplemental compensation.** For *supplemental life insurance,* see **split-dollar insurance.** *Supplemental medical insurance* may be any health insurance that supplements a regular health policy, and may be a special **fringe benefit,** usually offered only to top management, in which all expenses from medical or dental care not covered by the general medical/dental policy offered by the company are reimbursable. *Supplemental unemployment benefits* are payments to laid off workers from private unemployment insurance plans that are supplements to state **unemployment insurance** compensation. There are two basic *SUB* plans—the individual account and the pooled fund. With the former, contributions are credited to each employee's account and a terminated employee may take benefits with him or her. With the latter, benefits are paid from a common fund and individual employees have no **vested** rights should they leave the company. *Supplemental* or *supplemantary proceedings* are a **judgment creditor's** in-court examination of the debtor and others to find out if there is any money or property available to pay the debt.

Supply In economics, the quantity of goods and services available for purchase if income and other factors are held constant (calculated so as to not affect the figure). Increases in price either induce increases in supply or ration supply. Increases in **demand** usually induce increases in price. A *supply curve* is a graph showing the relationship between general market prices for an item and the quantity of the item that will be available at each price. The *supply of effort* (or *total supply of labor*) is the theoretical number of hours that a total population (for a plant, a company, a city, etc.) will work in a given time period. A *supply schedule* is a tabular display of the quantities of a given product offered at differing prices. *Supply-side economics* is a belief that lower tax rates, especially on **marginal** income, will encourage fresh **capital** to flow into the economy; which will, in turn, generate jobs, growth, and new tax revenue.

Support level A price level below which **securities** prices will normally not fall because the price attracts additional buyers.

Surcharge An extra charge on something already charged; a special payment; or an overcharge.

Surety A person or company that insures or guarantees that another person's debt will be paid by becoming liable (responsible) for the debt when it is made. See **guaranty.**

Surplus 1. Money left over. A **corporation's** *surplus*, or its **capital** *surplus*, has been defined in several different, overlapping, and sometimes conflicting ways, including "**assets** minus **liabilities,**" "assets minus **stock** value," and "assets minus stock value, liabilities, and **reserves,**" etc. There may also be a difference between a *financial surplus*, as variously defined above, and a *legal surplus*. The former may be used for business expansion, contingencies, etc., while the latter may also be used to pay **dividends.** A legal surplus depends on, among other things, the value put on each stock share. The word *surplus* is being replaced for many purposes by **retained earnings** and **accumulated retained earnings.** 2. Anything paid to a **factor of production** over what it would have taken to draw it into production; also called *surplus value*. A *consumer surplus* is what a buyer would be willing to pay for a product in addition to its market price. A *producer's surplus* is what a producer gets for selling a product at market less the price at which he or she would have been willing to sell.

Surtax 1. An additional tax on what has already been taxed. 2. A tax on a tax. For example, if you must pay a hundred-dollar tax on a thousand-dollar income (10 percent), a 10 percent *surtax* would be an additional ten dollars, not an additional hundred dollars.

Survivorship The right to property held by more than one person when one of them dies.

Suspension Removing an individual from employment for a specified period. Suspensions, by their nature temporary, are disciplinary acts—more severe than a **reprimand** yet less severe than a discharge.

Swap arrangement A reciprocal short-term credit agreement (which is renewable) between **central banks** to obtain **foreign exchange** for intervention in the foreign exchange market. A central bank obtains foreign exchange in return for domestic currency and, at a future specified date, the transaction is reversed.

Swap maternity A provision in **group** health **insurance** plans providing immediate maternity benefits to a newly covered woman, but terminating coverage on pregnancies in progress upon termination of a woman's coverage.

Sweat equity The increase in property value due to an owner's making improvements.

Sweat shops Work sites where employees worked long hours for low wages, usually under unsanitary conditions.

Sweetheart Someone loved. A *sweetheart clause* is that portion of a contract that makes a general policy statement about the harmonious manner in which both sides will live up to the spirit and letter of the agreement. A *sweetheart contract* is a **labor contract** containing unusually favorable terms for one side or the other. Many *sweetheart contracts* are gained by actions unrelated to the employment relationships (such as bribery).

Swing shift An extra shift of workers in an organization operating on a continuous or seven-day basis. The *swing crew* rotates among the various shifts to compensate for those employees who are absent, sick, on vacation, etc.

Switch sale See **bait and switch.**

Sympathy strike A **strike** by one union solely to support the aims of another union in an effort to exert indirect pressure upon an employer.

Syndicate 1. An association of individuals formed to conduct and carry on some particular business transaction, usually of a financial character. A syndicate often resembles a **joint adventure.** Syndicates are generally, but not always, temporary associations or firms. They may terminate automatically when the purpose for which they were formed has been accomplished. In the **securities** business, a *syndicate* is an association formed by one or more **dealers** who will act as managers of the group for the purpose of **underwriting** or distributing an **issue** of securities. 2. Slang for an organized crime network.

Syndication In real estate, a **limited partnership.**

Synthetic time study A **time study,** not dependent upon direct observation, in which time elements are obtained from other sources of time data.

Systemic discrimination The use of **employment practices** that have the unintended effect of excluding or limiting the employment prospects of women and minorities.

Systems analysis A methodologically rigorous collection, manipulation, and evaluation of organizational data to determine the best way to improve the functioning of the organization (the system) and to aid a decisionmaker in selecting a preferred choice among alternatives. A *systems approach* is an analytical framework which conceives of an enterprise as a set of objects with a given set of relationships and attributes (all connected to each other and their environment in such a way as to form an entirety). *Systems management* can be the application of this approach to organizational problems or the management of a subsystem of a larger organization.

T

T 1. In newspaper financial transaction tables, an indication, lowercase (t), that a **stock** has paid no cash **dividend;** or that a **bond** has a **floating rate.** 2. In newspaper stock transaction tables, an indication that the stock is traded on the Toronto Stock Exchange.

T-Account A form of keeping financial records in which the title is above the top part of the "T," the **debits** are on the left side of the vertical bar, and the **credits** are on the right.

T-Bill See **Treasury.**

T-Group See **laboratory training.**

TM Trademark.

Tacking Attaching something later, smaller, or weaker to something earlier, larger, or stronger. For example, if the owner of a third **mortgage** buys the first mortgage on a property and joins them together to get **priority** over the owner of the second mortgage, this is called *tacking.*

Taft-Hartley Act The federal statute that modified the **Wagner Act** of 1935. It provided that "National Emergency Strikes" could be put off for an 80 day cooling-off period during which the president might make recommendations to Congress for legislation that might cope with the dispute; a list of **unfair labor practices** by unions, which balanced the list of unfair labor practices by employers delineated in the Wagner Act; that the "closed shop" was illegal (this provision allowed states to pass "right-to-work" laws); that supervisory employees be excluded from coverage under the act; and that the **Federal Mediation and Conciliation Service** be created to mediate labor disputes.

Take To gain possession. A *take-down* is the time when a deal is actually performed, such as when goods have been both delivered and paid for, or the time when prearranged credit is actually used. *Take-home pay* is pay after deductions for such things as taxes, insurance, savings plans, etc. A *take-out loan* is a permanent **mortgage** that pays off a construction loan. A *takeover* is the gaining of control, but not necessarily majority ownership of a company (see **tender offer**). A *friendly takeover* occurs when the executives and directors of the target corporation support the takeover; a *hostile takeover* occurs when they do not. To *take up* a **note** or other **negotiable instrument** is to pay or **discharge** it.

Taking indicators An investment banking practice of seeking out potential buyers of a new **issue** before setting a price.

Tall organization See **flat organization.**

Tare Box or container weight subtracted from the total weight of goods.

Target The thing aimed at. For example, a *target company* is the subject of a **takeover** by a **tender offer.** And under a piece-rate wage system, a *target* represents expected earnings; it is usually set at a fixed percentage, 10 to 15 percent, above the base rate. A *targeted job credit* is a **tax credit** for employing a member of a *targeted group* of disadvantaged workers who have been so designated by an appropriate state employment security agency. *Target* (or *target return*) *pricing* is determining the sales price of a product by seeking a specific return of total dollars.

Tariff 1. An import tax; the rate at which imported goods are taxed; or a list of articles and the import tax that must be paid on each of them. An *autonomous tariff* is one that is determined solely by the country imposing the tariff; a *conventional tariff* is one that is arrived at as the result of negotiation between countries—a tariff by treaty or convention; a *protective tariff* is to protect local businesses from foreign competition; a *retaliatory tariff* is imposed in exchange for a foreign country's tax on goods from your country; and an *antidumping tariff* is designed to prevent foreign countries from selling cheaper here than there. A *single column tariff* is a tariff **schedule** listing only one **duty** rate for each imported commodity. A *specific tariff* is levied on the basis of some physical unit, as so many cents a pound, bushel, or yard in contrast to one that may be **ad valorem.** *Tariff escalation* is a situation in which tariffs on manufactured goods are relatively high, tariffs on semiprocessed goods are moderate, and tariffs on raw materials are nonexistent or very low. A *tariff quota* is the application of a higher tariff rate to imported goods after a specified quantity of the item has entered the country at the usual tariff rate during a specified period. A *tariff schedule* is a comprehensive list of the goods which a country may import and the import duties applicable to each. 2. A public list of services offered, rates charged, and rules of a public utility (such as an electric company).

Task A unit of work. *Task analysis* is identifying the various elements essential to the accomplishment of a task. A *task-and-bonus plan* is a wage incentive plan paying a specific percent of the base wage rate (in addition to the base wage rate) when a specified level of production is maintained or exceeded for a specified period of time. A *task force (task group, work group,* or *interdisciplinary team)* is a temporary organizational unit charged with accomplishing a specific mission. It is aggressively oriented, in contrast with committees, which tend to be chiefly concerned with the assessment of information to reach a conclusion.

Tax A required payment of money to support a government. There are hundreds of types of taxes. Those most important in a management context (such as **ad valorem tax, capital gains tax, progressive tax,** etc.) are defined separately, as are many other *tax* words (such as tax **assessment,** tax **assessor** and others) which are not found below. *Tax avoidance* is planning finances carefully to take advantage of all legal tax breaks, such as **deductions** and **exemptions.** A *tax base* is the thing or value on which taxes are levied. Some of the more common *tax bases* include individual income, corporate income, real property, motor vehicles, estates, etc. The *tax benefit rule* states that if a loss or expense deducted from taxes in one year is recovered in another year, the recovery will be taxed as income in that later year to the extent of the deduction. For *tax certificate,* see *tax deed. Tax court* is a U.S. court that takes **appeals** from taxpayers when the **IRS** has charged them with deficiencies (underpayments) in their payments of income, estate, and gift taxes. A *tax credit* is a direct subtraction from tax owed (for other taxes paid, for certain special purposes such as a part of child care expenses, etc.) See **deduction, exemption,** and **exclusion.** A *tax deed* is a proof of ownership of land given to the purchaser by the government after the land has been taken from another person by the government and sold for failure to pay taxes. (Also, a *tax certificate* is a temporary proof of ownership that can be turned into a **deed** if the original owner does not **redeem** the property by paying the taxes due by a certain date; and a *tax lease* is a proof of ownership for a number of years when state law prohibits **absolute** sales for tax reasons. All of these are *tax* **titles** given at a *tax* **sale** after a *tax* **warrant** has been issued for a *tax* **foreclosure** on a *tax* **lien**.) A **tax deferred annuity** is an **annuity** with employee contributions not subject to taxes at the time that the contributions are made. Contributions are later taxed as they are paid out after retirement when the annuitant is presumably in a lower tax bracket. A *tax equalization policy* is a program that has an employer deduct from the salary of employees sent overseas, the amount of taxes that would have been due if they had resided in the U.S. In return, the employer assumes the total burden of both U.S. and host nation income taxes. See **progressive taxation.** *Tax evasion* is illegally paying less in taxes than the law allows. It is committing **fraud** in filing or paying taxes. *Tax exempt(s)* is a phrase referring to property (such as that belonging to schools, churches, etc.) that is not subject to property taxation; investments (such as **municipal bonds**) that give income that is not subject to income taxation; income that is free from taxation (such as income received by a **charitable** organization); or certain charitable organizations themselves. For *tax foreclosure,* see *tax deed.* **Tax fraud** is the deliberate nonpayment or underpayment of taxes that are legally due; *tax evasion. Tax fraud* can be *civil* or *criminal*, with criminal fraud having higher fines and the possibility of a prison sentence upon the showing of "willfulness." The line between the two types of fraud is fuzzy. A *tax haven* is a jurisdiction, usually abroad, with slight or no taxes on the income of foreigners. A *tax home* is that base of business operations from which, if you travel on business, travel expenses may be deducted from taxes as business expenses. *Tax incidence* is the effect of a particular tax burden on various socioeconomic levels. *Tax-increment financing* is the ability of local government to finance large-scale development through the expected rise in the property tax to be collected after the development is completed. This permits the issuance of **bonds** based on the expected tax increase. For *tax lease* and *tax lien,* see *tax deed.* A *tax rate* is the percentage of **taxable income** (or of inherited money, things purchased subject to sales tax, etc.) paid in taxes. The federal income tax has a *graduated tax rate.* This means, for example, that the first ten thousand dollars of a person's taxable income might be taxed two thousand dollars and the next one thousand to two thousand dollars at 25 percent. This percentage is called the *tax bracket* or *marginal rate.* A **tax-reimbursement allowance** is additional money paid to an employee assigned overseas to compensate for the additional taxes that must be paid (both U.S. and foreign) over what would have been paid had the employee remained in the United States. A *tax return* is the form used to report income, **deductions,** etc., and to accompany tax payments and requests for refunds. For *tax sale,* see *tax deed. Tax selling* is the selling of **securities** near the end of the year in order to establish desirable tax gains or losses. For *tax shelter,* see **shelter.** A *tax sheltered annuity* is a *tax deferred annuity.* A **tax subsidy** is a tax advantage designed to encourage specific behavior that furthers public policy; for example, **mortgage interest** deductions to encourage citizens to buy houses, investment tax credits to encourage businesses to expand and create new jobs, etc. For *tax title,* see *tax deed.* For *tax* (or *taxable) year,* see **fiscal year.** A *taxable estate* (or *gift*) is the property of a dead person (or a gift) that will be taxed after subtracting for allowable expenses, **deductions,** and **exclusions.** *Taxable income,* under federal tax law, is either the **gross income** of businesses or the **adjusted gross income** of individuals minus **deductions** and **exemptions.** It is the income against which *tax rates* are applied to compute tax paid before any **credits** are subtracted. A *taxpayer identification number* for most individuals is their social security number. But partnerships, corporations, trusts, etc. must have an *employer identification number* available from the **IRS.** A *taxpayer suit* is a lawsuit brought by an individual to challenge the spending of public money for a particular purpose.

Taylor Differential Piece-Rate Plan An incentive plan in which different **piece rates** are established for substandard, standard, and higher than standard production.

Technical analysis Deciding whether to buy or sell a particular **stock** or other **security** based on its price and its sales patterns. See **fundamental analysis.**

Technological life The estimated number of years before the existing or proposed equipment or facilities become obsolete due to technological changes.

Technology transfer The application of technologies developed in one area of research or endeavor to another, frequently involving a concomitant shift in institutional setting; examples include the application of space technology developed under the auspices of NASA to the problems of public transportation or weather prediction.

Teleconferencing Connecting several people for a meeting by computer or T.V.

Telex Western Union's international telegram service.

Teller A person who counts (such as a *bank teller*, who takes in and pays out money).

Ten shares unit See **inactive stock.**

Tenancy The condition of being a **tenant;** the **interest** a tenant has; the **term** (amount of time) a tenant has.

Tenant 1. A person who holds land or a building by renting. *Tenants* include persons who have a **lease;** tenants *at will* (started out with a lease and still living there with permission); tenants *at sufferance* (started with a lease, but holding onto property against the wishes of the owner); etc. 2. A person who holds land or a building by any legal right including ownership. For example, *tenants in common* each hold a share of land that can be passed on to heirs or otherwise disposed of; *joint tenants* are like *tenants in common* except that they must also have *equal* interests in the property and, if one dies, that person's ownership interest passes to the other owner(s); and *tenants by the entireties* are like *joint tenants* except that they must also be husband and wife and that neither has a share of the land, but both hold the entire land as one individual owner. Different states vary these definitions slightly.

Ten day window The SEC requirement that whenever an individual or a company buys 5 percent or more of a corporation's **stock** the purchase must be made public within ten working days in order to inform the **target company** and its investors of a potential **takeover.**

Tender 1. An **offer,** combined with a readiness to do what is offered. 2. An offer of money. 3. Cash on the line.

Actually putting money forward, as opposed to merely offering it. In this sense, U.S. cash is *legal tender* in the U.S. 4. A *tender offer* is an offer (usually public) to buy a certain amount of a company's **stock** at a set price. This is often done to get control of the company. A *creeping tender offer* is the gradual buying of a corporation's stock on the open market. A *self-tender offer* has a corporation buy back some of its own stock to keep the shares out of unfriendly hands. A *two-tiered tender offer* is an offer of cash for some shares at one price; then a lower offer for subsequent shares at a later date. This tactic seeks to get shareholders to rush into the cash offer.

Ten-K (10-K) The annual report required by the **SEC** of publicly held corporations that sell **stock.**

Tenor The time between the date a debt is taken on and the date it must be paid.

Term 1. A word or phrase (especially one that has a fixed technical meaning). *Terms of sale* are the conditions that govern payment. *Terms of trade* are a measure of the relation of export to import prices; terms of trade are said to be favorable if the prices of imports fall in relation to prices of exports. 2. A fixed period; the length of time set for something to happen. A *term loan* is a bank loan for over a year, *term insurance* is **insurance** for a fixed period of time only, and a *lease term* is how long the **lease** lasts. 3. A part of an agreement that deals with a particular subject; for example, a *price term.* 4. For *term* **bond,** see that word.

Terminal 1. A device for computerized information exchange. It may be a typewriter keyboard plus printer, keyboard plus screen, etc. 2. *Terminal arbitration* is **arbitration** that is called for as the final step in a **grievance** procedure. 3. *Terminal value* is an estimate of the value of a proposed investment at the end of its economic life.

Termination Any ending; an ending before the anticipated end; an ending as specifially defined under some law. For example, under the **Uniform Commercial Code,** *termination* marks the end of a **contract** without its being broken by either side. A *termination contract* is an agreement between an employer and a new employee that provides for salary continuation for the employee in the event of termination. The length of time that compensation continues to be paid typically varies from six months to two years. *Termination pay* is the same as **severance pay.**

Test check A method of verifying the accuracy of an entire **account** or record by testing selected portions of the whole. The usual test check consists of a **random sample** of the whole. The percentage of errors or other deviations that appear in the sample tested is considered to exist in the same proportion in the whole.

Testamentary Having to do with a will.

Testator A person who makes a will.

Testimony Evidence given by a witness under oath.

Theft of services An employee's unauthorized use of company equipment and resources.

Theory X and Theory Y Contrasting sets of assumptions made by managers about human behavior. *Theory X* holds that the average human being has an inherent dislike of work and will avoid it if possible. Most people must be controlled with punishment to get them to put forth adequate effort toward the achievement of organizational objectives. *Theory Y* holds that the average human being does not inherently dislike work. Depending upon controllable conditions, work may be a source of satisfaction (and will be voluntarily performed) or a source of punishment (and will be avoided if possible). A central motif in both Theory X and Theory Y is control. With Theory X, control comes down from management via strict supervision. Theory Y, on the contrary, assumes that employees will be internally rather than externally controlled.

Theory Z An approach to management, generally associated with Japanese industry, that emphasizes **participative management** from employees who are committed to their work through cultural tradition, shared socioeconomic values and communal forms of decisionmaking.

Thin corporation A **corporation** that owes its stockholders so much money that the **IRS** will call some of the debt **equity** and call some of the debt payments **dividends,** thus raising the owners' taxes.

Thin market An inactive **market** with wide fluctuations in price due to the apparent undesirability of the current price level. The term may be applied either to the market as a whole, or to a particular **security.**

Think tank A colloquial term for an organization or organizational segment whose sole function is research.

Third *Third country invoicing* is a method of **transfer pricing** to avoid currency controls. The *third market* is the sale, outside the usual **exchange,** of **stocks** and other **securities.** This is also called "off-board," and is sometimes done by institutional traders of large blocks of stock. See also **over-the-counter.** A *third party* (or *person*) is a person unconnected with a deal, lawsuit, or occurrence, but who may be affected by it. For example, a *third party beneficiary* is a person who is not part of a **contract** but for whose direct benefit the contract was made. And a *third party payment* is a payment by a health insurance company for services by a doctor (second party) for a patient (first party). The *third sector* is all those organizations that fit neither in the public sector (government) nor the private sector (business). The *Third World* includes those countries with underdeveloped but growing economies and low per capita incomes, often with colonial pasts.

Thirty-day letter An **IRS** letter to a taxpayer stating a tax **deficiency** (or refusing a refund request) and explaining **appeal** rights.

Threshold effect The total impression a job applicant makes by his or her bearing, dress, manners, etc., as he or she "comes through the door."

Thrift institution A **savings and loan association** or **mutual** savings bank whose primary function is to encourage personal saving and homebuying through **mortgage** lending.

Thrift doctor A manager, consultant or lawyer who helps financially troubled banks deal with government regulators, design new operating plans, and find **merger** partners or new **capital.**

Through bill A **bill of lading** for goods that will be carried by more than one shipper in sequence.

Throughput A large middle step in data processing or a system's operation; it comes after input and before output.

Tickler 1. A file in which documents are arranged by the date they must next be acted upon. 2. Any reminder or follow-up file.

Tie-in sales See **tying in.**

Time Gradations of a calendar. The *time adjusted rate of return* in the **internal rate of return.** A *time and materials* contract is used primarily where services, rather than goods, are acquired. The services are paid for at an agreed hourly rate which covers labor, **overhead,** profit, and materials. These contracts are used for such services as repairs and consulting work. *Time and motion studies* measure the time required, under **standard** conditions, to complete any task requiring human effort. These studies then analyze the work (sometimes motion-by-motion) to find and eliminate inefficient work methods and replace them with the most efficient methods. A *time bill* is a **bill of exchange** with the date of payment fixed (as contrasted with a **demand** or **sight** bill). A *time deposit* is an account at a bank or other depository institution on which limitations on withdrawal are imposed; the depositor contracts to leave the funds deposited for a certain period of time or until a certain date in return for receiving a certain rate of **interest.** These include savings accounts, **certificates of deposit,** etc. A *time draft* is a **draft** payable at a certain time. The *time horizon* is that distance into the future to which a planner looks when seeking to evaluate the consequences of a proposed action. *Time is of the essence* is a phrase in a **contract** that means that a failure to do what is required by the time specified is a **breach** (breaking) of the contract. The *time-price doctrine* is the idea that a higher price may be charged for things bought on **credit** than for the same things paid for in cash. This is a way for a seller to get around state **usury** laws. A *time series* is a series of measurements or observations taken over time. They have one or more of these characteristics: long-term trends, seasonal fluctuations, cyclic variation, and partial randomness. An example would be annual consumer expenditures for each year during the years 1950–1990. *Time sharing* is the simultaneous use of a central computer by two or more remote users, each of whom has direct and individual use of the central computer through the use of a terminal. *Time sharing* is also a real estate term for property, usually a vacation condominium, that is purchased only for use at a set time (such as the first two weeks of August each year). In some contracts, partial ownership is bought; in others, only the right to use the property. For *time ticket,* see **job ticket.** *Time utility* is having a product available when a customer wants it. See also **form, place,** and **possession utility.** The *time value of money* is a concept that holds that a dollar ten years from today is not the same as a dollar in five years or a dollar today; an investor needs to take this into account when analyzing an investment proposal involving expenditures and receipts at varying points in time. In order for a meaningful comparison to be made, such costs and returns should be converted into equivalent costs and returns occurring at a single point in time. A *time wage rate* is any pay structure providing for wage payments in terms of an hourly, weekly, or monthly time interval. This is in contrast to a **piece-rate** structure where an employee is paid only for the amount that he or she produces.

Tippee   A person given information about a company by an **insider** whose duty to the company and the general public forbids giving out such information.

Title   1. The name for a part of a **statute.** For example, *Title VII* of the 1964 Civil Rights Act is known to specialists in the field of employment **discrimination** as simply *Title Seven.* It prohibits employment discrimination based on race, color, religion, sex, or national origin, and created the **EEOC** as its enforcement vehicle.   2. The formal right of ownership of property and the document that shows it. For **abstract of, chain of, clear, color of, document of, marketable, paper, perfect, record, torrens,** etc., *title,* see those words. A *title search* is a search of the land records to see if *title* is good or restricted. A *title guaranty company* makes this search, then guarantees the title for the buyer, often through *title insurance. Title standards* are criteria set up by state organizations of banks, real estate lawyers, etc., to evaluate whether or not a title is good. A *title state* or *title theory jurisdiction* is a state in which the title to **mortgage** property is held by the lender until the debt is paid. See **lien theory state.**   3. A formal **job description** or a description of a **class** of jobs.

Tombstone ad   A **stock** (or other **securities**) or land sales notice that clearly states that it is informational only and not itself an offer to buy or sell. It often has a black border.

Tonnage tax   A tax on ships based on either their weight or carrying capacity.

Tontine   A reverse type of life **insurance,** now illegal, in which many persons pay into a fund and only those living by a certain date split up the proceeds.

Topheavy market   A **market** whose prices are too high, making it ready for a fall.

Torrens title system   A system of land ownership **registration,** used in some states, in which the actual **title** is recorded and formally approved (usually by a judge) as a "Certificate of Title," rather than the more usual procedure of recording only evidence of title (such as a **deed**). *Torrens* registration is supplemental to the regular title system and is voluntary for each purchaser.

Tort A legal *wrong* done to another person. A *civil* (as opposed to *criminal*) wrong that is not based on an obligation under a **contract.** For an act to be a *tort*, there must be a legal duty owed by one person to another, a breach (breaking) of that duty, and harm done as a direct result of the action.

Total 1. Complete for legal purposes. For example, a *total disability* may not be "total" in the common language sense, but merely be that which stops a person from doing his or her normal work; and *total loss* by fire need not be a burning to the ground, but merely be a complete commercial loss. 2. *Total assets turnover* is an activity ratio: sales divided by total assets. *Total cost* equals fixed plus variable costs for a given output. *Total product* is the amount produced over a given period of time by all of the **factors of production** then in use.

Totten trust Putting your money into a bank account in your name as **trustee** for another person. You can take it out when you want, but if you do not take it out before you die, it becomes the property of that other person.

Touch and stay A ship's right, under its insurance policy, to stop and stay at certain ports, but not to carry on any trade there.

Tract index A public record containing all recorded **deeds, mortgages, liens,** etc., piece of land by piece of land according to numbered lots with map references. If you know exactly where the land is, you can easily find out about transfers of ownership and other recorded matters. Compare this with a **grantor-grantee index.**

Trade 1. Buying and selling; commerce. 2. A job or profession. 3. Barter; swapping. 4. For *trade adjustment assistance,* see **adjustment assistance.** A *trade agreement* is an agreement among countries to allow the sale of certain items (and at certain import tax rates); a *trade association* is a group of similar businesses organized for idea exchange, maintaining standards, and lobbying; *trade credit* is **credit** sales made by one business to another (commercial **accounts receivable**); *trade debt* is credit purchases by one business from another (commercial **accounts payable**); a *trade discount* is a price reduction to certain types of business customers (from a lumber dealer to building **contractors**); a *trade dispute* is any **labor dispute** (excluding such things as the refusal to cross picket lines); a *trade diversion* is a shift in the source of imports which occurs as a result of altering a country's import policies or practices; a *trade name* is the name of a business that will usually be legally protected in the area where the company operates and for the types of products in which it deals; a *trade-off* is either the selection of one of several alternatives, or a concession made in response to the other side's concession; a *trade secret* is a process, tool, chemical compound, etc., that is not generally known to the public and is not patented; for *trade union,* see **craft union;** and *trade usage* is common, regular practice or custom within a type of business or trade.

Trademark   A distinctive mark, motto, or symbol that a company can reserve by law for its own exclusive use in identifying its products (identified by the symbol® for **registered**). *Trademark rights* may be used to prevent others from using a confusingly similar mark, but not to prevent others from making the same goods or from selling them under a non-confusing mark.

Trading posts   Locations on the floor of an **exchange** at which specific **securities** are bought and sold.

Traditional economy   A society largely dependent upon subsistence agriculture.

Tramp steamer   A ship not operating on regular routes or schedules.

Transaction account   Any bank or similar account with withdrawals by **negotiable** (or transferable) **instruments,** telephonic and preauthorized transfers, payment orders of withdrawal, or other similar items. Examples of transaction accounts are **negotiable order of withdrawal accounts, demand deposits,** automatic transfer service accounts, accounts at savings and loan associations accessible by remote service units, and credit union **share drafts.**

Transaction costs   Costs incurred while engaging in market transactions; for example, billing costs, bad debts, etc.

Transaction statement   A document that delineates the terms and conditions agreed upon between an importer and exporter.

Transfer To change or move from person to person (sell, give, or sign something over, etc.) or from place to place (court to court, etc.). A *transfer agent* is a person (or an institution such as a bank) who keeps track of who owns a company's **stocks** and **bonds**. Also called a **registrar**. The transfer agent sometimes also handles **dividend** and **interest** payments. *Transfer authority* is the **statutory** power granted the executive to shift **appropriated** funds from one **account** to another. *Transfer of training* is the theory that knowledge or abilities acquired in one area aids the acquisition of knowledge or abilities in other areas. When prior learning is helpful, it is called *positive transfer*. When prior learning inhibits new learning, it is called *negative transfer*. *Transfer payments* are payments by government made to individuals who provide no goods or services in return; for example, welfare payments, social security payments, etc. See also **business transfer payments**. *Transfer pricing* is setting prices for sales or other exchanges between international **subsidiaries** or branches, usually to avoid **foreign exchange** controls, to avoid taxes, etc. *Transfer tax* is the name for different types of taxes in different places; for example, an **estate** tax, a gift tax, a tax on the sale of **stocks**, etc. See **unified transfer tax.**

Transformational leadership Leadership that strives to change organizational culture and directions, rather than continuing to move along traditional paths. It reflects the ability of a leader to develop a values-based vision for the organization, convert the vision into reality, and maintain it over time.

Transit zone A port of entry in a coastal country established as a storage and distribution center for the convenience of a neighboring country which lacks adequate port facilities or access to the sea. Goods in transit to and from the neighboring country are not subject to the customs duties, import controls, or many of the entry and exit formalities of the host country. For comparison, see **free port** and **free trade zones.**

Treasurer The person in charge of an organization's money (taking in, paying out, etc.), but not necessarily its financial decisions.

Treasury 1. Department of the Treasury. The U.S. cabinet department that handles most national financial, monetary, and tax matters. It runs the Internal Revenue Service (taxes), the Mint (coins), etc. ***Treasury securities*** are obligations of the United States sold to finance government operations. Treasury securities may be marketable (capable of being traded in organized markets) or nonmarkable (not subject to sale to third parties). Forms of marketable securities include Treasury **bills, notes,** and **bonds.** Treasury *bills* are issued in denominations of $10,000 or more, for **maturities** of 13, 26, and 52 weeks. Treasury bills are issued on a discount basis and the investor receives **face value** at maturity; the **return** to investors is the difference between the price paid and the amount received when the bills mature. Treasury *notes* and *bonds* are issued in denominations of $1,000 or more. Treasury notes are for maturities of 1 to 10 years and bonds for over 10 years. Notes and bonds carry **coupon** rates of interest. U.S. savings bonds, a form of nonmarketable security, are designed for the small investor. Investors can buy all of these without incurring a **commission** directly from a **Federal Reserve Bank** or the Bureau of the Public Debt. Government securities can also be purchased from banks, government securities dealers, and other broker/dealers. Income from Treasury securities is subject to federal income tax, but is exempt from state and local taxes. See also **open market operations.** 2. *Treasury stock* is shares of **stock** issued by a corporation, paid for in full, and later reacquired by the corporation by gift or purchase. Some states permit a corporation to repurchase shares only out of **retained earnings.** Such stock may either be kept in the corporate treasury or disposed of in any manner benefiting the corporation.

Trend The change in a series of data over a period of years, remaining after the data have been adjusted to remove seasonal and cyclical fluctuations. For example, the annual increase in output over a period of several years excluding fluctuations due to the **business cycle.**

Trend analysis An analysis of successive **balance sheets** or **statements,** which stresses the changes in items between periods. **Ratios** between items on each balance sheet are computed, then compared with similar computations from previous periods. This helps determine whether the business is growing, standing still, or losing ground if adjusted or standardized statements are available. *Ratio trend analysis* is the study of successive periodic changes in

ratios. *Horizontal trend analysis* is a year-to-year comparison of the actual figures of a series of statements rather
than of ratios between sets of figures. Horizontal trends
can be expressed in dollar changes or percentage changes,
with either one base year or a progressively changing base
year for calculations.

Trial balance A separate totaling of all **credit** entries and
all **debit** entries in an **account** (or of all accounts with a
credit balance and all accounts with a *debit balance*) to
compare the two. If they are not equal, there is a
bookkeeping error in a **double entry** system.

Trigger price The price *below* which a domestic sale of a
foreign product will *trigger* a **dumping** investigation.

Trolley car policy A facetious name for an **insurance** policy from which it is so hard to collect **benefits** that it is as
though it provided benefits only for injuries resulting
from being hit by a trolley car.

Trophy wife The second wife of a status-conscious **CEO**
who is noted for her attractiveness, professional accom-
plishments, and especially her youth when compared to
the usually much older CEO.

Trough The bottom of a **business cycle.** If a trough is big
enough, it is a depression.

Truck line A large main transportation or communication
line.

True lease A **lease** that qualifies under **IRS** rules for the
lessor to claim ownership benefits (such as investment tax
credits and **deductions** for **depreciation**) and for the **lessee**
to deduct payments from income. *True leases* are differ-
ent from **installment** sales.

True value rule If corporate **stock** is not fully paid for in
"real money" or its equivalent, stockholders may be **liable**
to **creditors** of the company for the difference.

Trust 1. Any transfer of money or property to one person
(or any holding onto it by one person) for the benefit of
another. For example, a mother signs over **stocks** to a
bank to manage for her daughter with instructions to give
the daughter the income each year until she turns thirty
and then to give it all to her. In this example, the mother
is the *settlor* or **grantor** of the *trust*, the bank is the
trustee, and the daughter is the **beneficiary.** However, a
trust need not be set up explicitly by name; for example,
if a father gives a son some money saying "half of this is

for your brother," this may be a *trust* too. Also, a trust can be set up in a will; created by formally stating that you *yourself* hold money in trust for another person; and created several other ways, both intentional and unintentional. There are hundreds of types of trusts. Those most important in a management context (**business trust, equipment trust, investment trust,** etc.) are defined separately. A *trust account* (or *trust deposit*) is money or property put in a bank to be kept separate (often for ethical or legal reasons) or used for a special purpose. A *trust certificate* is a document showing that property is held in trust as **security** for a debt based on money used to buy the property. See **deed of trust.** A *trust company* manages trusts and acts as a will trustee, **executor,** and guardian. Trust companies also act as **fiscal** agents for corporations, attend to the **registration** and transfer of their **stocks** and **bonds,** and serve as trustee for their bond and **mortgage** creditors. Most state laws permit trust companies to perform all the functions of a bank and federal law permits national banks to engage in trust activities. A *trust deed* is a **deed of trust.** A *trust deposit* is a *trust account.* A *trust fund* is money or property set aside in a *trust* or set aside for a special purpose. For example, federal government trust funds are for carrying out specific purposes and programs according to terms of a trust agreement or **statute,** such as the social security and unemployment trust funds. The *trust fund theory* (or *doctrine*) says that certain funds (such as those improperly used by a corporation's **directors** or others) will be considered as held in trust for **creditors** or others. A *trust indenture* is a document that spells out the details of a *trust.* The *Trust Indenture Act* is a federal law requiring certain investor-protection provisions in documents used to **issue** some kinds of bonds. A *trust instrument* is a **deed of trust** or a formal *declaration of trust.* A *trust officer* is a person in a *trust company* who manages *trusts.* *Trust powers* include the authority to act as **fiduciary** for personal (and corporate) accounts, or in capacities such as trustees, executors, administrators, or guardians. A *trust receipt* is a document by which one person lends money to buy something and the borrower promises to hold the thing in *trust* for the lender until the debt is paid off. These deals are now usually handled by **security** agreements. A *trust state* (or *trust theory juris-*

diction) is a state in which title to mortgaged property is transferred to a **trustee** to hold until the debt is paid. See **title** state and **lien theory** state. 2. A group of companies that has a **monopoly.**

Trustee 1. A person who holds money or property for the benefit of another person (see **trust**). 2. A person who has a **fiduciary** relationship towards another person; for example, a lawyer, an **agent,** etc. 3. A *trustee in bankruptcy* is a person appointed by a court to manage a **bankrupt** person's property and to decide who gets it. 4. A *trusteeship* exists when one person or organization is appointed to manage the affairs of another.

Truth-in-Lending Act The **Consumer Credit Protection Act.**

Turkey farm An office or division having little work and slight, if any, responsibility. Managers frequently find it easier to place troublesome or incompetent employees on turkey farms rather than go through the hassle of **adverse action** proceedings.

Turnaround management Taking a failing enterprise and improving it to the point where it is making a profit.

Turnkey control 1. A **contract** in which a builder agrees to complete a building to a specific point, usually "ready to move in," and in which the builder assumes all construction risks. 2. A drilling contract in which the driller does all the work up to the point when a well can begin production and in which, for a set fee, the driller assumes all construction risks except the risk of a dry hole.

Turnover (or turnover rate or ratio) 1. The number of times that an **asset** is replaced during a time period. See **capital turnover, cash turnover, fixed asset turnover, inventory turnover, receivables turnover,** and **total assets turnover.** 2. The movement of individuals into, through, and out of an organization. *Turnover* can be statistically defined as the total number (or percentage) of separations that occur over a given time period. The turnover rate is an important indicator of the morale and health of an organization.

Twisting Misrepresenting policies to convince a person to switch **insurance** companies.

Two-tier method Double taxation of **corporate** income (when the company gets it and when the owners get it).

Two-tier offer A takeover bid in which stockholders who respond quickly to a **tender offer** get a better deal than those who delay.

Tying in A seller's refusal to sell a product unless another product is bought with it. If a seller has a **monopoly** on a product, *tying in* the sale of another product may be a violation of the **antitrust** laws, especially if the *right* to sell a **patented** product is tied into selling a non-patented product.

U

U In newspaper stock transaction tables, an indication, lowercase (u), that a **stock** has reached a new 52-week high.

UCC Uniform Commercial Code.

UCCC Uniform Consumer Credit Code. (Also called the UC3 or U3C.) A **uniform act** adopted by some states to **regulate** the way merchants and lending institutions give **credit** to **consumers.**

ULPA Uniform Limited Partnership Act.

UPA Uniform Partnership Act.

USC United States Code. The official lawbooks where all federal laws are collected by subject matter.

USU Unbundled stock unit. A **security** which gives the owner a limited portion of the value of a given stock such as the right to **dividends** or the right to any appreciation in the stock's price.

UTI Undistributed taxable income.

Ultimate purchaser A consumer or business purchaser who intends a product for use, not resale.

Ultra vires (Latin) "Beyond the power." Corporate actions outside the scope of activities permitted by **articles of incorporation** are *ultra vires.*

Umpire A person chosen to decide a **labor dispute** when the original **arbitrators** disagree.

Unadjusted rate of return An approximation of the rate of **return** determined by dividing income by average investment for a given period. Also called *accounting rate of return.*

Unaffiliated union A **union** that is not a member of the **AFL-CIO.**

Unconscionability Sales practices that are so greatly unfair that a court will not permit them. For example, the use of small print and technical language in contracts with poorly

480

educated persons combined with prices that were three times higher than normal, was called *unconscionable* by one court. The **Uniform Commercial Code** permits **rescission** ("unmaking") of unconscionable contracts.

Undercapitalization 1. Too little **working capital.** 2. Too few shares of **stock** in relation to total profits. This can be changed through a stock **split** or stock **dividend.**

Underground economy Economic activity that evades tax obligations; work done "off the books," for cash only. Examples of *underground economic activity* include a medical doctor accepting a cash payment from a patient and not recording the payment for income tax purposes; a carpenter doing work for a small business and accepting an in-kind payment, whose value is not recorded for income tax purposes; and, of course, traditional criminal activity. *Underground* in this context does not necessarily mean "secret"—except to the Internal Revenue Service.

Undertaking 1. **Bonds** or other financial **securities;** the process of putting out these bonds. 2. A **venture** of any kind. 3. A promise; a legally binding promise.

Underwrite 1. To **insure.** An *underwriter* is an insurer (and in a more limited sense, a person who evaluates insurance **risks**). A *lead underwriter* is the organizer of a **syndicate** of investment bankers. 2. To guarantee to purchase any **stock** or **bonds** that remain unsold after a public sale, or to sell an **issue** of stock or bonds *for* a company or purchased *from* a company. The person (or organization) who does this is an *underwriter*. See **investment banking** for more.

Undistributed (or undivided) profits tax A tax on a company's profit that is kept (rather than paid to stockholders) in excess of reasonable needs (paying bills, expansion, contingencies, etc.). The federal tax is called an **accumulated earnings tax.**

Undivided right (or title) Property held by two or more persons under the same right. These persons may have different financial stakes in the property, but they all have full rights of possession.

Unearned income 1. Money that has been received, but not yet *earned*; for example, a landlord's receiving a January rent payment in December. 2. Income from investments, rather than from salary or wages. This may or may not be taxed at a higher rate than **earned income.**

Unemployment Persons able and willing to work who are actively seeking, but unsuccessful at finding, work at the prevailing wage rate are among the *unemployed*. The *unemployment rate* is probably the most significant indicator of the health of the economy. *Unemployment benefits* (or *compensation* or *insurance*) are specific payments available to workers from the various state unemployment insurance programs. Unemployment benefits are available as a matter of right (without a **means test**) to unemployed workers who have demonstrated their attachment to the labor force by a specified amount of recent work or earnings in *covered* employment. To be eligible for benefits, the worker must be ready, able, and willing to work and must be registered for work at a public employment office. A worker who meets those eligibility conditions may still be denied benefits if he or she is disqualified for an act that would indicate the worker is responsible for his or her own unemployment. A worker's monetary benefit rights are determined on the basis of employment in work covered by the unemployment benefit law over a prior reference period (called the **base period.**) Under all state laws, the weekly benefit amount—that is, the amount payable for a week of total unemployment—varies with the worker's past wages within certain minimum and maximum limits.

Unfair competition 1. Too closely imitating the name, product, or advertising of another company in order to take away its business. This is called "passing off." 2. Some states recognize various other dishonest trade practices, such as using someone else's work unfairly, as *unfair competition.* 3. *Unfair methods of competition* is a slightly broader phrase, used by the **Federal Trade Commission,** to bring in more types of unfair conduct than the courts had previously recognized.

Unfair labor practices The **National Labor Relations (Wagner) Act** of 1935 specifically forbade certain actions—unfair labor practices—by *employers*. These prohibitions, which serve to protect the right of employees to organize themselves in labor unions, are **interference** with, restraint or coercion of employees in the exercise of their guaranteed rights under the law; domination of, interference with the organization and administration of, or financial support of any labor organization; **discrimination**

in hiring or firing of employees, or in the conditions of employment aimed at the encouragement or discouragement of membership in a labor organization; discrimination against an employee who files charges or gives testimony under the Wagner Act; and refusal to submit to **collective bargaining.** Twelve years after the passage of the National Labor Relations Act, Congress became convined that both employees and employers needed additional legal protections against unfair labor practices of **unions.** So the **Labor-Management Relations (Taft-Hartley) Act** of 1947 amended the National Labor Relations Act to include the following union prohibitions: restraint or coercion of employees in the exercise of their rights guaranteed under the law or of an employer in the selection of representatives for collective bargaining or the adjustment of **grievances;** causing or attempting to cause an employer to discriminate against employees in order to encourage or discourage membership in a union or against employees who have been denied membership in, or ejected from, the union for reasons other than their failure to pay regular **dues;** refusal to bargain collectively with the employer whose employees it represents; requiring employees under a **union shop** or **maintenance of membership** agreement to pay excessive or discriminatory union initiation fees; forcing an employer to pay any money or other valuable consideration for services that are not to be performed; forcing any employee or self-employed person to join a union or any employer or other person to stop doing business with any other person; forcing any employer to recognize or bargain with a union that has not been formally certified by the NLRB; and forcing any employer to recognize or bargain with a union if another union has been certified as the representative of the employees.

Unfair trade practice acts Laws in about half of the states which prohibit wholesalers and retailers from selling goods below their cost; some states even require a minimum percentage markup.

Unified transfer tax A federal tax on transfers by gift or death. It replaced the separate federal gift and **estate** taxes. The *unified transfer credit* is a **credit** against the unified transfer tax. It replaced the lifetime gift and estate tax **exemptions.**

Uniform Regular; even. Applying generally, equally, and evenhandedly. *Uniform acts* (or *uniform laws*) are laws in various subject areas, proposed by the Commissioners on Uniform State Laws, that are often adopted, in whole or in part, by many states. The *Uniform Commercial Code* is a comprehensive set of laws on every major type of business law. It has been adopted by almost every state, in whole or in major part. It replaced many older uniform laws, such as the Uniform Negotiable Instruments Law and the Uniform Sales Act. *Uniform cost accounting* is the use of a common set of **accounting** definitions, procedures, terms, and methods for the accumulation and communication of financial data. These uniform systems are developed by trade associations and government regulatory agencies. *Uniform Guidelines on Employee Selection* are guidelines adopted by the four federal agencies most concerned with employee selection processes: the Equal Employment Opportunity Commission, the Civil Service Commission, the Department of Justice, and the Department of Labor. The guidelines are designed to assist employers, labor organizations, employment agencies, and licensing and certification boards to comply with requirements of federal law prohibiting **employment practices** that **discriminate** on grounds of race, color, religion, sex, or national origin.

Unilateral One-sided. For *unilateral contract,* see **contract.** A *unilateral mistake* about a contract's *terms* usually will not get a person out of the contract unless the other side knew about the mistaken idea all along.

Unincorporated Not a **corporation;** but some organizations that are *unincorporated* and have certain corporate characteristics may be taxed as corporations.

Union 1. An organization of workers, formed to **negotiate** with employers on wages, working conditions, etc. Labor unions include *closed* (highly restricted in members by small numbers, long **apprenticeships,** high fees, etc.; see also **closed shop**); *company* (sponsored by an employer; now usually forbidden by labor laws); *craft* or *horizontal* (persons in the same craft, no matter where they work); *independent* (persons working for one employer who form a union with no affiliations); *industrial* or *vertical* (working in one industry, regardless of job type); *local* (workers in one company or place who affiliate their union with a larger one); *open* (easy to get into; see also **open shop**); and *trade* (refers to either a labor union generally or a *craft* union). For other types of unions (such as **business** or **international**), see those words. For *union certification*, see **certification proceeding**. A *union label* is any imprint attached to an item that indicates that it was made by union labor. For *union scale*, see **journey worker pay**. A *union-security clause* is a provision in a contract between a union and an employer that sets out the union's status and explains which types of employees must belong to the union. Union-security clauses typically provide for such things as the **checkoff**, the **closed shop**, the *union shop*, the **agency shop**, preferential hiring, etc. It seeks to protect the union by providing for a constant flow of funds by, typically, requiring every employee in the **bargaining unit**, as a condition of employment, to be a member of the union or to pay a specified sum to the union for its bargaining services. A *union shop* is a business in which all workers must join a particular union once employed, typically within one month. For *union steward*, see *steward*. 2. Any joining together of persons, organizations, or things for a particular purpose.

Unit A thing, person, or group regarded as a single entity for calculation and accounting purposes. For *unit* in a labor-relations context, see **bargaining unit**, and **employer unit**. *Unit costs* are the costs of a single representative unit of production or service. Unit costs are determined by dividing total costs by some related base. A *unit investment trust* is a type of investment company with a fixed, unmanaged **portfolio**, typically invested in **bonds** or other debt **securities**, in which the interests are redeemable at their net asset value at the option of their holders. In addition, there often is a secondary trading market for the shares of unit investment trusts. Units are often sold to the public in $1,000 denominations. A *unit of production* is one barrel of oil (or an equivalet measure of a different natural resource) out of the estimated number that will be produced from a particular well, **lease**, or property. The *unit* is each barrel's fractional part of the whole estimated production. The total costs and profits of each venture are divided among each barrel for tax purposes. *Unit ownership acts* are state laws on **condominiums**. *Unit pricing* is pricing by item and not by a flat **contract** price on a total deal involving many items. *Unit pricing* may also mean pricing by each unit of weight (per ounce of peanut butter rather than per jar), by length (by board-foot, rather than by board), etc. The *unit rule* is a way of valuing **stocks** and other **securities** by taking the sale price of one share of stock sold on a stock **exchange** and ignoring all other facts and assumptions about value. The *unit rule* is also a rule binding all members of a group to vote the way the majority of the group votes. A *unit trust* is either an inflexible **portfolio** of **securities** yielding a fixed **return** that is managed by a **trustee,** or a **mutual fund** in the United Kingdom.

Unitary tax   A business tax of a percentage of worldwide profits, not just profits earned in the taxing jurisdiction.

Unitrust   A **trust** in which a fixed percentage of the trust property is paid out each year to the **beneficiaries.** To qualify for special tax benefits, a unitrust must comply with several **IRS** requirements.

Unity of command   The concept that each individual in an organization should be accountable to only a single superior. *Unity of direction* is the concept that there should be only one head and one plan for each organizational segment.

Universal product code   A **bar code** that can be used by a retailer to control **inventory,** print receipts, etc.

Unjust enrichment   The legal principle that when a person obtains money or property unfairly, it should be returned. (This does not include merely driving a hard bargain or being lucky in a deal.)

Unliquidated   See **liquidated.**

Unmarketable title   See **marketable title.**

Unsecured note (or loan)   A loan granted on the basis of a borrower's credit-worthiness and signature; not **secured** by **collateral.** A decision to grant an unsecured business loan usually results from a highly favorable evaluation of the company's four *C*s: character, condition, capital, and credit. *Character* refers to an owner's or manager's reputation in the trade for honesty and proper handling of company **assets.** *Condition* refers to the company, the industry, and the product; a bank wants to understand a company's competitive position in an industry. *Capital* refers to the owner's investment in the company; a bank wants the same protection for its funds. And *credit* refers to the reputation the owner or manager has for meeting obligations as they become due.

Unstated interest Because both buyer and seller must sometimes treat a part of each **installment** sale payment as **interest**, certain amounts of each payment may have to be considered "unstated" interest. This reduces the stated selling price and increases the seller's interest income and the buyer's interest expense. Unstated interest is **imputed** (considered to exist) under various **IRS** rules.

Upset price A **reserve** price.

Uptick 1. A **stock** selling at a price higher than it was for a preceding sale. 2. A minor upward trend in the price of a stock. A *downtick* is the reverse of either case.

Urban enterprise zone See **enterprise zone.**

Use tax A tax on some prodcuts brought into a state without paying the state's **sales tax.**

Useful life The normal operating life of a **fixed asset** or group of fixed assets for a particular owner. For example, the useful life (or *service life*) of automobiles for a fleet leasing concern may be one year; for a manufacturing company using them for sales transportation, two years; for a company providing automobiles for executive use only, three years. The useful life of an asset depends upon its *expected* life, not its actual life. Determining an asset's useful life is an essential first step in determining the annual **depreciation** to be charged to the asset.

User charges (or user fees) Specific sums that users or consumers of a government service pay to receive that service. For example, a homeowner's water bill, if based upon usage, would be a *user charge. User fees* has recently also become a euphemism for *taxes.*

User-friendly A computer system that is easy to learn and to use.

Usary laws State statutes that limit the maximum legal rate of **interest** that lending institutions can charge on their loans, varying from state to state.

Utility 1. The real or fancied ability of a good or service to satisfy a human want. Usually synonymous with *satisfaction, pleasure,* or *benefit.* 2. See *public utility* under **public services commission.** 3. *Utility player* is a baseball term for a business manager who can competently perform any of a variety of jobs.

Utter Put into circulation; **issue** or put out a check.

V

VAT Value added tax.

VDT Video display terminal. A computer screen (usually with a typewriter keyboard).

VRM Variable rate mortgage.

Valuation 1. The process of appraising the value of imported goods on which duties are assessed. The **duty** is then assessed according to the **tariff** schedule of the importing country. 2. Determining the value of a business based either on expectations of future profits and **return** on investment or on the **appraised** value of the **assets** at the time of negotiation (which assumes that these assets will continue to be used in the business). 3. *Valuation reserves* are **reserves** that provide for losses in **asset** value. They may be applied to **accounts receivable,** investments, marketable **securities,** plant and equipment, **patents,** and **intangibles** that have a limited life.

Value Worth. This may be what something *cost*, what it would cost to *replace*, what it would bring on the open market, etc. *Actual value, cash value, fair value, market value,* etc., may all mean the same. See **market value.** *"For value"* or *"value received"* means "for **consideration."** These phrases often go in a **contract** or **note** to show that it is meant to be valid even if no *consideration* is mentioned in the document itself. A *value-adding partnership* consists of a group of independent companies who work closely to produce a flow of goods and services along a *value-added chain*. A *value-added tax* is a tax on each step of a manufacturing process based on the value of what is produced minus the value of the materials bought. *Value analysis* is a formal approach to identifying and eliminating costs of products or services that are not necessary. The *value date* is the date on which a bank deposit is recognized as effective. The *value of money* is its purchasing power; what it will buy at any given time. *Value engineering (or analysis)* is systematically looking at alternative materials and methods to get the best product at the lowest cost and systematically looking at alternative products to best meet customer needs. A *valued policy* is an **insurance** policy in which the items insured are given an exact value. This is in contrast to an *open policy* in which a value need not be placed on items until they are lost, damaged, etc.

Variable   1. Any mathematical quantity that varies or any qualitative characteristic that may be varied in an experiment; any factor or condition subject to measurement, alteration, or control.   2. A *variable annuity* (or *insurance policy*) is an **annuity** (or **insurance** policy) with payments that depend on the income generated by particular investments. It is also called "**asset**-linked." These annuities are sometimes convertible to fixed-income plans upon retirement. *Variable costs* are those costs that change in total with increases or decreases in volume of units produced, while remaining the same on a per unit basis. The change in total variable costs is in proportion to changing volume. This contrasts with **fixed costs** where the opposite is true. A *variable levy* is a **tariff** subject to alterations as world market prices change, to assure that the import price after payment of duty will equal a predetermined gate price. It is a *protective* tariff. A *variable rate mortgage* is a home **mortgage** whose **interest** rate can be varied in accordance with some predetermined index (such as the **prime rate**). Rate increases may be limited over the life of the mortgage, while rate decreases are mandatory.

Variance   1. Official permission to use land or buildings in a way that would otherwise violate the **zoning** regulations for the neighborhood.   2. In a **standard cost system,** this is the difference between standard and actual costs. Variances may be analyzed for changes in labor and materials costs, **productivity,** etc.

Velvet ghetto   An organizational unit (such as a **public relations** department) that is overloaded with women in response to an **affirmative action program** and in compensation for their relative scarcity in other professional or management categories.

Vendee   Buyer.

Vendor Seller. Also, a provider of goods and services. *Vendor rating* is the process of scoring providers of goods, materials, and services based on objective criteria, both for comparative purposes and to maintain minimum standards. As a part of a **quality control** program, vendors are rated on such criteria as deviation from acceptable quality levels per batch, promised delivery dates, and costs. *Vendor's lien* is a catchall phrase for various types of **liens** held by the seller of property, including the *purchase price lien* (not usually recognized by law) of a person who sells land with no **security**, and the lien of a seller who holds goods until the price is paid.

Venture 1. *Venture capital* is money available for or invested in a new business. It ranges from a few dollars saved by a child to buy a used lawnmower for summer jobs to the organized raising and investing of billions of dollars by organizations formed for the sole purpose of new business investment. Between these extremes are such things as a company raising money for new product expansion and the buyout of other companies that will expand the product line. A typical *venture capital investment corporation* will have employees and consultants who specialize in raising investor funds; finding and evaluating promising new ventures for investment; evaluating these companies both before investment and during ongoing operations and continued investment; providing technical assistance to these companies in marketing, financing, and other areas where new companies may be weaker than in the production of products and services; and eventually bringing in **institutional investors** for later, larger phases of the new business. A typical investment by one such company might require heavily documented information on the company's history, key people, products or processes, market and competitors, financial history, and financial projections including projected financial statements for several years. For a large investment, detailed flow charts and diagrams might be required for processes, planned uses of space and capital, and many other subjects as well as detailed breakdowns on special areas such as patents, key technologies involved, and cost-volume ratios. Most often important, however, is the subjective evaluation of the company's owners' and managers' strengths and weaknesses (such as drive, integrity, and intelligence). Investment firms sometimes specialize. One venture capital firm, for example, concentrates on areas of new technology where the firm can take a majority ownership of a company with no significant competition.   2. *Venture management* is the use of a corporation's own personnel and financial resources to build new businesses. Companies usually do this in one of three basic ways: by forming a separate venture management company that is wholly owned and that seeks out new areas for development; by forming a new venture management department within the company to develop these outside ventures; or by forming a less formal **project management** team or **task force** to look into external venture possibilities. This last team approach may involve bringing in employees, as long as their skills are needed, without detaching them from their regular responsibilities. All of these approaches are relatively new; but there are several reasons why more and more companies will move into venture management. These reasons include allowing diversification without the problems of **mergers** and **acquisitions;** using profits wisely and creatively; giving venture-skills opportunities to creative and aggressive managers without driving them out of an otherwise tightly constrained large organization; reaching long-term growth projections; and increasing the likelihood that **research and development** projects can follow up on promising leads outside of the normal course of the company's business.   3. A *venture team* is a group of specialists from a company's marketing, engineering, finance, and other departments who work outside of normal departmental control to develop new products.

Vertical   In a chain, such as from manufacturer to wholesaler to retailer (as opposed to among various manufacturers, among various retailers, etc.). In **antitrust** law, a *vertical trust* is the combining of several of these levels under one ownership or control. *Vertical distribution* (or *marketing*) is a professionally managed coordinated product distribution (or marketing) system, controlled by a corporation, coordinated by one company for several, or agreed to by contract. *Vertical integration* is the control by a company of all the economic steps in the production of a product (from raw material to retail purchase). For *vertical loading,* see **job** loading. *Vertical training* is the simultaneous training of people who work together, irrespective of their status in the organization. A *vertical work group* is a work group containing individuals whose positions differ in rank, prestige, and level of skill. A *vertical union* is an **industrial union.**

Vest Give an immediate, fixed, and full right; take immediate effect; deliver complete ownership of property regardless of whether actual possession is postponed to a future date. *Vested* means **absolute, accrued,** complete, not subject to any **conditions** that could take it away; not **contingent** on anything. A *vested interest* is a claim or privilege that has become legally established as a present right to future property or benefit. For example, if a person sells you a house and gives you a **deed,** you have a *vested interest* in the property (even if the sale **contract** allows the seller to stay in the house for ten years); and a pension is *vested* if you get it at retirement age (even if you leave the company before that). There are several types of **pension plan** *vesting.* For example, *cliff vesting* (until you work a certain number of years, you get nothing; after that, you get all your **accrued benefits**); *graded vesting* (additional percentages of your accrued benefits are added the longer you work); and *rule of 45 vesting* (if your age plus the number of years you have worked for the company equals 45, part of your accrued benefits become vested, with the rest vested in the next few years). There are variations on all of these methods.

Vetoing stock See **voting stock.**

Vicarious liability Legal responsibility for the acts of another person because of some relationship with that person; for example, the **liability** of an employer for the acts of an employee.

Vice president A position that can vary from second in command to one of innumerable subordinates.

Visible supply The quantity of a particular commodity (such as wheat) which is in storage, in transit, or otherwise immediately available to the market. It does not include new plantings or unharvested crops, which are known as the *invisible supply.*

Void Without legal effect; of no binding force; wiped out. For example, a *void contract* is an agreement by which no one is (or ever was) bound, because something legally necessary is missing from it.

Voidable   Something that can be legally avoided or declared **void** but is not automatically void. For example, a *voidable contract* is a **contract** that one or both sides can legally get out of, but is effective and binding if no one chooses to get out of it.

Voluntary arbitration   **Arbitration** agreed to by two parties in the absence of any legal or contractual requirement. *Voluntary bargaining items* are those items over which **collective bargaining** is neither mandatory nor illegal.

Voluntary restraint agreements   Informal bilateral or multilateral agreements in which exporters voluntarily limit exports of certain products to a particular country to avoid economic dislocation in the importing country and the imposition of mandatory import restrictions. See **orderly marketing agreements.**

Voting stock   Usually **common stock.** However, other types of stock can sometimes vote on matters that directly affect their *class* of stock (usually **preferred** stock). This may be called *vetoing stock* or *contingent voting stock,* and often comes into play if **dividends** are not paid. A *voting trust* is a deal in which stockholders in a company pool their *shares of stock* for the purpose of voting in stockholders' meetings.

Voucher   1. A document that authorizes giving out something (usually cash).   2. A **receipt** or **release;** the **account** book that shows these receipts.

W

Wage *Wage* (or *wages*) can mean **salary;** salary *plus* **commissions,** bonuses, company housing, tips, etc.; or regular payments based on hours worked or work produced, as *opposed* to salary. *Wage and hour laws* are federal and state laws setting minimum wages and maximum hours of work, especially the **Fair Labor Standards Act.** *Wage and price controls* are laws or regulations that attempt to restrain inflation by limiting prices and wages. These controls were in effect during World War II and the Korean War and from August 1971 to April 1974. A *wage area* is a national or regional area selected on the basis of population size, employment, location, or other criteria for a *wage survey.* A *wage assignment* is an arrangement in which a person allows his or her wages to be paid directly to a creditor. It is illegal in most situations in many states. See **garnishment.** *Wage differentials* are differences in wages paid for identical or similar work that are justified because of differences in work schedules, hazards, cost of living, or other factors. *Wage drift* is a concept that explains the gap between basic wage rates and actual earnings, which tend to be higher because of overtime, bonuses, and other monetary incentives. For *wage earner's plan,* see **Chapter Thirteen.** A *wage floor* is a minimum wage established by contract or law. For *wage parity,* see **parity.** A *wage progression* is progressively higher wage rates that can be earned in the same job. Progression takes place on the basis of length of service, merit, or other criteria. For *wage reopener clause,* see **reopener clause.** A *wage survey* is a formal effort to gather data on compensation rates or ranges for comparable jobs within an area, industry, or occupation. Wage surveys on both a national and regional basis are available from such organizations as the Department of Labor, the

American Management Associations, the International Personnel Management Association and the International City Management Association. A *wage tax* is any tax on wages and salaries levied by a government. Many cities have wage taxes that force suburban commuters to help pay for the services provided to the region by the central city.

Wagner Act The 1935 National Labor Relations Act applying to all interstate commerce except railroad and airline operations (which are governed by the **Railway Labor Act**). The Act seeks to protect the rights of employees and employers, to encourage **collective bargaining,** and to eliminate certain practices on the part of labor and management that are harmful to the general welfare. It states and defines the rights of employees to organize and to bargain collectively with their employers through representatives of their own choosing. To ensure that employees can freely choose their own representatives for the purpose of collective bargaining, the Act establishes a procedure by which they can exercise their choice at a secret ballot election conducted by the National Labor Relations Board. Further, to protect the rights of employees and employers, and to prevent labor disputes that would adversely affect the rights of the public, Congress has defined certain practices of employers and unions as **unfair labor practices.** The Act is administered and enforced principally by the *National Labor Relations Board,* which was created by the Act. In common usage, the *National Labor Relations Act* refers to the *Wagner Act* as amended by the **Taft-Hartley Act** of 1947 and the **Landrum-Griffin Act** of 1959.

Waive Give up, renounce, or disclaim a privilege, right, or benefit with full knowledge of what you are doing. This voluntary giving up of a right is called *waiver.* It is the surrender, either **express** or **implied,** of a right to which you are entitled by law. For example, a stockholder might sign a *waiver of notice of meeting,* or might impliedly waive that notice by participation in the meeting. The essence of *waiver* is conduct that indicates an intention not to enforce certain rights or certain provisions of an agreement; for example, a buyer may waive delivery on a certain date by accepting the goods at a subsequent date. Also, *waiver of premium* is a provision included in some **insurance** policies which exempts the insured from paying **premiums** while disabled during the life of the contract.

Wall Street A street in New York City around which is concentrated the New York financial community. It is sometimes referred to as "the Street."

Warehouse receipt A *receipt* given by a person who stores goods for hire. This person is called a *warehouser* (or *warehouseman*) and must usually be **licensed** and **bonded** by a state or the federal government, though some are licensed locally. The receipt must identify the goods, the terms of agreement of storage, and the persons involved. It may be either **negotiable** or non-negotiable. If negotiable, it represents **title** to the goods, and transfer of the receipt is the same as transfer of ownership of the goods. Also, if negotiable, the receipt may be used to secure a loan on the property. This is often done in the case of agricultural **commodities.** See also **field warehousing.**

Warrant 1. To promise, especially in a **contract** or in a **deed** (see **warranty**). 2. Permission given by a judge to a police officer to arrest a person, conduct a search, seize an item, etc. 3. An **option** to buy **stock** that is initially sold along with the sale of other **securities.** For example, a corporation might sell shares of **preferred** stock accompanied by *warrants* to buy a certain amount of **common** stock at a certain price by a certain time. It may either be attached to the security or issued as a separate instrument. Warrants that are attached to the security may be either detachable or non-detachable. If detachable, the warrant may pass from hand to hand and may be used without the original security. In some cases, a warrant may be non-detachable until a certain date. The word *warrant* ·is sometimes used to mean both warrants and *pre-emptive rights (see* **pre-emption**). But, strictly speaking, they are different; pre-emptive rights are the right to *first* buy *any* new stock if it is issued; warrants are merely a way to lock in a price on existing stock. Warrants may be issued by a corporation for several different purposes. Most often, they are used to give a speculative value to normally non-speculative securities such as preferred stock or **bonds.** By giving the buyer a chance at getting common stock later at a below-market price, sales of the non-speculative securities can be stimulated by the hope that the common stock will go up. Warrants are also sometimes used to maintain control of a company in its current hands by allowing certain stockholders to exercise stock purchases if challenged for control by a grouping of other owners. Warrants are a useful device to give incentive payments to executives who, in theory, will work hard to make the company stock go up. And warrants are sometimes bought by persons who want to protect themselves against large losses due to massive **short sale** of the underlying stock.   4. A short-term obligation issued by a government in anticipation of revenue. The instrument (a **draft** much like a check), when presented to a disbursing officer, such as a bank, is payable only upon acceptance by the issuing jurisdiction. Warrants may be made payable on demand or at some time in the future. Local governments, in particular, have used delayed payment of warrants as a way to protect cash flow.

Warranty   Any promise (or a presumed promise, called an *implied warranty*) that certain facts are true. In land sales, a *warranty* is a promise in a **deed** that the **title** of land being sold is good and is complete or **marketable.** See **special warranty deed** and **quitclaim deed.** In building, a *construction* or **homeowner's warranty** is the promise that it was built right; and a *warranty of habitability* is the implied promise to buyers or renters that a house is fit to live in. In commerce, a *warranty* is similar to those above; and in **consumer** law, a *warranty* is the same as above plus any obligations imposed by law on a seller for a buyer: for example, the *warranty* that goods are **merchantable** and the *warranty* that goods sold as fit for a particular purpose, *are* fit for that purpose. Also, under recent federal law, if a written consumer warranty is not "full" (as to labor and material for repairs) it must be labeled *limited warranty* in the sales contract. See also **breach of warranty.**

Wash sale   1. Selling something, and buying something else that is basically the same thing. The word is often used to describe the nearly simultaneous buying and selling of shares of the same stock or of the same commodity. When this is done as a fictitious set of sales to maintain the illusion of trading activity at an artificial price on an **exchange,** it is illegal. When it is done to create a *tax loss,* the loss may be disallowed by the **IRS.**   2. Rescission is sometimes called a *wash* because all original rights, **liabilities,** and property are returned.   3. Breaking even financially on a sale.

Waste-book   A merchant's log of rough notes of transactions as they occur. Also called a "blotter."

Wasting Can be used up. For example, a *wasting asset* (or property) can be an oil **lease** or **patent** right that has a limited useful life and can be given a **depletion allowance** for tax purposes; and a *wasting trust* is one that uses up the **principal** to make payments.

Watered stock (or captial) A **stock issue** that is put out as if fully paid for, but that is not because some or all of the shares were sold (or given out) for less than full price. It is often created by overvaluation of property given in payment for the stock, by improper **depreciation,** or by a declining price level. If stock is proved to be watered, the holders may be **liable** for the difference between the actual appraised value of the property given for it and the **par** (or stated) value or legal subscription price of the stock.

Waybill A travel document for shipped goods that usually contains shipping point, carrier, shipping method, description of goods, destination, charges, signing information, etc. See also **bill of lading.**

Webb-Pomerene Act The federal law which exempts associations of exporters from some **antitrust** legislation.

Weight 1. In compiling **stock** averages, *weight* is the multiplier assigned to a stock to reflect a **split** of its shares. For example, if three shares have been issued for each old share that was selling at 120, the new price of 40 will be multiplied by 3. 2. In compiling price indices, *weight* is the relative importance of each **commodity** in the "market basket" whole. Thus, in the **Consumer Price Index,** purchase of newspapers may represent 0.99 per cent of the average family's expenditures. If the index of the price of newspapers rises from 100 to 110, the weighted index for newspapers will rise to 1.089. 3. On a *weighted application blank,* weights or numeric values can be placed on the varying responses to application blank items. After a **job analysis** determines the knowledge, skills, and abilities necessary to perform the duties of a position, corresponding personal characteristics can be elicited. Applicants who score highest on the weighted application blank would be given first consideration.

Welfare funds Employer contributions, agreed to during **collective bargaining,** to a common fund to provide welfare benefits to the employees of all of the contributing employers.

Well pay Incentive payments to workers who are neither "sick" nor late over a specified time period.

Wharfage A charge assessed by a pier or dock owner for handling incoming or outgoing cargo.

Wheel of retailing theory As new retailers enter the market, they sell goods at low prices. As they become more successful, they offer more services and charge higher prices. Then, newer retailers enter the market offering goods at lower prices, thus starting the cycle or *wheel* again.

When-issued Trading in **securities** that have not been finally approved by the **Securities and Exchange Commission,** or for which certificates are not ready for delivery. **Contracts** arising from such transactions are all **contingent** upon the actual issuance of the security.

Where-got, where-gone analysis A **statement** of sources and application of funds that is significant in determining the cause of changes in the **balance sheet** or **statement of income.** Computations for the analysis are based on the rise and fall of **net worth.** Net worth rises with any increase in **assets** or decrease in **liabilities;** it declines with any decrease in assets or increase in liabilities. All changes producing increases in net worth are tabulated in the *where-gone* column. All changes producing decreases in net worth are tabulated in the *where-got* column. This provides no more information than is evident from a comparison of two successive financial statements, but it makes obvious the flow of funds in the business.

Whipsaw strike 1. A **strike** against a company in which the union uses the added pressure of allowing the company's competitors to continue working by not striking them. 2. A strike that is particularly harsh to convince other companies to give in to union demands.

Whistle blower An individual who believes the public interest overrides the interests of his or her organization and who publicly reveals the facts if the organization is involved in corrupt, illegal, fraudulent, wasteful or harmful activity.

White collar The dress of office workers. *White-collar crimes* are commercial crimes like **embezzlement, price-fixing,** etc. *White-collar workers* are employees whose jobs require slight physical effort and allow them to wear ordinary clothes.

White knight A corporation that intervenes in a **takeover** attempt to save a company faced by a **tender offer** that the company's officers do not like. It does this by offering more for the shares and "protectively" buying the company, swallowing it whole for better or for worse.

White paper A formal statement of an official government policy with its associated background documentation.

Whole Entire. *Whole dollar accounting* is a technique applied to general **accounting** procedures in which the last two digits of dollar and cents amounts are eliminated and amounts are recorded in whole dollars. This elimination is accomplished by raising amounts of 50 cents or more to the next highest dollar, and lowering amounts of 49 cents or less to the next lowest dollar. *Whole life insurance* provides **insurance** protection for the insured person's entire life, usually for a flat yearly **premium.** While the **face value** of a policy will be paid only at death, a cash surrender value builds up, against which the insured could borrow at favorable rates. Most whole life policies provide for the cessation of premiums at a certain age and the conversion of the policy to an endowment or cash settlement. This is also called *straight life insurance* or *ordinary life insurance.* A *wholly-owned subsidiary* is a company that is completely controlled by a **parent** or **holding company.** The parent or holding company owns all of the **voting stock** of the **subsidiary** company.

Wholesale Selling (usually in quantity) to intermediaries or to retailers rather than to consumers of the product. For *Wholesale Price Index,* see **Producer Price Index.** A *wholesaler* is an intermediary between producers and consumers. The most common wholesaler is the *merchant wholesaler* who buys from manufacturers and sells to retailers and other merchants or to industrial, professional, institutional, and commercial users, on his or her own account; for example, **jobbers,** importers, exporters, textile converters, and industrial distributors. Generally, the merchant wholesaler does not purchase goods for final sale to consumers and is differentiated from other wholesalers (e.g., the agent or broker) because he or she actually takes **title** to the goods handled.

Wildcat strike A work stoppage not sanctioned by union leadership and usually contrary to an existing labor contract.

Wind up   Finish current business, settle accounts, and turn property into cash in order to end a **corporation** or a **partnership** and split up the **assets.** See **dissolution.**

Windfall   Profits that come unexpectedly or through no effort or financial cost.

Wink   A unit of time equal to ½₂₀₀₀ of a minute, which is used in **time and motion study.**

Wire transfer   An electronic communications network used for transferring funds and messages. Examples include the *Federal Reserve wire network* and *Bank Wire,* a communications network owned by commercial banks. See **electronic fund transfer systems.**

Withdrawals   1. The earned income of a household or firm that is saved rather than used to purchase goods and services. 2. The ways in which money is removed from a bank. A *withdrawal plan* allows an investor to receive regular (monthly, quarterly, etc.) payments more or less equal to the income of the investment. 3. Those items from a **consignment** of goods that have been bought or sold.

Withholding tax   The money an employer takes out of an employee's pay and turns over to the government as prepayment of the employee's **income tax;** or the money a bank or company holds back from **interest, dividends,** or other profit payments and similarly turns over to the government.

Without recourse   Words used by an endorser (signer other than original **maker**) of a **negotiable instrument** (check, etc.) to mean that if payment is refused, he or she will not be responsible.

Without reserve   A term indicating that a shipper's agent or representation is empowered to make definitive decisions and adjustments abroad without approval of the group or individual represented.

Word processing   Computerized text creation, editing, and printing. There are four basic kinds of setups: *stand alone* (or *dedicated*) systems are self-contained (with a complete **terminal,** computer, storage medium and printer); *shared logic* systems are terminals that share all other facilities; *distributed logic* systems share only printers and optional peripherals; and *mainframe-link* terminals are hooked into a large computer.

Work   According to Mark Twain, in *The Adventures of Tom Sawyer,* "Work consists of whatever a body is obliged to do, and play consists of whatever a body is not obliged to do." A *work analysis* is a **time and motion** study. A *work* (or *output*) *curve* is a graphic presentation of an organization's or individual's **productivity** over a specified period of time. For *work design,* see **job design.** The *work-in-progress inventory* includes all those products upon which production has begun but not finished. The *work-in-progress turnover* is a ratio: amount of work in progress turned into finished goods divided by average work in progress for the same period. *Work measurement* is any method used to establish an equitable relationship between the volume of work performed and the human resources devoted to its accomplishment. Concerned with both volume and time, a work measurement program is basically a means of setting **standards** of work measurement (numerical values applied to the units of work an employee or group can be expected to produce in a given period of time) to determine just what constitutes a fair day's work. See **time and motion study.** A *work order* is a form used to authorize and control work in a factory. The **cost accounting** cycle begins with the issuance of work orders. A *work premium* is extra compensation for work that is considered unpleasant, hazardous, or inconvenient. **Overtime** is the most obvious example of a *work premium. Work-ready* is a term used to describe a handicapped person who, if given employment, would be able to perform adequately on the job without being a burden to others. *Work rules* are formal regulations prescribing both on-the-job behavior and working conditions. They are usually incorporated into a **collective bargaining** agreement at the insistence of the union in order to restrict management's ability to unilaterally set production **standards** or reassign employees. *Work sampling* is a technique used to discover the proportions of total time devoted to the various components of a job. Data obtained from *work sampling* can be used to establish allowances applicable to the job, to determine machine utilization, and to provide the criteria for production **standards.** While this same information can be obtained by time-study procedures, work sampling—dependent as it is upon the laws of probability—will usually provide the information faster and at less cost. *Work sharing* is a procedure for dividing the available work (or hours of work) among all eligible employees as an alternative to **layoffs** during slow periods. There are three types: reduction in hours (by far the most common), division of work, and rotation of employment. *Reduction in hours* requires each employee to reduce weekly hours of work below normal schedules to spread the work. *Division of work* is normally found in agreements covering employees on piecework or incentive systems, and emphasizes earnings rather than hours of work (although reduced hours may also occur). *Rotation of employment* (or *layoff*) provides that short, specific periods of layoff be rotated equally among all employees, in contrast to the more common practice of laying off junior employees for longer or indefinite periods. See **job sharing**. *Work simplification* is an **industrial engineering** function designed to find the one best way to do each job in a plant, based upon economy of time, effort, material, and other criteria. A *work station* is either the assigned location where a worker performs his or her job, or a computer terminal with access to a variety of functions such as **word processing,** computing, **electronic mail, databases,** etc. A *work study* is either a **time and motion study;** or a part-time employee who is also a full-time student. *Work to rule* is a work **slowdown** in which all of the formal work rules are so scrupulously obeyed that productivity suffers considerably. Those *working to rule* seek to place pressure on management without losing pay by going on **strike.** *Workaholic* is a word used to describe a person whose involvement in his or her work is so excessive that health, personal happiness, interpersonal relations and social functioning are adversely affected. *Worked off* refers to a **security** or **commodity** whose price has declined only slightly. *Workers' compensation* provides cash benefits and medical care when a worker is injured in connection with his or her job and monetary payments to survivors if killed on the job. In most states, workers' compensation is paid for entirely by employers who either buy insurance or **self-insure.** *Workers' councils* are any of a variety of joint labor-management bodies for the resolution of problems of mutual interest. Workers' councils are usually associated with concepts of **industrial democracy** and are found mostly in Europe. *Workfare* is any public welfare program that requires welfare recipients to work or enroll in a formal job-training program. *Workforce planning* is the determination by management of the numbers, kinds, and costs of the workers needed to carry out each stage of the organization's program plan. **Working capital** consists of a company's **current assets** minus **current liabilities.** It is one measure of the company's ability to meet its obligations and to take advantage of new opportunities. See **current ratio** and **quick assets.** For a manufacturing or sales company, sufficient *working capital* is needed to maintain the flow of money from cash to **inventories** to **receivables** and back again to cash. This would include a cash balance sufficient to **discount** all **bills,** to purchase **raw materials** or inventory to carry a stock of finished goods large enough to make prompt deliveries, to meet payrolls, and to maintain **accounts receivable** for the time demanded by industry practices. For *working certificate,* see *working papers.* The *working class* consists of all who work. When the term is used politically, it tends to exclude managers, professionals, and anyone who is not at the lower end of educational and economic scales. *Working conditions* are those factors, both physical and psychological, which comprise an employee's work environment. *Working control* is controlling enough **stock** in a corporation to effectively direct its policies. While in theory you need 51 percent of **voting stock** for control, for all practical purposes it is usually sufficient to own (or have voting with you) the largest block of shares for working control; with large corporations this can be as little as 20 to 30 percent of voting stock. The *working hours method* is a method of **depreciation** used where the major depreciation factor is hours of use rather than time periods. Rotary oil drilling rigs, for example, may wear out from a fixed amount of use rather than from the mere passage of time. *Working papers* are federal certificates of age showing that a minor is above the oppressive **child labor** age applicable to the occupation in which he or she would be employed. Such proof of age is required under the provisions of the **Fair Labor Standards Act.** *Working papers* are also the preliminary analyses prepared by an **auditor** prior to issuing an opinion. The *working poor* are employees whose incomes are not adequate enough to pull them out of poverty (often defined by government as an income below a minimum standard). For *workmen's compensation,* see *workers' compensation.* A *works* is a factory. A *works manager* is a factory manager. A *workweek* is an expected or actual period of employment for a "normal" week, usually expressed in number of hours. According to the **Fair Labor Standards Act,** a *workweek* is a period of 168 hours during 7 consecutive 24-hour periods. It may begin on any day of the week and any hour of the day established by the employer.

World Bank   The **International Bank for Reconstruction and Development.**

World Bank Group   A closely integrated group of international institutions providing financial and technical assistance to **developing countries.** Included are the **International Bank for Reconstruction and Development,** the **International Development Association,** and the **International Finance Corporation.**

WOTS-UP analysis   *WOTS* is an acronym for *weaknesses, opportunities, threats,* and *strengths.* An analysis of these factors seeks to determine how able an organization is to cope with its environment. A *WOTS-UP analysis* is usually prepared as part of a **situation audit** for **strategic planning.** Its basic purpose is to help policy makers find the best fit between an organization's capabilities and opportunities.

Wraparound   1. A second **mortgage** on a property that includes payments on a low-**interest**-rate first mortgage. This is done by buyers who don't want to lose the first mortgage and sellers who can't finance the sale without being willing to keep their names on the first mortgage. It is also done by lenders who finance work on older buildings. *Wraparounds* may cause problems if the original lender or the holder of the original mortgage is not aware of the new mortgage. Upon discovering this arrangement, some lenders or holders may have the right to insist that the old mortgage be paid off immediately.   2. A new mortgage that makes payments on old mortgages on several properties at once.

Wrap-up clause   See **zipper clause.**

Writeoff   1. An uncollectible debt.   2. A business or investment loss that can usually be claimed as a tax loss.

Writer   A person who sells **options.**

X

X In newspaper stock transaction tables, an indication, lowercase (x), that a **stock** trades **ex-dividend.**

X-Axis The horizontal axis on a graph.

X-Theory See **Theory X.**

Y

Y-Axis   The vertical axis on a graph.

Y-Theory   See **Theory Y.**

Year-end bonus   See **nonproduction bonus.**

Yellow-dog contract   Any agreement (written or oral) between an employer and an employee that calls for the employee to resign from, or refrain from joining, a union. These are illegal.

Yield   Profits, as measured by a percentage of the money invested. For example, a ten-dollar profit on a hundred dollar investment is a 10 percent *yield.* For a **bond,** *nominal yield* is annual **interest** compared to the bond's **face** value; *current yield* is annual interest compared to its purchase cost; and *net yield to maturity* is current yield plus a factor that accounts annually for the difference between face and market values. For a **stock,** *prospective yield* is annual **dividends** compared to the stock's purchase cost; while *retrospective yield* can also take into account an annualized figure for the difference between the stocks purchase and sale prices.

Yield variance   In a **standard cost system,** the difference between what has been produced and what should have been produced according to a standard.

York-Antwerp rules   Agreed international rules for **contract** provisions dealing with **bills of lading,** for settlement of disputes about maritime losses, etc.

Yo-Yo   A **stock** whose price varies widely.

Z

Z 1. *Regulation Z* is the set of rules put out by the **Federal Reserve** Board under the Truth-in-Lending law. It describes exactly what a lender must tell a borrower and how it must be told. 2. *Z* is the mark used to fill in unused blank spaces on a document to keep them from being filled in later. 3. For *Z-Theory*, see **Theory Z.**

ZBA Zero balance account.

ZBB Zero-base budgeting.

THE ZBB PROCESS: OVERVIEW

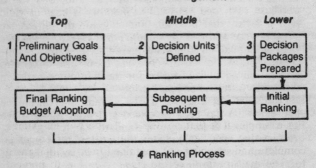

Levels Of Management

Top — *Middle* — *Lower*

1 Preliminary Goals And Objectives → 2 Decision Units Defined → 3 Decision Packages Prepared

Final Ranking Budget Adoption ← Subsequent Ranking ← Initial Ranking

4 Ranking Process

Zero Nothing. A *zero balance account* is a bank service to commercial customers in which subsidiary accounts with no funds are permitted to write checks. At the end of each day, the bank transfers funds from the customer's *master account* to bring each account back to zero. *Zero-base budgeting* is a system of looking closely at an entire program's funding when planning its next budget, rather than looking only at that program's need for additional money. It is a rejection of the *incremental budget* concept (which essentially respects the outcomes of previous budgetary decisions, collectively referred to as the budget base, and focuses examination on the margin of change from year to year). A major tool of *ZBB* is **decision packages,** or lists of priorities for funding, so that higher-level managers can reorder or cut *any* "package," not only newly proposed ones. A *zero-coupon bond* does not pay any **interest** until **maturity;** its `yield` comes from its deeply discounted price. A *zero-defects program* is a formal effort at quality assuredness aimed at eliminating human errors during production. *Zero growth* can refer to an economy that has had no growth during a specific time period; a conscious policy on the part of a company or government to maintain a present situation and not grow larger in any appreciable way; or an economic policy that discourages growth to conserve natural resources (*zero population growth* is one element of this). A *zero-rate mortgage* is a **mortgage** in which a large down payment is made, and the rest of the purchase price is paid off in equal **installments** with no interest. These mortgages are unique in that they appear to be completely or almost interest-free. But the sales price may be increased to reflect the loan costs. Thus, one could be exchanging lower interest costs for a higher purchase price. Also, there is no interest to deduct from taxes. A *zero-sum game* is a concept from **game theory** in which for every amount won there is an equal amount lost; one player's loss is another's gain.

Zipper clause   A statement in a **contract** that it is **integrated.** For example, it is that portion of a **collective bargaining** contract that specifically states the written agreement is complete and anything not contained in it is not agreed to. The main purpose of the *zipper clause* is to prevent either party from demanding a renewal of negotiations during the life of the contract. It also serves to limit the freedom of a **grievance arbitrator** because his or her rulings must be based solely on the written agreement's contents.

Zone   1. A geographic area.   2. An area of concern.   3. A *zone of employment* is the physical area (usually the place of employment and surrounding areas controlled by the employer) within which an employee is eligible for

workers' compensation benefits when injured, whether or not on the job at the time. *Zone pricing* is charging everyone within a geographical area the same price for the same delivered goods. When different sellers of the same goods charge the same price despite differing shipping costs, it may be an **antitrust** violation. *Zone pricing* is also charging a buyer for *delivery* based on distance as defined by the number of geographic zones.

Zoning The division of a city or county into mapped areas, with legal restrictions on land use, architectural design, building use, etc., in each area.